'TIS NOT OUR WAR

ALSO BY PAUL TAYLOR

*My Dear Nelly: The Selected Civil War Letters of
General Orlando M. Poe to His Wife Eleanor*

*The Most Complete Political Machine Ever Known:
The North's Union Leagues in the American Civil War*

Old Slow Town: Detroit during the Civil War

Orlando M. Poe: Civil War General and Great Lakes Engineer

*Give My Love to All Our Folks: Civil War and Post-War
Letters of Clinton DeWitt Staring and Charles E. Staring*

*Glory Was Not Their Companion: The Twenty-Sixth
New York Volunteer Infantry in the Civil War*

*He Hath Loosed the Fateful Lightning: The Battle
of Ox Hill (Chantilly) September 1, 1862*

Discovering the Civil War in Florida: A Reader and Guide

'TIS NOT OUR WAR

Avoiding Military Service in the Civil War North

PAUL TAYLOR

STACKPOLE
BOOKS

Essex, Connecticut
Blue Ridge Summit, Pennsylvania

STACKPOLE BOOKS

An imprint of Globe Pequot, the trade division of
The Rowman & Littlefield Publishing Group, Inc.
4501 Forbes Blvd., Ste. 200
Lanham, MD 20706
www.rowman.com

Distributed by NATIONAL BOOK NETWORK

British Library Cataloguing in Publication Information available

Library of Congress Cataloging-in-Publication Data Available

ISBN: 978-0-8117-7538-0 (cloth : alk. paper)
ISBN: 978-0-8117-7539-7 (ebook)

♾️™ The paper used in this publication meets the minimum requirements of American National
Standard for Information Sciences—Permanence of Paper for Printed Library Materials, ANSI/
NISO Z39.48-1992.

"The real difficulty was, and will be again, to obtain an adequate number of good soldiers."

—MAJ. GEN. WILLIAM T. SHERMAN

"War hath no fury like a non-combatant."

—CHARLES EDWARD MONTAGUE

"Memory is the king of shadows. . . . How two people—three, four, a score of them—can witness the same moment yet have vastly different memories of it, thus throwing shadows over the absolute truth."

—ROBERT MCCAMMON, *THE KING OF SHADOWS*

CONTENTS

CONTENTS

ACKNOWLEDGMENTS

I began this book in August 2019 with the kernel of an idea; the impression that with the exception of the war's first few months, the Civil War North's slave-free states were never the unified and homogenous pro-war front portrayed within much of America's collective Civil War memory. In addition, I came to realize that while numerous books and essays were written over the decades examining why the average Northern man went off to fight, there had never been—to the best of my knowledge—a full-length published book that studied the issue from the other side of the looking glass, that is, why an even greater number made a carefully considered decision to stay out—or get out—of the Union army by any means necessary. Hopefully this work will properly convey those period realities to the general reader.

Over the intervening years, numerous individuals and institutions cheerfully answered my various questions and requests as well as offering excellent suggestions. As has been the case with several of my past books, Patrick Kerwin at the Library of Congress's Manuscript Division always assisted with all of my in-person and long-distance requests. I also want to acknowledge the research support provided by the reference staffs at the many archive repositories cited in the bibliography. In particular, the suggestions offered by the respective staffs at the US Army Heritage and Education Center in Carlisle, Pennsylvania; the Ohio History Center Archives in Columbus; the Western Reserve Historical Society in Cleveland, Ohio; the Library of Virginia in Richmond; and the Indiana Historical Society in Indianapolis have all made my visits to their archives more fruitful and productive than they might have been.

Of course, I would be remiss if I did not express my gratitude to my daughter, Sofia Taylor, for her wonderful research assistance while away at college. Lastly, but certainly not least, I want to thank Dave Reisch, Tricia Currie-Knight, Stephanie Otto, and the entire team at Stackpole Books for our partnership in bringing this work to fruition.

INTRODUCTION

In Shakespeare's *Hamlet*, Prince Hamlet asks Queen Gertrude for her opinion regarding a play actress's extravagant performance. The queen replies, "The lady doth protest too much, methinks." As with the Bard's legendary drama, that iconic line is often used today to imply that someone who asserts or denies something with excessive vigor is often hiding all or at least part of the truth. Such was also the case for many Civil War–era Northern men of military age who exuberantly proclaimed their patriotic integrity at every public opportunity, yet always found reason *not* to enlist and fight in putting down the great rebellion.

The reasons for their reluctance—and the social culture behind them—offer fertile ground for exploration. For on the other hand, the American Civil War's historiography examining why average Northern men left their homes and families to fight in the conflict is deep and rich. Chandra Manning's *What This Cruel War Was Over*, James McPherson's *For Cause and Comrades*, James Robertson Jr.'s *Soldiers Blue and Gray*, Gary Gallagher's *The Union War*, and William Marvel's *Lincoln's Mercenaries* are but a few of the scholarly works that explained how patriotism, preserving the Union, boredom at home, pay, slavery's abolition, and proving one's manliness were some of the motivating factors for the approximate 33 to 40 percent of all White, military-age Northern men who fought for the Union in the Civil War. Those men participated in what was the largest military mobilization in US history. Of the approximately five million men who fell between the ages of eighteen and forty-five during the years from 1861 to 1865, those enlistment percentages included the 75,000 who initially served for only ninety days and the 640,000 enlistees who were still in the army at the end of 1861.[1]

Furthermore, the vast majority of Civil War books and documentaries produced after the guns fell silent depicted the four-year rebellion as one dominated by great battles and campaigns, famous generals, and well-known political figures. The modern casual reader and armchair general will often see a war portrayed as one of grand glory waged by two deeply devoted home fronts fighting in lockstep with their armies to obtain their respective visions of what their nation should be.

But what, then, of the North's remaining 60 to 67 percent who made a carefully considered, conscious decision *not* to enlist or serve in some formal capacity? Did those other men throughout the North not feel the same patriotic impulses as their fellow citizens who rushed to the enlistment office? Did they not believe in the sanctity of the Union that was bequeathed to them by their revolutionary forefathers? Was freeing men held in chains under chattel slavery not a righteous moral crusade? The fact that the federal government felt compelled to threaten conscription in order to refill the Union armies' ranks only a little more than a year into the war indicates that many did not. Patriotism, while wonderful in theory, had its apparent limits in reality.

Clearly, some men could not serve due to obvious reasons such as poor health. Others felt a higher duty to family or community, for example, maintaining their farms, owning businesses that employed many, or having substantial employment elsewhere. Newspaper editorials repeatedly urged farmers to stay home and produce food for the burgeoning army needs. Such necessary work was considered every bit as patriotic as shouldering a musket. Other men may have considered going off to war as an imposition on their economic lives and, by extension, a threat to their families' financial security. Young men enrolled in college viewed enlisting as a threat to their academic life. Civil War volunteers were essentially farmers and shopkeepers with no prior bonds to or aspirations for military life.

Perhaps others knew in their heart that they were simply cowards (also commonly referred to then as "poltroons") and in the antebellum and Civil War eras, there was no social stigma worse than being labeled a coward. Within the context of battle, what many soldiers yearned for was a simple "honorable wound" that would prove beyond a doubt that they were not a coward. The ideal "red badge of courage" would showcase their martial manhood to their friends and families back home but would not hinder their normal return to civilian life in the slightest. In this regard, Capt. Orlando M. Poe explained to his wife how he was a proponent of such wounds and held great respect for those men who bore them. As for himself, Poe admitted he "wouldn't object to a few slight wounds, such as show well, but are not dangerous."[2]

Conversely, one of a soldier's greatest fears was to be shot in the back because such a wound would indicate to others that he was running from the fight, even though soldiers' perspectives of what constituted battle-field cowardice and bravery altered as the war progressed; especially with regards to *other* companies and regiments. These men sensed what mod-ern social psychology has now asserted; that in the military or any large civilian group that consecrated honor and loyalty, the man who displayed cowardice in front of his peers would suffer for it. His new battlefield reputation would repel both employers and women back home. As Chris Walsh noted in his excellent work on cowardice, "the cowardly begin the book of Revelation's list (21:8) of those damned to burn forever in a lake of fire, and they are the most despicable souls in Dante's *Inferno*." Walsh also gives us a solid working definition of a coward: A coward is someone who, because of excessive fear, fails to do what he is supposed to do. For much of the Civil War's four-year duration, the pro-war Northern press and citizenry put forth that what a real man (in other words, a courageous man) was "supposed to do" was to enlist and fight for flag and country in the Union army. With only a relative few publicly acknowledged exceptions, those who did not were often deemed cowards, laggards, and shirkers even though what constituted cowardice was never a fixed defi-nition during the war. Its meaning, and Northern society's responses to it, altered with the fortunes of war.[3]

***

This book is a historical narrative that examines Northern resistance to military service during the Civil War as set within the context of the era's culture, social mores, and gendered expectations. It then addresses what modern society may learn from those period realities. It rests on the premise that except for the war's first few months, the Northern slave-free states' home front was never the united solid column portrayed within much of America's collective Civil War memory. That while there was a patriotic outpouring and rush to enlist early on, the statistical majority of the North's White men of military age remained anywhere from apathetic to unequivocally hostile with regard to answering their nation's call throughout the four years of conflict. In fact, within fifteen months after the war commenced in April 1861, the initial rallying 'round the flag had all but vanished.

This study focuses on a "bottom-up" social history lens, concentrating on the beliefs and opinions of average civilians, rather than a top-down approach that emphasizes the thoughts and words of generals and political leaders. To that end, it highlights the letters and diaries written by those at the home front, relatively scarce objects when compared to the colossal number of letters and diaries written by the soldiers in the field and preserved to this day. In addition, it will examine the not insignificant portion of Union soldiers who, after enlisting, came to regret their decision and sought a way out of the ranks by any means, honorable or not. They decided it was no longer their war, either.[4]

This work also sets out to examine the North's Civil War–era social culture and the ethos—both personal and public—that allowed so many hale and hearty Northern White men of military age to confidently refuse voluntary enlistment throughout the war's early years. It will explore the subtle and sometimes violent actions some men took to avoid possible conscription once that became a reality only sixteen months after the rebellion commenced. Many of these men and their families believed that as free private citizens, they had no constitutional obligation to take up arms solely because a distant federal government said so. They opposed the Lincoln administration's then-new assertion that it possessed the right to forcibly take a man away from his home—literally at the point of the bayonet—and subject him to military discipline under national authority.

President Abraham Lincoln's administration, of course, viewed the matter differently. It relied upon the maxim that every citizen not hampered by physical or mental disability owes his country military service in time of domestic emergency. This newly claimed national authority was a serious diversion from the sense of individualism that dominated the nation's collective mindset since its founding and was still a core trait of American values. This belief held that it was the citizen who had control over how he was going to dispose of his talent and himself and not a distant national government. It was not coincidental that the recently created Republican Party's foundational beliefs centered on the twin ideals of free labor and free men. Historian James Kettner described

DON'T YOU SEE THE POINT?

"Don't You See the Point?" (*Harper's Weekly*, August 29, 1863).
COURTESY OF HARPWEEK

this concept as "volitional allegiance"; the theory that a free man's loyalty was one of choice and not subjection. After all, these citizens reasoned, the philosophical cornerstone for the Declaration of Independence was the idea of individual liberty. The Constitution and especially the Bill of Rights were formulated precisely to protect that liberty.[5]

While some men were willing to take a temporary step back from individualism, many were not. During the Civil War and as we sometimes see in our modern era, many citizens were keenly aware of their individual rights but saw little in the way of personal obligation or civic duty to the collective whole. This paradigm has shown itself again in twenty-first-century America, regardless of whether the war in question was a hot one on foreign soil against a shadowy enemy or a home front "war" against a deadly, worldwide pandemic. In the case of the Civil War era, Brig. Gen. James Fry summarized this widely held opinion in his end-of-war report on the congressional creation in early 1863 and subsequent activities of the Office of the Provost Marshal General. "The people had become more accustomed to the enjoyment of privileges than to the fulfilment of duties under the general government," wrote Fry, "and hence beheld the prospect of compulsory service in the army with an unreasonable dread."[6]

Gerald Linderman wrote in his 1987 book, *Embattled Courage: The Experience of Combat in the American Civil War*, how every war begins as one war but eventually becomes two; one fought by the soldiers and one watched by the civilians. I will slightly alter his insight by suggesting there is the war the soldiers fight in and then a second war that the home front's competing factions do not merely watch, but even eventually engage in; a home front war that can and will viciously argue the merits of and manner in which the soldier's war is being fought. Communal infighting within the Civil War's Northern home front often turned contentious and violent over who would serve (or not) as the North's cannon fodder and why, for as Peter Carmichael observed in *The War for the Common Soldier*, there was no boundary in the Civil War between the home front and the battlefield. Battlefield and home front enemies were deemed to be cut from the same cloth. They were traitors, pure and simple.[7]

Yet much of that Northern home front combativeness seemed to vanish after the war ended. Throughout much of the war and especially after, Unionist soldiers and civilians came to regard their efforts as the selfless and courageous response of a people willing to pick up the musket to save their nation or properly care for those left behind. By so doing, these Northerners believed they had reclaimed God's favor through their holy war. Within that self-righteous context, however, any admission or even discussion of cowardice or apathy was problematic, especially with regard to post–Civil War histories. For within memoirs, published letters and diaries, as well as later accounts of the rebellion, decisions born of dissent, indifference, or cowardliness often became sanitized for the sake of the nation's confidence, national reconciliation, and other social needs, if not outright ignored. A case in point is the 1884 volume on the history of Indiana's Morgan, Monroe, and Brown Counties. The editor offered up more than twenty pages of the three counties' valiant contributions to the Union's Civil War effort. In contrast, the one page to follow that touched upon the subject of regional "disloyalty" started with the sentence, "The least said on this subject the better." The post-war North considered it more appropriate to forget than remember such unsavory topics and therefore became slowly engaged in a form of self-induced forgetfulness. More than 100 years after the rebellion ended and amid the contentious Vietnam War era, such disregard for the non-heroic side of the war sometimes remained in place. While working in the early 1970s on his doctoral dissertation that focused on Civil War draft resistance in the northern Midwestern states, Robert Sterling wrote of having encountered archivists and librarians who openly expressed their reluctance to offer him any papers or records that may have presented their local communities' historical image in an unflattering light.[8]

Accordingly, within these malleable post-war "cycles of selective memory," only the hero remained. "Remembrance! Of what? Not the cause but the heroism it invoked," spoke ex-Union general Lew Wallace at the 1895 dedication of the Chickamauga and Chattanooga National Military Park. At a gathering of New York veterans in the early 1890s, Brevet Brig. Gen. Peter Michie dryly spoke of this fact by acknowledging "The greatest heroes of the war are still in the land of the living, for they are ourselves." Michie knew the old veterans told their war stories in such a way so that with every retelling, each soldier's personal prowess was slowly magnified while any errors or hesitations gradually vanished. The inevitable result, according to Michie, was that "we end with actually believing ourselves to be the very heroes our stories make us out to be." It was as if there had never been any home front or battlefield cowards and that the reasons for enlisting throughout the war were always purely noble and patriotic. These subtle, self-generated deceptions were part of what the famed poet Walt Whitman had in mind when he wrote in 1882, "the real war will never get in the books." As a corollary, every soldier's selective memory recalled both his town's and his personal enlistment motives as only of the highest principle and never for base reasons such as money or boredom.[9]

***

In his book *Liberty, Virtue, and Progress*, Earl Hess argued that Americans rallied together to back the war, however, that support was far from unanimous. He noted that such well-known, ardent war proponents as Ralph Waldo Emerson and Walt Whitman became dismayed as the all-encompassing war fever of spring 1861 began to dissipate as the year progressed into the fall and beyond. According to those men, the North's citizens had lost the spirit of sacrifice that so animated them initially and now began to refocus their energies on personal matters such as entertainment, parties, and business. The rich elite returned to their resorts and operas while the working-class saloons were as crowded as ever. Many from both social classes enjoyed watching the then-new game of baseball.[10]

Whitman described this return to normalcy as "very flippant & shallow somehow," for he believed it exemplified a lack of moral fiber that would harm the Union war effort. In Whitman's opinion, Northern society's shared sacrifice had to be in alignment with the soldier suffering he witnessed in Washington's military hospitals.[11]

Visiting Englishman George Sala observed this growing apathy by noting in his diary, "The gay and impulsive people of New York have run away with the delusion that all signs and symptoms of the existence of civil strife have been banished from their sumptuous streets." Yet as a stranger, Sala knew that any foreign visitor could not walk Broadway's streets for thirty minutes "without becoming disagreeably aware of the fact that at nearly every hundred yards, a great, insatiate monster is fuming for men to come and be killed." It was obvious to Sala that New York's residents had grown desensitized to all of the martial banners and recruiting posters calling for "Thirty thousand more volunteers" as well as the huge bounties promised to recruits. Sala experienced firsthand what historian Peter Parish termed the "comfort factor" because, with few exceptions, the war was fought far away on Southern soil. Like innumerable citizens across the North, the war had grown distant to them and was no longer an intrusion into their daily lives. That distance led to indifference as much as commitment.[12]

Despite Hess's and Parish's assertions that Northern citizens generally came together to back the war, or at least accept it, I contend that while Northern Unionists may have been vocally supportive in public, in reality, most became disconnected to any practical degree precisely as Emerson, Whitman, and Sala witnessed. They were certainly aware of the war, however, it did not fundamentally change their day-to-day lives other than their desire to *avoid* the war after conscription became a reality in the summer of 1862. A significant portion of the Civil War North became engaged in what segments of twenty-first-century society refer to as "virtue signaling": the public sharing of one's opinion on a social or political issue in order to gain communal praise or acknowledgment of one's moral virtue, though in absence of any actual physical or time-consuming commitment to the issue at hand. Social psychologist Dr. Jonathan Haidt argued this point in his modern classic, *The Righteous Mind*, by showing that modern man is a "Glauconian"; one who is more concerned with appearing virtuous in public rather than quietly behaving in that manner away from the public eye. The legendary US Supreme Court Justice (and Civil War veteran) Oliver Wendell Holmes Jr. deliberated on this point 140 years ago when he wrote, "a man may have as bad a heart as he chooses, if his conduct is within the rules." Scores of Northern American men of military age (along with their families) had no intention of serving in an army whose mission they were indifferent to at best or strongly against at worst. Concurrently, there was a similarly immense number who spoke and publicly acted wholly in support of the war, though privately, knew in their hearts that they had no desire or intention of going anywhere near the front lines. This book will tell their story, which was buried in the post-war desire—and continuing to this day—of remembering the Civil War as a righteous holy war dominated by a Northern home front fully devoted to restoring the Union and then freeing Black people held in bondage.[13]

"Somebody Must Go; and Who Can Go Better Than Young Men Like Myself"

Patriotism Was Hardly the Sole Reason Why They Initially Volunteered—An Overview

THE CIVIL WAR COMMENCED IN THE EARLY MORNING HOURS OF APRIL 12, 1861, with the Confederate bombardment of Union-held Fort Sumter in Charleston harbor, South Carolina. The fort's commander, Maj. Robert Anderson, was compelled to surrender his garrison the next day. The new Confederacy's threatening words and paper-based state secessions were replaced by military aggression against federal property. Those first shells fired signified the new Confederacy's earnestness and that national reunification was not going to occur at the negotiating table. Outraged cries of "treason!" were lobbed against the South from every corner of the Northern states. It became imperative for most of the North's citizenry—*but not all*—that the South be taught a military lesson and the Union preserved.

A resultant war fever quickly took hold and then consumed the Northern states from coast to coast in the days and weeks following Fort Sumter. Young men and older teen boys by the tens of thousands rushed headlong to their local enlistment office for a chance to retaliate and "put down treason." Almost everyone believed the war would not last long, certainly no more than the summer. One grand battle, probably somewhere along the 100-mile corridor between Washington, DC, and the new Confederate capital in Richmond, Virginia, would settle the matter. Those who disagreed that the war would be short and relatively bloodless were viewed as crackpots. War was viewed as all glory, filled with pomp and circumstance, and what little death there might be would surely only happen to someone else. Moreover, no one could foresee the carnage that awaited. For most living Americans, their only past military reference point was the Mexican War from thirteen years prior, and its active operations phase had lasted only sixteen months. For those with a broader worldview, the 1859 Franco-Austrian war lasted less than three months.[1]

Separating the good, healthy volunteers from the unfit was an unknown science with many men accepted wholesale without even a cursory examination. In the moment's adrenaline-driven exhilaration, few gave any serious thought to the hard realities that might lie ahead. In fact, one soldier recalled some "stay-at-homes" saying that in those heady days, it required less courage to enlist than it did to say no. For the most part, the deep political differences between President Abraham Lincoln's Republican Party and the Democrats were set aside under the bipartisan banner of "no party now." Lincoln, for his part, astutely appointed some Democrats to key positions in his administration, knowing he would need Democratic support if the North was to prevail. That unifying principle also applied to those men eager to volunteer, who readily set aside their political party affiliations, if they even had any. Religious, ethnic, and class divisions played little part in who initially enlisted. Most were scornful of the South and eager to avenge the national insult.[2]

In the days and weeks that followed, patriotic and poetic paeans to Old Glory and the new abstract nationalism appeared in popular literature and newspapers throughout the North. Concurrently, red, white, and blue symbolism permeated every town; a first, for in the republic's early days, the national flag was generally limited to naval or merchant ships. Symbols of national unity were not common. Now, however, "Everywhere the stars and stripes of the Union floated in the breeze, while every man wore a patriotic badge in his buttonhole," wrote the correspondent for the *London Illustrated News* from Boston on May 24. In Bellefonte, Pennsylvania, so many flags were reported flying from public and private buildings that they could not be accurately counted. In Chicago, the demand for American flags was so great "that not one yard of bunting can be procured in the whole city at present." Adding to the new nationalism were town bands who played martial tunes from street corners and public squares. Writing from Columbus, Ohio, on April 23, Nelia Moler informed her sister how "There is nothing done in town now but enlisting . . . almost any time [of the day] you will listen you can hear Yankee doodle or hail Columbia." Since the pro-war argument at the outset was only about reuniting the nation and stamping out alleged treason—and *not* as a war to end slavery—the North initially presented a united front against secession. In those early weeks, whether or not a young man volunteered to put down the rebellion was regarded by most Northerners as the best test of his loyalty and manhood, rather than any particular party affiliation. As a consequence of the North's initial and widespread pro-war consensus, those who believed the war to be a huge mistake felt obliged to stay silent for the time being.[3]

Unfortunately for Lincoln and the Northern states, all of those volunteers were necessary because the nation's Regular army was nowhere near up to the task of forcing the recalcitrant seceded states back into the Union. In the winter of 1860–1861, the North simply refused to believe that secession was a viable possibility as evidenced by its complete lack of war preparations, even as the South was carrying off arms and seizing federal forts.

On January 1, 1861, the US Regular army numbered only a paltry 14,657 men present for duty, a number that one historian surmised was adequate only for properly policing New York City, which according to the 1860 census was the nation's largest city, with a population of just more than 813,000. There were only about fifty soldiers posted in Washington, DC, and most of those were aged, senior officers. The nation's War Department, led by Secretary of War Simon Cameron, was woefully understaffed and underfunded, as was most of the military. The War Department's eight bureaus were staffed by ninety employees in 1860, but when the war came that already low number was whittled down to fifty-six after secession-related resignations. There was no general staff to head the army and no map collection necessary for battle-planning.

Furthermore, most of the Regular army's soldiers were scattered at remote outposts west of the Mississippi River or along the southern Atlantic and Gulf coasts, out of sight and mind. It would have taken several months to gather 3,000 regulars just to protect Washington, DC. The army's ranks were further thinned by the 313 well-trained officers who joined the Confederate cause after either resigning or being dismissed. Unless a person lived in a distant frontier town or near a port where those soldiers might be posted, it was quite possible for most citizens to never come into contact with a uniformed Regular. Therefore, with no real foreign threats, the army's primary functions were to maintain order through-out the vast West and to suppress the occasional Indian uprising. For a nation founded on the belief in utilizing the volunteer citizen-soldier for its defense and which disdained the idea of a large standing army, this reality was quite acceptable to the nation's citizens and their political representatives.[4]

The founding fathers, while reluctantly admitting the need for a professionally trained officer class to lead its volunteers, were nonetheless highly suspicious of established armies such as those maintained by the European powers. Thomas Jefferson, for one, viewed a standing military as incompatible with democratic principles as well as an unnecessary drain on the public treasury. Their idealized American citizen-soldier was not a professional warrior permanently engaged in war for pay or plunder. Instead, the founders had embraced both the military and civic virtues of the unprofessional citizen-soldier who would rally together in state-run militias (a type of standing reserve force) when the need arose but then return to civilian life after the emergency had passed. As with ancient Rome, the new republic's egalitarian ideal held that all (White) men were equal and therefore, his citizenship and voting rights were balanced by a duty to serve when necessary. After all, it seemed obvious to the new nation that a free man's natural desire to defend his home and land would surely exceed that of any "hireling." In this way, the typical militiaman viewed his service as an agreement with his state government, rather than a distant federal one.[5]

A militiaman's natural love of country, manly courage, and possession of the proper martial spirit were deemed by some to be more important virtues than any type of military training. Moreover, it had always been this way for the fledgling nation. In no prior American war had the nation's Regular army been a numerically significant force. As a result of this citizen-as-volunteer mentality, the federal government along with the twenty slave-free and four slaveholding yet loyal "border states" (Missouri, Kentucky, Maryland, and Delaware) went into the war with a small cadre of professionally trained West Point army officers ready to lead almost no army.[6]

With armed insurrection at his doorstep and Congress not in session until July, President Lincoln found himself with almost unlimited emergency powers. He initiated his temporary manpower solution by turning to the ossified Militia Act of 1795. That congressional act—which was sustained by the Supreme Court in *Martin v. Mott* (1827)—allowed the president to call up state militias for national duty in order to "suppress rebellions" or "repel invasions." The act, however, did place an aggregate limit of 75,000 men to serve for no more than ninety days. So it was that on April 15, three days after the Fort Sumter bombardment commenced, Lincoln issued his proclamation calling for the maximum 75,000 state militiamen—between the ages of eighteen and forty-five—to serve

THE AWKWARD SQUAD.

"The Awkward Squad" (Johnson and Buel, eds., *Battles & Leaders of the Civil War*, vol. 1, 84)

ninety days to "maintain the honor, the integrity, and the existence of our National Union" and to "repossess the forts, places, and property which have been seized from the Union." Despite his legal limitations, Lincoln's initial call for 75,000 men to serve just ninety days buttressed the belief in a short war.[7]

With the notable exception of Massachusetts and despite the country's professed devotion to the citizen-soldier, those state militias were hardly the crack, war-ready units the North needed. For decades, the states' lofty rhetoric regarding their militias far outpaced the financial commitments necessary to maintain them. Maine's militia was in a typically "neglected and unprepared condition." Its enrollment lists numbered about 60,000 men, however, no more than 1,200 were in any condition necessary for immediate military service. An Illinoisan remarked how his state had neglected the "mimic show of war" while Michigan's militia was described as little more than "a burlesque of the military profession." In a portent of what would follow five years later, Michigan's adjutant general remarked in 1858 that its few viable companies were composed almost entirely of foreigners, "while Americans shrunk from duty." Due to its "indolent apathy," a New Yorker wrote how the Empire State's militia was "long neglected, run down, half disbanded, [and] only kept dully alive by the activity and the purses of a few martial spirits." Overall, the situation was just as bad. The Regular army's adjutant general had reported on January 1, 1861, that the total enrolled militia in the slave-free states (except for Iowa and Oregon, of which there were no returns) comprised 2,197,236 men, but of this formidable paper-based host, not more than 1 percent was remotely ready for meaningful military purposes.[8]

Given the nation's lack of any real internal or external threats, the consequences were predictable. One historian likened volunteering in a state militia as more like joining a weekend bowling league than serving in the armed forces as we think of it today. The martial parades and drills militiamen occasionally gathered to learn were often performed with broomsticks rather than muskets due to a lack of proper weaponry. In any case, the muskets stored at state arsenals were generally antiquated while gunpowder and other military provisions were likewise outdated. The reality for many militiamen was that these gatherings often served as more of an excuse for a hard-drinking weekend with the fellows. For the country, however, the situation was more disconcerting. In the event of a crisis, its ragtag volunteer militia was initially useless, while the idea of a large professional army, trained and ready for war, was a political impossibility.[9]

The North's initial tidal wave response to Lincoln's call to arms both in speed and numbers was overwhelming and served as the apolitical template for what the Civil War generation and its children chose to remember. So many men initially rushed forward to enlist in those heady days of April and May 1861 that scores were turned away; the desired number of companies and regiments already filled to capacity. In vain, state governors and prominent federal politicians warned Secretary of War Cameron that rejecting such numbers had the potential to dampen volunteering enthusiasm, which might be dearly regretted later. That was especially the case in the Midwestern states though a few Eastern states failed to reach their quota. Ohio's quota, for example, was 13,000 men. Yet within a few weeks, as many as 80,000 Ohioans answered the call, six times its quota and just slightly more than Lincoln's call for the entire North. The national number called, however, was soon learned to be nowhere near what was needed. Lincoln, the federal government, and the North's populace for that matter had all naively underestimated the manpower necessary for the task ahead and, in some instances, being turned away did indeed dampen the spirit of some would-be volunteers.[10]

The war fever gripping the North was likened to a religious awakening. The Northern "saints" of Union, flag, and country were metaphorically blessed and sanctified from both the podium and the pulpit. In the next breath, Southern secessionists were damned and excommunicated. Their secession was deemed a sin to be purged from the national consciousness. Disregarding Napoleon Bonaparte's supposed maxim that God was on the side of those with the heaviest battalions, Northern ministers used their lecterns to portray the war as part of the eternal battle against Satan and that God would surely bless the Northern cause. For many Northern ministers of Puritan descent, this new strain of patriotic love of country was no different from religious devotion. American patriotism was presented as hardly a secular matter, but rather a manifestation of religious sentiment. Southern treason against the national banner was likened to treason toward the Almighty. The result was that the nascent rebellion quickly took on spiritual overtones with the phrase "holy war" becoming omnipresent in Northern sermons and newspapers from Maine to Iowa. By logical extension, Christian men were proclaimed to be the best and bravest soldiers because their heavenly reward was consistently their main focus. Those who fell in battle would therefore be blessed as martyrs. "If ever there was a 'holy war' on earth, I solemnly believe that this in which we are now engaged is that war," thundered Rev. George F. Wiswell from his Delaware church. From his New York pulpit, Rev. Henry Bellows told his congregation only eight days following Fort Sumter that, "We have a holy war on our hands," and now "we must wage it in the name of civilization, morality, and religion." In Akron, Ohio, Rev. Adams counseled some local recruits that they were marching off to war to combat not merely treason but religious sacrilege. "This conflict therefore . . . is a holy war," he stressed. To these men of the cloth, the idea of a beneficent God averting war through his merciful touch was unappealing, for as Robert Penn Warren later observed, "The man who is privy to God's will cannot long brook argument, and when one declines the arbitrament of reason . . . one is making ready for the arbitrament of blood."[11]

This *rage militaire* was not limited only to younger men seeking to enlist. In Philadelphia, fifty-two-year-old Sidney Fisher noted in his diary how "The town is in a wild state of excitement. Everybody is drilling." Though he was well past military age and not a healthy man, Fisher still wanted to do *something*. "I feel that I ought not to remain inactive," wrote Fisher, but given his ailments, "I would not be a very effective soldier." At forty-one years old, the wealthy New York City lawyer and diarist George Templeton Strong felt the same as Fisher. He immediately pledged personal funds to equip a new regiment and also signed up for a potential rifle corps, but then conceded that his nearsightedness was a "grave objection" to becoming a proper marksman. Though not a military organization, thirty-nine-year-old Frederick Law Olmsted, already a famed landscape architect, helped to create the US Sanitary Commission in June 1861 and served as its executive secretary. "It is a day for heroes," he later wrote, "& we must be heroes along with the rest." For numerous men unable or unwilling to enlist into the army, their martial solution lay in joining "home guard" units then forming within their hometowns. Age was no barrier to the fervor sweeping the North and for those men who were reluctant to enlist, serving in such a capacity might help to reclaim their social status as well as garner respect from the soldiers.[12]

Home Guards

Those able-bodied men older than the army's maximum allowable age of forty-five or those younger men who chose not to enlist sometimes enrolled into local volunteer units known as "home guards." Based on the antebellum militia concept, these informal home front units were formed by local communities ostensibly to defend their homes and property from any external or internal wartime threat, such as enemy invasion or local-ized insurrection. Defending their local community was a more powerful motivating force for mid-nineteenth-century Americans than any notion of nationalistic obligation. Watson Smith of St. Louis, for example, wrote to his father on April 25 explaining how he had enlisted into a home guard unit the night before and that it was "composed mostly of Amer-icans, many fine fellows, for the purpose of protecting Federal & private property and the lives of citizens." That was not hyperbole, for as one Boston mother wrote to her recently enlisted son in May 1861, that city's newly formed home guard was a necessity because "there is no [more] police to protect the town and the rowdies are very numerous."[13]

The unofficial aspect was crucial because home guards—as compared to the recognized state militia—were adamant that their offers to protect their towns or even government property did not equate to any formal enrollment into state or federal service. Furthermore, wealthier men of military age or workingmen who felt they could not abandon their fam-ilies or business responsibilities also quickly discovered how volunteering in a home guard unit might satisfy their patriotic impulses while shield-ing them from potential public opprobrium for not enlisting straight away into the army.[14]

As mentioned in the introduction, a town's leading businessmen or area farmers viewed their financial or manufacturing support to the local economy and their desire to protect those assets as a legitimate contribution to the war effort that was every bit as patriotic as serving in the army. In October 1861, even though he did not enlist, Kansan Samuel Reader made that very point by explaining to his sister how fourteen of his neighbors had just enlisted in the home guard but he had not, although strongly urged to do so by his neighbors. As an avowed Unionist, "It certainly looked bad to see some of them men of families leaving for the war while a great strapping healthy fellow like me stayed at home," he confessed, perhaps somewhat apologetically. "But maybe I will yet have a chance to show myself as patriotic as my brother . . . I solace myself with the thought that if I cannot help our cause as a soldier I certainly can as a farmer." Across the country, Philadelphian Sara Wister observed less than a week after the war started how, "Everyone is enlisting in *at least* the Home Guard," further sensing how all of her neighborhood's young men would eventually join the guards. New enlistee Ambrose Hayward, however, was not impressed with such displays. While waiting for his Philadelphia regiment to be mustered in, he wrote to his brother on June 9 explaining how the city's home guards often paraded around town but apparently did little else. "They have splendid Gray Uniforms and with nice clean choakers and Kid Gloves they have the appearance of ladies Soldiers," he wrote. "They are not thought much of here with the exception of the ladies of Walnut St." Hayward's home guard mockery spoke to the war's initial gendered ideal that dictated a real unmarried man stepped forward to enlist and not remain behind in domestic spaces dominated by feminine influences. Unlike Hayward, Wister believed that serving in a home guard unit offered the man who could not—or would not—formally enlist an opportunity to showcase his patriotic manly bearing while avoiding the front lines. These were men like twenty-eight-year-old Artemus Ward, who confessed in a May 24, 1861, letter to a friend, "Something within tells me, in a still small voice, that I am better adapted for the Home Guard than anything else."[15]

The importance of home guard units was most pronounced in those areas where the perceived threat from "Secesh" elements was greatest. Frontier communities felt a growing need to create home guard units for some sort of protection as they watched those Regular army soldiers in their area now transferred to the East. Towns and citizens located in the rural Western states or within the volatile lower Midwest generally had more to fear than a New England village. In southern Illinois, for example, loyal citizens formed home guard units as a means of countering those Southern-sympathizing elements who, they sincerely believed, were plotting insurrection and violence against the local and national governments. From the war's outset, Iowa governor Samuel Kirkwood feared guerilla incursions from Missouri as well as hostile Indian raids along the state's northwestern frontier. By early May, Iowans were "waking up to the importance of organizing home guards." In August 1862, Illinois governor Richard Yates asked Secretary of War Edwin Stanton for permission to create four, one-year home guard regiments to defend their homes against Rebel-sympathizing guerrillas. These guards would be comprised of men older than the age of forty-five and would serve only within Illinois, Kentucky, and Missouri. Stanton, for his part, had little use for such units. Writing again to Yates in July 1863, Stanton declared, "Regiments for home service interfere materially with the organization of troops either by draft or volunteering for the general service of the country." If a man felt he was performing adequate patriotic duty by serving in a home guard, there might be, Stanton reasoned, little incentive for him to volunteer into the ranks. Stanton was on the mark because for many men, that was the entire point of serving in the home guards; avoiding the front lines.[16]

Border and town defense against feared Confederate attacks was an additional motivating factor. During Brig. Gen. John Hunt Morgan's famous Confederate raid through southern Indiana and Ohio in June–July 1863, a Chillicothe, Ohio, home guardsman recalled how martial law was declared in the town and to prepare for defense. He was given a squad of ten men equipped with muskets and fixed bayonets whose orders were to seek out any store, saloon, or restaurant where liquor was sold and to ensure they were closed up. Those who resisted were to be arrested immediately.[17]

In the East, such units worked on their martial drills, often to the amusement of local citizens as they paraded about in their civilian clothes or a variety of uniforms. In many instances, the home guards and their chosen officers became more valuable as a symbol of pro-war inspiration

NOT USED TO IT.

Home Guard.—Well—'swonderful howerdrill wearsout a m'ran's legs—fearf'lly f'tiguing.

"Not Used to It" "Home Guard.—Well—'swonderful howerdrill wearsout a m'ean's legs—fearf'lly f'tiguing." (*Vanity Fair*, June 1, 1861)

than actual fighting. For some men, the realization of easy duty had quietly supplanted patriotic words that admonished one to volunteer into the ranks. In one instance, the Gettysburg, Pennsylvania, newspapers urged men to enlist in the then-forming home guard *because* of the "easy and pleasant" duty.[18]

Historian Robert Sandow observed that based on newspaper accounts from the war's opening months, Northern home guard service was not initially regarded as any less patriotic than serving with the army. That eventually changed, however, as enlistments slowed following the July 1861 battle of Bull Run debacle and then into the summer of 1862 as the army's manpower shortages crystallized, which prompted one paper to refer to home guards as "a much slandered and persecuted class." This was especially the case within the more heavily populated and urban East. In one example, the Pennsylvania authors of Allegheny County's early contributions to the war effort admitted how the greater Pittsburgh area's home guards were "made the target of not a little idle and malicious wit, and finally succumbed to ridicule and loss of novelty."[19]

Soon enough, newspaper cartoons and editorials began to lampoon such men and service, such as "Our Fat Contributor in the Home Guards," a satirical, "on-the-scene report" from an excessively obese home guard member describing his various travails. The famed physician and poet Oliver Wendell Holmes Sr. chastised those men who opted for such light work in a scathing September 1861 poem titled "The Sweet Little Man," which he dedicated to the "Stay-at-Home-Rangers." It included the verses:

> Bring him the buttonless garment of woman!
> Cover his face lest it freckle and tan;
> Muster the Apron-String Guards on the Common,
> That is the corps for the sweet little man!
> Give him for escort a file of young misses,
> Each of them armed with a deadly rattan;
> They shall defend him from laughter and hisses,

SWEET LITTLE MEN OF '61.

"Sweet Little Men of '61" (Billings, *Hardtack & Coffee*, 27)

Aimed by low boys at the sweet little man.
All the fair maidens about him shall cluster,
Pluck the white feathers from bonnet and fan,
Make him a plume like a turkey-wing duster, —
That is the crest for the sweet little man![20]

In Logansport, Indiana, the young ladies of that town passed a resolution in late October 1861 declaring that cowardice was the only fit
excuse for any young man not to enlist. Further, they declared, "we will
have nothing to do with young men who refuse to go to the war, and
that 'Home Guards' must keep their distance." The *Lancaster Daily Intelligencer* wrote of men who were always publicly spoiling to fight Rebels
but never apt to enlist, "unless in the 'Home Guards,' but whenever there
is enlisting to be done his voice is heard above all others in urging others

to do so." In Cleveland, the *Plain Dealer* reported how two men from the Union army's engineer corps had inspected a bluff overlooking Lake Erie as a possible defensive site against Rebel incursion. The paper then noted somewhat sarcastically that manning any artillery placed there would be "nice, pleasant business" for the home guards, all the while still being able to take their meals at home.[21]

Thomas Hicks's 1863 painting *The Home Guard* seemed to encapsulate this form of mocking. The painting depicts a thin, seated man in a Union uniform holding yarn for a young woman who cannot bring herself to look directly at him. Concurrently, the man is under the contemptuous gaze of the young woman's older chaperone, who, while knitting, is thinking the man should be at the front lines rather than in a home front living room. The clear propaganda message in all such literary or artistic efforts was that a healthy man's honorable duty was at the front and not at home.[22]

Moreover, the home guards began to generate a level of annoyance from the "real" soldiers already enlisted within the army. With no small amount of sarcasm, Charles Church of the 3rd Michigan Infantry wrote to his father in October 1861 asking the man to tell the local home guards that he wished them success. Church then asked his father to find out how far the local guards sent out their pickets and how many regiments were engaged in that duty; the clear implication was that such men were only imitation soldiers. The 19th Massachusetts Infantry's Lyman Blackington wrote to his sister in January 1862 complaining about his regiment's current inaction. He wanted to be "smelling gunpowder" because all of their current laying around felt like home guard duty. A New York soldier writing under the name of "Hank" sent a letter to his hometown newspaper jeering those "brave boys" who thought about enlisting several times yet "always returned to their mother's apron strings." This comment was in line with other home front–generated satire alleging that men who wished to remain at home in domestic spaces were feminized and would be pampered by their feminine protectors. "Hank" felt they "ought to be organized into a 'Home Guard' to be armed with broomsticks and paper wads." Later that summer, Lt. James Wade wrote to his mother expressing sarcastic amazement how their town's home guards "were really <u>so rash</u> as to <u>offer their services</u>" after learning of a Union setback in Virginia.[23]

Daniel Perry of the 14th New York Infantry was another who openly decried the home guards and their elaborate, martial-tinged festivities and balls. While being forced to sleep in the Virginia snow, Perry groused to his sister, "If they want a ball, let them come down here and live and sleep on a ball of mud. I think it would do some of them good." After the March 1863 Conscription Act became law, Pvt. Edwin Weller expressed approval of the measure as did all of his comrades. "Let a lot of those home guards . . . come down here and go through what we have," he wrote to his lady friend. "They will not croak quite so much about the Army and why it does not do more." Especially in the Eastern theater, numerous soldiers like Perry and Weller resented having to do all the dirty work while the home guards garnered the public respect of soldiers but never really faced any imminent danger; all of which resulted in some late-war and post-war animosity between Northern soldiers and civilians. Later in the war, a Pennsylvanian in the 62nd Infantry mentioned the possibility of an upcoming draft, which would give his town's home guards "something to do besides laying around." He stressed, however, that he was not referring to workingmen with families, "but those young gents that have nothing to care for but themselves, and think that the young ladies cannot do without their presence." As the war was winding down, Bvt. Maj. Osgood Tracy wrote to his mother in Syracuse, New York, explaining how he hoped to be home within six months and that his heavenly Father would continue to watch over him. If he did fall, however, Osgood wrote that it should be a consolation to his mother that he tried his best to do his duty and "did not belong to the 'Home Guards.'" These soldiers believed that by volunteering in the army, they had sacrificed far more than the home guards and, in the process, proven their courage and honorable manhood while the so-called stay-at-homes had neglected their patriotic duty.[24]

EMPLOYMENT NEEDS

While a patriotic impulse to reunite the nation and avenge the insult to Old Glory—all cloaked in the garments of righteous morality—were certainly what drove many men to enlist, that was hardly the sole, ubiquitous reason as so often portrayed within our collective memory of the Civil War. Most young men could hardly be considered Republican or Democratic ideologues. As historian Bell Wiley recorded in his classic *The Life of Billy Yank*, "Patriotism was indistinguishably blended with practical urges." The majority of Northern men who enlisted in 1861 did so for a variety of mixed reasons, none of which was preeminent. Civil War scholar James McPherson also noted this by citing Mexican War historian James McCaffrey, who wrote that "a desire for personal glory and adventure in a foreign land" was "sometimes masked in the rhetoric of patriotism." Seeking to preserve the glorious "Union" and defeating treason were publicly applauded enlistment motives, self-aggrandizement was not. Nevertheless, like most wars throughout history, the public and private reasons why men volunteered to serve in the nascent Union army were never black and white but colored in various shades of gray.[25]

If "putting down treason" and maintaining the Union's sanctity were the most prominent reasons men proudly and *publicly* proclaimed for enlisting in the Union army, the need for a steady paying job was another motive that men generally kept within themselves and their families. When the Civil War commenced in April 1861, the Northern economy was ailing and had not been robust for years. For years imports had vastly exceeded exports, which resulted in a slow but steady drain of precious metals within the economy. Europe's Crimean War sent its traditional agricultural markets into turmoil, which presented a windfall to Western grain-producing states as they stepped in to fill the void. But when that war ended in 1856 and Europe's customary markets reopened, those Western states were left in the lurch with excessive crops, which caused prices to plunge.[26]

Following his November 1860 election victory, President-elect Lincoln was greeted with a recession that began the prior month and did not end until the following year when the Union's demand for all manner of military supplies sent factory demand for labor and its attendant output surging. Meanwhile, Lincoln's 1860 election victory rang the alarm bell for the Southern slaveholding states who were convinced that Lincoln and the Republicans posed a mortal threat to their economy and way of life. After all, here was a president-elect and party who had no historical or ideological links to the South. Despite Lincoln's words, the Republicans' entire public image seemed opposed to Southern power and culture. Secession talk and preparations began almost immediately, including boycotting Northern products. Southerners renounced their debts to Northern banks and manufacturers, angrily remembering how New York bankers lopped off forty cents of every dollar they paid for Southern cotton for various charges such as credit, insurance, shipping, and storage. All of this prompted a stock market plunge that only worsened the North's recession, manufacturing economy, and related employment.[27]

As the New Year commenced, the commercial reporting agency R. G. Dun and Company informed investors that January 1861 saw 859 business failures, more than double that of the previous January. Demand for goods fell, causing unemployment to spike. Socialite Elizabeth Blair Lee wrote to her husband in early February 1861 how in St. Louis, "all business is prostrate." In Columbus, Ohio, *The Crisis* reported on February 21 that it had never seen so many men out of work. By late March, Pennsylvania's *Clearfield Republican* estimated that at least half of that town's unemployed were now "vibrating between moderate poverty and extreme starvation." In Detroit on May 31, Elizabeth Stuart observed that "None can or will pay . . . Saw mills &c all stopped—No work—No money."[28]

The ongoing recession and its attendant unemployment drove many out-of-work men to consider a volunteer private's pay of thirteen dollars per month to be much better than nothing. After enlisting for lack of steady work, Peter Welsh reminded his wife just how "heartsickening" it was "trying to get along at carpenter work the way times were." In any event, Welsh argued that his soldier's pay was better than what he would make as a carpenter, even assuming he could find it and then having to beg for that work. For those urban civilians who remained behind in economically struggling communities, the prospect of unproductive and excess men leaving for war was often a welcome sight.[29]

Dollars also trumped patriotism for some family members who pressured their single sons or brothers to enlist in order to draw benefits from community relief funds, recently created across the North to financially assist those families whose male breadwinners were now serving in the Union army. These familial support promises were crucial for those family men weighing enlistment. Public "war meeting" speakers assured potential recruits that their dependent wives and children left behind would never feel the cold hand of want. In Connecticut, for instance, numerous legislators and citizens alike with long memories recalled how the state's returning Mexican War veterans were greeted with stony disregard, forcing many to roam the streets in search of a meal. Such callous indifference could not occur again, especially with the new volunteers' wives and children. Recruiting posters across the North touted the need for "good men" or "able-bodied men" but then in smaller print included assurances that the state would provide for needy families left behind while providing relief to any veteran and his family who suffered from the war, thus acknowledging the competing claims between duty to country and responsibility to family. Nonetheless, the posters primarily appealed to manly pride, not family obligations. In Dubuque, Iowa, for example, a group of the town's leading men quickly created an organization "to receive and disburse funds for the benefit of families of volunteers." Known as the Volunteer Fund Board, the association reassured Dubuque's potential initial volunteers that their families would not financially suffer in their absence. This tacit agreement allayed the fears of Dubuque's first two companies of ninety-day soldiers who left town on April 23, 1861.[30]

Dire personal finances even influenced older, would-be officers. After granting his teenage son permission to enlist in a newly formed Connecticut infantry company, Edward Hawley then informed his son that he had written to Connecticut's secretary of state offering to train and lead a company of young men. Requesting confidentiality from his son, Hawley admitted that his business was performing poorly and that a company captain's pay of sixty dollars per month was far better than what he was currently earning. Fighting for flag and Union was not mentioned by the father. Unemployed twenty-seven-year-old William Bolton of Norristown, Pennsylvania, had found work for only four weeks during the six months preceding the April 1861 start of the rebellion. Completely bankrupt, he accepted an officer's commission and its attendant salary of $115.50 per month in the 4th Pennsylvania Infantry once the war started. In an era when a skilled blacksmith or carpenter might average around $570 per year, Bolton's $1,386 annual salary was quite handsome indeed. Moreover, Bolton and others like him who had struggled to find work knew that the army also offered an unemployed man an added incentive in the form of employment stability rarely found in civilian life. The 13th New York Infantry's captain Samuel S. Partridge conceded that point, writing in early August 1861 how the current certainty of his military pay and position served to stifle his civilian lawyerly ambitions. Nonetheless, if his ninety-day enlistment ended soon, as he expected, any potential reenlistment would be based mainly upon his law practice's prospects or lack thereof.[31]

Plenty of young men held to that employment logic. If reliable work was to be had at decent wages, then potential army enlistment was cast off to the side. A Connecticut man with good employment who eventually enlisted in August 1862 rationalized his decision not to enlist at the war's opening sixteen months earlier in part by writing, "there were men enough out of employment who considered it a privilege to enter the army because they had no other means of support." In that group was young Edwin Worthington, who confessed to his mother, "I could find nothing to do anywhere so . . . I went off to New York and enlisted." Another young man, Phinias E. Johnson, wrote to his cousin lamenting that he could not find work nor did he have any decent prospects. A few months later, Johnson's uncle clarified his nephew's decision, "He enlisted . . . in a fit of dejection and discouragement at not being successful in getting steady work or a proper remuneration." Both Worthington and Johnson were dead within a year. In the border state of Kentucky, a Union man wrote to a federal officer on May 5, 1861, pointing out that money was the primary inducement for getting men to enlist since there were so many unemployed who needed the pay for their families' subsistence.[32]

Even with the new war, tough economic times still permeated the North. In St. Louis, the *Republican* refuted claims that the city was suffering from a labor shortage because of so many men enlisting in the army. Rather, it asserted the reverse; that it was the lack of work that compelled so many workingmen to enlist. In Abington, Massachusetts, Rufus Robbins Sr. wrote to his son serving with the 7th Massachusetts Infantry in mid-August 1861 that "Business is as dead here as it was when you went away." On August 25, Samuel Dickerman informed his brother from Pepperell—about sixty-five miles northwest of Abington—that "business of all kinds is dead as can be here & is likely to be for some time." Vermont's *Daily Green Mountain Freeman* spoke for many men like Bolton, Partridge, Harris, and others when it opined, "In these hard times no business promises better pay than enlisting in the army." Though on a less overt scale, the pecuniary considerations that prompted countless young men to enlist in the spring and summer of 1861 were fundamentally no different from the lucrative bounties that spurred others to enlist in the summer and fall of 1862.[33]

The North's excessive labor supply was somewhat absorbed in mid-1861 by both the government's call for ninety-day militia and the seasonal need for agricultural labor. Nevertheless, the Northern economy's employment situation remained tenuous off and on until 1863. A Pennsylvanian summed up the hard financial realities faced by many men when he urged his wife in early November 1861 not to cry over his enlistment because "you know if i could have got work i wood not have left you or the children."[34]

***

Considering their conviction that the war would be short, young men and teen boys rushed to enlist believing their ninety-day service would be a quick, relatively easy summer outing; a chance to gain martial glory while parading in their new uniforms. Numerous employers even offered volunteers to hold their positions open for them because every Union volunteer seemed convinced that one stern look at the Rebels and the latter would turn tail and run. Personal bravery itself would settle the matter. A then-unknown man from Galena, Illinois, named Ulysses S. Grant—who would command all Union armies three years later—wrote to his father on May 6, 1861, stating his belief that the war would be of "short duration." In his first letter home written from his training camp on

June 2, Chandler Bertram of the 28th New York Infantry characterized this short war sentiment when he informed his wife how the prevailing opinion was that his regiment would be disbanded by fall at the latest. They would then return home to a hero's welcome, thereby burnishing their public claims to the era's definition of "honorable manhood." Ohio's Thomas Evans acknowledged this. "We supposed the war would be only a short duration," he explained in his diary. Then, once the war ended, "in our view we were soon to return and then bearing the name of a soldier would lift us above all common people. Alas, how vain were our thoughts." Nineteen-year-old Frank Rieley clarified to his mother in his first letter home why he had enlisted without either her approval or knowledge. He primarily considered it a duty that every family should send at least one man to help save the country. Moreover, if he survived the war, he reasoned his service would help him along in life as "people will know that I have grit in me." Proving one's manliness was a powerful motivator for teen boys and young men of the era. "I think it is evry young man's duty who feels any interest in his Country . . . [to] go and fight for it and prove himself a man," wrote twenty-two-year-old Symmes Stillwell in a letter to his mother typifying this important cultural value.[35]

Maintaining a positive public reputation mattered as well. Men who were already successful had to evaluate the potential costs of enlisting or not because men in the middle or near the top of the economic and/ or social ladders of success certainly had more to lose than a relatively unknown man near the bottom. A struggling unmarried man generally had nothing to hold him back whereas a stable family man had much to consider, including his family or business's cash flow as well as his social status should he not volunteer. William H. L. Wallace was already a highly successful thirty-nine-year-old lawyer when the rebellion commenced, however, as a man with Mexican War military credentials, he wasted no time in accepting the colonelcy of the 11th Illinois Infantry when it was formed at the beginning of the war, despite his wife's misgivings. He reminded her that the country needed such men as him and therefore, "Being thus situated in having the opportunity of going into the service for the war, we would justly and doubtless receive censure of all loyal people should we decline." In referring to her cousin and lawyer,

William Lister, Sarah Wister noted in her diary how thirty-three-year-old William's enlistment decision weighed heavy since, like William Wallace, he was also well-entrenched in his successful law practice. However, she also sensed that William's public reputation would be more damaged by staying at home rather than by enlisting. What others might say and think was a matter worth considering for many successful men.[36]

Various middle- and upper-middle-class men did not want to merely enlist per se but rather sought officer's commissions as a way of maintaining or even improving their current social status. Healthy ambition as exhibited via military promotion displayed a key Victorian value of moral self-improvement and proper masculinity. As a result, such "spreading renown" as the father of one junior officer referred to it, could lead to post-war financial prosperity, business success, or even political power. For an ample number of bourgeoisie young men and their parents, enlisting in the war with a junior officer's commission was considered the first step in what was hoped would be a promising career.[37]

Furthermore, numerous middle- and upper-class men feared that enlisting as a mere private might harm one's current social standing. When one young woman was asked why her wealthy father had not gone into the ranks after realizing that "not everybody could get places," she wrote that she found the question rather insulting and then replied to her questioner, "My Father is made of better stuff." Maine's B. F. Smart responded to his father's question regarding promotion possibilities by stating that an officer's commission in the Regular army "would satisfy my highest ambition" but acknowledged that such an appointment was unlikely if he did not first distinguish himself in the volunteer service. "If doing my duty well will entitle me to any consideration, I mean to come out of this matter at least a lieutenant," admitted Samuel Partridge in early June 1861 to his brother. As an assistant adjutant and aide-de-camp, Partridge knew he didn't have to "get my name up by any great bravery, but by doing my duty every day in a manner to meet the approbation of my officers." When his desired officer's commission did not arrive as quickly as expected, Charles Brewster expressed some jealousy toward those who were reaping the financial advantages of an officer's pay. "It seems everybody got their nests feathered but me," he complained to his sister and then added, "at any rate everybody that can't earn their living any other way." Within their personal calculus, those men who were not farmers were quite cognizant of the post-war benefits they quietly expected to gain, such as the enriched opportunities that would be accorded to honorable veterans as well as an enhanced social standing among women.[38]

PROVING ONE'S MANLINESS AND APPEALING TO WOMEN

Feminine influence—especially from younger women—regarding male enlistment was predictable and certainly obtained the desired effect. Pro-war newspapers dutifully put forth the propaganda message via editorials, poems, and cartoons that mothers, wives, sisters, and sweethearts should urge their men to enlist. A small-town Connecticut newspaper, for example, encouraged the town's women to "hurry along your husbands, sons, and brothers to the field!" Iowa's *Cedar Falls Gazette* suggested that "the girls" should "put their shoulders to the wheel" and tell their lovers they would be discarded if they did not enlist. In other instances and what might be compared to England's World War I "White Feather Campaign," unmarried young women went door to door armed with recruitment forms and coquettish smiles as they asked single men to sign their names and serve their country.[39]

If smiles and appeals did not spur men to enlist, then shaming tactics just might. While recognizing he wasn't initially quite brave enough to face Rebel guns, Illinois' J. F. Skinner also admitted how "chafed" he felt when he heard one of the local ladies sarcastically remark "how nice it was to have an able-bodied young man that did not care enough about his country to expose his precious self." A "Volunteer's Sister" mocked and pitied such "chicken-hearted fellows" who refused to enlist. She then asked what shall be done with these "Home Pets," since it was everyone's duty to elevate them and turn these "Dooryard Rangers" into honorable men. In the case of married men, some of the relatively few who chose to enlist in the war's early months were certainly inspired by their wives to do so and most likely for patriotic reasons. Their wives may have even

HOW WIVES MAY MAKE THEIR HUSBANDS ENLIST.
LADY—"*Either you or I, sir.*"

"How Wives May Make Their Husbands Enlist" "Lady—'Either you or I, sir.'"
(*Frank Leslie's Budget of Fun*, October 1863)

linked their own community honor with that of their husbands who were stepping forward to answer the nation's call.[40]

Charles Biddlecom of upstate New York hinted in his letters that he enlisted solely to prove his manliness not only to himself and his wife, but to his extended family as well. "I don't care a (—) for the Union and think it is not worth the life of one man," Biddlecom confessed. "To me, I fight because I'm too proud to be called a coward." At twenty-nine years old and married, Biddlecom was much older than most recruits, yet he enlisted in the 28th New York Infantry when the war began convinced that the war would not last more than a few months. When he found the war and his place in it still ongoing in early August, Biddlecom decided he had seen enough of "soljerin'" and obtained an honorable discharge due to his purported rheumatism.[41]

Army recruiters, government officials, pro-war newspaper editors, and pro-war women emphasized that female attraction would naturally flow toward those men who patriotically responded to their nation's call. They stressed that desirable young ladies would rebuke the rich man's supposedly cowardly son with soft hands who had no intention of enlisting. Instead, they sought the manly, therefore courageous rough-hewn volunteer who risked all for flag and country because the era's gendered ideal dictated that a coward could not be a noble father or faithful husband. This was a conviction that cut across both the North and South. The paradigm was illuminated in a later conversation at a Mississippi hospital between an ex-Confederate soldier who had escaped his forced enlistment and noted Unionist Sarah Edmonds. The man explained to Edmonds how young Confederate women were the South's best recruiters because "they absolutely refuse to tolerate, or admit to their society, any young man who refuses to enlist." According to the soldier, such men were apt to receive a package containing skirts and crinoline with a note from a young woman explaining why such an outfit was appropriate for him unless he immediately donned a Con-federate uniform. Even Confederate president Jefferson Davis added to this debate by remarking how young women should prefer the wounded soldier with the "empty sleeve" rather than "the muscular arm of him who staid at home and grew fat."[42]

Historian Gerald Linderman noted that the female "secret weapon" in this regard was "sexual intimidation" as exemplified in Sarah Edmonds' conversation. For in mid-nineteenth-century America, the concepts of male duty and honor were closely associated with the era's gendered ideals pertaining to proper masculinity. With regards to soldiering and single men, those who refused to enlist might as well be women. "I would not give a copper for a man who would not volunteer to the rescue of his country, when her institutions, her property, and lives of her citizens were assailed by traitors," wrote Eliza Tomlinson to her husband in a letter later published in the *Cincinnati Gazette*. Twenty-one-year-old Ellen Wright struck a sterner tone when she wrote in 1861 how she "wouldn't look at" a man not in service. Emma Moody made clear her scorn for those not in uniform when she declared to a soldier friend, "If ever you hear of me maring An Abolition or a home coward you please tell me of it for if there is any I dispise it is these two classes of men." Other women were a bit more introspective, such as Demia Butler, who asked her army brother rhetorically, "Don't you think it were better to select our gentleman friends from those who at least appear to love their country and are trying to defend it rather than from those staying at home who have brains too weak and souls too narrow ever to feel a lofty sentiment of patriotism?"[43]

A proud man of the era did not want to be seen on the receiving end of a woman's chastisement for his unwillingness to serve his country in its hour of need. A single woman might object to the war's rationales as a matter of personal principle, but it was another issue entirely to abide her beau's reluctance to serve. Those young unmarried men who did enlist were often rewarded with a steady stream of letters from female friends and relatives urging them to remain proud and steadfast in their duties. As one youthful Indiana lad admitted, "If a fellow wants to go with the girl now he had better enlist. The girls sing 'I Am Bound to be a Soldier's Wife or Die an Old Maid.'"[44]

Moreover, there was an unspoken social consensus that younger single men should be the first to volunteer, given their relative lack of obligations to family and community or their successful establishment within a given occupation. Married men or those who owned productive property and businesses were higher up on the pecking order. After enlisting into the 2nd New Hampshire Infantry, Ai Baker Thompson admitted these sentiments to his father, who Thompson knew would be disheartened over his son's enlistment. "Tell mother that I should consider myself but little better than a traitor . . . if in this hour of my country's peril, situated as I am, without wife or children . . . I should hesitate a single moment to volunteer my feeble services in defense of the stars and stripes." Ohio's Alvin Morris, though married, also sensed this dynamic when he wrote to his wife shortly after the war started, "Were I a <u>single</u> man I should seek glory in the tented field." Morris then reassured her, "my obligation [is] to you and our little ones." As it turned out, unmarried eighteen-year-olds were the largest single age group for Northern enlistees. Most married men, in contrast, worked their family farm or held jobs in which they were their family's breadwinner. They knew that in most cases, leaving to "go a soljerin'" would most likely impose severe economic hardship on their families.[45]

One historian estimated that of the men in Vigo County, Indiana, who initially enlisted into the 11th Indiana Infantry, no more than one-third were married. In Parke County's (Indiana) Penn Township, of the 104 married men of military age, only nine enlisted before the first draft in 1863. This collective belief was also on display in Adrian, Michigan, when Henry Brown wrote to his friends observing how the town's initial volunteers were practically all single men from Adrian or nearby. Brown noted, "Some married men enlisted but the single men turned out so freely that the others got their discharge & are not going." In Iowa, George Burmeister wrote in his diary on April 29 how "All the married men and some others were dismissed in order to reduce the company to one hundred men." Twenty-three-year-old Madison Bowler of Minnesota summed up this widely accepted conviction: "Somebody must go," he conceded, "and who can go better than young men like myself without business and without family to demand my attention."[46]

MALE AND COMMUNITY PEER PRESSURE

In addition to women's influences on one's perceived masculinity, male peer pressure also enacted a tremendous pull on young men. It was an example of the herd instinct for no man—especially a young, vibrant single man—wanted to be perceived as a shirker or coward by his community when his peers were enlisting all around him. Moreover, young men often enlisted voluntarily in family or friend groups so they could all serve together, rather than risk being drafted later as individuals once conscription became a factor in August 1862. This herd instinct was important, for in the Civil War era, a man's honor was intrinsically linked to his courage, which was viewed by both men and women as the manliest of all character traits. Who better for a man to showcase his manly courage than to those who knew him best? Courage and cowardice were viewed as issues of character, not context. "Character is what involuntarily commands respect . . . what makes itself felt," opined *Putnam's Monthly Magazine* in 1854. Hence, those men who possessed good character as civilians would therefore show themselves as having good character in war. Conversely, those who did *not* enlist lacked character or manly courage, or so the belief went.[47]

John Haley of the 17th Maine Infantry admitted to these values in his journal, explaining how once one friend enlisted, "the rest thoughtlessly followed, like sheep over a fence." In that heady moment of enthusiasm, Haley realized he had to either enlist with his friends or "show a white liver by backing out." John Billings remembered that unless a young man's reasons for not enlisting straightaway were unimpeachable, "he was hooted at for his cowardice, and for a time his existence was made quite unpleasant in his own immediate neighborhood." Leander Stillwell of Illinois would certainly have concurred with Haley and Billings. Though only seventeen years old at the time and therefore legally too young to serve, he somehow enlisted in the summer of 1861 against his father's wishes because "It was simply intolerable to think that I could stay at home, among the girls, and be pointed at by the soldier boys as a stay-at-home coward." Borden Hicks likewise admitted later in life that patriotism played no part in his June 1861 enlistment at age seventeen. "All I wanted was a chance to don a uniform, to march and fight, to do some heroic deed," Hicks confessed, so that he could "come back home and be admired by the girls, as a hero." Such teen angst generated by coercive communal pressure was not uncommon for there appeared to be no greater barometer of a boy traversing the rite of passage into manhood than by his willingness to enlist and march off to war. Abner Hard, the surgeon for the 8th Illinois Cavalry, acknowledged in his post-war regimental history that there had always been ample discussion throughout the army regarding the so-called "stay-at-home cowards." With a hint of sarcasm, Hard speculated the reason why these men stayed home was because "it was their duty to remain that those who enlisted might have someone to 'huzzah' for them." Another veteran, however, saw a perverse benefit in such men remaining at home, believing it was better to have loyal men stay at home rather than the disloyal. In essence, and as then-Capt. Julius Hinkley of the 3rd Wisconsin Infantry later opined, "There is nothing that so quickly arouses the combativeness of men, and especially of young men, as the intimation that they are cowards."[48]

As the war dragged on, however, veteran soldiers learned the potential pitfalls of youthful men hurriedly enlisting for such reasons. They saw how a green, teenage recruit's naive desire for adventure or glory could quickly dissipate and how those men might vanish once hot work was at hand. This concern was especially disconcerting for one army doctor who criticized eighteen-year-old boys enlisting as they were the ones most susceptible to homesickness or what the army termed "nostalgia." Months after the war started, a 144th New York Infantry veteran flatly told a friend not to enlist for any motive other than a keen sense of personal duty to his country. "There would be less skedaddling and more good soldiers" if others took that advice, he surmised. Capt. Samuel Merrill of the 70th Indiana Infantry also felt that men who enlisted under such circumstances did not make good long-term soldiers. He bitterly complained to his wife that nine-tenths of the volunteers he saw "enlisted just because somebody else was going, and the other tenth was ashamed to stay at home."[49]

Once the initial wave of war fever subsided, community "war meetings" were another popular and continuous method of exerting local peer pressure. By the end of October 1864, for example, the town of Brockport, New York, had held at least thirty-one such meetings over the previous thirty-eight months. These public gatherings frequently occurred in churches or town squares and took on a celebratory festive air, not unlike a religious revival. Such rallies were popular and efficient in more rural areas where a town's leading men would organize companies and sometimes even regiments. These town leaders, well-known and generally respected by all, were then, in turn, usually elected by their new recruits to serve as company captains and lieutenants. Liquor was often liberally shared by army recruiters with prospective recruits. Local bands played all manner of martial music, women sang patriotic songs and read similar-styled poems, while current army officers, preachers, and old veterans from the Mexican War and even the War of 1812 were trotted out to make rousing patriotic speeches urging men to enlist.[50]

It was also common for boisterous civilian men to publicly proclaim their patriotic support for the war at these rallies while loudly declaring their intent to enlist *if* certain other men or a specific number of volunteers enlisted then and there. Pvt. Warren Goss recalled how one such speaker called for volunteers and then boldly proclaimed how "human life must be cheapened." Goss dryly noted that he never learned if the man ever contributed to that cheapening. More often than not, such men and all in attendance knew their prerequisites were unrealistic. As the desired consequence, they acquired whatever patriotic virtue their overblown oratory may have bought them while knowing that the odds of them actually having to follow through on their promises were slim to none. These were the men who were described as "invincible in peace and invisible in war." This was what Pennsylvanian L. S. Shorton had in mind when he urged a friend not to dissuade a mutual acquaintance from enlisting, "but rather use your influence to get others to go." Their stirring words harkened back to the Revolutionary War and served not only as an immediate call to action but often included some not-so-subtle shaming tactics, such as when a newly minted captain boldly proclaimed at a Wisconsin rally, "I would rather fill a soldier's grave than stay at home a coward." Even worse for an unsuspecting young man at such a rally was if his lady friend, spurred on by the hoopla and excitement, publicly urged him to enlist without his prior approval or even knowledge that she would do so. "John, if you do not enlist I'll never let you kiss me again as long as I live!" proclaimed one young woman to the embarrassment of her male friend and the jeers of his mates who had already volunteered.[51]

A WAR MEETING.

"A War Meeting" (Billings, *Hardtack & Coffee*, 39)

This type of zero-sum peer pressure had the desired effect on the burgeoning "manly pride" of boys and young men, many of whom were still in their late teens, because the era's romanticized and dominant culture—essentially White, male, and middle class—dictated that no self-respecting man could gain communal approval without projecting his manly courage. "We could not bear the thought of seeing two thirds of the men in our town leaving their business and rushing to the battle-field . . . and we staying at home like cowards," acknowledged William Tebbetts, who eventually enlisted into the 45th Illinois Infantry in December 1861. Tebbetts realized that stepping up to enlist was viewed as the "manly courage" benchmark's first litmus test. All it usually took was one man to sign his name to the enlistment rolls and then, like dominoes falling, others followed, always to the sound of the crowd's rousing cheers. The next day, after the excitement and perhaps the liquor had worn off, some men inevitably regretted their decision. Then-Capt. Isaac J. Wistar later wrote, "In short, for every hundred men, drunk and sober, actually got by hook and crook safely on board the [train] cars, at least a hundred and fifty had to be [coerced], in consequence of the ever-changing views of themselves and their anxious relatives . . . even after the trains were in motion, many jumped off, with courage worthy of a better cause." Such shenanigans were uncommon, however, for as one old soldier later recollected, "Pride, that tyrannical master, rarely let them turn back."[52]

Bored at Home and Seeking Adventure

In 1861, most of the North's population lived in small rural towns or on farms, and most had never ventured more than twenty-five miles from their homes. For young men everywhere who wanted to see the country or were perhaps bored at home, enlisting into the rapidly filling volunteer regiments afforded them a golden opportunity to see another part of the country without personal expense since the army would be providing them with food, clothing, pay, and transportation. After a group of his college friends enlisted, Henry Alvord suspected, "there is but little real patriotism in the movement. Most go for novelty, for the sake of going." Eighteen-year-old Thomas Christie freely admitted that motives other than patriotic influenced his enlistment but did not see those motives as wrong. "I do want to see the world, to get out of the narrow circle in which I have always lived, to make a man of myself." For teenage boys like Alvord and Christie, the possibility of being on the receiving end of a Johnny Reb minié ball barely registered. This sense of adventure was reinforced by the army's recruiting posters, which stressed the manly prestige afforded to the "good," "brave-hearted," or "able-bodied patriots" who volunteered for a given regiment.[53]

Others knew that volunteering into the army meant they would be out from under the watchful eyes of parents and preachers for the first time in their lives; many were seemingly eager to embrace what were deemed the most masculine of military vices: drinking and fornication. With regards to this eagerness, Michigan's Charles Haydon dryly noted from his Detroit training camp in May 1861 how, "If the men pursue the enemy as eagerly as they do the whores, they will make very efficient soldiers."[54]

The 1860 census revealed a fall in the marriage rate over the preceding decade along with a rise in the initial marriage age for both men and women. This was due no doubt, in part, to additional census data showing that single men noticeably outnumbered single women

33

in most urban areas during the 1850s, which led, in turn, to a growing and robust sex trade industry in those towns by the time the Civil War commenced. By 1862, there were 450 registered brothels—also known as "bawdy houses"—in Washington, DC, alone and almost 600 operating in New York City. When war reporter Franc Wilkie left Washington in the autumn of 1862, he described it as "the most pestiferous hole since the days of Sodom and Gomorrah" while "most of the women on the street were openly disreputable." From Wilkie's vantage, the number of drunken Union officers in uniform who haunted the bordellos and bar-rooms every night would have been sufficient to capture Richmond. For many pious men, the long-term effects were predictable. "Whiskey and sexual vices carry off more soldiers than the bullet," Cyrus Boyd noted in his diary in January 1863.[55]

For country boys or farmhands, many of whom were still teenagers, speculative concepts like "Union" or "nation" had little initial impact on their localized lives and small-town values. What concept of nationalism existed was more likely a feeling of regional or class pride because the country had grown up with its citizens believing that one's primary loyalty was to family and community. Familial and community roots ran deeper than those attached to the nation, which helps to explain why the war and its attendant communal infighting became so intense. Most national events in the past were distant and often had little impact on citizens' day-to-day lives. In fact, for most adults, their only interactions with the national government were voting (for men), the occasional trip to the post office, or perhaps engaging in a land purchase from the federal government.[56]

The initial journeys from home for young men like Christie, Smith, Boyd, and others to far-off towns or training centers were viewed by them as a grand adventure, not unlike the romanticized, manly tales of the era. The more literate of those young farm boys and urban men had been raised on such stories and poems as Lord Tennyson's "The Charge of the Light Brigade," Timothy Flint's *Biographical Memoir of Daniel Boone*, or Longfellow's then-recent "Paul Revere's Ride." These masculine works focused on action and heroism, which therefore helped to imbue young men with a stirring sense of male honor that, secretly perhaps, made a youthful male view himself as the noble knight off on a glorious mission. For such boys and men, *not* enlisting would be interpreted by his peers and community as a public failure of what it meant to be a man.[57]

Country lads marveled at the technological wonders of modern trains and steamboats during their initial trip from home to training camp. Cheering crowds, martial bands, buffet-style meals, and pretty young women frequently greeted them at the various train stations. At one such stop, a then seventeen-year-old lad remembered how he was told by an attractive young maiden that she would "rather kiss a soldier than eat her dinner." The boy later admitted that he did not take the hint, opting instead to accept the cup of hot coffee in her hand. A young New Yorker recalled how throughout his journey, men filled his pockets with cigars and even insisted he accept the money they offered him. If he kindly refused, they forced it into his pockets. At the very least, the prospects of a short, ninety-day war and personal glory generated a sense of martial excitement within these young men and a welcome break in what may have been viewed as an otherwise dull existence.[58]

While some younger men left their families seeking adventure, other, usually older, men sometimes joined the army as a means of escaping problems at home. For example, if a man was facing a criminal or debt proceeding, enlistment might prove a temporary solution. As another means of encouraging enlistments, thirteen loyal states enacted statutes during the war that authorized postponing any ongoing court action against a man engaged in military service. Judges, in fact, routinely "suggested" that some just-convicted men show their patriotism and remorse by voluntarily enlisting rather than being sent off to jail.[59]

In other instances, a man's problem may have been with the bottle rather than the courts. One Northern woman sensed that getting her drunkard husband into the army was a viable means of helping him find sobriety. After losing every dollar he owned during a weekend bender in Boston, Peter Welsh enlisted into the 28th Massachusetts Infantry as a means of gaining back some income. "There is hundreds of men here who got in to it in the same way I did," he admitted to his wife, but only *after* he enlisted and arrived in Washington.[60]

Family or marital issues were also contributing if not primary factors for those men seeking a new life and then often under assumed names.

Nineteen-year-old James Horrocks did just that after being named in a paternity suit by a sixteen-year-old girl in his hometown of Farnworth, England. Though he proclaimed his innocence, he nevertheless fled his home for the Liverpool docks in the summer of 1863, where he quickly boarded a New York–bound ship. Once in the States, he enlisted into the 5th New Jersey Light Artillery under the name of "Andrew Ross" only after his attempts to find acceptable civilian employment had failed. In his first letter home dated September 5, the well-educated Horrocks seemed quite pleased with himself because his decision and chosen service branch had netted him the largest cash bounty possible. (Bounties are discussed in detail in chapter 5.) As additional bonuses, Horrocks explained that he would have light work, suffer no picket duty or carry heavy knapsacks around, plus he would have the benefit of riding a horse. With no stake in or care for the war's larger issues, the foreign-born Horrocks epitomized the "Yankee hireling" that many Confederates asserted had filled the Union armies' rank and file.[61]

These possible enlistment scenarios were not only the case for new volunteers but had existed that way in the Regular army for decades. Whereas the volunteer citizen-soldier exemplified the essence of civic duty and patriotic integrity, any man who had sought enlistment into the Regular army in the mid-nineteenth century was generally regarded as a ne'er-do-well; a man who had something to hide or at the very least, something he wanted to forget. Such service then did not carry with it the respect and public gratitude that many in our modern era convey to those men and women in uniform. Rather, the army was viewed as the last resort of the drunkard or idler, especially when the burgeoning nation was considered a land flowing with economic opportunity for any man and his family. One antebellum army journal reported that during an investigation of a particular fifty-five-man company, "It appeared that nine-tenths enlisted on account of female difficulty; thirteen . . . had changed their names, and forty-three were either drunk, or partially so at the time of their enlistment." As late as 1863, the army's manual on how doctors should evaluate recruits noted that serving in the army during peacetime presented "so few attractions that men of good reputation, having other means of earning a livelihood, avoid it, and the ranks are filled up from the idle, the dissolute, and the unfortunate."[62]

A man may have been able to erase and escape his background, but his habits and character traits usually remained. Pennsylvanian Henry Armprister abandoned his civilian life for the army at age fifty-two, leaving behind a wife and seven children. His problems with alcohol, however, shadowed him to the front. His commanding officer considered Armprister a good soldier when he was not drunk, but that was a moot point because the man was rarely sober. Eventually, Armprister was court-martialed for deserting the army, just as he had earlier forsaken his family.[63]

Foreign immigrants sought to serve in the Union army for many of the same reasons as native-born recruits. At least in the early years, patriotic and nationalistic devotion to their new homeland was part of their mix but rarely the sole reason. For many who had experienced some form of ethnic prejudice, especially the Irish and Germans, their choice to voluntarily enlist into the Union ranks would showcase their desire and commitment to becoming "real" Americans.[64]

Constant hunger created by poverty was another tyrant poor men sought refuge from, especially for the wretched Irish immigrants wallowing in New York City's slums. All but driven out of Ireland by the 1840s potato famine, the United States became the preferred destination for poverty-stricken Irish emigrants, who were attracted to these shores not only by the nation's political and social freedoms but also by what they believed to be the sheer quantity of available work. All of which would surely help fill their families' empty stomachs. America's decades-long laissez-faire attitude toward immigration bespoke an open-door policy for the downtrodden Irish.[65]

A correspondent for the *Illustrated London News* reported after the July 21, 1861, Bull Run battle that, "Many of the recruits from New York City care not a jot for the integrity of the Union, but have enlisted to escape from starvation." George Sala, the *London Daily Telegraph*'s correspondent, wrote in his diary how after years of observing American society, he was convinced that those immigrants who enlisted were simply "aliens who have sold themselves for certain sums of money."

Perhaps that was because poverty could be a powerful motivator. In their study of letters written by German immigrants in the Civil War, Walter Kamphoefner and Wolfgang Helbich noted how at least one-third (and maybe more) of the men in their soldier group had enlisted primarily because they were unable to find gainful employment. One of those men was Gustav Keppler, who admitted "I went and enlisted only when I had no other choice," while another man, August Strohsahl, wrote of his frustration in not being able to find work on land or sea. Therefore, Strohsahl lamented, "there was nothing I could do but become a soldier." Though obviously not true for all immigrants, a new suit of blue clothes and the prospect of steady meals and pay proved to be ample inducement for the many poor immigrant men who had little to no knowledge of the political issues surrounding the new rebellion.[66]

SLAVERY'S ABOLITION

Though modern scholarship places slavery as central to our understanding of why the Civil War was fought, relatively few men who chose to enlist in the war's opening months did so with slavery's abolition as their *primary* motivator. This was especially true for conservative Democrats, who supported the war only as a means of restoring the Union and thereby reestablishing the federal government's legitimate authority, but not to abolish slavery, which, after all, was still constitutionally legal. To those men, the North's "Radical Republican" abolitionists were just as guilty of bringing on the war as were the South's "fire-eaters." Such explosive political matters, they believed, should be settled at the negotiating table or the ballot box, not at the cannon's mouth.[67]

In his seminal 1935 work, *Black Reconstruction*, the famous African American historian and civil rights activist W. E. B. Du Bois, acknowledged "The North went to war without the slightest idea of freeing the slave." Decades later, historian Randall Jimerson estimated that only one in ten recruits enlisted with slavery's abolition as a personal, primary war aim. Given that almost 99 percent of citizens in the Northern free states were White, it is not surprising that most recruits knew no Black people much less ever laid eyes on a slave. Dennis W. Brandt noted in his social history of the 87th Pennsylvania Infantry and its community that none of the many pre-1863 soldier letters he examined from that regiment contained the words "slavery," "slave," or "abolition." Any "rights" the soldiers wrote of, Brandt explained, were in reference to their own. That perspective had not changed in the months immediately following the war's end. In their respective analyses of dozens of Union regimental histories written and published during the years 1865 to 1866—which therefore accorded them a still-fresh perspective—historians Peter Luebke and Gary Gallagher both concluded there was a strong consensus among those books' veterans-turned-historians: The war had been fought primarily to preserve the Union; freedom for the slave was an additional outcome with the soldiers having supported emancipation first and foremost as a war measure, rather than on overtly humanitarian grounds.[68]

Almost all Northern volunteers were more concerned at the war's start with "stamping out treason" rather than ending slavery. "Put down the rebellion 1st say I and let the niggers take care of themselves" was seventeen-year-old Pvt. Charlie Brandegee's succinct yet widely held opinion. Francis Bliss put forth a similar belief, believing there was too much hand-wringing about slaves and not enough focus on the rebels. "Let us let the negroes alone, and all hands take right hold of this Rebellion and put it down and it will be done in less than three months," he asserted to his mother in November 1862. O. W. Norton of the 83rd Pennsylvania Infantry reminded his sister in January 1862, "This is not a war against slavery, but for the Union." For those who felt it should be about abolition, Norton was dismissive: "Away with such nonsense, I say, and the soldiers all say so."[69]

Famed poet Walt Whitman, who worked as a volunteer in Washington's military hospitals during the war, later wrote, "Not the Negro, not the Negro. The Negro was not the chief thing. The chief thing was to stick together." Even Abraham Lincoln admitted where his original priorities were in his famous August 22, 1862, letter to *New York Tribune* editor Horace Greely when he declared, "My paramount object in this struggle is to save the Union, and is not either to save or to destroy slavery." The perspectives put forth by men like Whitman and Lincoln were also apparent in the North's newspapers. In his modern representative survey of Northern newspapers, Nathan Kalmoe calculated that ending slavery appeared as an early, primary war goal in only 4 percent of the papers.[70]

White Northerners lived in an ambivalent world regarding slavery and race. While most Northern Americans had decried slavery as barbaric and wrong since the beginning of the nineteenth century, probably no more than 15 percent supported its immediate abolition. Furthermore, the majority of those who did support emancipation as a war aim had no intention of seeing the freed slaves remain in the United States in what they feared would be a permanent state of idleness. Democrats and Republicans both subscribed to the era's racist stereotype that depicted Blacks as inherently lazy, but while Democrats felt that way due to their belief in the African's racial inferiority, Republicans blamed it on slavery's characteristic barbarism and degradation. Their goal was to see the freedmen sent elsewhere, perhaps to Western lands set aside for Native Americans or even colonized onto some Caribbean island. This sentiment was typified by Ohio housewife Jane Evans, who wrote to her son, "I would not mind freeing the Negros if they could be sent off and not come back here again." Thinking upon the matter, a Wisconsin private concluded, "I think I have a good degree of sympathy for the <u>Slave</u>, but I like the <u>Negro</u> the farther off the better." Such matter-of-fact racial prejudice also perversely helped to lessen the North's initial hostility to Black soldiers, once Whites realized that a Black man in a blue uniform could stop a Rebel bullet just as easily as a White one. Moreover, Northern free Blacks enlisting into the army would be sent far away to Southern battlefields where they would hopefully remain once the war ended. Kansan Sam Reader realized this "benefit" when he wrote in August 1862, "I consider myself a philanthropist in regard to African Slaves, still I do not carry this so far as to wish to see men of my own Race dragged from home and business which urgently requires their presence, while these same Slaves ought & are willing to fight for their freedom." Slavery and the appropriate place for Africans within American society were issues most Whites preferred to ignore.[71]

Nonetheless, there were Northerners who, from the outset, viewed slavery as the real issue. Those abolition-centered men who eagerly enlisted into the Union army were clear within their letters as to why they had donned the Union uniform. The nascent war allowed them to turn their idealism into social action. Though far older than most recruits, forty-year-old Taylor Pierce enlisted into the 22nd Iowa Infantry in August 1862. In one of his first letters to his wife on September 13—one week *before* Lincoln issued his Preliminary Emancipation Proclamation—Pierce stressed that it was his duty to "try and be one of the many that God has raised to put down this rebellion and blot out the institution of slavery." At the other end of the country, a Vermont corporal proclaimed, "Slavery must die and if the South insists on being buried in the same grave I shall see in it nothing but the retributive hand of God."[72]

The war's harsh realities—such as a camp's tedium and its unsanitary conditions, communicable diseases, supply and ration shortages, as well as the battlefield's mangled corpses and cries of the wounded—all had a profound effect on those Union volunteers. What they saw and experienced was a far cry from their earlier idealized imagery. It did not matter whether they were young or older, nor whether they had enlisted for purely patriotic or other sundry reasons. The bloody carnage and subsequent rout that the Union suffered at the first battle of Bull Run near Manassas, Virginia, on July 21, 1861, served as an unwelcomed splash of icy water on the North's collective face. A smaller though no less psychologically dismal defeat occurred outside of Leesburg, Virginia, three months later on October 21 at the battle of Ball's Bluff. After that engagement, Washingtonians were treated to the grisly sight of dead Union soldiers whose bloated corpses had floated down the Potomac River into the North's capital city after they had drowned near the battlefield's riverbanks only forty miles away. Then in southwestern Tennessee at the battle of Shiloh on April 6–7, 1862, more men fell in two days of fighting than in all other American wars combined up to that date. Northern citizens and soldiers alike realized the war was not going to be the brief and grand affair many had earlier predicted.

Young men and teenage boys who had raced to the enlistment office brimming with bullet-proof naivete and youthful fantasies of martial glory saw their illusions vanish like June snow upon those battlefields. Meanwhile, those Northerners who stayed home had read the newspaper accounts with their grim statistics. They learned of the war's hard truths directly from fathers, husbands, brothers, sons, and friends in the army who had come home after their initial ninety-day enlistment or on furlough. They read the letters home from those same men. Any notion of "glory" was washed away as a cold reality set in, and for those Northern men who carefully assessed the personal costs and benefits of a potential enlistment within their own figurative balance sheet, many determined that the price to self and family was not worth it. They would not enlist especially when it seemed like so many others were willing or better suited to go. For some, the calculations had begun on day one, for others months later. They concluded this was not their war and for *approximately two-thirds* of the North's White men of military age—whether single or married—*not* having to don a blue uniform became a paramount concern.

"It Is Only Greenhorns Who Enlist"

A Philosophical Reluctance to Volunteer

THE CIVIL WAR'S EARLY MONTHS MARKED THE ONLY TIME OVER THE four-year conflict when the North was essentially unified. Most Democrats and Republicans had come together in a joint commitment that the Union must be preserved. Party differences were set aside for the time being since slavery's abolition was not an admitted reason for war. Indeed, patriotic outpourings were so pervasive that those who maintained severe doubts about the war's merits knew better than to speak out. Most newspapers that were openly critical of war prospects in the weeks and months leading up to Sumter were now strangely silent. New Yorkers J. Ansel Booth and O. R. Gross both wrote in mid-April how all of the opposition newspapers were obliged to hang out the Stars and Stripes. "No sentiment but for the Union allowed to be uttered now," Gross further noted. Those individuals who had doubts felt the pro-war winds blowing as well, such as former Michigan governor and Democrat Robert McClelland, who urged his daughter to stay silent on the war. "The less you say about it the better," he advised. When a young Kentucky woman asked her uncle which side he supported, he counseled her that he deplored the condition of affairs and hoped he would never do anything to add to the current troubles, "but talking too much does a great deal of harm." The older man knew it was better to stay silent when hotheads all around in that border state were stirring for action. In St. Louis, a town that held significant Confederate sympathy, private feuds appeared everywhere. Sarah Hill remembered her Unionist husband imploring her to stay close to home, keep quiet, and say nothing in public regarding the rebellion.[1]

Nor were all parents pleased with how their ministers and pastors were exhorting their sons to enlist. Mrs. Margaret Rieley of Cleveland, Ohio, berated her pastor for encouraging her teen son to enlist; who then did just that without first consulting or even informing his parents. Now she demanded to know from the pastor what company or regiment her son had enlisted in. From her perspective, if her son was being taught to act in such a manner, then she needed to withdraw her other children from such a church.[2]

Those few who did speak out in empathy or agreement with the rebellion or who offered a sneer toward a friend who had enlisted often received a well-dealt blow in return or worse. "It was one of the common incidents of the day for those who came into the [Ohio] State House," recalled Gen. Jacob Cox, "to tell of a knock-down that had occurred here or there, when this popular punishment had been administered to some indiscreet 'rebel sympathizer.'" Philadelphia diarist Sidney Fisher wrote after having assessed the city's public sentiment how, "It is at the risk of any man's life that he utters publicly a sentiment in favor of secession or the South." When antiwar Philadelphian Charles Ingersoll wrote a letter to Connecticut's former governor in October condemning Lincoln and the Union war effort, he signed his missive with the instructions to "read and burn," a clear warning from Ingersoll revealing his belief that it was no longer safe for anyone to promote antiwar opinions—even in private. In Indiana, a newspaper editor who approved of Southern secession was thoroughly beaten by a Union recruiting officer, one of the first of many such retributions. Just to the north in Michigan, George Farr remembered how his former employer came into Adrian a few days after the war started and began criticizing everything Northern while praising the South. Soon enough, "a crowd got after him with a rope and proposed to hang him to a lamp post. Only a quick retreat through an alley saved him."[3]

Most antiwar men may have realized that remaining quiet was the best course for the time being, however, they were certainly not going to enlist, either. Senator and "War Democrat" James A. McDougall recalled traversing the loyal Northern states from one end to the other after the war commenced and witnessing that very mindset. While he saw numerous localities where bold leaders successfully recruited almost all of the young men and then led them into the field, he also experienced far too many districts where a lack of concern or interest dominated. "There were whole towns and cities," McDougall later wrote, "where no one volunteered to shoulder a musket, and no one offered to lead them into the service." The vehemently anti-Lincoln New York *Daily News* avoided quiet indifference and took a more openly acerbic position. "He is no Democrat who will enter the army or volunteer to aid this diabolical policy of Civil War," it proclaimed to its primarily urban, working-class readers on April 15. Their reasons were varied; some believed that since any state had joined the federal compact voluntarily that they then had every right to leave in the same manner. In essence, the North had no constitutional right to force the seceded states back into the Union at the point of the bayonet. Others felt that the probable cost of blood and treasure just was not worth it. Let the South go. Still, others said good riddance. Who wanted a state and its people to be part of this great land if they believed slavery to be proper and justifiable? Regardless of the reason, it all boiled down to a refusal to participate in what they saw as a fool's errand, even if the war lasted only the ninety days that most suspected.[4]

Their perspective hardly changed once Lincoln asked men to enlist for possibly up to three years. "Tell all our friends not to enlist in the cause for their chances will be small for getting back at the end of three yrs," advised N. A. Chandler to his wife. One officer in Iowa's pre-war state militia announced that he had "no ambition to embark in such a war, but would prefer to see those who have been and still are so active in bringing about the present state of things lead the van." Harlow Orton of Wisconsin was a staunch Union man, yet he believed the war to be a folly that would "destroy all hope of Union forever." Nevertheless, wrote Orton, "if Government so orders, I will obey as a good citizen . . . but I shall not volunteer to go just now . . . I shall go on the even tenor of my way, attending to my own business, and watch and pray." Baltimore's 1861 mayor, George Brown, later admitted, "I refused to enlist in a crusade against slavery, not only on constitutional grounds but for other reasons." His rationales included a conviction that if freed slaves were given the right to vote, they would be incapable of using it properly. And if they were denied that right, then they would still suffer from White oppression but without the basic protections previously afforded them by their masters. From Brown's lofty and privileged vantage, it was better to leave well enough alone. In Detroit, twenty-five-year-old attorney Henry B. Brown groused into his diary only ten days after the war started that he faced another day with nothing to do. "Nothing but war and rumors of war," he complained, for Brown had no desire or intention of enlisting and never did.[5]

Though there may have been disagreement as to why the war should be fought if at all, most Northerners agreed that the South needed to be taught a lesson. It is important to note that those Northerners who truly sympathized with the South and cheered its secession were a distinct minority even within the Democratic Party. However, many men who signed up for ninety days had a serious change of heart when they learned that on May 3, President Lincoln had issued an additional call for volunteers to serve for three years or until the war ended, whichever came first. These men asked themselves who would tend to their crops or help run the family business. A ninety-day lark and a chance to see the country on the government dime was a world away from what the distant national government was now asking, which resulted in many new recruits refusing to serve the lengthier time frame.

It only took a few months for an innumerable number of the Union's raw recruits to lose their euphoria. Much of that shine had worn off after months spent in dismal camps or on the march, if not sooner. In western Virginia, a Unionist man wrote to a friend relaying a mutual acquaintance's fresh counsel from within the army who now "advises all boys that have good homes to stay there." The army friend told of having to sleep on a hard board on the ground, having to eat sour bread, wearing poor shoes, and, seemingly worst of all, having to drink his coffee without cream. Farther to the west, Cyrus Boyd told his diary how his new company had barely left home when the first frosty Iowa evening they encountered prompted some teen boys to begin talking about their mothers and returning to their cozy comfortable homes. As historian Kenneth Noe observed, inclement weather often acted as a "third army" that had to be dealt with every bit as much as the human blue- or gray-clad enemy. Moreover, poor weather could have a harmful effect on a man's morale and his subsequent desire to fight. Further into the conflict, a young, war-weary son confessed to his father in early November 1862 how, "If I live to get out of this war, I think I shan't care about roving any more." A pensive Democratic soldier in the 72nd Indiana Infantry felt the same as he admitted to his parents on the first anniversary of his recruitment that, in retrospect, he had no idea why he had enlisted. "I did it without reflecting what the life of a Volunteer was," and "I dident appreciate the comforts and Blessings of home. In fact I done it just to be doing." Decades later as an elderly man, an Ohioan looked back on those early days of naive exuberance and concluded that any young recruit's greatest asset was his inability to peer into the future.[6]

As with Lincoln's call for up to three years of service rather than ninety days, the war's first major battle on July 21, 1861, at Bull Run creek near Manassas, Virginia, was a disastrous watershed moment for the North as well as for the initial ninety-day volunteers. The day had started well enough for the green Union forces, however, equally inexperienced yet newly arrived Confederate reinforcements turned the tide later in the afternoon. The Union defeat turned into a disorganized rout with scores of Union troops fleeing back into the safety of Washington. The lack of training and martial discipline prompted a Prussian military observer to describe such battles as "two armed mobs chasing each other." As a consequence, many ninety-day volunteers chose to reenlist while others had seen enough. They felt they had done their duty and returned home to their normal lives. The day after the Bull Run debacle, Lincoln called for another 500,000 volunteers to serve three years, however, at a national level, those heady days in April when young men everywhere rushed pell-mell to the recruiting office were gone. Enlistments had begun to slow noticeably after the initial war fever had subsided. "It is useless to shut our eyes to the fact that recruiting is progressing very slowly, not only in this city but all over the North," noted the *New York World*. "The same story comes from every quarter—an abundance of organizations and officers, and very few privates." By the first week of August, Connecticut's Democrats began holding "peace meetings" featuring white flags and passionate speeches with the hope of dampening any remaining war enthusiasm. In Illinois, Republican governor Richard Yates warned the secretary of war how "Apathy is stealing over even Illinois." Hard army life and the roar of actual battle were not part of the ninety-day summer frolic many had expected.[7]

Moreover, the economy had improved across the North as the initial wave of volunteering had siphoned off much of the unemployed, plus the government's need for all manner of war material was creating lucrative business contracts and factory jobs. In Illinois, J. F. Skinner was initially reluctant to enlist because he calculated he could earn as much money in five days working at his painting trade as he would make in an entire month as a soldier. In late September 1861, an older man in Gallipolis, Ohio, wrote to a friend mentioning that he was so consumed of late with business and home life that he had little time to read up on the latest war news. Farther across the country in Chambersburg, Pennsylvania, sixty-five-year-old shopkeeper William Heyser remarked in his diary that his town was greatly changed by the war and mostly for the better. "Business is so good," he wrote on October 4, "our small town is taking on a city appearance of activity." By late 1861, Boston had become so normal again that a music critic from that city observed, "It is hard to realize we are in the midst of civil war."[8]

Meanwhile, those home front voices who were dubious about the war's merits and had remained quiet now began to voice their dissent. Antiwar Democratic politicians and newspapers who had urged a peaceful, negotiated settlement sensed vindication as the body count began to rise. The Bull Run defeat was "bad for the army that fought there, bad for the country, [and] bad for the prestige," admitted the Republican *New York Times*, however, "it was a God-send for the croakers. If it saddened patriotism, it made their hearts glad—brought them into the foreground." Republican papers such as the *New York Daily Tribune*, the nation's most widely circulated newspaper, began firing back at the state's Democratic politicians who, the *Tribune* alleged, were now busily sowing mischief and fomenting discontent within the army.[9]

Antiwar men and women on the street also chimed in. In Darien, Connecticut, after a Southern sympathizer fired off a cannon celebrating the Confederate victory, pro-war men seized the piece and tossed it in the river. Twenty-seven miles to the north in Danbury, a group of jubilant Democratic women led a brass band down Main Street, reveling in the Union defeat. When a pro-war shopkeeper in Du Page County, Illinois, expressed his sorrow over the Bull Run defeat to a local antiwar dissident on the other side of the street, the latter expressed his delight and asserted that such a whipping served the Union army right.[10]

Vocal antiwar partisans such as those mentioned above became known as "Copperheads." That label was a broad-brush pejorative term used by pro-Lincoln, pro-war Republicans to describe antiwar Democrats, regardless of the latter's reasons. The term first appeared in July 1861 in an attempt to compare those dissenters to the poisonous and deadly snake slithering along the ground, ready to silently strike its enemy from behind. The name stuck in the Republican press even as antiwar Democrats attempted to embrace that moniker by wearing the "Lady Liberty" copper penny as their symbol of constitutional fidelity. Most of these dissidents were politically conservative with their vision of constitutional loyalty holding to a narrow interpretation of that document's tenets. As historian Jennifer Weber pointed out, they were the philosophical antecedents of modern-era Supreme Court justices Antonin Scalia and Clarence Thomas. In a general sense, most (but certainly not all) Copperheads came from three demographics within American culture. They were Southern by birth or had a strong Southern ancestral heritage; they were German or Irish immigrants, most likely Catholic, who had come to this country within the preceding generation to provide for their families' welfare, not engage in war; or they were believers in a small central government with most legal power residing with the states. They saw themselves as speaking truth to power as they sought a return to what they described as "the Constitution as it is and the Union as it was," that is, a negotiated settlement with slavery remaining intact. Most were Union loyalists who were simply opposed to the war's rationales and the manner in which the Lincoln administration fought it. Especially egregious to the dissenters were what they regarded as the administration's flagrant disregard for a citizen's constitutional civil liberties as well as any administration's constitutional limitations. Few genuinely favored an independent Confederacy. Nevertheless, to most Union soldiers and much of the pro-war civilian public, the Democratic Copperheads became malevolent, peace-at-any-price traitors. During the war, a relative few did indeed do everything in their power to discourage enlistments, disrupt the draft, and aid deserters. Most, however, simply wished to be left alone, and while they were not going to engage in any overt acts to subvert the Union war effort, they also had no intention of doing anything to aid the Union war effort either, for example, enlisting. The Confederates likewise had little use for the Southern-sympathizing Copperhead, for they had no respect for a so-called friend or ally unwilling to join them on the field of battle.[11]

For many pro-war Unionists, there was a distinct difference between a Northerner privately questioning the war's necessity or its constitutional legalities—and publicly celebrating Union defeats. Moreover, there was an even larger difference between civil debate and making veiled, public threats against the government like the one made by Wilbur Storey, who was the fiery and highly partisan Democratic editor of the *Detroit Free Press*. On January 26, 1861, two and a half months before the war commenced, Storey vowed in his paper that if the North attacked the South, a "fire in the rear" would be set loose by Northern antiwar adherents. Storey's words and sentiments were routinely used by Unionists as proof of treasonous threats lurking throughout the North.[12]

Patriotism became synonymous with loyalty to the pro-war administration while antiwar Copperhead-driven dissent became tantamount to treason. William D. Sedgwick of Massachusetts encapsulated this growing belief in an August 1861 letter to his mother. "I used to think it was only necessary in order that we might have a respectable country, to exterminate about 4/5 of the population of the South," Sedgwick explained. But after only four and one-half months of war, Sedgwick revised his calculation, now convinced that "the extermination of 3/5 of the north would have to be added, in order to rid the whole country of its damned fools and cursed thieves & hypocrites." To the majority of the pro-war North, such despicable displays were all part of a conspiracy to discourage enlistments, generate soldier complaints, and generally embarrass the Lincoln administration with an eye to negotiating peace with the Rebels. Their conviction that a treasonous conspiracy was underway proved to be every bit a powerful motivating force as any known plot.[13]

Due to the softening war fever, appeals to patriotism alone no longer seemed sufficient for potential volunteers. Finding willing recruits to replenish the army was the responsibility of the army's recruiting agents, and they were starting to experience some difficulties by the late summer of 1861. It was not easy work, and after the Bull Run debacle in July, it could seem like finding the proverbial needle in a haystack. After almost half a year of war and still no end in sight, some in the North were beginning to wonder if the costs in blood and treasure were truly worth it. One recruiting officer recalled that several visits to a somewhat willing man's home were often required to garner his consent. If he agreed to serve, family, sweethearts, and friends then had to be consulted as well. A young woman in Michigan wrote to a friend in late August 1861 describing how two recruiting officers had recently attended a local dance but met with no success in finding recruits. "It seems that they are more for dancing than they are for the war," she observed, nevertheless "they could not get any. There was no one that had courage enough to enlist." In Milan, Ohio, and after being told by a young man that he could make more money teaching school at twenty-five dollars a month than by enlisting, Lt. Sheldon Colton expressed dismay in a letter to his brother regarding his recruiting efforts: "One needs all the patience of which a man was ever possessed to keep his temper and listen to all the excuses of able bodied young men who are asked to enlist."[14]

Republican newspapers, therefore, began to change their messaging by touting the economic advantages of enlisting in the still hard times that were gripping much of the non-urban North. To entice recruits, some states and counties began to offer cash bribes—known as "bounties"—as a further inducement for men to enlist. The federal government announced that any man enlisting for three years would receive a $100 cash bounty payable at the end of his term. Meanwhile, towns and counties throughout the land had also created relief funds as a form of social welfare that a soldier's family might draw upon to relieve the financial distress created by their breadwinner's absence. While it was apparent that the war was not going to end in ninety days, most Northerners still believed the war would be over within one year. Newspapers stressed that it was imperative for a man to enlist now while he could still take advantage of such lucrative offers.[15]

In a moment when the initial patriotic call to "duty" was so intense, how was it that only a few months later, so many men and women could appear so ambivalent toward the war's publicly professed goals? It appeared the glorious republic that the revolutionary-era forefathers had fought so mightily to bequeath to their descendants was on the verge of being torn apart so that the South could maintain its gang-labor form of slavery.

THE AMERICAN INDIVIDUALISM IDEAL

At the core of the mid-nineteenth-century American national character was the concept of individualism. It was a belief that held that no matter how high or low a man's station in life, he was an autonomous being, free to make his way in life as he saw fit. The "united states" were grammatically thought of by many as a lower-cased plural noun; a land teeming with individual rights and opportunity that offered any man the possibility of advancing up the economic ladder as far as talent and energy might take him. Social class or ancestral lineage played no part as it did in the autocratic lands of Old Europe that most Americans' ancestors had emigrated from. The mid-nineteenth-century man realized that the late-eighteenth-century standards of community consensus and tradition, rigid hierarchy, and the deference that went with it were giving way to individualism, political equality, and self-reliance. He was hindered in his movements and decisions only to the extent that his actions did not impede upon the equal rights of his fellow man. Countless young men swept into the recruiting office in April and May 1861 believing they were protecting those cherished ideals. Those opportunities and rights, however, proved to be a two-way street, for just as many men believed in their right to ignore a war that they viewed as an imposition on their individual lives, their families, their educations, their livelihoods, and especially their adult male children. American society at the time possessed laws and cultural limitations on what a man could *not* do, but very few on what he *must* do. Writing in the seventeenth century, British philosopher John Locke declared man as the primary component from which all sociological studies should begin—rather than the state in general or his social class or community in particular. Even into the eighteenth century, social thought dictated that one's local community surpassed the state in importance, with the latter being merely a system of functions created by the former.[16]

Locke reasoned that the individual had to come first since he was the one who ultimately created a society and then a government. Most importantly, that government existed only with the consent of the governed. Since man was endowed by the creator with reason and freedom, his natural rights needed to supersede duties to the state. Therefore, the essential purpose of government was to protect the individual's natural rights. America's founding fathers had created the Declaration of Independence with its very ethos steeped in the concept of individual liberty rather than past governments whose laws were based on a shared culture, blood, or the religion of its people. The Constitution and especially the Bill of Rights were precisely worded in such a way as to protect that liberty. Though the word individualism had become somewhat synonymous with selfishness and social anarchy in Old Europe into the nineteenth century, in America the word still held strong connotations of self-determination, moral freedom, man's self-dignity, and the laws of liberty. Frenchman Alexis de Tocqueville observed this dichotomy in the early 1830s during his famous North American travels. Americans' individualism arose, Tocqueville wrote, not out of any selfish love of self at the expense of others, but rather from the "mature and calm feeling" that any man's destiny was in his own hands and from the belief that "they owe nothing to any man, they expect nothing from any man." In this burgeoning new land, a man's fate was now directly tied to what he did or did not do, not who his father was. For these reasons, many Americans believed that if a man decided *not* to enlist in 1861, his right to make that choice eclipsed any coercive obligation to serve that the federal government may have wished to impose on him. This is why the Union's attempts to force men into the army via the threat of conscription in 1862–1863 met with such strong pushback. Many Americans believed that any man might decline to enlist yet could—and should—still be considered properly patriotic and loyal by virtue of his other honorable actions. This mid-nineteenth-century form of rugged individualism stood in stark contrast to the mid-twentieth century when individual sacrifice for the greater public good became a national expectation.[17]

Plenty of elite Americans throughout the land believed those self-determination rights and the consent of the governed born of the Revolutionary War were still valid. For example, Lincoln's new minister to Great Britain, Charles Francis Adams Sr., felt a strong reluctance to see his upper-class sons engage in soldiering. When one of Adams' sons, Henry, wrote to his brother, Charles Jr., early in the war, he advised his sibling on what their father was currently thinking regarding Charles' potential enlistment. "His idea is that the war will be short," explained Henry, "and that you will only destroy all your habits of business without gaining anything." Judge Thomas Mellon of Pittsburgh was equally dismayed when he learned that his son, James, wanted to enlist in a Wisconsin regiment. "It is only greenhorns who enlist," declared the elder Mellon. "You can learn nothing useful in the army . . . In time you will come to understand and believe that a man may be a patriot without risking his own life or sacrificing his health. All now stay if they can and go if they must. There are plenty of other lives less valuable or others ready to serve for the love of serving." Such a perspective of "good for thee but not for me" even took place at the height of Union authority—in the Lincoln White House. Lincoln's son, Robert Todd Lincoln, turned eighteen years old in 1861 but spent almost the entire war enrolled at Harvard University. Only in January 1865, when the rebellion seemed almost over, did the president relent and allow his son to join the war. But not as a mere private in the ranks. Lincoln made arrangements with Lt. Gen. Ulysses S. Grant to have his son placed on the general's staff with a cushy captain's commission and well away from Confederate shot and shell. Such elite concerns that serving would *give* nothing useful to their sons along with Mellon's reference to "less valuable lives" illustrated the class consciousness highlighted by the workingman's conviction that the conflict was "a rich man's war but a poor man's fight."[18]

Illinois schoolmaster Levi Ross unintentionally countered Mellon when he spoke for workingmen by writing in March 1863, "I believe that a poor man's life is as dear as a rich man's." Since the wealthy had more material wealth and property to lose in the event of a defeat, Ross reasoned they should sacrifice more in suppressing the rebellion. The Civil War exacerbated social class divisions, as upper-class elites publicly urged their less-privileged citizens to boldly support the North's war effort with their bodies and by extension, their families' welfare. Yet, those working-class men and yeoman farmers instinctively realized that what they stood to lose was much greater, relatively speaking, than their bourgeois counterparts and as a consequence, decided in many instances *not* to walk away from their communities, families, and farms. Historians from Merle Curti to Melinda Lawson have noted how the proposition that one's loyalty to country may be measured by the sacrifices they are willing to make is a theory that many Americans found difficult to grasp.[19]

The mid-nineteenth-century concept of individualism dovetailed with the cultural conviction that an American ultimately owed a greater sense of loyalty and obligation to his family, local community, and culture than to any theoretical sense of national duty. Moreover, the North and South were viewed as two distinctly different regional cultures. In many quarters, the concept of national reunification lacked the moral power or influence to galvanize the North. National politics was viewed as little more than a collective forum for the states to debate and resolve their competing interests. The voice that the early volunteers gave to nationalistic duty was most likely a sense of community pride or even a feeling of class loyalty. Some of these citizens and their communities were often indifferent to the war's aims, regarding secession or abolition and its national consequences as irrelevant to their localized existence. Other Northern citizens even sympathized with the Southern cause, having kin and relations in the Upper South that went back generations. Few men wanted to raise a musket against cousins or even siblings. The southernmost counties of Illinois, for example, had a strong pro-Southern culture and had voted by a six to one margin for Democrat Stephen Douglas over Abraham Lincoln in the 1860 presidential election. The town of

Marion, Illinois, even raised a company of men for Confederate service in May 1861 while the editor of the local pro-Union newspaper was forced to flee the city. Indiana's J. B. Otey crystallized the matter for many when he wrote in a private letter, "I cannot take sides against the South. The bones of my ancestors lie mouldering there. My connections are there. Everything dear to me in the way of kindred is there, and I must and will be there."[20]

The deep bonds of clannish loyalty that the citizen-soldier felt toward his family and community resulted in a soldier's strongest devotion centered on the smallest army unit to which he belonged. That was generally the company, which was usually recruited entirely from his hometown or geographic region and ideally contained about one hundred men, many of whom the new volunteer knew personally. Following that was his regiment, which initially started from home generally with one thousand men distributed into ten companies. The volunteer regiments were then given state designations. States had the responsibility for raising an army because individual men and women of the era, whether Northerner or Southerner, considered themselves first off and foremost as citizens of a particular state rather than of the country. According to historian Gerald J. Prokopowicz, "the regiment, more than any other unit, was a self-aware community, held together by bonds based on common geographic, social, cultural, or economic identities, strengthened by months of training and campaigning as a unit." The dominant social and cultural factors present in a new recruit's hometown certainly influenced his thinking, which could then bleed into a unit's outlook. Victorian-era Americans realized that communal ideals and perceptions often clashed with their individualistic desires. Yet those desires were generally subordinated to the community's standards, such as the desire for social order. For example, a staunchly Democratic town whose dominant antiwar opinion would have influenced a pro-war recruit or may have prompted a potential volunteer to stay at home.[21]

These small-town, rural values that stressed self-reliance and highlighted the preeminence of familial and communal obligations also put forth that any young man should enlist *if* he had no such responsibilities. The converse of that belief was also well understood by all. If a man had ample obligations to his family and/or community, there was no shame in him not enlisting as long as he was not hypocritical in his actions or took advantage of the situation to the detriment of others. For some Americans, especially those living in more rural areas, the new notion put forth by federal authorities that duty to the country supplanted local obligations was deeply resented due to the potential negative impact on a household's labor and finances. The likely poverty that any family might face if the husband/breadwinner was carried off to war was deemed a proper excuse for avoiding voluntary enlistment. These polar convictions—the opposite sides of the same coin—were deeply embedded into the era's culture and found agreement across the country, regardless of party politics or social-class perspectives.[22]

A further example of local primacy was the long-standing democratic tradition of enlisted men having the right to elect their own company-level officers such as lieutenants and captains. Moreover, it was established practice that any man who had the wherewithal to recruit a large number of men would generally have the privilege of then leading those men. If volunteering to serve in the army in time of war was a citizen-soldier's political statement in support of the war's aims, then his right to elect the men he would serve under was an equally cherished political belief. More often than not, a company captain, the lieutenants, the noncommissioned officers, and the privates in the ranks all knew one another because they were often recruited from the same town or rural area. Everyone knew the other's character strengths and weaknesses. Much to the initial chagrin of company officers, the privates often referred to them by their first names. A bit of electioneering and campaigning for the coveted junior officer commissions was common, with the defeated candidates sometimes resigning from the service rather than being forced to serve as a mere private. As a consequence, it was a challenge for some men to take orders from those they felt were their social inferiors, or in some instances, more mature men with real-world life experience objected to taking orders from inexperienced younger men.[23]

Sgt. Austin Stearns of the 13th Massachusetts' Company K later recalled a new lieutenant who joined the army straight from college and was therefore completely devoid of the knowledge or experiences a commander of men must have. Though Stearns admitted the young man meant well, Stearns also felt fully one-fourth of the newly recruited men in his company were better qualified than the boyish lieutenant. In this regard, the *Chicago Daily Tribune* saw one palpable benefit as the army looked to transfer from three-month regiments to three-year regiments. "The drunken, incompetent or unpopular, officers will be got rid of," it observed. "Their worthlessness having been discovered, the boys will give them a wide berth when they come to fill up new regiments for the duration of the war."[24]

The privates themselves sometimes refused to serve or reenlist when officers were appointed or elected who the privates did not approve of. Those negative opinions quickly made their way to friends and family back home and sometimes served as a recruiting deterrent. In more than a few instances, the outright incompetence displayed by some regimental officers quickly came to the fore upon reaching the field, especially with those who had gained their appointment solely through political patronage rather than any degree of military merit. In the case of New York's first thirty-eight regiments, the result according to Col. Silas Burt was that about two-thirds of the regimental officers resigned or were discharged at some point during their initial two-year term. Furthermore, a full one-third had resigned during the first six months. By the summer of 1862, Maj. Gen. George McClellan was compelled to admit to New York governor Edwin Morgan that "while many noble exceptions are to be found, the officers of volunteers are, as a mass—perhaps I should say were (for the worst are sifted out)—greatly inferior to the men they command." The short term of the initial enlistments—only ninety days—and the political nature of how inexperienced volunteer officers came about within state regiments combined to create a notable lack of training and discipline among Union regiments in the first few months of the war.[25]

***

All of this internecine company conflict as well as the war's virtues and whether or not a man should volunteer were burgeoning debates that had been and still were argued endlessly in the nation's newspapers. As the 1860s dawned, there were more than four thousand newspapers in the United States, most with small, localized circulations. As opposed to a century later, Civil War–era newspapers were proudly and overtly partisan with little forethought given to strict objectivity. They were often owned and operated by one prominent, politically partisan man who functioned as everything from typesetter and editor to distributor. There was little separation between opinion and straight news as one often bled into the other. As for the war, these newspapers routinely published soldiers' letters from the field whose praises or criticisms generally aligned with the paper's political views. They opined on how the war had impacted their local economies, the recruitment process, who and how many were volunteering from the local area as well as the various mobilization efforts. Through this medium, owners and editors used their papers to serve as the local party spokesperson on the war's merits as well as the unvarnished voice of the public. They used their partisan platform to serve as a reminder to the White male voting public why the reader adhered to one political party or the other in the first place, or, as Lawrence Kohl noted, "the rhetoric of political persuasions was designed more to reassure the faithful than to convert the infidel." The opinion columns of twenty-first-century newspapers, partisan cable news networks, and internet news websites serve the same social identity function. During the Civil War, this quickly evolved into a public discourse on the meaning of loyalty during an internal rebellion and therefore, who was a loyal citizen or a "traitor" based on their speech or actions. This mindset was aptly illustrated in the war's opening weeks when a young, single man's enlistment served to showcase his patriotic bona fides and martial masculinity, or lack thereof if he did not volunteer.[26]

As with newspapers, popular literature of the era was also used to promote enlistment as well as a cudgel to lambast those who refused to answer their nation's call. This litany of literature included sensational and romanticized novels, newspaper satire, stories, cartoons, poems, and songs, all working together to create what Alice Fahs described as "a cultural politics of war." While this literature often portrayed mothers as making the ultimate sacrifice in offering up their husbands and sons to the war, the overarching political message from their daughters was that those young single men who refused to volunteer were cowards.[27]

Carry Stanley's *The Volunteer's Wife*, from October 1861, typified this perspective as it portrayed a workingman named George Campbell who enlisted at the war's beginning to care for his wife and young son because there was no other paying work to be had. His wife, Margaret, tearfully agreed, reassured by George that he would be home in three months after his enlistment term expired. Stanley put forth the North's feminized ideal that to be a volunteer's wife or mother was a "patent of nobility" within her community. As his company marched by her window, Margaret realized how "The whole company [was] sent forth by the women, with prayers and hopes, and the certainty that each particular man was a hero." Margaret barely survived on what little she could earn, always looking forward to the day when George's pay arrived. Then near the end of his ninety-day enlistment, she saw his name in the newspaper indicating he had been killed at the battle of Bull Run. In the weeks and months to follow, Margaret and her young son were reduced to a pauper's life. Near the end, however, as Margaret is close to succumbing, George miraculously reappears, his death notice an error as he was wounded, captured, and imprisoned by the Confederates, but then ultimately escapes. He returns home to a hero's welcome, his life and his family's well-being restored. George intends to reenlist in due course, most likely with an officer's commission and his loving wife's full blessing. The story's heartrending and romanticized lesson was that the potential short-term suffering to families generated by manly enlistment and female support would be rewarded in the longer term. Moreover, such fiction asserted that both men and women should curtail their individual wants and needs for the new nationalism's greater good.[28]

The flip side of the noble volunteer as portrayed in *The Volunteer's Wife* was Kate Sutherland's *The Laggard Recruit*, which appeared in January 1862. While it was another short tale that urged manly volunteerism, it also illustrated the female-generated consequences that would inevitably follow for those men who did not step forward. "The test of [our] favor now, is courage," advised the young lady to her as-yet-to-enlist male suitor. "Men who stay at home, court our smiles in vain" was the woman's not-so-subtle threat. Though fictional, its propaganda message aptly warned how the foppish "stay-at-home coward" should not and would not garner the affections of young single women who desired manly, courageous men. As Gerald Linderman referred to in his book *Embattled Courage*, females had no qualms about utilizing sexual intimidation to encourage male enlistment and shame those who did not.[29]

Henry Morford was a satirist and newspaper editor who penned several popular novels during the Civil War, including 1864's *The Coward: A Novel of Society and the Field in 1863*. The book commences around the time of Lee's June 1863 invasion of Pennsylvania, however, is only loosely connected to the then-ongoing Civil War and is set heavily in New Hampshire's White Mountains and overseas. Like Sutherland's *Laggard Recruit*, the book was a popular tale that utilized a fictional young woman decrying cowardice.[30]

The one-act play *Off to the War!* was another satirical effort that lampooned the alleged stay-at-home coward. In the play, the audience meets the pompous Mr. Dobblewobble, who held a colonel's commission at one time in the peacetime militia but recently resigned now that the bullets have begun to fly. When his wife subtly questions his motives, Dobblewobble explains that it was not due to cowardice but rather an honorable and patriotic act on his part in order to make room for those men better suited for warfare. After his wife reflects on the honor that he may have gained by serving in the Union army, Dobblewobble replies, "Think of the honor of coming home full of holes!" As with *The Laggard Recruit*, the play lampooned those men who talked of supporting the war yet always found an excuse for not serving.[31]

The lone antiwar novel from the Civil War years was Benjamin Wood's *Fort Lafayette; Or, Love and Secession*. Forty years old when the war started, Wood was the brother of New York City mayor Fernando Wood and a partisan Democrat who served in the US House of Representatives throughout the war. In addition, he was also the fiery, Copperhead editor of the New York *Daily News*, whose pre-war editorial position consistently sympathized with Southern grievances though stopped short of endorsing secession. With the onset of war, Wood's paper was effectively shut down by Union authorities in late 1861 due to its consistent anti-Lincoln and antiwar diatribes. With his paper gone, Wood turned his considerable literary talents to fiction, hoping his anti-war convictions would reach a much wider Northern audience and just as importantly, mobilize them against serving in the war. *Fort Lafayette* was published in January or February 1862, less than a year after the war started. It was a typical melodramatic potboiler of the era that featured sentimentalized romanticism and intrigue, all covered with unmistakable messaging against war in general and the folly of the Union position in particular.[32]

In addition to lengthier novels and short stories, newspapers used short pieces of humor or satire as a means of shaming those who had not enlisted. A Michigan newspaper joked of a "young exquisite," who, when rhetorically asked why the man had not yet enlisted, the paper remarked how "He always thought the war was best when taken in home-opathic doses."[33]

CHAPTER 3

"Tis Not Our War"

A Plethora of Specific Reasons to Stay Home

WHY BOTHER WITH A SHORT WAR

As discussed in chapter 1, grown men and teenage boys rushed to enlist by the tens of thousands following the Confederate attack on Fort Sumter, most touting patriotic motives, but also because they thought the war would be over quickly and therefore not an impediment to their "real" lives. This was especially the case for younger unmarried men. "Putting down treason" and "teaching the South a lesson" would be a jolly lark, a quick ninety-day opportunity to gain martial glory and the enhanced civilian stature that would surely follow. The majority consensus was that everyone would most likely be home by summer. If not by then, then certainly home in time for the fall harvest season. Many initial recruits agreed to sign up for ninety days but not for potentially three years after Lincoln made that call on May 3. For those who did agree to the three years or until the war ended—whichever came first—most never dreamt that the three-year term would come to pass.

Yet for every eager volunteer who was convinced the rebellion would be over quickly, there was another man who decided not to enlist precisely *because* of the widespread conviction that the rebellion would not last long. With the belief that the war would be settled somewhere in the East between the Washington, DC, and Richmond, Virginia, corridor, some men in the West felt everything would be over by the time they could travel to the seat of war. Therefore, why bother? Though he did later enlist, Leander Stillwell admitted he ignored Lincoln's first two calls for volunteers because "the belief then was almost universal throughout the North that the 'war' would amount to nothing much but a summer frolic, and would be over by the 4th of July." Maine's Daniel Sawtelle felt the same, disregarding the war until he opted to enlist in February 1862. "Everyone seemed to think that we would go through the South as our army had gone through Mexico," he later recalled, "forgetting that the people of the South were of the same race and blood as ourselves." The distance to a recruiting station and the time it would take to get there also contributed to a young man's ambivalence, especially for those who lived in remote rural areas. After all, they could always enlist later if necessary. For these men, their fundamental question was why should they disrupt their personal or family lives for something so distant and brief, especially when there were so many others willing to go?[1]

Married men with families and those with farm or business obligations were most prone to seriously ponder that question. West Point graduate and future Union major general William T. Sherman certainly felt that way. When the war began, Sherman was the civilian president of a St. Louis streetcar company. While seeking to rejoin the Regular army in a suitable position, he admitted in a May 8, 1861, letter to Secretary of War Simon Cameron that he "did not, and will not volunteer for three months, because I cannot throw my family on the Cold support of charity." Arthur Farquhar later wrote that as a then twenty-two-year-old, recently married man, men like him were not even expected to enlist at the war's beginning, and far fewer ever considered doing so. "And when they did try, their wives often dragged them back," he added.[2]

Joshua Lawrence Chamberlain of future Gettysburg fame was another who waited until the war was well into its second year before offering his services. As a thirty-three-year-old modern languages professor at Maine's Bowdoin College, as well as a married father of two, enlisting in 1861 was deemed out of the question due to a myriad of pressing family matters coupled with the common belief that the war would be a brief affair. After Lincoln's call for 300,000 more men in the summer of 1862, Chamberlain experienced a change of heart after watching dozens of his students abandon their studies and march off to war during the past fifteen months. He asked Maine's governor for and soon received a commission as a lieutenant colonel in the then-new 20th Maine Infantry. Though his aging father had once dreamed of a military education for "Lawrence," his devoutly religious mother had vehemently protested against it. Now with war raging across the land, Lawrence's Democratic-leaning parents grudgingly accepted their son's martial desire even if they did not agree with his reasons. "We hope to be spared," wrote Lawrence's sixty-two-year-old father, because "tis not our war." The elder Chamberlain was a taciturn yet successful self-made man with conservative Calvinist religious beliefs and a man who lived by the Puritan work ethic's creed of self-discipline, hard work, and devotion to family. Leaving family responsibilities behind to march off to a distant war that did not directly impact the family or community was no longer part of his worldview. His choice of words became the rationale for almost every antiwar position involving US military forces in the future.[3]

SHODDY

Those men who proudly marched off to war in the spring and early summer of 1861 did not think about clothing and weapons quality, ration shortages, or any other logistical matters that fell under the purview of state governments or the Regular army's Quartermaster Department. The initial inadequacies in all of these areas left many bewildered, confused, and ultimately angry. These young men who offered up their lives to the government in defense of their country simply assumed that uniforms, food, muskets, and all other military necessities would be properly provided for. The initial reality was anything but that. State and local governments had to take the lead after the War Department asked them to do so because that department had nowhere near the personnel or other resources to carry out the task. State governments ended up outfitting their regiments through local contractors and even civilian groups with the result being a mishmash of style and qualitative differences, assuming they were even provided.[4]

A soldier writing from Ohio's Camp Dennison on May 30 observed how numerous recruits were "in rags, wearing nothing but drawers; and on account of their mean appearance positively refusing to come out on dress parade." Furthermore, he noted that such a condition was not limited to any one company or regiment but was evident in every regiment he had inspected. Franc Wilkie was a reporter traveling with the 1st Iowa Infantry and he was shocked to see the 2,000 decrepit muskets that were delivered to the regiment in mid-May, drolly concluding how it would be "a master stroke of policy to allow the secessionists to steal them." They were so antiquated that they were "infinitely more dangerous to friend than enemy." Wilkie's observation was not uncommon in the war's earliest days.[5]

Two months later in some areas, proper supply matters were still so degraded that the ninety-day volunteers could not wait to head home, having seen and experienced enough ragged glory. In western Virginia, Maj. Gen. Robert Patterson telegraphed Washington on July 18 how, "Many of the regiments are without shoes; the Government refuses to furnish them; the men have received no pay, and neither officers nor soldiers have money to purchase with." The next day brought more of the same. "Almost all the three-months volunteers refuse to serve an hour over their term, and except three regiments which will stay ten days the most of them are without shoes and without pants."[6]

Uniform suppliers rarely had sufficient quantities of a desirable cloth and often ended up substituting an inferior grade to the point that the new uniforms quickly disintegrated. The 3rd Wisconsin Infantry's Julian Hinkley recalled that the first uniforms they were given *looked* splendid, however, "they were of such poor quality, especially the trousers, that within ten days it was necessary to furnish the entire regiment with common blue workingmen's overalls, in order that we might with decency be seen upon the streets." An Ohio newspaper chimed in only weeks after the war started by reporting how "the blankets served to the men at first were so rotten that they almost fell to pieces." By summer, almost every Northern state saw its primary contractors under fire by both the press and state legislators for incompetence, malfeasance, or both. "For one pound of necessary metals, one yard of fabric, one gallon of liquid, the price of two was paid," complained Col. Henry Olcott in describing this "carnival of fraud." Moreover, "Our soldiers were given guns that would not shoot, powder that would only half explode, shoes of which the soles were filled with shavings, hats that dissolved often in a month's showers, and clothing made of old cloth, ground up and fabricated over again." In Washington, it seemed to Capt. Henry Young as if everyone had their hand in the government till. After explaining to his wife of a recent instance of colonels and quartermasters pocketing several hundred dollars each, he concluded that financial malfeasance was carried out to such an extent that small amounts as he described were barely mentioned.[7]

One unexpected result of this corruption was that the word *shoddy* soon permanently entered the nation's lexicon as a word used to describe any product or service of poor, inferior quality. It is important to note, however, that the word *shoddy* was initially a legitimate technical term used to describe the bits of wool fiber left over from normal clothing production. Often these scraps would then be mixed in with newer materials as a legitimate means of creating softness and lowering costs. Much of the new uniforms provided to the army, however, were discovered to contain excessive quantities of the cheap filler, resulting in clothing that was thin, flimsy, and quickly fell apart.[8]

The initial supply problems with arms and munitions were no different than those with clothing and shoes. Modern rifled muskets were lacking in sufficient quantity to outfit companies and regiments, much less armies. Instead, the North possessed an overabundance of obsolete, rusty weaponry coupled with insufficient factories to make new ones. In some cases, eager volunteers were turned away simply because their states had no arms to issue them. In other instances, new recruits who were issued such inferior weapons refused to go into battle against what they thought would be a properly outfitted enemy. After William F. Patterson requested the latest rifled muskets for his Kentuckians, Brig. Gen. George Thomas replied, "As you allude to the passion which the men have for the rifle, I will inform you that I can see no prospect for getting any for them. They will have to take the [smoothbore] musket." That unfortunate situation remained in place in the Western theater until late 1862. When Jacob Cox accompanied Gen. George McClellan to inspect the weaponry at the Ohio state arsenal following the war's commencement, they found essentially an empty warehouse. Only a few crates of rusty and antiquated smoothbore muskets were found along with several damaged cannons and a pile of mildewed horse harnesses. "A fine stock of munitions on which to begin a great war!" McClellan sardonically remarked upon leaving the building. Once the federal government understood the gravity of the situation, federal agents were forced to seek out new muskets from overseas suppliers.[9]

The quality and quantity of camp rations were often no better than the uniforms or weapons and had a similar adverse effect on the new soldiers' morale and, by extension, their family and friends back home. Men who had any manner of aptitude for cooking were discovered only by the slow process of natural selection, which resulted in many disagreeable meals early on. Like the uniforms, though, poor quality was more often due to supply chain issues and unscrupulous contractors or inspectors rather than any government indifference. Michigan's Charles Haydon pointed his blame primarily at the contractors and the way they prepared the food, which, he asserted, appeared to have "a good deal of dirt mixed with it." Moreover, Haydon was convinced that whatever they were served for dinner was generally made from that day's leftover breakfast scraps; all of which led to rampant intestinal disorders among the recruits. A reporter traveling with the 1st Iowa Infantry described that regiment's initial supply of butter as "a chemical combination of a dozen colors, a fierce odor, and strong enough to run an eighty horsepower engine." Nevertheless, it was served in ample quantities so that the butter "seasoned with a liberal sprinkling of curses and a few honest growls" was quickly consumed. Another recruit disparaged the "nasty half cooked beef . . . coffee resembling rain water & vinegar mixed," all the while wishing for food "that is not full of . . . all other kind of uncleanliness." Such supply and culinary tales of woe from a friend or loved one in the army surely gave pause to those men still at home who may have been contemplating enlistment.[10]

The lack of military supplies and its attendant concerns quickly reached the highest levels of the federal government. By summer, state politicians and army officers were warning Secretary of War Cameron about their ever-growing recruitment difficulties, which they felt were directly related to a lack of proper uniforms, weaponry, and rations.

Union loyalist John Carlile wrote to Cameron on June 19 begging for provisions for his newly recruited men in western Virginia since "delay in getting them tends to discourage enlistments, while the men armed and well equipped and drilled have the opposite effect." In September, Iowa governor Samuel Kirkwood pleaded for proper equipment to be furnished immediately to newly mustered companies because the continued delays harmed enlisting. Just more than a month later on October 22, Quartermaster Gen. Montgomery Meigs likewise complained to Cameron, informing him how "troops before the enemy have been compelled to do picket duty in the late cold nights without overcoats, or even coats, wearing only the thin summer flannel blouses." The inevitable consequence from Meigs' vantage was that a lack of clothing rather than a lack of pay was the real culprit for demoralization and slow recruiting.[11]

If antiquated weaponry, "shoddy" clothing and blankets, and poor food were not bad enough, new recruits soon learned that there was more to army life than martial pomp and chasing Rebels. They never dreamed that most of their early days would be spent in camp practicing military drills up to five times a day and which lasted one to two hours per session. Then they had to complete all manner of dreary, menial tasks, such as building latrines, gathering wood for cooking, and picking up trash. Later in the war, veterans would remark that a soldier's life was 99 percent boredom followed by 1 percent of sheer terror on the battlefield. Then the process started over again. Initially, this camp dreariness overtook many men. One young officer wrote to his mother informing her that he would advise a friend not to enlist; that he might as well stay at home rather than sit around camp performing such tedium. Any recruit, especially those who did have proper muskets and related provisions, wanted to get after "Johnny Reb" and fight. After all, that was why they had volunteered in the first place.[12]

"Camp Sickness"

In addition to the lack of proper military supplies, word of the new recruits suffering from strange illnesses and what was called "camp sickness" soon made its way to the Northern home front. Many of the stricken men, especially those from the more rural Western states, had never ventured far from their homes and farms nor had they routinely circulated in a larger urban setting. As medical science now knows, a consequence of this somewhat isolated life was that they had not developed any type of natural "herd immunity" to many of the era's deadly diseases. Exposure to measles, typhoid, chicken pox, mumps, whooping cough, diphtheria, smallpox, and other communicable diseases to which rural-born soldiers were vulnerable affected roughly half of green soldiers. In fact, throughout the war two-thirds of all Union casualties were ascribed to disease and illness while battle deaths accounted for the remaining one-third. This type of daily exposure, enhanced with poorly ventilated and overcrowded tents, helped facilitate the spread of disease. Improperly prepared food and tainted liquor often added to the woe. "I would sooner risk the bullets of the enemy," a Wisconsin man disclosed to his wife in late February 1862 after witnessing the rising body count. Within days, he informed her that his regiment was now carrying out two or more funerals per week due to illness-related deaths. As a consequence, new recruits quickly learned to fear disease as much if not more than the Confederates. Charles Wills exemplified that concern when he described how he and his training camp comrades had to sleep in old cattle stalls. "Eight men are allowed the same room that one cow or jackass had," he calculated. The result being, "We are more afraid of ague here than of the enemy."[13]

Even worse than being afflicted with "camp sickness," according to the *Daily Pittsburgh Gazette*'s field correspondent, was that the debilitated soldiers had nothing on hand to make them somewhat comfortable or to give them cheer, thereby keeping their spirits from sinking further. The Union army manpower shortage soon became striking. Pvt. H. H. Matthews estimated in early December 1861 that his Company C of the 33rd Indiana Infantry could field only twenty-five to thirty able-bodied men, the rest down with camp illnesses. At the beginning of 1862, the *Cedar Falls Gazette* reported that 20 percent of General Crittenden's brigade stationed at Calhoun, Kentucky, were seriously ill. In the East, some regiments within the Army of the Potomac did not have enough healthy men to properly care for the sick.[14]

The medical community's knowledge of infectious diseases and their treatments was highly limited when the rebellion commenced in 1861. Antibiotics had yet to be invented while sanitary precepts regarding battle wound treatment were still in their infancy. Illnesses such as measles and dysentery shadowed soldiers who were now on the march. By the summer of 1862, the citizen-soldier's romanticized image of war was replaced by the daily grind of camp diseases, fatigue duty, and hard marching. Following the April 7, 1862, battle of Shiloh fought on the banks of the Tennessee River, the 14th Wisconsin Infantry was posted to remain as a provost guard, which was the Civil War forerunner to the modern military police, though with minimal rations, no tents, and continually exposed to rain. Two months later, a soldier in that regiment wrote home declaring that because of the inevitable illnesses, "Our regiment is almost decimated." After a quick head count, he concluded there were "hardly enough well ones to take care of the sick, and still we stay here dying by inches." Union soldiers and their friends and family remaining at home were learning quickly that disease was a deadlier foe than Rebel bullets.[15]

WHERE'S MY PAY?

Those men who voluntarily left their farms or other jobs and families in order to wage war certainly expected to be paid for their efforts. As discussed earlier, many of these men had wives, children, aging parents, or other family members to help care for, and in the tough economic times still gripping the nation, a steady paycheck from the federal government was why many had enlisted in the first place. It was a *quid pro quo* for these men. If the government reneged on its promise to pay, then the soldier's service obligation was likewise absolved. Yet all too often, an overwhelmed federal government struggling to find funds meant that the soldiers' pay did not arrive in camp in a timely fashion if at all. Some congressmen even rationalized that it was more important to pay suppliers than the soldiers. Between a lack of proper supplies and pay, some ninety-day soldiers became so disgusted that they would not even remain in the army for an extra day, which in one instance forced the army to concede an important piece of territory to the Confederates due to a lack of men willing to stay and hold it.[16]

Every state had regiments that could tell the same tale. Like all of the other initial ninety-day regiments, the men of the 19th Ohio Infantry had marched off to war filled with visions of martial glory. After they had performed honorably during the June 1861 Rich Mountain campaign in western Virginia, they returned home in a foul mood because they had not been paid. Many of the regiment's men had left farms half planted or lost income because they were gone from their shops for several months. Now they accused the federal government of not holding up its end of the bargain. Meanwhile, those potential recruits who had yet to enlist took notice. In Pennsylvania, thousands of ninety-day men were penniless when they arrived home at the state capital at Harrisburg. Then the War Department mustered them out of the service without paying them. With no money, food, or shelter, some Pennsylvanians were forced to steal food and then sleep anywhere they could. Even by mid-September, some men had yet to be paid. One Indiana private wrote home complaining that his 15th Indiana Infantry had yet to receive one cent from the government. "A more ragged looking set I never saw," he complained.[17]

All of these stories eventually reached Lincoln's desk, and he was certainly no less pleased than the privates. One apocryphal tale told of an army paymaster who stopped by the White House to "pay his respects" to the president. "From the complaints of the soldiers," replied Lincoln, "I guess that's about all any of you do pay."[18]

***

Men who were successful in business viewed the jobs they offered at home or the taxes they paid as patriotic and sufficient contributions to the war effort that were every bit equivalent to enlisting in the army. One month into the war on May 15, 1861, Harrisburg's *Pennsylvania Daily Telegraph* argued this point, stating, "There is no necessity for men of business, particularly those with families, to enlist in the ranks. Money and supplies will be needed far more than men, and will be exhausted first." Therefore, from the paper's vantage, "A man who has no taste or special qualifications for military duties, can serve his country just as efficiently by contributing a portion of his income towards the support of the army in the field."[19]

Productive farmers in particular were also granted a cultural exemption from military service if those men were caring for their families while providing necessary foodstuffs for the community and military. After all, since the US economy was still primarily an agricultural one in 1861, how could farmers and their various field hands abandon their fields when crops had to be planted and then harvested during the summer and fall seasons? Numerous newspaper editorials urged farmers to plant as many crops as possible in order to help feed the army. "Let every man plant and sow every available acre of ground within his reach," counseled the *Brooksville Republican*. Such activity, therefore, was deemed every bit as patriotic as enlisting.[20]

LET OTHERS FIGHT IT OUT

The patriotic image the Northern press presented of women everywhere waving handkerchiefs and urging their men off to war was not entirely accurate. While young unmarried women commonly applauded single men who enlisted, most married women did not encourage their husbands to leave their families behind and march off to war, in spite of the historical image of the tearful yet dutiful wife bidding her husband goodbye. Civil War historians have estimated that no more than a third of married men ever served. An analysis of various National Archives sources for the town of Cortland, New York, for example, showed that only ten of the ninety-eight men who enlisted into the town's company at the war's commencement were married and only six of those ten had children.[21]

As a married father, Michigan's Isaac Beers urged his similarly situated brother to give up the idea of enlisting. Yet he admitted, "If I had no children to depend upon me for a living and education I should volunteer to fight for the stars and stripes." Albert Wilder of the 39th Massachusetts Infantry later told his sister, "The best place for any married man is at home with his wife there is single men enough to crush out this rebellion." After recently married David Walters enlisted in late 1862, Walters' new brother-in-law expressed his misgivings to his sister: "I think it would have been more credit to him to have taken care of his family than to have gone to the army—but everyone to their own notion."[22]

As keepers of the home, married women often viewed the war differently from their husbands. Whereas the Civil War husband was sometimes pulled to enlist by prideful emotions of an abstract duty to country, a desire for manly recognition, or even the need for a steady job to support his family, he saw his rival duties to country and family as complementary. His complex emotions and stay-at-home rationales were constantly stirred by conflicted reasoning and societal pressures to enlist. As a married man, thirty-one-year-old George Gray of Waltham, Massachusetts, felt these competing pulls when the war began. Gray wanted to enlist at the war's outset, but felt confused as to "which was my duty, to give my services to my country, or to my family."[23]

A man's wife, on the other hand, often saw his service as taking her husband away from family responsibilities, regardless of the family's political sympathies. Ohioan Julia Jackson certainly characterized that sentiment. Though she had reluctantly agreed to her husband's enlistment in November 1861, Jackson felt compelled to remind him five months later, "You are sworn to me before you are to your country."[24]

On the antiwar side, army surgeon Seth Gordon later wrote of many women—married or single—who were opposed to the war from honest motives, believing it should have been somehow averted in the first place. They were completely indifferent to the war's rationales and sought to prevent their male loved ones from entering the army even considering the later financial inducements. The net effect according to Gordon was that "The influence of such women hindered enlistments." Even staunch Republican women had some doubts. For instance, George Kryder of the 3rd Ohio Cavalry occasionally felt compelled to address his wife's 1863 regrets when she wished in retrospect that he had never enlisted back in 1862. Kryder reminded her that his enlistment was his duty and, in any event, it was far better for him to have volunteered rather than to be forcibly drafted. When Mortimer Leggett accepted the lieutenant colonelcy of the 78th Ohio Infantry in late 1861, his wife began her new

1862 diary by admitting, "I do not know how we can get along at home without him."[25]

A wife may have supported the reasons for the war philosophically, however, she frequently resisted the idea that those male loved ones closest to her should go off to fight. Better to let those who started the war fight it out between themselves. To that end, the wife of a Democratic New York judge suggested to her diary—and perhaps not entirely in jest—that the best solution would be for the North's female abolitionists to meet the South's female fire-eaters in a fair fight so they could "mutually annihilate each other." Duty to country and family were not complementary to the Northern wife, but rather, they were obligations that were hostile to each other. Netta Taylor, for example, repeatedly reminded her husband, Tom, a captain in the 47th Ohio Infantry, that his first duty was to his family, not the nation. "I am so tired living this way, so unhappy and dissatisfied living without you, indeed at times I am perfectly miserable," she admitted in late October 1862. This dynamic was generally most apparent with married farmers. Unless the family was well off enough to be able to afford modern machinery such as reapers and mowers or to hire additional labor, or perhaps had extended family nearby who could assist, the wife realized that the daily manual labor previously performed by her now-absent husband would have to be completed by her and her children, if any.[26]

Just as fathers and husbands mostly chose not to enlist because they believed their primary responsibility was to their wives and children, many adult sons desired to stay home if they were the only source of support for aging and/or infirm parents. That was the case for William Mitchell of Piqua, Ohio, who felt compelled to clarify to his cousin in an August 1862 letter why he had not enlisted. First stressing that it was not due to any level of cowardice, Mitchell wrote that if he left, the family business would fail. "The old man could not get along without me," Mitchell explained, "& then mother is so near gone with the consumption that it would about kill her." Twenty-four-year-old Pennsylvanian Jacob Zorn eventually enlisted in August 1862 with his widowed mother's reluctant consent, however, he freely admitted in his diary that he had possessed "little or no intention of ever enlisting" during the previous sixteen months due to family concerns. Additionally, adult male sons would stay home to assist with running a family farm if one or more male siblings had already enlisted. No mother or father was expected by Northern society to send all of their adult male children off to war.[27]

Parental wealth and not their old age or poverty compelled some fortunate young men to stay out of the war. The popular phrase describing the Civil War as "a rich man's war but a poor man's fight" certainly came about in part because of those healthy and fit single young men who chose not to enlist because their parents were wealthy and, therefore, they stood to inherit significant money and property. Once the draft came about, they could easily afford to buy their way out of serving by hiring a substitute. "They cannot enlist in defense of the 'Stars and Stripes,' and the protection of property, for fear they might possibly die, and someone else would inherit their expectant estates," complained Pennsylvania's *Agitator* in October 1861. "But so goes the world."[28]

FOPS, SWELLS, DANDIES, AND "SHOULDER STRAPS"

In a classic example of style over substance, some generally wealthier and younger civilian men who had no intention of enlisting took to wearing quasi-military attire as a means of showcasing their purported patriotism and martial seriousness. They considered their shopping and purchasing as legitimate patriotic acts undertaken in lieu of enlisting. Clothing became just one of the numerous commercial products entrepreneurs created so that consumers might show off their patriotism. In such costumes, they could talk of honor and gallantry with an air of importance while appearing to be men of substance and means. They believed that "clothes made the man" in a manner similar to the garish uniforms worn by numerous officers at the war's beginning. This civilian "uniform" served as a means of projecting the wearer's sense of self-control and order while concealing his known internal weaknesses. Such men were often considered "fops," "swells," or "dandies"—nineteenth-century terms used to describe a man who displayed an excessive interest in clothing, fashion, and style. In an era when White citizens were calling for a growing sense of responsibility and energy, the dandy stood out as a model of selfish irresponsibility and lack of commitment. He considered his fashion as a form of elite rebellion against the republican ideals of hard work and modesty but indicated a level of equality and therefore moral righteousness with the true Civil War volunteer.[29]

Many if not most citizens saw through the facade. As with the military-inspired fashion trends that had emerged in Britain during the Napoleonic era, *Vanity Fair* lampooned these men as "an army of stout, good-looking fellows, who stand all day and night about street corners, dressed in blue, with gilt buttons, and shields, and locust maces." Bloomsburg, Pennsylvania's *Star of the North* also ridiculed these men, initially pointing out that the typical age of the "silent, languid dandy" was twenty-five to thirty. In the paper's final jab, it asserted that even women had no use for the dandy, except to laugh at. As but one example, in the post-war novel *Sibyl's Influence; Or, the Missing Link*, Miss Therwin remarks with scornful emphasis, "I have found even during my few years of social life, that there is quite a difference between fops, swells, dandies, and—*men*."[30]

Somewhat similar to the dandy who wore quasi-military attire yet sought to avoid the war was the man who entered the army with an officer's commission but who had no desire of going anywhere near the front lines. His goal was rank and title as an end in itself. These were the fraudulent soldiers, also known derisively as "shoulder straps," who maximized their pre-war social influence to position themselves well away from the front while exploiting their new titles, such as the regimental officer who was always back home, ostensibly on recruiting duty. Much of the North viewed these men with more disdain than the quasi-uniformed swell or home guard member, for while the latter was often seen as somewhat clueless about the war's realities, the "shoulder strap" was a fraud, a hypocrite who sought to personally profit from the war without becoming actively engaged in it. Nathaniel Hawthorne lambasted these characters in a July 1862 *Atlantic Monthly* essay penned under "A Peaceable Man" pseudonym. Written just a year into the war, Hawthorne lamented the "incalculable preponderance" of military titles and pretensions every town and community would be forced to deal with well into the future. Hawthorne rightly feared that military title rather than battlefield merit would be the upcoming measure to all claims of social distinction.[31]

ABUNDANT DISQUALIFICATION.

"Ugh! How d'you make out that *you* are exempt, eh?"

"I'm over age, I am a Negro, a Minister, a Cripple, a British Subject, and an Habitual Drunkard."

Attending College Equated to Patriotism

It was common for youthful middle- or upper-class young men attending a Northern university to equate their studies with a properly patriotic contribution to the war effort, and therefore they avoided the war with a clear conscience. Furthermore, they were told that if they provided some emotional and/or perhaps financial assistance to those families whose fathers, sons, or brothers were off fighting, then such patriotic displays would fulfill their duty to the Union cause. Some rationalized their educational investment, the knowledge they were acquiring, and how they would use that to advance society as more important to the nation's collective betterment in the long term than whatever piece of insignificant cannon fodder they might become in the short term. Still, other students, such as twenty-six-year-old Gideon Allen, were outspoken against the war and considered the Lincoln administration's policies as a tragic betrayal of a citizen's constitutional civil rights. Allen admitted to his love interest that he was a proud Copperhead, as well as his opinion that the war was becoming ever more illegitimate as the months swept by. His decision to remain at the University of Wisconsin and not enlist was every bit as much a political statement of resistance against the war as it was a young man's personal goal to obtain a college education.[32]

Though numerous college students and some professors rushed off to the war, many did not, and for most, their decision was often not an easy one. For those who stayed, they continued teaching and attending classes as in the antebellum days, often seeming blissfully unaware that a war was underway. If they did write of the conflict, they often viewed it as a faraway event with little impact on their everyday lives. The historian of Yale University during the Civil War later wrote how the majority of its students, "either lukewarm or indifferent, remained merely spectators through the entire conflict." One student at upstate New York's Hamilton College admitted in October 1861, "If it were not for the daily papers, we would almost forget there was a war." Redsecker Young illustrated that reality as a seventeen-year-old Pennsylvanian studying at a private school in Ellington, Connecticut, when the war broke. For three years, he diligently kept a diary, usually making daily entries that spoke to his studies, socializing, friendships, and that seemingly favorite topic of diarists, the weather. What stands out, however, is how the great rebellion then underway makes barely a ripple in his world and consequently, his diary. Another student at Pennsylvania's Dickinson College penned a patriotic poem at the beginning of Robert E. Lee's 1862 Maryland campaign. By so doing, he supposed he "had evinced sufficient patriotism, and consequently felt relieved."[33]

Discussing the Lincoln administration's decisions through a university's debating societies and fraternities served as a metaphorical training ground for the national or state leadership positions many felt they would assume following the war's end. Less than a year into the war, the two student editors for the University of Michigan's annual fraternity magazine compared their home front exertions to their brothers in blue in the field and concluded "Ours is the harder lot, to stay behind, and envy their noble, patriotic self-sacrifice."[34]

Faculty and staff often agreed with those rationalizations. In some instances, school officials urged their students to form military companies. The school would then hire a drillmaster to conduct on-campus martial exercises so that the students might mollify their soldierly urges and hence, remain enrolled. George Robinson wrote while enrolled at the University of Michigan in June 1861 how the school's president had urged his students to stay in class until they graduated. By so doing, Robinson believed he could then enter the army with a lieutenant's commission, and therefore be of more service to the country than if he enlisted now as a mere private. This stay-or-go conundrum was also wonderfully rationalized by twenty-two-year-old Charles Kroff, who wrote in his diary on July 10, 1861, "My position this time is exceedingly critical, if I join the army it will be a great sacrifice on my part both in a pecuniary and intellectual point of view. By joining the army at this time, three years of the best portion of my life would be spent with a low groveling set of men, taking them as a mass . . . It seems to me as though it [would be] folly for me to go south to be shot at by rebels; rebels whom are far inferior in intellectual propensities, but perhaps superior with the rifles." Nonetheless, Kroff sensed his duty to the country outweighed his education and enlisted two days later.[35]

J. F. Ellis was a student at Illinois' Wheaton College when he explained to a classmate in November 1861 how any man's enlistment should be made according to his personal convictions regarding duty. As previously discussed, American culture emphasized the *voluntary* aspect of the citizen-soldier volunteer. "I have done this, and have concluded that I can affect more good by educating myself than by enlisting at present." Ellis believed the war was folly unless emancipation was a key aim, in which case he would then serve. Young Ellis was good to his word, for following Lincoln's Emancipation Proclamation, he enlisted into the 106th Illinois Infantry.[36]

Scores of younger Americans subscribed to the same logic and/or apathy as college students. Historian William Frassanito wrote of owning two diaries—one from 1862 and the other from 1864—of a seemingly stalwart and healthy twenty-two-year-old man named Albert Cruttenden who worked on his family's farm in central New York throughout the Civil War. He apparently never enlisted nor was drafted. What struck Frassanito was that of the two diaries' combined 700+ entries, only one referenced the great rebellion then underway. Frassanito concluded that if these two diaries were read by someone with no knowledge of American history, the reader would assume that these were two of the most peaceful years in the nation's history. The 1862–1863 diary of eighteen-year-old Alice Hawks revealed a similar disconnect. Her diary of Indiana home front life is filled with incidents about home, school, work, and society yet, as the diary's editors pointed out, the war intruded only slightly into her diary pages "like an unexpected and unwelcome visitor." In a letter to his sister in January 1862, twenty-nine-year-old John Vance Lauderdale confessed his ignorance and apparent indifference regarding the war's progression. "If I hear of a Generals army defeated, I always have to ask a friend of mine here whether he was Fedr'el or Rebel," Lauderdale admitted. Lauderdale did enter the war within a few months as a civilian contract surgeon working for the army, however, his reasons were purely career- and financial-oriented, and not for any heartfelt conviction toward the Union cause. The North was filled with many people like Hawks and Lauderdale, who lived far from any battlefront. While the Northern citizenry in the collective sense were obviously aware there was a war going on, for most it simply did not consume or change their daily lives tangibly as it did Southern civilians. As the mayor of Cleveland,

Ohio, Irvine Masters, admitted in April 1864 as his city continued to grow and prosper, it had "not directly felt the shock of war."[37]

NOT MY SON

Even if their child was not attending college, numerous Northern parents were not willing to grant enlistment permission to their sons who were younger than twenty years old; a consent that was, theoretically at least, required by law. Not only did they not want to put their sons in harm's way, fathers, mothers, and even older brothers viewed serving in the army as a potential moral hazard to their sons or siblings, many of whom were raised in the church. They considered the likelihood of their "boys" consistently being exposed to hardened men with profane and hard-drinking ways as a peril they had no desire to subject their sons to. "A ruffer set you never saw" was how Lewis Haviland characterized that concern when he described the eight hundred men in his Adrian, Michigan, training camp as part of his first letter home in early June 1861. In his initial letter home that November, Pennsylvania private James Miller told his father that he liked soldiering well enough but that "the boys are very rough and profane." Such descriptions were common and hardly placated parental concerns over what their young sons had signed up for. When Kansan Sam Reader learned that his younger brother had enlisted into the volunteers, Reader informed his father, "Had he wished to enlist into the Regular service I would myself have used every argument in my power to dissuade him from such a step, as many demoralizing influences would be thrown around him if I may judge from what I have seen of the Regular[s] in this part of the Country."[38]

Succumbing to moral hazards seemed to be as great a concern to parents as well as the obvious physical dangers of battle, especially mothers. They knew the perils their inexperienced teen boys and young men would find in army life, well away from the guiding and softening influences of his family's women. Ai Thompson's mother regretted her son's enlistment because she feared "you will have hardships to indure that you little think of." Her greatest concern based on what she wrote in her initial letter to him was wondering what kind of company her son would keep as well as urging him "not to indulge in any bad habits such as drinking and swearing and anything that will prove fatal to your character." The possibility of getting shot and killed by a Confederate bullet seemed a secondary concern.[39]

Charles Brown of the 13th New York Infantry opined to his sister that many of the men he encountered were morally fit to serve their country only by wielding a spade or rifle within the army. From Brown's vantage, the era's romanticized ideal of principled men sacrificing for a moral value "is pretty thoroughly wiped out by contact with the class who are in the army so far as I have seen." Echoing Brown was Frank Badger, who dryly reported to his mother in upstate New York that the only way a full one-quarter of the men in his regiment would know it was a Sunday was because the stores were closed and therefore they could not buy liquor. Meanwhile, eighteen-year-old Alfred Woods admitted to his aunt that whatever fears his family may have had for his moral welfare were legitimate. Writing from his Albany, New York, camp, Woods confessed he anticipated some trials and hardships, however, "I never expected to see so much vice as I have seen here. Swearing, drinking, fighting, quarrelling and sensuality have no end here."[40]

Some young recruits eager for action soon realized that their parents' concerns were on the mark. They saw how their idealized image of righteous and upstanding men marching off to war for a holy cause was an illusion. By late November 1861, a thirty-four-year-old Norwegian man serving in the 2nd Minnesota Infantry confessed to his family that prostitutes, aka "camp followers," were everywhere. "We have about forty women in the regiment, some of them make lots of money natures' way," he gently explained. In every town where Union soldiers were stationed, legions of such women gathered to sell their bodies to lonely men in uniform in a business process that was old as war itself. This was especially the case after Union paymasters had visited a camp. A later medical report revealed that during the war's first year, one in twelve Union soldiers was inflicted with syphilis, gonorrhea, or some other form of sexually transmitted disease. These reports were hardly the type that might sway churchgoing parents to allow their teen sons to march off to war and therefore served as another reason to avoid the conflict.[41]

After Maj. Gen. George McClellan arrived in Washington in September 1861 to assume command of what became the Army of the Potomac, he attempted to address this apparent problem by issuing a general order that urged "a more perfect respect" for the Sabbath among his soldiers. The *Christian Messenger* applauded McClellan's directive, now believing that "Christian men will the more cheerfully enlist in the army," since before the general's arrival, "Parents and friends have been reluctant as to subject young men of good moral character to the ordeal of camp-life, so long as that life was understood to be Sabbathless, and of course immoral."[42]

By November 1862, reluctant parents of teenage boys had an unlikely ally in William A. Hammond, the army's surgeon-general. Hammond had seen enough teenage recruits to realize that change was needed "both for the interests of the Army and the welfare of individuals." Hammond knew that even though the minimum age was eighteen, it was common to find boys of sixteen years old shouldering a musket. Wisconsin's Elisha Stockwell Jr. even managed to enlist when he was only fifteen years old. "Youths of these ages are not developed and are not fit to endure the fatigues and deprivations of the military life," Hammond argued. "They soon break down, become sick, and are thrown upon the hospitals." For the sake of the army, Hammond recommended that a recruit's legal minimum age should be fixed at twenty years. Nevertheless, his recommendation was not acted upon.[43]

Innumerable parents and guardians who would have wholeheartedly agreed with Hammond ended up petitioning Union authorities and state courts to reclaim their underage children who, they alleged, had enlisted without their consent. For these parents, having final control over the personhood and labor of their minor children was a fundamental aspect of American liberty. Army officials were routinely frustrated by the long-standing tradition of parents or guardians filing a writ of habeas corpus to regain their underage children who had enlisted without their approval. Long a foundational cornerstone of Anglo American law, the writ of habeas corpus (which literally translates to "produce the body") is the only common law process cited in the US Constitution. The writ dictated that the arresting authority had to bring the accused before a court and show cause for their arrest and/or detention. If the judge found the authority's reasoning insufficient, the detainee could be set free. In our modern area, habeas corpus is viewed primarily as a defense tool, however, nineteenth-century Americans routinely used it as a measure to settle other disputes such as child custody to the aforementioned underage military enlistments. Once having gained the writ, a parent or guardian legally forced the pertinent army officer to leave his camp or barracks, often at considerable cost or inconvenience, and to appear in court along with the enlistee to make the army's case for keeping the young man in the service.[44]

COMMUNITY AND ETHNICITY

Ethnic loyalties and their attendant concerns—which changed over time—also influenced prospective volunteers one way or the other. A significant number of both German and Irish immigrants desired to enlist when the war began both as a means of showcasing their Union loyalty as well as finding a steady paying job. Irish leaders also saw the war as an opportunity to dispel nativist fears about their Catholicism and its harmony with the American democratic tradition. These immigrant communities were under no illusions as to the overarching deep prejudice exhibited toward them within their civilian past by native-born Americans. All too often, native-born Americans simply disliked German citizen-soldiers and distrusted Irish ones.[45]

Yet other immigrant families felt this was not their war for it signified an unwelcome invasion into their daily lives. When twenty-one-year-old John Fruehauff enlisted in April 1861, he expressed dismay that his German-lineage parents felt their family should be "exempt from doing anything for the country or incapable of any sacrifices for the safety of those homes & home duties you so highly extol." He denied that his enlistment was a "hasty act" born out of a roaming desire but was actually a personal call of duty.[46]

Nonetheless, and especially in the case of the Irish, much of their immigrant population became convinced this was not their war. They remembered Ireland's Great Famine of 1845–1852 and how it destroyed more than half of the country's population. Many survivors fled to the

United States looking only for honest work as a means of feeding their families and escaping what they viewed as a tyrannical English government. In most instances, that work was little more than hard manual labor. Now, they resented how multitudes of their brethren had been misled by foreign worker importers back in Ireland, believing they were coming to America only for the promised jobs. "I said and so did others of those who came from London that it was not for to be soldiers we came out, but to get the work appointed for us in London," claimed a new Irish émigré. Another Irishman already tricked into the Union army lamented that he was "sorry to the heart that [I] should become the dupe of a Federal agent." He also noted, "I am not the only one . . . the moment they land they are drafted to the battlefield."[47]

After all, what was the point of defending a Union that was so traditionally and overtly antagonistic to Irishmen? Nativist hostility to the so-called "savage Irish" was part of their lives since the 1830s as they witnessed Protestant gangs attack Irish Catholic churches. Nor could the Irish not notice how American newspapers stereotypically portrayed them as routinely drunken and possessing "ape-like" features. In some instances, Democratic newspapers used satirical articles illustrating how their foreign-born partisans were willing to enlist in new ethnic regiments *if* the state's governor also called for a new regiment comprised of abolition-minded Republicans *and* succeeded in getting it filled to quota. The point was their party loyalists would not have to enlist soon if they waited until their proviso was met. Once the war started, Catholics often felt the sting of discrimination and reacted in kind. After hearing how non-native workers employed at a Boston naval yard were dismissed in the fall of 1861, a local priest counseled his parishioners *not* to enlist in the army until the government instituted fairer employment practices. By the spring of 1862, German and Irish Catholic immigrants began to reconsider their role in it. For these predominantly conservative communities, their overarching desire was to prove their loyalty to the Union that *was*, not to what they saw as changing war goals predicated on radical abolitionism.[48]

That change of heart became most apparent to Col. Silas W. Burt, New York's assistant inspector general, who reported to Gov. Edwin

"This Is a White Man's Government" A post–Civil War image depicting reconstruction as a nefarious conspiracy between the "savage ape-like" Irish, ex-Confederates, and wealthy northern Democrats. (Library of Congress Prints and Photographs Division)

D. Morgan during an Essex County tour that "scarcely a single Irishman, citizen or alien, has been enlisted since July 1 [1862] . . . in spite of every inducement and appliance." The exceptions, Burt noted, were "so few as scarcely to merit attention." Once the federal government enacted the militia draft in August 1862, which was closely followed by Lincoln's Preliminary Emancipation Proclamation on September 22, German and Irish immigrants all but stopped enlisting in the Union armies; both recalling how the notion of compulsory military service in a national army they despised was one reason they had fled their homelands in the first place. Such was the case for Julius Wesslau, who, in writing from New York to his family in Germany on October 26, 1862, wrote of the new militia draft with all its pitfalls. It is "especially not to my liking," he explained, "and if I was unwilling to be treated like a piece of government property in Prussia, I am just as unwilling to do so here." Out West, the Milwaukee *Seebote*, the voice of the Wisconsin German Catholic community, likewise expressed its horror that European immigrants would be "used as fodder for cannons" and that the "Germans and Irish must be annihilated, to make room for the Negro." Many Germans stopped all manner of support for the war and some even refused to vote.[49]

Antiwar Irish and German Catholics disliked how their reluctance to take part in what they interpreted as a Protestant religious crusade rendered them traitors in league with the Confederacy in the eyes of pro-war nativists. Immigrants had not sought out this war and resented how Republicans likened their neutrality to disloyalty. It is little wonder that Irishmen especially paid little attention to the various bounties and offers. Even though they overwhelmingly abhorred slavery and secession, a German Catholic priest attempted to summarize the position of his countrymen in America when he said, "I did not leave Germany to be shot for the Negros. Let me alone."[50]

This racial indifference to the plight of the slave manifested itself in the North across all ethnic, class, and religious lines and certainly played a part in the North's recruiting challenges from August 1861 through July 1862. The vast majority of Northern White Americans, though anti-slavery, nevertheless sincerely believed and took it for granted that Blacks were an inferior race and should not be made armed soldiers. The potential sight of a Black man in a blue uniform shouldering a musket next to a similarly outfitted White man presented an image of racial equality that most Whites would not abide during the first year of the war. Moreover, the prospect of armed Black men shooting down White men under lawful military authority was deemed equally intolerable. Most White Americans were not willing, initially at least, to risk life and limb in order to end slavery especially when all had seemed to agree at the outset that the war would be fought solely to preserve the Union. Furthermore, many Northerners, especially conservative Democrats, reminded the citizenry that slavery was still legal in the slave states. For most Northern Americans, the only legitimate reason for war was to bring the recalcitrant Southern states back into the federal compact, thereby preserving the sanctity of the Union. Men routinely stated (and wrote) that they were willing to fight and die for Old Glory so as to restore their nation. As historian Gary Gallagher aptly illustrated in *The Union War*, preserving the Union was their primary motivator in going off to war. Risking their lives and livelihoods to emancipate what was generally regarded as an inferior race then became acceptable as a means of ending the war and punishing the South.[51]

While most Northerners may have abhorred slavery, there were those relative few who nonetheless agreed with the South that it had the constitutional right to secede and decided to avoid the war for that reason alone. Others felt it better to just let the South leave than have the North wage a war of subjugation. Two days after Lincoln's November 1860 election victory, the Republican-leaning *New York Daily Tribune*—the nation's largest and most influential newspaper—urged the South not to secede. On the other hand, the paper editorialized that if the "Cotton States" believed they could do better outside of the Union than in, then let them go in peace. "The right to secede may be a revolutionary one," the paper opined, "but it exists nevertheless . . . We hope never to live in a republic, whereof one section is pinned to the residue by bayonets." Ex-president Franklin Pierce's former attorney general, Caleb Cushing, essentially agreed with the *Tribune*. In a December 10 speech at Newburyport, Massachusetts, he claimed that it was up to the North to now determine the best course of action since the South had apparently made its choice. Cushing believed that fervent Republican agitation over slavery lay solely at the heart of the quarrel. If the North could not "overcome" that, then "it may be best to separate; best for us at the North as for them at the South."[52]

All of this Northern debate about the war's purpose and merits was not overlooked by the South and had an important impact on how the Confederacy decided to wage their rebellion. Realizing the shortfall they faced in men and material, their overarching strategic plan was to simply outlast what they believed was the North's finite will to fight. Rather than trying to conquer the North, the South decided to fight a defensive war that would result in the North eventually believing it was no longer worth the blood and treasure required to force the South back into the Union. Better to just let them leave.

"CONSCIENTIOUS SCRUPLES"

The term "conscientious objector" that we often hear today did not exist during the Civil War even though the concept was well-known within the country. These were citizens of certain religious faiths or other pacifist groups whose tenets opposed participation in all wars because of their conviction that shedding human blood went against their Christian beliefs. For some, participation even meant conducting business with a government at war. Peace activist Arthur Love urged a friend in an August 22, 1861, letter not to sell goods to the Union army and to reject the idea that doing so was the lesser of two evils. "Patriotism used to mean love of country," wrote Love, describing patriotism as a virtue. Now, he complained, "it seems to be a love to have our own way, in our country, and is now ambition." For these men, any war-related activity should be shunned, which included serving in the military in any capacity, including as a chaplain or even as a hospital nurse. "There has never been a time in my life when I felt that I could take a gun and shoot down a fellow human being," wrote evangelist Dwight L. Moody, typifying their beliefs. They took God's Old Testament commandment literally that proclaimed "Thou shalt not kill." Their primary obligation was to serve in the army of the Lord and not any armies of man.[53]

Persons who held to such convictions were referred to in the war's *Official Records* as holding "conscientious scruples." They included the

Quakers (the largest such group), Amish, Mennonites, the Church of the German Baptist Brethren (also known as the Dunkers), and, toward the end of the conflict, the Seventh-day Adventists. Initially, the Lincoln administration as well as most soldiers generally acquiesced to their pacifist beliefs, thereby distinguishing mainstream Protestants or Catholics and the smaller pacifist sects. That sentiment changed when the draft became an issue in August 1862. Once the 1862 militia draft was announced, some states acceded to their opposition to personal service in the state militias without caveat. Other states required some manner of cash payment in order to grant a religious exemption. Other states, such as Michigan, offered no exemptions whatsoever.[54]

Of course, not all of the boys in blue were convinced that any man who claimed such status was being completely sincere. Edward Wright noted in his history of conscientious objection during the Civil War that the North's generals seemed more disposed toward the objector's requests than were many of the regimental officers and privates. The enlistees knew which men from their hometowns had always held to such lofty principles and who had not. Sgt. Jacob Zorn, for example, saw how his hometown of Berlin, Pennsylvania, held a meeting in September 1862 for all who held "conscientious Scruples." Zorn noticed how the town's pacifist Dunker congregation was more than willing to avail themselves of the opportunity to remain at home. "My opinion," Zorn concluded, "is many of them have no more Scruples than I or any other person has." The 4th Vermont Infantry's major Stephen Pingree spoke for many who believed Caesar should come before God when he wrote, "I do not think a man is entitled to have religion in times like these—if it interferes with the duty he owes his country."[55]

Once a national draft was formalized in early 1863 via the Enrollment Act (to be discussed fully in chapter 7), these objectors were no longer granted an exemption. A circular dated August 1, 1863, from the War Department directed that any man holding to such scruples could hire a substitute or pay the federal government's commutation fee just like any other man wishing to avoid service. Yet almost three months later, Gen. John Dix wrote to General-in-Chief Henry Halleck suggesting that Quakers be allowed to serve as hospital nurses or attendants in place of frontline soldiers. "They do not object to being employed in nursing the sick and disabled," Dix reasoned, "as it is a duty of humanity and . . . without any sacrifice of principle on the part of the Government." By mid-December, the War Department agreed that any man who opposed the war or even paying commutation money due to his conscientious scruples would be placed on parole until called if he happened to be drafted.[56]

The anti-slavery abolitionist cause was another moral crusade that generated some strange bedfellows. The movement was mostly in full support of the war even as it had harshly criticized the Union for allowing slavery in the antebellum years. Leading abolitionists, such as William Lloyd Garrison, backed the North and the war, believing the conflict would lead to their emancipationist ends even if that was not an initial goal. On the other hand, and though relatively few in number, ardent "immediatist abolitionists" refused to enlist or even support the war unless it became overtly about emancipation *and* full equal rights for Blacks, for there were a healthy number of what we now call special-interest groups whose primary loyalty was to their cause rather than any burgeoning nationalism. In this camp was the husband-and-wife team of Stephen and Abby Kelley Foster, who insisted that moral ends required moral means. Their brand of "moral nationalism" rejected a war to preserve the Union as it was with slavery intact. Their anger was highlighted by what they viewed as the president's appeasement when he disclaimed any intention of eliminating slavery in the key border states of Missouri, Kentucky, Maryland, and Delaware. Franklin Jacob Ellis of Wheaton College wrote emphatically in November 1861, "I say emphatically that I shan't strike a blow against secession unless I am permitted to strike it under the proclamation of unqualified emancipation to every creature within our boundaries." When coupled with the racial bigotry they saw all around them in the North, Northern immediatist abolitionists became convinced that the Union had no intention of ascending to the moral high ground by delivering full racial justice to the oppressed.[57]

Famed New England novelist and abolitionist Lydia Marie Child held to similar convictions. At fifty-nine years old when the rebellion commenced, she expressed her wish that "Old Glory" would now become worthy of being honored in the sense that US soldiers acting under governmental authority would no longer allow slaves to be sent back to their masters in chains and whipped to near death. "When it treats the colored people with justice and humanity, I will mount its flag in my great elm-tree," she wrote to a friend in early May 1861, "but, until then, I would as soon wear the [Copperhead] rattlesnake upon my bosom as the eagle." For radical abolitionists like Child and the Fosters, a definitive loyalty to their political cause trumped abstract loyalty to the nation. To support such a war was seen by them as anathema; supporting a war for the flawed Union that *was*, rather than the righteous one that *should be*.[58]

These "mad abolitionists," as New Yorker Maria Daly referred to them, generated considerable contempt from much of the Democratic North. Samuel Medary, editor of the highly incendiary *Crisis* in Columbus, Ohio, described them as "infidels in black coats and white neck ties, with Bibles in one hand and Bowie knives in the other—with prayer books and torches." Meanwhile, Daly complained to her diary how none of these abolitionists would ever go off to war but rather sought every flimsy excuse to escape serving. "Their fine, patriotic, virtuous, philanthropic principles stand them in lieu of great patriotic action," she wrote with no small amount of sarcasm. "How one despises such creatures!"[59]

POLTROONERY

Few considered those men who had always held to "conscientious scruples" to be cowards or hypocrites. As mentioned earlier, not acting in a hypocritical or duplicitous manner was a key tenet as to whether one's rationales for not enlisting were accepted or not by a man's home front community. Nonetheless, as in all wars and all times, some men who could have readily served quietly chose not to because they knew in their hearts that they were simply a coward. Given the era's conviction that a real man displayed "manly courage," no one would ever make such a humiliating admission. Those men who had already stepped forward to enlist with no expectation other than to serve their country certainly felt that way toward the "stay-at-homes."

In the Civil War era, both cowardliness and courage were viewed as character traits shaped by social class and upbringing rather than by a convergence of irrepressible external factors such as those found on the battlefield. In other words, nurture trumped nature. To be seen as a coward was to be seen as morally weak and therefore a moral failure. For historians, correctly interpreting a person's motives both during and after the war presents an immense challenge given human nature and its desire to conceal our own shortcomings.[60]

The famous American writer William Dean Howells noticed this tendency to sanitize. His conscience never seemed at ease over his decision to not enlist. His post–Civil War comments on the rebellion always appeared to reflect on what he may have viewed as his cowardly inaction or, at a minimum, his ambivalence. "Every loyal American who went abroad during the first years of our great war," he later wrote, "felt bound to make himself some excuse for turning his back on his country in the hour of her trouble." Another American literary icon, Henry James Jr., also decided not to enlist in April 1861 after he had just turned eighteen years old. James had always spurned competitive endeavors, consequently, he chose early in life to be an avid chronicler of the human experience rather than an active participant in it. Therefore, it is perhaps not surprising that he always remained somewhat reticent about not volunteering when so many others, including his two younger brothers, were enlisting all around him. Not until 1914 in his *Notes of a Son and Brother* did James lament about his not serving—and then only in the vaguest way—explaining his absence due to a "physical mishap" that prevented his enlistment but did not preclude extensive travel soon thereafter. James' equally famous older brother, William, also admitted years later that he too had been "much gnawed by questions as to my own duty of enlisting or not." His absence from what was his generation's defining event was, he later suspected, due to his "own pusillanimity."[61]

Henry Baker was a New Hampshire furniture maker of far more humble means than Howells or the James brothers yet had no such need for self-reflection. He knew when the war started that if he did not enlist then and there, he would one day share Howells' troubling regrets. Baker wrote in 1861 how his voluntary enlistment was a moral *duty* and if he did not go, "I know that in after years, I shall feel ashamed to confess that I have left others to do my duty for me." Samuel Storrow of Massachusetts felt a similar tug. In explaining to his father why he enlisted without his parents' consent or knowledge, he wrote that he did not want to play "the part of a coward" by staying at home and allowing others to fight his battles for him. "What a shame," he explained, "what mortification would it cause me years hence to be obliged to confess that in the great struggle for our national existence I stood aloof, an idle spectator without any peculiar ties to retain me at home." Other men who could not or would not go felt compelled to do something. Thirty-year-old Theodore Roosevelt Sr.—father of the future president—did not volunteer when the war began in deference to his Southern-leaning wife, yet he soon became a New York allotment commissioner helping the needy families of Union soldiers as well as a future Union League and Loyal Publication Society member. "I would never have felt satisfied with myself after this war is over if I had done nothing," he wrote to his wife, "and that I do feel now that I am only doing my duty."[62]

Capt. Godfrey Trachpy would certainly have agreed with men like Baker, Storrow, and Roosevelt. As a veteran officer in the Austrian army who was in the States to observe the war while on an extended furlough, Trachpy wrote a long letter in January 1862 commenting on the North's conduct so far. He praised the young Union men who, in later years after having grown old with hair turned gray, would be able to look back with pride knowing they answered their nation's call. As for those who chose not to step forward, the captain rhetorically asked, "What then will be the feelings of the laggards, who, through cowardice and carelessness, remained at home?" Trachpy minced no words with his answer: "Their after days will be spent with the knowledge that they are undeserving the name of men." Such cowardice accusations, however, were not leveled at those who had a viable excuse for not volunteering, such as the man who was the sole caregiver to elderly or infirm parents. Moreover, whether poltroon or loafer, such pejoratives rarely applied to the letter writer or recipient, but only to the unseen "other" who did not step forward to enlist. Whatever their myriad reasons, the fact that approximately two-thirds of service-eligible Northern White men made a conscious decision *not* to volunteer at any time during the four-year rebellion presented a manpower dilemma to the federal government that historian

Fred A. Shannon referred to as "the slacker problem." It indicated a level of willing sacrifice that settled somewhere between indifference and anti-war hostility. As 1861 ended, few realized that the North had reached its zenith of purely patriotic enlistment.[63]

CHAPTER 4

"Patriotism Is Well-Nigh 'Played Out' in the Army"

Changing Perspectives, the Militia Act of 1862, and the Rise of the Mercenary

As the 1861–1862 winter made its way into spring, the North began to realize that the war was not going to be the jolly lark many had earlier predicted. The Confederacy did not seem like it was going to melt away anytime soon, and that was nowhere more apparent than on the battlefield, where Rebel forces had shown themselves more than able to take on Billy Yank. Inevitably, such realities had a palpable effect on Northern morale. In a speech on the House floor, Ohio congressman Samuel Cox bemoaned how "Thousands of our people now regard with dampened spirit and sad silence the condition of our country; and they are almost dismayed by our terrible present and still unpropitious future." Cox's words applied to those who gravely pondered the matter. For many civilians, however, the war's initial excitement had long worn off with life returning to normal. In St. Louis, twenty-eight-year-old attorney Franklin Dick bemoaned how the North's ongoing prosperity had resulted in a lack of earnestness and growing apathy. Thomas Lowe wrote to his soldier brother from Ohio relaying how home front routines had resumed. "Our people all attend to their usual avocations our streets seem as full as usual, we are buying and selling, working & playing, loving and hating just as we have always done," Lowe wrote, but with one important exception.

He also noted how occasionally "and rather frequently indeed of late . . . we see a Procession preceded by a muffled drum, a hearse and the Light Guard with arms reversed, and this is all we see of the war." Northern men who were still contemplating enlistment were constantly reminded by sights such as Lowe's, as well as antiwar critics and even friends that they should carefully consider the full gravity of their decision.[1]

If the battlefield situation was not bad enough, the administration and public were also reminded of how the war's financial costs were rapidly escalating. The army's daily payroll alone was at least $325,000 with almost 700,000 people in the government's employment; a number far more than expected. Meanwhile, the federal treasury was almost empty. To alleviate the situation, Congress passed the Legal Tender Act on February 25, 1862, which authorized the use of paper money to finance the war effort. Known colloquially as "greenbacks," this marked a serious diversion from the government's previous standard of using only gold or silver specie to pay its bills. This act, its inflationary impact, and the resultant effect on enlisting will be discussed further in chapter 9.[2]

While the government was struggling to make ends meet, much of the public was doing the same. Mrs. Bethiah McKown wrote to her son from St. Louis on May 18 discerning how the city's streets were filled with Union soldiers who were fighting not from patriotism, "but for their bread and butter." Particularly hard hit were the southernmost counties of Ohio, Indiana, and Illinois, which in the case of the latter two, were geographically located farther to the south than much of Virginia or Kentucky. Long a Democratic stronghold and one of the North's most outspoken and dangerous areas, the 1850 census showed that in Indiana, the number of the state's residents who were born in slaveholding states was greater than the total number born in New England, New York, and Pennsylvania combined. Ten years later, the 1860 census revealed that 475,000 of those three states' residents were Southern-born or their parents had migrated from the South. The South's culture remained strong within their communities, while many even had friends or relatives serving in the Confederate army. This lower Midwest was a formidable economic and political region that overall was pro-Union but not necessarily anti-slavery. Its growing antipathy toward the federal government was not mitigated when they learned that one of the government's first actions to subdue the rebellion was to cut off the flow of goods and food into Dixie. Farmers and working families suffered greatly when Union forces effectively shut off the Mississippi and Ohio Rivers by early 1862. According to the *Cincinnati Gazette*, the region's farmers had suffered a loss of $6,000,000 just in bacon alone due to the closing of their Southern markets. "Times are very hard here at present," Ohioan George Brown wrote to his brother in Michigan on April 22, personifying the regional sentiment. Within five months, Brown had enlisted in the Union army solely to help make ends meet.[3]

In addition to requiring funds to pay for the war, the North's need for more men by the summer of 1862 was not helped by the administration's earlier conviction that the army's ranks held all the men necessary. In order to stem the tide of volunteers still flowing into recruiting offices, on December 3, 1861, the War Department ordered that no more regiments, artillery batteries, or independent companies were to be raised by state governors unless the War Department made a special requisition for them. This decision was due in large measure to the frustrating fact that the federal and state governments still could not outfit them properly. Then during a ten-week period from February through early April 1862, one repeated military success after another from Virginia to Florida and even New Mexico prompted a sense of elation to wash over the North. Politicians and Northern newspapers were convinced the rebellion's end was imminent. Secretary of War Stanton was also caught up in the euphoria, and at practically the same time the Confederacy was delivering its first-ever conscription bill, he issued General Orders No. 33 on April 3 directing all recruiting efforts to be immediately discontinued in every state. In addition, every recruiting office was to be closed, with all furnishings and government property sold at the best price possible. Once completed, those officers and soldiers detached for recruiting duty were to report immediately to their respective regiments.[4]

With twenty-twenty hindsight, historian Brooks M. Kelley referred to this decision as "perhaps the prime blunder of the war." Edwin Stanton's modern biographer, William Marvel, deemed it "incomprehensible" and a "grievous error" that prolonged the war. Some officers in the field quickly realized how the numbers were inflated and the error of Stanton's decision. Brig. Gen. William T. Sherman wrote how he considered the stoppage "a great mistake" because while he may have had sufficient men on paper, he knew he did not have enough in reality. In the east, the Army of the Potomac was prepared to take the field for what would become known as the Peninsula campaign yet now there would be no fresh recruits forthcoming to replace the inevitable casualties. Indiana's adjutant general later described Stanton's edict as "a most unfortunate step" and how "all efforts to have the order recalled were unavailing." Leading pro-war Democrat August Belmont was likewise mystified, writing to Republican politico Thurlow Weed in mid-July that the decision was "a fatal blow to our army." Now, as a result, wrote Belmont, "Where we would have found last winter ten men eager to enlist, anxious to share in our triumphs, we will scarcely now find one."[5]

The effect of such actions on the Northern public was profound and gave a ring of truth to Belmont's prediction. Newspapers generally applauded Stanton's order. The reliably Republican *New York Times* wrote approvingly and with Shakespearean allusion how Stanton, unlike King Lear, apparently no longer wanted or needed soldiers. Detroit's staunchly Democratic *Free Press* cheerfully assumed the order was given not due to the war's imminent end but because the purported 750,000 men now on the army's rolls were more than adequate. From that paper's perspective, if the army was admitting that it had all the men it needed, then why would any man not yet enlisted give further consideration to the matter? Perhaps even more importantly, why would any potential recruit risk life and limb—not to mention his family's security—when an improving economy offered many men the opportunity to gain significant wealth by providing goods and services to the North's ever-hungry war machine? The loud and clear answer to those rhetorical questions in late spring 1862 was that they would not.[6]

Stanton soon realized his error, though he never gave any adequate clarification as to why he issued it in the first place. On May 1, he explained to Maj. Gen. Henry Halleck that the order was merely to compel returns from the state governors and that the desired reports were now in hand. Stanton eventually reversed himself, issuing general orders on June 6 for recruiting to begin anew.[7]

The North's optimism generated by the battlefield successes from 1862's late winter and early spring was wiped away with the carnage and defeat that awaited the Union army throughout the upcoming summer. Only three days after Stanton's edict and though ostensibly a victory, the Union suffered 13,000 killed, wounded, or missing at the April 6–7 battle of Shiloh in southwestern Tennessee; a butcher's bill that was inconceivable at the time and dashed any further illusions of a relatively bloodless and quick war.

In the East, Maj. Gen. George McClellan's 1862 Virginia Peninsula campaign started well enough with victories at Yorktown and Williamsburg, in late April and on May 5, respectively. By the time his 120,000 men reached the gates of Richmond in late May, however, matters had turned precipitously. A drawn battle at Fair Oaks (also known as Seven Pines) on May 31–June 1 was the bloodiest engagement in the Eastern theater up to that point, with casualties four times that of Bull Run from the previous summer. The Seven Days battles from June 25 to July 1 featured six major engagements in the fields and forests east of Richmond, all but one Union victories. Yet McClellan seemed to react as if they were defeats. On August 4, his army was ordered off the Virginia peninsula and back to the Washington environs. Total Union casualties for the Seven Days were estimated at more than 16,000, a ghastly number that stunned home front Northerners. Lt. Sam Partridge of the 13th New York Infantry summed up what every volunteer was starting to realize when he wrote home on June 16 acknowledging, "War isn't fun. Fighting is hard work and mighty risky."[8]

Union soldiers also came to realize that the Confederates were not their only enemy as they made their way through the swampy, sweltering, mosquito-laden Virginia peninsula. Adam Gurowski was a Polish-born translator working in Washington, DC, at the State Department and, after reading the incoming reports from that army, he correctly surmised in his diary how "the malaria there must be more destructive than many battles." Hospital steward John Henry of the 49th New York Infantry didn't have to deduce like Gurowski because he was on the scene, allowing him to easily count the bodies and do the math. With his regiment and the army positioned just east of Richmond, Henry wondered whether disease or the Rebels were to be feared more. "We cannot muster as effective more than two thirds of our original number," Henry asserted. Such routine reports of rampant disease and illness in the North's newspapers or direct from loved ones in the army surely gave pause to any man considering enlistment. On a broad scale, the elite executive committee members of the US Sanitary Commission made that very warning in a letter to Lincoln on August 5 after having spoken with scores of its commission members. "The great loss of life from other causes than injuries received in battle," the committee wrote, "is alleged to have materially discouraged volunteering."[9]

One manner in which Northern civilians learned of those immense casualties was by the extensive casualty lists published in Northern newspapers. These daily lists horrified civilians, angered administration and army officials, and contributed to a decline in enlistments. John Miller of the 76th Pennsylvania Infantry wrote to his brother in early August 1862 declaring, "If they would know what I know it would be pretty hard to raise one Company in York [Pa.]." Silas Burt recalled how officials had argued against publishing the lengthy lists of killed, wounded, and missing since they acted as a serious impediment to army recruitment, and they most certainly did. Northern readers breathed a sigh of relief when they did not see a loved one's name. Countless civilian men then quietly reminded themselves that they were not going to give a Rebel marksman an opportunity to add their name. Yet, Burt correctly surmised the downside of not admitting the truth when he wrote, "the repression of such facts would have bred imaginary horrors a hundred fold more vivid."[10]

COWARDS AND SHIRKERS VERSUS FRIENDS AND FAMILY

From the day a new recruit first left home in 1861, his relations and friends had implored him to write home as often as possible and share all of the exciting details of army life. Soldiers with ready access to pen and paper generally did write frequently, and initially they relayed all of the stirring aspects of their new adventure. Those men who enlisted for patriotic reasons proudly viewed themselves as the noble citizen harking to their nation's call during a time of emergency. The flip side of that perspective, which held for at least the first year of the war, was that those healthy, single men back home who did not enlist were cowards and skulkers. "They are wrapped up within themselves," thought New Yorker Thomas Owen of those who shirked their patriotic duty, "and care not how humanity progresses, so long as they enjoy freedom and the blessings somebody else has won for them."[11]

Yet as spring 1862 bled into summer, the tone of the soldiers' letters began to change and, in countless instances, would remain that way for the remainder of the war. While these missives had normally ridiculed those unmarried, able-bodied men who had never enlisted as shirkers, they now started to gain a different perspective with regards to their male family members or close friends still at home. This was especially true if a male sibling had stayed behind to help run a family farm or business while another—often older—sibling had already enlisted into the army. A year's worth of camp boredom, illness, hard marching, and brutal warfare taught these men that many of their friends and relatives were simply not physically or psychologically cut out for army life and would quickly succumb. Writing from Falmouth, Virginia, in late June, Pvt. William Greene stressed to his brother, "You could not stand 1 week," and then added, "All the fat ones are continually dropping out while the lean ones and those that come in winter can stand it better." Cavalryman William Wells likewise implored his sister not to allow their brother, Charley, to enlist because he could not tolerate the rigors of a soldier's life. As a test, Wells suggested that his brother should put forty pounds onto his back and then walk in the high heat of the day to their nearby river and back repeatedly until he had traversed sixteen to twenty miles. Then repeat that march two or three days in succession. Lastly, he should sleep on the grass in front of their Vermont home for one week with only a light blanket, getting up every third night to stand guard for two hours. "See how he likes that," Wells instructed. In December 1863, LaForest Dunham of the 129th Illinois Infantry gave his then seventeen-year-old younger brother another typical warning from the front, urging the glory-seeking lad that if he knew what was good for him, he would stay home and help their parents all he could. "You would not stand it six months." Dunham then added, "If you think anything of me, stay at home." Pvt. Rufus Robbins of the 7th Massachusetts Infantry similarly explained to his brother, "I want you to stay at home with father and mother. You can be a patriot there as well as here and such," indicating that the Union soldier's perspective on what was and wasn't proper patriotism was starting to shift.[12]

At the same time that he was lashing out at secessionists at home and in the army, Henry Johnson was advising his father and younger brother not to enlist, not so much due to any perceived physical limitations, but rather that since both he and another brother, Ike, were already in the service, the family had met their patriotic obligations. Furthermore, "Father is too old & Jay too young, and neither of them stout enough," Johnson warned in an August 1862 letter to his sister. Johnson's rationale was simple. There were plenty of men eligible for military duty who could easily go and whose families had not sent anyone. William Greene likewise urged his brother, Marlon, not to enlist after learning the latter was still contemplating the matter. "You remember one of our family is here now and that is our share." It was far easier for someone to approve of a distant war fought by strangers than to support a war fought by their loved ones.[13]

These men were not being duplicitous. After a year or so in the army, men like Johnson and Greene as well as countless others now saw their enlistment as representing not only themselves but their immediate families as well. As the war progressed, a growing and widespread Northern belief dictated that after a family had provided a father or son to the military, it should not be called upon to provide another family member until less patriotic families had done their part by providing someone. With another brother already in the ranks, twenty-five-year-old Francis Bliss of the 1st Massachusetts Cavalry implored his mother not to let her youngest son enlist, convinced that his family had more than fulfilled their duty by already having two sons in the army. "Tell William not to think of enlisting. Tom and I will do fighting enough for our family, if they will give us a chance. He will be serving his country better on the farm than he will in the ranks . . . He must not go," Bliss warned. Three days later, Francis wrote directly to his nineteen-year-old brother, William, with an identical admonition. "There will probably be another call for troops before long, but I don't think you ought to enlist. You must look at the necessity of your being at home while Tom and I are away . . . It is not the duty of all to go. Be contented and stay at home."[14]

The youthful enthusiasm and desires for patriotic glory that filled so many letters one year earlier were now replaced by the sobering realities of war and campaigning. They included reports of disease and killing on a scale never before witnessed by Americans. With twenty-twenty hindsight, many Union recruits who had rushed pell-mell to the enlistment offices in the heady days of April and May 1861 and with visions of a quick adventure now began to not only advise their friends and relatives not to enlist, some also began to openly regret their own enlistment decision. Furthermore, they minced no words regarding the matter in their letters to family and friends. In his post-war poem titled "Shiloh: A Requiem," author and poet Herman Melville neatly captured this change of heart with the line "What like a bullet can undeceive!"[15]

By the early summer of 1862, the learned realities of a soldier's life and what seemed like military defeat or stalemate prompted army morale to nosedive. Joseph K. Taylor of the 37th Massachusetts Infantry wrote how he could not recall talking with a single soldier who did not consider himself a fool for enlisting. Taylor asserted that if he knew then what he knew now, nothing could have induced him to enlist. Many men like Taylor now realized that their loyalty to the uniform did not equate to a taste for army life. Only a month after his regiment's recruitment, Henry Walker of the 117th New York Infantry wrote to his wife from the Washington defenses as to how many of his comrades quickly felt the same. According to Walker, "the most of them say that if they was at home they would not go to war any more." Capt. Tom Taylor of the 47th Ohio Infantry had also seen enough and now sensed why soldiers stayed. "Patriotism is well-nigh 'played out' in the army," he informed his wife on July 7.[16]

In a July 8, 1862, letter to his brother written from the sweltering, mosquito-infested Virginia peninsula, Francis Channing Barlow wrote of his desire to escape the death, illness, and drudgery the front lines represented. "Be assured that I am eagerly watching my opportunity to get out of it," Barlow confided. "If I can't resign I should like to get a position as Inspector General or something of that kind. I am thoroughly disgusted." In June 1861, just after he enlisted, Lt. and Quartermaster Samuel Partridge of the 13th New York was buoyantly writing about his lofty goals and likelihood for promotion within the army. Now only a year later, he, too, was having serious second thoughts. "If this [Peninsula] campaign continues with its late severity, with its more than usual deprivations and hardships, I am afraid I shall be obliged to quit," he advised his grandmother, "unless I can get a position of a little more ease, and less headwork too." For men like Partridge, their primary goal in enlisting appeared to be promotion and advancement. While wading and sleeping in "mud shoe deep, the wind a blowing like the [devil] and the rain leaking through," in front of Yorktown, Virginia, a New York lad described his minimal four-man tent that some would not deem adequate for their hogs. He then confessed, "I think if I was home I would not enlist." Nineteen-year-old George Daggett had also experienced enough glory. Though he acknowledged that his enlistment term had another ten months to go, he confessed to his cousin that knowing what he now knew, he would not enlist if he was still at home. Daggett concluded his missive by offering some advice, "Will, I don't want to say anything that would discourage you but if you know when you are well off you will stay at home." Charles Benton of the 150th New York Infantry was even more forthright about just how far in the distant past enlisting for flag and Union had become: "Whoever announces that he enlisted because he loved his country is sure to become the target for the shafts of ridicule."[17]

The monetary incentive had also lost its glitter for many. In the East, an improving wartime economy provided well-paying jobs for those who wanted them. Furthermore, the upcoming fall harvest season and the hope for a good crop made it hard to attract men whose fields were hundreds or even a thousand miles away from Southern battlefields. An Iowa newspaper admitted as much. "We know that at this season of the year—in the midst of harvest—it is a difficult undertaking to recruit men. But that should not stay effort." Unless a farm family had a relative or close friend in the war, the distant rebellion often seemed like an abstract rather than a reality.[18]

All of these soldier comments were in line with what John Baynes noted in his mid-twentieth-century study of military morale; those who volunteer into the service out of a belief in a cause tend to display both enthusiasm and energy, which evolves into an inspired devotion to duty. When that belief fades, so does energy and as a consequence, morale suffers. Moreover, such letters as these surely had a stifling effect on those men still at home who may have considered entering the army.[19]

Horrid Hospitals

The men who went forth to do battle with the Confederate army were well aware that death awaited some of them. That was the nature of war and accepting the risk was part of martial manhood. Relatively few, however, knew of or expected the deadly diseases that also awaited them. Disease killed more Union men than Rebel bullets, and once Billy Yank learned that dire reality, his warnings to the folks back home became pervasive. A letter from Alvah H. Marsh of the 7th Michigan Infantry to his brother was typical. He admonished his sibling to forgo enlisting due to rampant scurvy and illness in his regiment's camp. "Take my advice for once [and] do not enlist at any rate," Marsh pleaded. "I know they will drum around and get you excited to enlist but do not for I have to suffer enough for all of the rest of my folks . . . God forgive if a man is sick here he may as well call himself dead."[20]

Stories of horrid army hospitals—whether makeshift field hospitals or large army hospitals in Northern towns—inevitably made their way back to the home front and served as ample inducement for other men not to enlist. In the antebellum and Civil War era, a town's public hospital did not connote a place of safe and professional care. Public civilian hospitals were considered "gateways to death" because of overcrowding and cross-infection. In reality, they were little more than charitable hostels reserved for the homeless urban poor or terminally ill. Middle- and upper-class individuals who needed personal medical care received it in their own homes. Now the sight of sickly, wounded, and maimed men arriving by the trainload dissuaded further enlistments.[21]

In addition, army field hospitals were rarely thought of by soldiers as places of healing. Recruits soon learned that their unsanitary, overcrowded conditions and often minimal care rendered them as somewhere to avoid at any cost. Soldiers who complained of having contracted camp illnesses or diseases were often viewed by their officers with skepticism, especially if those men were reluctant to report to the field hospital. "We have two that are very sick with the measles but they refuse to go to hospital and I don't blame them," lamented Ohio cavalryman Albinus Fell. From his perspective, the outcome was inevitable: "When a person is sick in camp they might as well dig a hole and put him in as to take him to one of these infernal hells called hospitals." Hospital steward John Henry also complained to his wife in late 1861 about the seemingly predictable process. "Men are kept in camp much longer than they ought to be after they're taken sick," wrote Henry. "[Then they] are taken to a hospital tent & are kept for a time until they become alarmed about them when they are sent to my ward as though I ought to almost raise them from the dead."[22]

Wounded soldiers also quickly realized that their battle injuries were merely to be repaired as quickly as possible in the same sense that a mechanic repaired a broken machine. Such dehumanizing "repair" often included the surgeon's on-the-spot decision to remove a shattered limb. Ether and chloroform were often in short supply, therefore the only comforts available to the wounded soldier were a shot of whiskey and a leather strap to bite down on. The sound of the surgeon's saw coupled with the wounded soldier's screams became so routine that the North's weekly newspapers published artistic depictions of such work. Hardly the type of war illustrations or reporting that would encourage current stay-at-homes to join the ranks.[23]

Of course, such scenes also had an indelible impact on the Union soldiers who witnessed them. One man likened the sounds coming from an army field hospital to that of a lively, religious revival meeting "where many pray in a low tone at the same time, mixed with loud exclamations such as 'O Lord,' 'O my God' . . . commingled with incoherent cries & groans." This was the "doleful music" every nearby soldier was forced to endure, and the results were foreseeable. "I would as soon be dead as to be confined in one of these Hospitals," wrote William Standard to his wife from Tennessee in early 1863. Any other non-visible ailments were to be suspected and doubted by surgeons. "I'm a great coward in sickness & fear it more than the enemy's bullets," admitted one Illinois soldier to his wife. Soldiers and their loved ones quickly learned that disease was a greater killer than Rebel bullets.[24]

Hospital fare and rations were equally bad. Furthermore, the food for hospital workers was no different from that of the soldiers, which often included mule meat. Few patients or staff found hospital food palatable, much less nourishing. In some instances, better food was reserved for surgeons while patients and nurses were forced to dine on what was termed "prison fare." Those men who had male relations or friends languishing in a fetid army field hospital often thought twice about volunteering and the possibility of ending up in a cot next to them.[25]

Soldiers in the field who were ill with some ailment sometimes sought to exacerbate their symptoms in order to obtain a medical discharge and skip hospitals altogether. Henry Clay Long had enlisted into the 11th Maine Infantry as a musician in late October 1861, yet his growing desire to get out was so pronounced by the end of April 1862 that he wrote to his wife explaining how he might fake an illness to obtain a medical discharge. Clay never attempted his plan because as he explained, "I am afraid that they would find me out and then I would be laughed at," an acknowledgment on Clay's part of the era's social stigma applied to perceived acts of cowardice. Clay convinced himself to stay because of his belief that the war would soon be over and that he would then head home in an honorable manner. "If I thought that I had got to stay here three years or even one longer, I would resort to some means of getting out of the circus," he admitted.[26]

As much as many soldiers abhorred the thought of languishing in an army field hospital, some realized that lying in a warm cot in a large Northern city hospital was preferable to being sent back to the front lines. William Fullerton, for one, admitted as much to his sister. "I know one thing," he wrote from his hospital bed, "every one that comes to a Hospital don't want to leave it, and they have good reason for wishing to stay." After the War Department authorized the chief medical officer in each city on April 7, 1862, to employ wounded or ill Union soldiers as nurses, cooks, or hospital attendants instead of a discharge, many convalescing men who could perform such tasks found that relatively easy duty to be a more desirable option than hard marching or fighting, especially if they had already experienced battle. The army quickly realized, however, that there was a negative trade-off: "The invalids thus occupied were useful indeed, but they ceased to be soldiers in fact and in spirit," wrote the Veteran Reserve Corps' adjutant general, "and in too many instances they continued to be mere hangers-on of hospitals long after they were able to resume the musket."[27]

These men became known as "malingerers" or "hospital rats"—derisive terms given to soldiers who prolonged their medical leave by faking various symptoms, illnesses, or injuries—with some soldier-actors making an art form of the process. John Beatty of the 3rd Ohio Infantry wrote in February 1863 that once a man "got away" into hospital duty it was almost impossible to get him back into the field. Another officer estimated at least one-third of soldiers in Union hospitals were in all actuality fit for frontline service. "It has come to be a thing expected, that those who are wounded, or sent to the hospital sick, even slightly and temporarily so, are lost to the regiment for the rest of the war in nine cases out of ten," reported Capt. Samuel Fiske of the 14th Connecticut Infantry. Fiske further noted that these men were often furloughed from the hospital only to return home, where they were routinely found working their farms all the while obtaining continuous certificates of illness from their easily persuaded family physicians.[28]

Other men did not even bother with feigning sickness in camp or elsewhere as part of their desire to avoid the front lines. They sought a full medical discharge and upped their game to whatever level that required. In a letter to his brother in March 1862, a Michigan man wrote of a mutual acquaintance who successfully obtained his discharge by pretending he was significantly lame "and now he can kick up his heels and laugh about it." The chief surgeon and medical director for the Army of the Potomac, Charles S. Tripler, complained in late May 1862 to that army's chief of staff how hundreds of men were found simply hiding in the woods after their commands had broken camp and set out on a new route of march. With medical recordkeeping still in a somewhat haphazard state, other perfectly fit men openly congregated at Virginia docks and then pushed their way onto crowded troop transports destined for Northern hospitals. Upon their arrival, they generally vanished for good.[29]

The realities of army life, death, and disease did not only impact those who sought adventure or even men who enlisted ostensibly for patriotic reasons. Many one-time mercenaries also became convinced that their lives were more valuable than a full purse. German-born Valentin Bechler, for one, had freely admitted in his past letters that he enlisted only for pay. By that summer, however, he was worn out. "I don't advise anybody to enlist," he admitted, because "By God, I don't know for what I should fight. For the rich man so he can make more money the poor man should risk his life and I should get slaughtered to pay the debts. Those are our prospects." A multitude of such letters were sent by the boys in blue to all corners of the North in the late spring and summer of 1862.[30]

All of the ominous-sounding letters from soldiers at the front warning friends and family back home not to enlist had a predictable effect on home front morale and enlistments. Michigan's adjutant general concurred, writing in his 1862 report that when a sick or wounded soldier returned home and told of the many privations, "recruiting ceases in his neighborhood." Moreover, the unwelcomed sight of pine coffins piled up at town train stations, newspaper reports of deadly field hospitals, and the battlefield setbacks in July and August 1862 only added to the North's depressed state. New enlistments had practically ground to a halt. Adding to the misery was how the triumphant Confederate Army of Northern Virginia appeared ready to attack the North. By early September, Washingtonians shuddered at the idea that the capital might be attacked any day following Gen. John Pope and his Union army's shellacking by the Confederates at the August 28–30 battle of Second Bull Run, only twenty miles west of their capital city. One New Yorker employed in that state's military department later recalled, "There probably never was a darker period in the whole war than after this last of General Pope's failures."[31]

Stanton's gaffe in closing recruiting offices, the North's military defeats, and the attendant decline in morale in the summer of 1862 had all worked together to create a serious manpower shortage. Moreover, the ongoing recession in 1861 had already siphoned off much of the unemployed who enlisted because they were looking for a steady pay-check. Volunteering had now all but dried up, which illustrated that the 700,000 White men who had eagerly enlisted in 1861 were the extent of the North's unshakable, no-inducement-needed "patriotic" outpouring. The federal government's seemingly insatiable appetite for bodies meant that it needed to find new ways to get more men into the ranks. Considering that the Union's nineteen slave-free states possessed a White male population of roughly 3,750,000 between the military ages of eighteen and forty-five, approximately 18.6 percent or just under one eligible man in five was willing to volunteer and shoulder a weapon during the past fifteen months or so. By the summer of 1862 and with the economy much improved, additional incentives were needed to lure men into the army since patriotic appeals had clearly run their course.[32]

At the same time, anti-administration newspapers had long abandoned the "no party now" bipartisanship from a year earlier and were now loudly calling the war and the administration's conduct of it into question. Democrats argued that there was a distinct difference between "the government" and "the administration." A true patriot never wavered in his loyalty to the constitutional principles of the former, but certainly could—and should—legitimately oppose the latter if he believed it was acting in purely partisan rather than national interests. Such loyal opposition could and should include a man choosing *not* to enlist in a war that many suspected had started to seriously veer off its initial righteous path.[33]

THE 1862 MILITIA ACT

Lincoln knew the armies needed more men, and in a display of keen political savvy, he first drummed up support from the North's governors to send more men. Having secured that behind-the-scenes objective, he then presented his call to the public as if the administration was accepting the states' offer to send more troops. On July 2, 1862, Lincoln issued a call for another 300,000 men to serve for three years or until the rebellion ended, whichever came first.[34]

The North's response to Lincoln's plea was lukewarm at best, underscoring how much of the Northern populace was tired of war and now viewed the conflict as somebody else's fight. A service-eligible man may have supported the war in theory, but that certainly did not mean he had any intention of officially volunteering into the army. As discussed in chapter 1, volunteering in a local home guard unit was still a preferable choice. To antiwar Democrats, these home guard men were the embodiment of the boisterous coward calling for ever more enlistments but never stepping forward themselves. When the North's most well-known antiwar politician, Ohio Democrat Clement Vallandigham, rhetorically asked in a July 1862 speech why 40,000 ardent, pro-war Ohio Republicans should not immediately volunteer, he replied, "They will never enlist; they never do. They are 'Home Guards.'"[35]

From Chicago, Charles Rowland wrote to Illinois governor William Yates declaring, "The recruiting business here seems positively dead." Rowland was convinced that the six recruiting officers currently at work in that city would not average one recruit per week. In Kansas, Sam Reader told his diary that there is "But little excitement and but little volunteering." A young woman wrote to her soldier brother in July 1862 claiming that the younger adults in their hometown of Thetford, Michigan, "get along just about as usual" with little concern over the war. A New England paper sought to alleviate that situation by proposing that store clerks—then a traditionally male occupation—enlist in the army and have their employment taken over by young women. The *Cleveland Plain Dealer* endorsed that suggestion because young ladies purportedly possessed the perfect fingers for handling "tape, calico, and the pen." Furthermore, the *Plain Dealer* opined how "many a pale and half consumptive young men" would then have the opportunity to gain a healthier lifestyle and the related benefits. Some Indiana women proposed to do just that, even going so far as to offer those clerks half of the salaries they earned and then even relinquishing their positions upon the men's return if only they would step up and enlist now. Throughout the North, pro-war newspapers began to sing "We are coming, Father Abraham, 300,000 more," yet the newly published song appeared to be a solo and not the nationwide chorus as the Lincoln administration had hoped.[36]

The lack of new volunteers was a country-wide problem. Indiana's *New Albany Daily Ledger* lamented in mid-July how the town's recent war meetings were a complete failure. "One looked in vain for those windy

Distributing Relief to, and Paying the Wives and Relatives of, the New York Volunteers (*Frank Leslie's Illustrated Newspaper*, September 7, 1861)

patriots who are so profuse in their abuse of secession and everybody who does not square to their standard," the paper editorialized. The *Ledger* heaped its scorn upon those upper-class men and their idling sons who "deem it almost a capital crime if poor men . . . do not enlist and leave their families to the patriotic charities of the valorous stay-at-homes." In Charleston, Illinois, one of Lincoln's friends reported on July 27 how close to five hundred able-bodied men attended a war rally the previous evening and that only three volunteered. Moreover, the town had about one hundred married men between the ages of eighteen and thirty. Yet, "not one of them will volunteer," the man concluded with ample frustration. It was much of the same in the more urban East. "There is no mincing the matter," wrote the *New York Herald*, "that the city is not doing its whole duty in furnishing volunteers, but the rural districts are fully alive with the necessity of hurrying reinforcements into the field."[37]

Wives whose husbands had already enlisted took to lambasting the speakers at those war meetings for their town's growing failure to live up to the familial support promises they had pledged a year earlier to the initial volunteers. They saw how the local efforts to provide meaningful assistance to soldiers' families had started well enough with the war's first ninety-day troops, but then slowly fizzled out when communities realized they could be doling out money for up to three years. Poor soldiers and their families were incensed that they were near destitution while many stay-at-home businessmen were profiting quite handsomely from the war.

Michigan's *Grand Haven News* acknowledged potential enlistees' concerns and that they were quite extensive. "Grievances of the kind . . . seem to prevail quite extensively, and many who are heads of families, knowing these complaints, and believing they are well founded, refuse to enlist unless a proper care of their families is pledged." In the case of Dubuque, Iowa's Volunteer Fund Board, its May 1861 pledges reached $6,000, but by January 1862, its funds were exhausted and the group disbanded. From then on, and for the most part in most Northern towns, community efforts seemed more focused on the more popular act of providing relief to soldiers in the field than to their families at home. At the same time, workingmen still at home saw how the families of neighbor friends off to war were struggling. *Frank Leslie's Illustrated Newspaper* drove that point home earlier by reminding its readers with a heart-rending illustration of how "Women who have never known what it is to receive a favor are compelled by starving children to turn suppliants." Those family men not suffering from want certainly did not wish poverty for their own loved ones and so many chose to remain at home.[38]

The decline of consistent assistance to soldiers' families had a predictable effect on potential recruits by the summer of 1862, as evidenced by the possible need for a draft in the first place. Dubuque farmer Ernst Renner captured the concerns. He and others had hesitated to enlist in August 1862 "because, from previous experience, we feared that our families would be neglected during our absence." He may have recalled the lofty community promises put forth in May 1861 that had vanished in the wind when the Volunteer Fund Board dissolved in January 1862.[39]

Those closest to the president were well aware of the administration's manpower predicament and the necessary solution. Secretary of State William Seward confided to his friend and Republican Party confidant Thurlow Weed back on July 8 how he had feared all along that mandatory conscription might be necessary. Moreover, Seward reasoned that it was crucial for the states to also see the need since they would be the entities carrying out the federal government's orders. Indiana governor Oliver Morton along with four other high-ranking Hoosiers fully agreed, writing confidentially to Lincoln on July 9 that conscription was vital given their knowledge of matters in the Northwest. Democratic Party boss August Belmont likewise admitted to Weed how the "apathy and distrust" that he met at every step and from men of unquestioned loyalty to the Union frightened him more than the recent battlefield reverses. Like Seward, Belmont believed that conscription was the only answer.[40]

To make sure the hesitant public realized the gravity of the situation, Congress passed the "Militia Act of 1862," which Lincoln signed into law on July 17. It represented the first substantial step toward a national conscription policy and seemingly enjoyed broad bipartisan support in the North's newspapers. The act declared that all able-bodied, single White male citizens between the ages of eighteen and forty-five were now legally part of the militia. The act empowered the president to call the militia into mandatory federal service for up to nine months. Married men between the ages of twenty and thirty-five fell under the same law. In addition, immigrant men who had previously voted or intended to become citizens were also deemed eligible; a declaration that prompted many émigrés to formally assert that they *did not* intend to become citizens as their means of avoiding the new federal law. The British consul officer in New York reported that his office was "literally mobbed" by applicants seeking shelter from the British Crown. Furthermore, he noted how the Irish, "who at other times are only too ready to spurn British nationality, are now among the most eager & obsequious applicants for my protection." Moreover, the initial congressional legislation allowed Black men to enlist and serve legally in the army, even as armed soldiers, however, Lincoln refused to go that far and opted only to allow Blacks to serve in manual labor support positions such as building fortifications,

"Resumption of the Draft—Inside the Provost Marshal's Office, Sixth District—the Wheel Goes Round" (Library of Congress Prints and Photographs Division)

serving as teamsters, or what legislators termed "competent" service. At this stage of the war, most Republicans and almost all Democrats were still against the notion of arming Blacks. Surprisingly, the administration then reversed itself on August 25, when Secretary of War Stanton authorized Brig. Gen. Rufus Saxton to arm, uniform, and equip Black runaway slaves for service in his South Carolina territory, perhaps as a trial run to see whether or not Black men under arms could be properly trained and disciplined as soldiers. It was the first time since 1792 that Black men were allowed to serve; an indicator of just how tepid White enlistment had become.[41]

Considering the overall disappointing returns from the July 2 call, Lincoln issued an order via Secretary of War Edwin Stanton on August 4 mandating an additional 300,000 militia volunteers to serve nine months "unless sooner discharged" under the guise of the recently passed Militia Act. As part of the act's provisions, each state was given a quota of volunteers. The state, in turn, apportioned that number to each town or county. A man who then enlisted in that locale was acknowledged as a "credit" to the town or county. Any locality, however, which had not met its required quota of volunteers by August 15 was to make up for the deficiencies through a special draft, a first for the Northern war effort. If a draft was required, Union authorities and the townsfolk would gather on the previously specified day and location. The names of all draft-eligible men were written on slips of paper and placed in a large draft wheel. A blindfolded man would then pull out the allotted number of names, which would be read aloud to the crowd. If called, a drafted man then had generally ten days to settle his affairs, report to the local provost marshal, and undergo his physical. The government also allowed a drafted man to avoid service by offering a competent substitute to go in his place. Furthermore, the government offered exemptions based on a man's occupation. Some examples of those who gained a coveted draft exclusion were telegraph operators who were fully engaged on August 5, 1862, locomotive engineers, armory workers, postal workers, ferrymen who were employed at any river ferry located along a postal route, and, of course, all members of both houses of Congress. In one novel example, firefighting companies found themselves flooded with new applicants, not out of any enhanced spirit of civic-mindedness, but because firefighters were supposedly exempt from the draft.[42]

Thus by "drafting" the militia rather than "calling forth" the militia as was the custom, the Lincoln administration laid the groundwork for the first compulsory military service law in the nation's history. Life and the previously held concepts of voluntary military service as Americans understood it had just ended. Never again could an American town or its citizens disregard a far-off war if they so desired. Quotas and credits were now the order of the new day.

CHAPTER 5

"Every Man That Is between 18 and 45 Years of Age Is Sick or Going to Be . . . Anything for an Excuse"

The North Reacts to a Changing War

THE IDEA THAT A MAN COULD BE UNWILLINGLY TAKEN FROM HIS FAM-
ily and forced to face death in a war many wanted no part of hit
the North like a thunderbolt. After learning of Lincoln's call for
300,000 nine-month men and the resultant draft that would occur if not
enough volunteers stepped forward, scores of reluctant men who had no
desire to don a blue uniform began to seek out some manner of official
exemption. Especially desirable was a permanent medical exemption,
which a man could obtain if he could "prove" that he possessed an illness or disability that prohibited him from properly performing military
duties. Throughout the North, men who seemed perfectly healthy to their
neighbors before the draft were now feigning deafness or blindness, or
had contracted internal afflictions such as rheumatism or hernias.

At the same time, localities frantically sought to avoid the ignominy
of having to hold a draft, for in an era where there was no social disgrace
worse than being labeled a coward, a town or district's inability to raise
enough volunteers clearly implied that its patriotism and collective backbone were lacking. Yet fifty-seven-year-old Hamilton Colton of Milan,
Ohio, immediately saw the equity in the draft. From his perspective, that

act would "relieve the best & bravest young men from taking the field for the benefit of sneaks & cowards." Yet in an overarching sense, Colton also believed that those men who could easily go would often be the last to enlist and therefore could only be reached via conscription. The draft quickly became the preeminent topic in any town across the North. By August 24, Elizabeth Pierce wrote to her sister how in Dayton, Ohio, "There is no talk but of recruiting, drafting, Provost Marshall, 'the regiment,' 'the battery,' subscriptions to aid recruiting . . . &c." The reason was the same everywhere for as she explained, "There is really a very earnest feeling, and a good deal of pride that so light a draft will be necessary." The same stigma applied to any male who was eventually drafted when he had been given ample opportunity to volunteer. "To a proud-spirited man, the idea of being a conscript in a nation of volunteers," wrote one man, "is repugnant to every feeling of self-respect."[1]

Nevertheless, the idea of mandatory military service via the draft and the military regimentation that went with it cut against the grain of what Americans believed their duty to be, especially with the citizen-soldier's long-standing, voluntary nature. Mid-nineteenth-century men were raised in a constitutional republic that placed a premium on personal independence and autonomy. Antebellum Americans offered only the most half-hearted nod toward George Washington's 1783 pronouncement that declared, "Every citizen who enjoys the protection of a free Government, owes . . . his personal services to the defense of it." A truly free government was one that left its citizens alone—in peace—if that was what the individual sought. As for wartime production and needs, many Americans believed in Adam Smith's concept of laissez-faire government: Let any man do as he wished within his capability and the law's limits, and the nation's collective interest would be best served. Any subservience a man felt was usually toward a father or older brother in managing the family farm or business, rather than any distant, faceless national government. He knew that he, too, might one day be in a similar position of patriarchal authority with the attendant responsibility toward family and community that went with it. Writing from the seat of war, Union colonel Charles Wainright admitted to these underlying precepts by remarking in his diary with frustration how, "Every man thinks that he is conferring a favor on the government by being here at all." For a nation that prided itself on its culture of individual freedom, mandatory conscription foretold despotic rule.[2]

Bounties

With volunteering having all but ground to a halt, states and localities revived the practice of offering cash bonus payments known as bounties. These incentives were necessary as a means of stirring up enlistments since, for the most part, patriotic appeals were no longer sufficient. Indiana's adjutant general deftly referred to these cash bribes as a "duty offering" from those who remained at home; a community's payment to men and their families who sacrificed in deference to their country's call. In essence, they served as a form of nonpartisan social welfare. As opposed to the $25 or $50 enlistment payments that sufficed in 1861, prospective recruits could now expect to receive bounty money that ran into the hundreds of dollars. Often they were able to collect a town, county, and state bounty on top of each other, which meant in some instances men could receive upwards of $1,000; a sum that in some places would have been almost sufficient to buy a small family farm. For example, buying an eighty-acre Illinois farm in 1860 required roughly $1,700 in initial expenses. Numerous men laboring as tenants on someone else's farm often viewed these bounties as the down payment to their own land and prosperity. Meanwhile, localities were so desperate to reach their volunteer quotas and thereby avoid a draft that the bounty frenzy created bidding wars in many instances. The obvious downside was that the generous bounty money had to come from somewhere, which normally meant increased property taxes levied against the town's citizens.[3]

The entire process was designed as a classic "carrot and stick" ploy. The carrot was the handsome cash bounties offered by the various governments and occasionally from wealthy private individuals. If not enough men volunteered from any given town or county, then the stick was the federal government's threat to conscript men into military service quite literally at the point of the bayonet with no bounty money paid out. After the War Department declared that no federal bounty money would be paid out after August 15 to any volunteers seeking to join a new regiment, scores of men stepped forward to grab their piece of the pie. In the case of Sandwich, Connecticut, eighty-five men enlisted in total, thereby eliminating the need for a draft in their community, however, it is noteworthy that about seventy of those men enlisted during the August 13–15 time frame, in order to beat the August 15 deadline. Ruth Whittemore of Owego, New York, had also observed this carrot and stick strategy in action when she wrote on August 10 to her brother who was serving in the 50th New York Engineers: "There is a great many enlisting around here now. They are afraid they will get drafted and lose their bounty." In Easthampton, Connecticut, Osmer Hills likewise informed his brother, "Everybody is afraid of being drafted." Therefore, the threat of having to conduct a draft was interpreted by the North as a warning, a public rebuke, and a humiliating symbol of a community's lack of proper patriotism.[4]

Vermont was one state that came up with creative bounties in the face of recruiting challenges. With harvest season drawing to a close in early fall, the state offered to pay new enlistees an additional $7 per month on top of their regular privates' pay. Towns also offered an additional $50 bounty to each soldier who enlisted. This stood in stark contrast to a man who would receive nothing if drafted. Moreover, a conscript would be forced to serve three years rather than nine months. These financial sweeteners and the allure of a short nine-month jaunt attracted scores of purported patriots who may have otherwise stayed home. A Massachusetts man enlisted into that state's 49th Infantry on August 4, admitting that doing so on such terms was "wiser than to join a three years' regiment." Another such man was thirty-nine-year-old Eben Calderwood, who took advantage of the ample bounties to enlist for nine months into the 21st Maine Infantry in early November rather than face the prospect of being conscripted. His financial euphoria was short-lived, however. Within months he was writing to his wife from sweltering Louisiana as to how "If I get out of this I shall never come again for 13 dollars per month." On the other hand, he reasoned, "If I could get second lieutenant pay 105 dollars a month I would talk about coming back."[5]

Bounties quickly became an expectation for potential volunteers as well as a primary enlistment motivator. As one perhaps not-so-surprising consequence, the army's examining surgeons as well as its junior officers learned early on that there were those men who may have been truly afflicted with some disqualifying infirmity, yet were so intoxicated by the prospect of easy bounty money that they tried to hide their ailments in order to enlist and collect the ready cash. Dr. Winston Somers of Illinois' seventh district witnessed such shenanigans firsthand. "They are anxious to enlist for the bounty offered," wrote Somers, and therefore, "they are consequently very supple and active, and have no consumption or disease of internal organs unless the surgeon can discover the same." A recently enlisted Michigan man saw both sides of the coin that the surgeon would later report on. The young man was undergoing his initial training in the town of Jackson when he wrote on October 24, 1862, of his astonishment as to how many men there were in the county who were claiming some type of medical exemption. Yet simultaneously, he was equally amazed at the number of genuinely frail or sickly men who were trying to enlist *solely* because of the bounty. Once in and with money in hand or sent home, they then made quick use of their condition to avoid duty or procure a medical discharge. Whether robust or physically unfit, by the late summer of 1862, money was the potential enlistee's bottom line.[6]

In letters to his sister in late July and early August 1862, twenty-one-year-old Charles Reed embodied this mindset when he described all of the various bounties he would collect up front, his monthly pay of twenty-one dollars, and other sundry benefits by enlisting as a chief bugler. He also mentioned his difficulties in finding acceptable civilian employment and the longer-term risk of volunteering for three years. He made no mention of serving for any higher sense of duty. Like Reed, Joseph Bishop of Danbury, Connecticut, also enlisted as a "chief musician" in August 1862 for a nine-month stint with the 23rd Connecticut Infantry. His letters to his wife revealed his ambivalence about the war's purposes, that he was not much of a fighter and admittedly could not stand the hardships of battle. What Bishop stressed was that between his bounty, monthly pay, and home front support for his family, "my going away will leave you more comfortable than if I stayed." At thirty-seven-years-old and a married father of three young children, shoemaker John Brendel enlisted on August 13. His first letter to his wife just more than

"Scene, Fifth Avenue." "He. 'Ah! Dearest Addie! I've succeeded. I've got a Substitute!' She. 'Have you? What a coincidence! And I have found one for YOU!'"
(Library of Congress Prints and Photographs Division)

two weeks later spoke solely of his bounties and how she could access the
money. Financial considerations also swayed a young Ohio woman when
she wrote to her brother in November 1862 counseling him not to come
home too fast if his company was disbanded as was being talked about
because it might jeopardize his bounty. On the other hand, if his unit was
disbanded, she advised that he should come home first before reenlisting
in another company. With another draft being rumored, she wondered if

he might go in their father's place if the latter was drafted. Or, he might reenlist by first offering himself as a substitute.[7]

The law allowed for a draft-exempt White man to offer himself up as a substitute to a drafted man for an agreed-upon fee that, in most cases, could be quite hefty. In essence, one man purchased personal relief—along with possible social emasculation—in exchange for the use of another man's body; an agreement not unlike prostitution. The two sibling's epistolary conversation had become one of bounties and money rather than the war's dangers and merits. Another apocryphal story told of three Ohio soldiers attending a Sunday morning church service. The minister paused to pay tribute to the men for their patriotic enlistment but then added that they should also become soldiers in the Lord's army. At which point one of the men loudly replied, "What's the bounty?"[8]

Wealthier individuals, such as affluent local politicians or thriving factory or business owners, also contributed to the mania through personal cash bounty offerings designed to help their town reach its enlistment quota. These were offered in addition to any municipal or state bounty. At a war rally in Cedar Falls, Iowa, on the night of July 30, 1862, businessman Thomas Walkup offered a five-dollar cash bounty to any man who enlisted then and there. In Montpelier, Vermont, James Langdon offered ten dollars each to the first twenty-five men who stepped forward, and in Ottawa, Illinois, a Democratic man of Irish descent serving on the LaSalle County Board of Supervisors made a similar generous proposition. He offered a twenty-dollar bounty to each of the first one hundred Republican abolitionists who would volunteer to serve in a company under his command. While these men certainly welcomed the public accolades their patriotic benevolence implied, the often unspoken goal was to generate enough local volunteers to keep themselves and their sons well away from the provost marshal's draft "wheel of fortune." For example, a textile mill treasurer in Laconia, New Hampshire, offered a twenty-five-dollar bounty to any mill employee who would enlist in one of the state's new nine-month regiments. As an added sweetener, he pledged to hold the man's job until he returned. Future Connecticut governor Joseph Gilmore, then a Concord railroad executive, also offered twenty-five dollars to the first nine men who would volunteer, thereby filling up a locally recruited company. Yet neither the treasurer, Gilmore, nor any of their sons ever volunteered, in 1862 or later.[9]

Northern White men had become so reluctant to volunteer in the aggregate that Secretary of State William Seward began to glance at foreign immigration as a potential source of reliable cannon fodder. On August 8, Seward sent a dispatch to all US diplomatic and consular officers in foreign countries reminding them that the nation's agricultural, manufacturing, and mining interests had never been more prosperous; this in spite of the war and high civilian labor demands driven by the growing need for ever more men to serve in the Union armies. The secretary asserted how "nowhere else can the industrious laboring man and artisan expect so liberal a recompense for his services as in the United States." Therefore, Seward directed his diplomatic corps to "make these truths known in any quarter and in any way which may lead to the migration of such persons to this country." With a steady paycheck and the possibility of lucrative bounty money, Seward hoped that an ample number of poverty-stricken European mercenaries would gladly sail to America to put on a brand-new blue uniform and escape poverty.[10]

The US Consul in Hamburg, Germany, James Anderson, replied to his Washington superiors that he received hundreds of letters every month from Germans in all parts of the country seeking information on enlisting into the Union army. Not surprisingly, most of it was economic in nature, such as inquiries into the price of labor in different governmental departments, the wages for officers or privates, and soldier bounties. The inquiries were so constant and consistent that Anderson disclosed he had prepared a form letter written in German that would invariably answer the writer's concerns.[11]

For some men and their families, however, no amount of bounty money was sufficient. This was not their war and they had no intention of putting themselves or their male loved ones in harm's way. "Don't you enlist unless you are quite sure you will be drafted," urged Sarah Keen to her brother in September 1862. That same month, Detroit lawyer and Democrat Henry Billings Brown weighed his flagging legal business against the various enlistment bounties. His personal calculus prompted him to remark in his diary that "Civil life is getting stale." Seeking a possible solution, Brown then asked his diary, "Shall I go into the army?" By the end of the year, however, Brown's business fortunes had changed. "Twice I thought very strongly of participating in the terrible civil war which has raged the entire year," he recalled, "but circumstances which I now regarded as fortunate prevented my entering the service." For men like Brown, the notion of enlisting as a citizen's duty to the country never seemed to materialize. The decision was simply a personal cost-benefit analysis.[12]

Furthermore, there was still some confusion as to the new recruit's term of service. When some men realized that they had signed up for three years or the war's duration, rather than three months, they changed their minds and went home. From their vantage, it was better to take their chances with the draft rather than commit themselves and their families to what seemed like an endlessly long time.[13]

Entire communities were often opposed to the war in general and the new militia draft in particular. Their rural day-to-day concerns focused on the welfare of their families and villages, not some distant federal government, a theoretical Union, or the so-called Confederacy and its slaves. They had no intention of abandoning their families, homes, or farms to fight in a far-off war they believed they had no stake in. Christian Isely wrote to his wife in August 1862 illustrating this reality. Then serving in the 2nd Kansas Cavalry, Isely described the bitter letter he had recently received from his sister in Ohio after their two other brothers were forcibly conscripted. "They are nearly all Democrats where they live and opposed to the war," wrote Isely, further remarking how the family placed all the blame on Republican abolitionists. Isely then added, "In the Township where they live—a piece of Land 6 miles square—47 had to be drafted. That shows how poorly they turned out in volunteering." In other instances, the draft hurt a town's businesses and the overall economy, as no man wanted to commit to anything until he knew whether or not he was clear of the draft.[14]

Seven weeks after Lincoln issued his 1862 call for 300,000 more men, Massachusetts' *Woburn Weekly Budget* mocked those "laggards" who had yet to enlist by describing their new stay-at-home uniform as featuring "a fringe apron strings around the shirt and a baby's rattle suspended around the neck. They will be armed with wooden swords and quill pop

Costume suggested for the Brave STAY-AT-HOME "LIGHT GUARD."

"Costume Suggested for the Brave Stay-at-Home 'Light Guard'" (*Harper's Weekly*, September 7, 1861)
COURTESY OF HARPWEEK

guns." One month later in late August after the town of Cambridge, Vermont, had successfully met its volunteer enlistment quota, the *Lamoille Newsdealer* sarcastically reported how the town had also managed to create "a Brigade of Home Guards from the *cowards* and *exempts*, who lately *rallied* to the doctor's for certificates, which are now below par." The "brigade" was to be led by Brigadier "General Debility," "Colonel Costiveness," "Major Piles," and other humorously named officers. Home guard units began to be derisively referred to as "fireside rangers," "stay-at-home guards," or "pasteboard patriots."[15]

The new draft law and the government's assertion of its new authority triggered violent disturbances and the ongoing threat of such action all across the North. Anti-draft strife and riots took place in Pennsylvania's Carbon, Luzerne, and Schuylkill counties and in Ohio. From Wisconsin, Gov. Edward Salomon told Edwin Stanton that there were serious disturbances within two counties. He explained that he had furnished six hundred armed men to protect the new draft's operations and make arrests; nevertheless, Salomon felt it was still too dangerous for his draft commissioners to serve draft notices personally and that the names of those selected should be published on public posters. Governors and politicians from Indiana and Iowa all begged the federal government for arms and men to quell the violence. Ex–Ohio congressman and renowned Copperhead Edson Olds was arrested on August 12 after he was alleged to have urged Democrats "to refuse to be mustered into service" even to the point of "the shedding of blood." Maryland's governor pleaded with the Department of the East commander, Gen. John Wool, to provide troops to help his enrollment officers safely carry out their duties in his contentious border state. From his Baltimore office, an exasperated Wool reported to Stanton that he had none to spare nor the time to reply directly to the governor given his myriad duties. "If a State cannot enforce its own laws without U.S. soldiers we may as well give up at once," Wool added. "I do not want men who are to be forced into the service."[16]

Other war-averse men decided it was better to just quietly leave town if a draft appeared imminent. The Washington press reported how numerous reluctant patriots had "packed up their duds and left—the cars taking off some two hundred fifty bound north in one day." In Baltimore, the *American and Commercial Advertiser* decried the process by which citizens were moving and exchanging their official residences to avoid a particular area's draft "with an eagerness marvelous to behold." The paper described how Baltimore's train station was thronged with Irishmen frantic to take the next train north to Philadelphia so as to avoid the former town's upcoming draft. In a similar manner, Connecticut's Richard Phelps told his diary of how five or six of his neighbors were preparing to flee into Canada. Phelps stressed they were all honorable hardworking men, but would rather leave than be forced into the war, adding how "a feeling of terror & dismay" pervaded over his community. Writing from Saratoga County in upstate New York, recently married Ellie Goldwaite informed her husband, who was serving in the 99th New York Infantry, that if there was a draft, numerous men from their town would be looking to escape into Canada. In fact, she mentioned one mutual friend who had already arrived from Albany to retrieve his cousin so both could leave for Canada as soon as possible. "I tell you," wrote Ellie, "the men will do anything rather than go to war."[17]

The desire to avoid the draft became so immense that the Lincoln administration ordered on August 8 that no draft-eligible man could leave the country. State borders were also closed off while travel within the nation was restricted. Despite these new laws, an ample number of men did successfully flee the country. In one novel instance, the *Cleveland Plain Dealer* reported how some men had even fled to Havana, Cuba, to escape the draft, yet now found themselves unwittingly surrounded by a far more lethal enemy: yellow fever. "The men who are so cowardly as to run away," the paper noted with smug satisfaction, "are just the ones who will be sure to die from yellow jack."[18]

Then there were those men who saw an opportunity for personal profit from all of the tumult. Newspapers speculated how—according to local recruiting officers—men were refusing to enlist because they were holding out for higher substitute pay, which they calculated would mean a better payoff than simply enlisting and receiving a bounty payment. In essence, these mercenaries were betting that if and when the draft took place, wealthier drafted men would dig deep into their pockets to avoid military service. For these men, war was a combination of roulette wheel and business solely to be profited from; any patriotic notions of fighting for one's home or country appeared to be secondary.[19]

As the first draft scheduled for October loomed over the North, some worried that only its Southern sympathizers and poltroons would remain at home. The peer pressure that communities exerted back in April and May 1861 to encourage men to enlist reared its ahead again. Letters to the editor began to appear in Northern newspapers admonishing men to volunteer and shaming those who did not. Newspapers took

"The Draft" "All other Methods of evading the Draft having failed, the above Disgraceful Scheme is to be attempted on the 10th." (Library of Congress Prints and Photographs Division)

to publishing lists of those men in their area who were draft eligible in an attempt to coax them into enlisting. The *Daily Democrat and News* in Davenport, Iowa, took matters a step further by publishing a "Coward List" and "Sneak List" of those men who refused to enlist by claiming an exemption on the grounds they were not citizens. The town of Windsor Locks, Connecticut, passed a resolution urging that a public record be maintained "of those who skedaddled, hoping to avoid the anticipated draft, so that their children and children's children may see who left the country in its greatest time of need." To be drafted was deemed a disgrace as the dominant cultural attitude dictated that any able-bodied man should want to enlist, unless he had an acceptable reason, such as being the lone son of aged parents who depended on him for their support or a widowed father with small children.[20]

Yet as summer rolled into fall and in the big picture, the carrot and stick process seemed to be working. Men who may not have enlisted if left to their own devices now began to volunteer by the tens of thousands so that they might take advantage of the lucrative bounty payments *and* avoid the public disgrace of having been forced to serve via the draft. That calculus would stay in play through the end of the war in April 1865.

Lawrence Van Alstyne was a twenty-three-year-old single man typical of those who did not enlist in 1861 but then eventually relented with Lincoln's call on July 2, 1862, for 300,000 more men. By that time, he knew he would also be pocketing a substantial bounty, which perhaps helped to sway his decision. Van Alstyne had deliberated about enlisting ever since the war began, yet he admitted his mind always came back to "this one could go, and that one, and they ought to, but with me, some way it was different" because "I was needed at home, etc., etc." When Alstyne finally "threw down my unfinished castles" and volunteered, everyone around him seemed to pat him on the back and offer all best wishes. A few were genuinely encouraging he observed, yet he sensed that "most of them spoke and acted as if I were on my way to the gallows." Northerners were willing to huzzah for the volunteers, but the numerical majority of those men able to serve still had no desire or intention of doing so.[21]

George Patch of the 19th Massachusetts Infantry told his parents in late July 1862 that half of the men he knew who were enlisting had done so because they were afraid of being drafted and then having to bear that stigma. Pennsylvanian Samuel Cormany also admitted as much, conceding to his diary how "The fear of being drafted, if I did not volunteer—had possibly some weight in inducing [my] decission." Of the 300,000 nine-month men called for by Lincoln, roughly 87,000 (or 29 percent) were conscripted into the army's ranks after all of the exemptions and substitutes were accounted for. In the post-war years, the North chose to remember the men who enlisted in the late summer and fall of 1862 as the second great wave of patriotic outpouring. The massive amount of bounty money that had to be paid by municipalities required to generate those enlistments was generally ignored. In his Civil War memoir, Bvt. Maj. William Lapham disparaged those who had gone to war only after being bought or hired. "People tried to make themselves believe that this was patriotism," Lapham wrote, "but it was really an act of cowardice and resorted to only to prevent conscription."[22]

For those boys who turned eighteen years old in 1862, their motives may indeed have been little different from those who enlisted in April

1861. Joseph Crowell was one such lad, and he later admitted that a fear of the draft was not an issue, nor could he ever really explain why he enlisted: "I think I am safe in saying that, at the moment, genuine patriotism hardly entered into the question." For older men, however, especially those with families, the fact that they stared at relatively huge sums of bounty money that was theirs for the taking if they enlisted, coupled with the existential threat of a government draft at their back if they did not, was often forgotten.[23]

The entire cash inducement–based process alarmed plenty of the Regular army's professional soldiers. Officer John Ames decried the mercenary aspects of "the miserable bounty business" and the blatant unfairness to those men who had first enlisted in 1861 when there were none to be had. As Ames saw it, the entire scheme appealed to money-grubbing impulses rather than patriotic. It was a short-term gain to the Union but at a significant long-term cost. If a man could comfortably wait at home for a year and then obtain both glory and bounty by waiting, then why would anyone step forward at the nation's first call, Ames wondered. Col. Silas Burt also saw the dangers. "What are the moral effects of this wholesale purchase of our citizens?" Burt rhetorically asked New York governor Edwin Morgan in late August with regards to the numerous private and local bounties being offered on top of state and federal. "Is there not a strong and increasing tendency to substitute mere mercenary considerations for that ardent and self-sacrificing patriotism?" Burt predicted the results of such bribery and likened the growing bidding wars to the Southern slave auction blocks. "Already the system is producing degrading and deplorable results," wrote Burt. "As the date fixed for the draft approaches, communities frantic from cowardice or contagious panic, are increasing their bounties, until in some localities is witnessed the debasing spectacle of an auction in humanity, a picture hitherto confined to our Southern states." Nothing really changed in this regard throughout the remainder of the war.[24]

The Bounty Man

Men who admitted they enlisted *primarily* because of the ample cash bounties quickly became known as "bounty men," and not surprisingly, they were looked down upon by those soldiers who had enlisted at the war's outset ostensibly for patriotic reasons. These lucrative bounties served to convince many that the war was now becoming a business. In his Civil War memoir, Frenchman Regis de Trobriand utilized the selective memory referred to in the introduction by referring to those initial 1861 enlistees simply as "unbought volunteers" whereas the men from the summer of 1862 he referred to as mercenaries. John Burrill of the 2nd New Hampshire Infantry confirmed in a September 15, 1862, letter, "It is true that those who come out here for $200 are reminded of it after they get here." Writing from Washington, DC, in mid-November 1862, George Spinney of the 1st Massachusetts Cavalry complained bitterly to his sister about the current crop of bounty men his regiment was receiving. He noted that practically all men who reported sick were new recruits and the ones most likely to seek a quick medical discharge with pay and bounty in hand. In Spinney's opinion, the whole bounty business "makes poor feelings between the men." As one consequence, the hardened veterans took great pleasure in ridiculing the softer bounty men who, initially anyway, were the ones who most often fell out of the ranks on marches, footsore and exhausted. A surgeon with the 13th Iowa Infantry explained to his wife with some jocularity how the men would often call out, "Halloa, Bounty . . . aint you glad you jined [sic] the army?" as they passed by those new recruits sitting and breathing heavily at the side of the road. One dog-tired greenhorn hoped for some sage advice from a veteran who asked him if he wanted to know how to keep his feet from getting sore, but anticipation turned to dejection when the trouper's sarcastic answer was for him to "wrap that $100 around your feet."[25]

In an overarching sense, the new bounty men were initially viewed by the veteran soldiers as little more than cowardly mercenaries who would probably run when the bullets started to fly. A recently enlisted New York surgeon described how he and the new recruits in his regiment were referred to as the "two hundred dollars sons of bitches" by the older veterans. Clarifying this resentment, New York's Winfield Perry wrote, "Mother you cannot imagine what a feeling there is between the old soldiers and the bounty men as these new Regts are called." Perry then told his mother of one hapless new enlistee who bragged of the $490 bounty in his pocket and how he had enlisted solely for the money. His bragga-docio earned him a thorough beating from a few soldiers while others simply watched and did nothing.[26]

Pvt. George Peck had no qualms over admitting in his post-war recollections how he waited to enlist until he felt the war was almost over and then did so only for the bounty. After having signed his enlist-ment papers and collecting his $300, Peck recalled his fiscal horror upon then learning that a nearby town was offering bounties as high as $1,200. Patriotic motives or stamping out treason played no role in his decision. Further driving his calculus was his expectation that the cavalry regiment he was to be assigned to would be sent home before he ever arrived. "In fact the recruiting officer told me as much," Peck explained, "and he said I would get my bounty, and a few months' pay, and it would be just like finding money." The reality is that Peck and men like him were little more than soldiers of fortune: Men who fought primarily for monetary gain with little to no interest in the war's politics.[27]

Since a potential recruit could enlist in any town he desired, it was perhaps not a bit ironic that the mercenary volunteer who shopped around for the best package of cash bounties was viewed by his local community as a good man wisely providing for himself and his family. Those healthy young men who did just that had waited more than a year to enlist and then only when they could line their pockets most hand-somely. Many felt compelled to do so because they also felt the figurative tip of a government bayonet poking their backside through the threat of conscription. The unspoken flip side of that coin was that the man who was drafted and received no bounty was viewed as little better than a fool and a coward. In his memoirs, Frederic Lockley admitted to all of these cultural values. The man who was forcibly drafted, Lockley explained, was robbed of any "patriotic sacrifice" and "all tinge of heroism." Nor did he receive any bounty money.[28]

Bounty Jumping

The bounties became so lucrative that thousands of men took part in a scam that became known as "bounty jumping"; a swindle that was born with the 1862 bounties and continued through the remainder of the war.

The bounty jumper would enlist in any given town—often under a fake name—and collect all of the available bounties. With cash in hand, he would desert at the first opportunity and then look to replace his new blue uniform with civilian clothes. At that point, he would make his way to another town where he might alter his appearance by cutting or coloring his hair, shaving a mustache, or donning eyewear. Then he would repeat the process. Literally jumping from a moving army train became a popular means of escape. While on duty at Boston Harbor's Long Island, where he was tasked with escorting new conscripts and bounty jumpers from that "cursed island" to the mainland, Ira Conine wrote to his wife explaining how seven such men had already drowned in the harbor while trying to swim their way to freedom. It was amazing to Conine how some men would risk life and limb to avoid risking life and limb in the military. "They certainly are the hardest men in the world," he added. Bounty jumping became a fine art and was so prevalent in some locales that new enlistees sometimes found themselves being escorted to the front under armed guard before the ink was even dry on their paperwork. Despite those efforts, many bounty jumpers escaped somewhere along the way and soon found themselves repeating their swindle in another town.[29]

Bounty jumping became a profitable business for those unsavory characters who had no interest in the war's goals or merits. Rhode Island's provost marshal, William Hamlin, reported how the Ocean State's generous bounties had attracted "a swarm of worthless men" like bees to honey. They came not only from the country's urban centers but from Europe, with the result that many had already deserted or were waiting for the first opportunity to do so. Provost Marshal General James Fry noted in his final report how one imprisoned man confessed to having "jumped the bounty" *thirty-two times*.[30]

Perhaps inevitably, more than a few Northerners became embittered when it seemed like the war had become more about making money than preserving the Union. The one-time "holy war" was transitioning into a business. The lucrative contracts created between the government and private enterprise to provide the foodstuffs and equipment the army needed were making many men rich. Individual working-class citizens were now selling their services to the army primarily due to the large cash bounties they and their families would receive. By mid-December 1862, New Hampshire's Margaret Harris was so fed up that she no longer cared who won the war as long as it ended soon. "It has got to be such a money making concern that I think it isn't much matter who beats," she rationalized to her brother, Leander. "I haven't got a spark of patriotism left things are carried on so," she admitted, and "It seems as though all our folks cared for was to see which could make the most out of the poor soldiers."[31]

***

If Northern civilians who remained at home expressed dismay at the prospect of a draft, those Union soldiers already in the ranks were generally delighted, for they held little tolerance for the great mass of healthy, *single*, enlistment-eligible men who had yet to volunteer. "I suppose the draft laws still occasion a great deal of excitement in the North," Pvt. John McKee wrote in August 1862 in a letter home to Ohio that characterized this viewpoint: "It meets with universal approbation with those now in the service as each one knows some coward at home that he would like to see drafted." They saw the draft as a tool that would apply fairness. Since all would share the fruits of victory, all should share the burdens of war. From the Union soldier's vantage, the principal injustice was that there were plenty of hale and hearty single men lounging at home who could easily serve yet refused to do so. It was those men who had already volunteered who were being wronged by the stay-at-homes' continued absence. Therefore, any man now drafted could not claim any inequity being done to him. After all, so the soldiers' belief went, it was his reluctance to fulfill his patriotic duty in the first place that now made the draft necessary. "I consider it a disgrace for any young man to suffer himself to be drafted especially one in my circumstances that has nothing to hinder him from going," asserted Charles Weller to his sweetheart after enlisting at age seventeen in mid-1862. Those Union soldiers in the ranks saw themselves as fighting to uphold the nation's values while others at home were not pitching in to help.[32]

When Byron Churchill learned from his mother that two soldier friends on a recruiting trip back home had met with little success, he replied with his wish that "all such cowards would be drafted and had to serve their life time in the army." Like almost every other Union private, Churchill was confident that if all able men stepped forward, the rebellion would be quickly crushed. From Churchill's perspective, those who refused were "to[o] big Cowards to come and face the Canons and the Enimies as we'd do." Pennsylvanian John Black also typified soldiers' resentments toward the "stay-at-homes" when he wrote to his sweetheart in the summer of 1862. "There are any amount of young men in Blair Co. that I would love to hear of being made to go and handle the musket. . . . I cannot see why under the Sun any young man can stay home, when his country is all the time calling with might and main for his help. Shame! Shame!! Shame!!!" Another young soldier in the 17th Illinois Infantry echoed Black, asserting, "Nothing would do us more good than to see these laggards drafted, and no such thing known as buying a substitute." "If men will not pay attention to the call of the Government they must be forced to do so," wrote Austin Smith of the 4th Michigan Infantry to his mother. "There is a number of young men in the town of Iosco that I am ashamed of," Smith continued, then calculating that only five or six had so far enlisted and that another fifty existed who could easily do so.[33]

MAIMING ONESELF

Once the provisions of the new 1862 militia draft law were rolled out, some perfectly healthy civilian men who were subject to the new act attempted to maim themselves in a way that would cause them to be rejected by army doctors but would not prevent any normal activity in their day-to-day civilian lives. These acts of self-mutilation were decried in the pro-Union press from one end of the nation to another once they became fairly well-known. Iowa's *Dubuque Herald* complained how some men who were "supposed to be in the prime of manhood" had fallen grievously ill just since the draft was announced. "Old crutches have been scoured up, and are now about ready for action," the *Herald* lamented. "Some men are lame, blind . . . have consumption, heaves and much general-debility." A Maine man sought out a dentist to have four healthy front teeth extracted so that he would appear unable to tear open a paper cartridge and load a weapon. It was quickly—and no doubt humorously pointed out to him by military surgeons—how the army was quite capable of finding other, more suitable work for him to perform. Then as cavalry regiments began to be equipped with breech-loading rifles as the war progressed, such dental matters became even less important, with the increased likelihood of a man with many missing teeth being assigned to that branch of the service. After learning of such self-mutilation, George Hupman of the 89th New York Infantry wrote to his parents stating that such men "are to be pitied if they are such fools as to pull out their Teeth . . . Chop of[f] their Fingers and cripple themselves for life" just so they could avoid the war. God forbid, wrote Hupman, if he should have any relations who bore such a cowardly mark.

Another reluctant warrior made a subtle threat claiming he should not be drafted at all since he was laboring with an eye impediment that "might make me shoot the captain as easy as not!" After the first potential draft was announced in early August, W. H. Faxon of Ovid, Michigan, told a friend how, "I am glad you enlisted when you did" because "every man that is between 18 & 45 years of age is sick or going to be, or lost a finger, or a thumb, or a great toe. Anything for an excuse." Faxon continued, "One man has been down to get the Town Board together to appoint him Constable so he could stay at home. Another man has offered $200.00 for a substitute if he is drafted. Another man came 6 miles to tell us that he expected to have the palsy before another winter. It is really laughable."[34]

Having an illness or injury, feigned or otherwise, that would prevent a man from serving in the military had to be approved by a military doctor. Other means included first obtaining a certificate of exemption from a local doctor, which quickly blossomed into a cottage industry for less-than-scrupulous physicians. "Certificate business has become the business of the day," complained Vermont's *Lamoille Newsdealer*. "Every man who wants one and has got his half dollar, can obtain one by giving his money to a couple of quacks, who stand with their mouths open ready to swallow." In upstate New York, one man wrote to his brother explaining how their local and well-paid, government-approved physician spent the required six hours a day examining men who applied for an exemption. After that, he was on his own time, for which he charged one dollar per head, sometimes pocketing up to an additional fifty dollars per day, which for the era was an immense daily sum. In some instances, desperate men paid as much as five dollars for an examination.[35]

It was the same sight everywhere. Countless men frantic to avoid the war were seeking any excuse that might gain them the desired release from the draft. Many of them obtained a government circular that listed fifty-one diseases that would secure the desired exemption for any man so afflicted. With list in hand, men desperate to avoid military service appeared before the enrolling surgeon with their circulars highlighted next to the diseases they thought appropriate. One Wisconsin man had thirty-one fatal diseases marked as "what ailed him," while another had nineteen diseases marked within his circular.[36]

After witnessing the long line of men seeking medical exemption outside of the local enrollment office, the editor of Ohio's *Stark County Democrat* cynically surmised that the country was actually a nation of cripples. Knowing the real reason for their attendance, the paper decided how "the large attendance shows the fear of being drafted, rather than an evidence of real disability." In Philadelphia, the lines were so long that hopeful exempts began lining up immediately after the office *closed* for the day so that they would be at the head of the line the following morning. Sensing an opportunity for profit, some perfectly healthy entrepreneurial types patiently waited in line overnight and then once near the front, they would auction off their prime spots to the highest bidder. In the Northeast, a Vermonter wondered how it was possible that any town in his home county of Addison could have only five able-bodied men. "I think our ancestors . . . must look down with wonder upon their degenerate sons, going about in crowds with certificates of disability in their pockets," he sadly concluded in a letter to the local paper. The soldiers already in the army could only shake their heads. After reading about such shenanigans in the papers, Levi Duff of the 105th Pennsylvania Infantry sarcastically assumed in a letter to his new wife in Pittsburgh that the city held a good many invalids at present. With regards to a mutual acquaintance who had ostensibly secured a medical exemption,

Duff wrote that he would be ashamed to walk the streets with a certificate of disability had he possessed the physical stature of their acquaintance. With a bit of a sigh, Duff concluded, "It is a pity that such men escape the draft."[37]

Sometimes family members and supposed loved ones ignored doctors altogether and took the matter into their own hands. The *Cincinnati Daily Press* reported how a Michigan woman was so determined not to see her husband enlist that she attempted to chop off his middle and forefingers while he was sleeping. Her tactic was to quietly lay a dull shaving knife against them and then strike a heavy blow. Failing to properly complete her mission, she quickly finished the job by sawing them off with a dull jackknife.[38]

New recruits who had already signed their enlistment papers occasionally arrived at the surgeon's office with second thoughts about what they had committed to. In their panic, they concocted all manner of creative reasons as to why, upon reflection, they were unfit for service. "I remember one of the excuses they would most frequently make was that they would not be stripped in order to be medically examined," recalled Brevet Brig. Gen. Reuben Williams. "This was required by the medical staff as early as the middle of 1862. They would declare that they would not undress to be examined before anybody!" The general, however, quickly found his remedy. "I would generally overcome this suddenly conceived excuse by deriding them for their lack of pluck and would end up offering to go before the medical examiner and strip off all my clothes with them. In almost every instance this method would succeed."[39]

Chronic rheumatism was an illness that many men and their families were familiar with in the mid-nineteenth century. Discernible by inflammation and pain in the joints or muscles, it became the most common feigned ailment during the war's early stages. According to one soldier on recruitment duty, another ruse was of men now arguing that they were at least sixty years old when they had earlier said they were forty. The *New York Daily Tribune* noted with some humorous sarcasm how this desire to look older had decimated the hair dye industry. "Gray hairs are not only honorable, they are fashionable," the paper proclaimed, noting how nobody, except "some ancient female" had used hair dye since the call had gone out for all men under forty-five years of age. "How suddenly some men grow old!" the *Tribune* concluded.[40]

If faked illnesses didn't work, then Michigan's *Grand Haven News* sarcastically pointed out that men could also avoid the draft by becoming a pauper "and get a ticket to the Poor-House" or "he may steal sheep and go to State Prison," since both paupers and convicts were draft exempt. The paper reasoned that any man who would seek draft exemption would also easily resort to either method.[41]

***

Civilians were not the only ones who would try to injure themselves so as to avoid war. Certain men already in the army became so disgusted with "soljerin'" that they took to injuring themselves as their means of escaping the war. Like their civilian counterparts, they sought a method that would preclude their ability to properly perform their duties but would not harm their normal return to daily life as a private citizen. Walt Whitman noticed in the Washington hospitals where he worked as a nurse that numerous soldiers in the first wave of wounded possessed only slight wounds and then often to the hand. In other words, a self-inflicted wound that would most likely offer a quick passport to the rear. Later in the war and with such self-mutilation still ongoing, Brig. Gen. John W. Turner announced to his division that "Such conduct is dastardly and despicable and none but arrant cowards will engage in it." Any man who would abandon his comrades in such a manner "should be stigmatized by the men of his regiment as a poltroon and coward." To combat these acts, Turner ordered all surgeons and their assistants to file a report with their regimental commander if they examined any man who they suspected of having maimed himself as a way to escape duty. A thorough and proper investigation should occur while the man was hospitalized "with the view that on his recovery he may be brought to trial and receive the punishment of [a] coward."[42]

The soldiers themselves usually knew whether such a wound was a legitimate accident or self-inflicted. Lying in a "horribly filthy" hospital filled with "lousy people," Valentin Bechler somewhat echoed Whitman by informing his wife that none of the wounded or sick soldiers there felt

I AM NOT SICK,
I'm over Forty-five,

I will make my Wife stay at home and give the Baby Catnip Tea.

AIR.—"I wish my Wife had no crying Baby."

I'm exempt, I'm exempt, I vow and declare
I'm exempt, I'm exempt, from the "draft" I will swear,
What, though the rebels our soil may invade,
And *wipe out* each general of pick-axe and spade?
Oh! what do I care though a million are slain;
And our starry-gemmed banner is tramped on the plain?
Oh! what do I care, who may fall or may thrive,
I'm exempt, I'm exempt, I'm o'er forty-five!

Oh! what do I care, what my neighbors may say,
That I've jumped o'er ten years in less than a day?
Oh! what do I care for my nation and laws?
I heed not her shame, I seek not applause;
But still for the Almighty Dollar I'll drive,
I'm exempt, I'm exempt, I'm o'er forty-five!

I always was healthy from heel unto nobe,
But now I have troubles as many as Job;
You may wink and may sneer, and say "it's all gas,"
That such a lame "HO'SE" with the doctors won't pass:
But I'm aches, I'm pains, from the head to the toe,
I'm exempt, I'm exempt, from the draft, you must know!

I'm free to confess that I find greater charms,
In a trip to England, than taking up arms;
I'm off, I'm off, with the very first train,
And when the war's over I'll come back again:
You call me a sneak—I heed not your twaddle,
I'm exempt I'm exempt, I mean to skedaddle!

"I Am Not Sick, I'm over Forty-Five" Song Lyrics (Library of Congress American Song Sheets Rare Books and Special Collections Division) they could get a discharge unless they first "maim their bodies with force." Illinois' William Standard informed his wife in late October 1862, only one month after his regiment was mustered in, how "one man shot off his right forefinger last night and Bill Gustine cut off one of his big toes today, or rather yesterday, I suppose to get rid of the war." Later in the war, he reminded her, "You must not think there is no coward among us. There is some that can't stand fire any to[o] well, and some that I think have played it off very well. . . . You have heard of fingers being shot off, toes shot, & some accidentally. . . . Now it may be that these things all happen by the fire from the enemy, but I fear not." While a noticeable number of men may have maimed themselves, there was an even small number who became so downtrodden that suicide became their only perceived avenue of escape. Less than 1 percent of all Union casualties—391 in total—took their own lives.[43]

GETTING CAPTURED BY THE ENEMY—INTENTIONALLY

The battlefield's 1862 carnage generated stories and reports that not only put a damper on civilian enlistments but also convinced some already in the army that they had earned enough martial glory. "Seeing the elephant" was a popular Civil War euphemism for a soldier's first combat action, a rite of passage that transitioned the civilian volunteer into a veteran soldier. If, however, that experience had come at a mass slaughterhouse like the April 6–7, 1862, battle of Shiloh in southwestern Tennessee or the July 1, 1862, battle of Malvern Hill outside of Richmond, then some soldiers decided that once was enough. Throughout the summer of 1862, countless Union soldiers sought escape from the front lines or a discharge from the army by any means, honorable or not.[44]

As with bounty jumping and faking infirmity, avoiding combat became a fine art for many enlistees. Some were able to acquire what the frontline soldiers termed "bomb-proof positions." These were rearguard jobs such as working in the Quartermaster Department, as a teamster, or as a hospital steward. After serving the original ninety-day stint as a private at the war's beginning, Robert Cary wrote to his friend Mack Ewing in December 1861 announcing his reenlistment into the 5th Illinois Cavalry and then his subsequent election as a company bugler. "And then the nice part of it is, I don't have to soldier," Cary proudly explained. Even though the company had already acquired two buglers at the time of his enlistment, Cary admitted how he, "worked the thing sharp and got a new Election." Cary's gambit worked and as a result, "I am excused from all duty. Get to ride with the Captain and have a nice time generally."[45]

No man instinctively sought out a firing-line death or even hard work. If he could acquire an honorable position that offered some measure of escape from either of those realities, he often seized the opportunity. Dow Webster of Otsego County, New York, had landed a position with the 1st New York Engineers and, though he considered its work hard enough, its biggest appeal to him, as he explained to his wife, was that he considered its duties as the freest from danger. For his part, Pennsylvanian David Keiholtz wrote to his recently enlisted brother on January 8, 1863, stating he was now assigned to his division's provost guards. Keiholtz explained that he much preferred this type of work to his prior regimental duties because "here we have no role [roll] calls, neither inspection, nor drills." Moreover, with only one post, Keiholtz wrote that no man had to perform standing guard duty more than once a week.[46]

Other soldiers who temporarily wandered away from their units were known as stragglers or sneaks, and they often enacted their vanishing act just prior to battle. These were the men who the historian of the 45th Pennsylvania Infantry described as "the skulkers and robbers in the rear of the army who never intended to do anything but rob, and who never get into battle." They would then reappear shortly after the engagement ended, grime wiped on their face, with a tale as to how they became inadvertently separated from their unit due to the smoke and din of battle. Others sometimes lagged behind early in the fight, seeking out wounded comrades who they could then assist to a field hospital in the rear.[47]

Still other anxious men sought out the enemy with the intent of being captured and taken prisoner; calculating that at this stage in the war, they would most likely be paroled and sent home, thereby gaining what one Yankee described as "a little rest from soldiering." It was a fairly simple yet dangerous process utilized by both sides. All a soldier who wanted out had to do was straggle in the enemy's vicinity and soon enough, he could find himself with his hands in the air, assuming he was not shot on sight first. Since both the Union and the Confederacy initially believed the war would be short, neither side had prepared for the means of housing and feeding great numbers of enemy prisoners of war, which prompted both sides to adopt the traditional European system of parole. To be paroled referred to the captured prisoner giving his word of honor that he would forgo further combat against his captors until formally exchanged for an enemy prisoner of equal rank. Once captured, a soldier was usually placed on parole by his captors within a few days, if not on the spot, and sent on his way. Both sides initially viewed the soldier's oath as a serious matter, given the era's culture, which held that holding to one's word of honor was a positive indicator of his manliness and good character. If a paroled soldier was later recaptured bearing arms and had not yet been formally exchanged, he was subject to execution by his captors.[48]

To be taken prisoner in battle generally brought a man no shame; however, to intentionally seek out the enemy for that end was quite another matter. The colonel of the 21st Ohio Infantry, Arnold McMahon, wrote after the war how, "The plan of parole which was recognized at the time worked great mischief, as it was soon understood in the army that to be taken prisoner was equivalent to an indefinite furlough." As a consequence, McMahon readily knew that "stragglers and skulkers became willing captives." Union soldier J. D. Paull wrote home in October 1862 disclosing how someone would be taken prisoner occasionally while on picket duty but only because he was usually "some lazy coward." Abraham Bope of the 61st Ohio Infantry told a similar tale to his sister, writing how a "coward" in his regiment was seen by several men intentionally waiting in a ditch with the intent of being captured by the Confederates. "Any man that will throw himself away on purpose to be taken a prisoner is no soldier at all," Bope reasoned. Realizing how quickly each army had paroled its prisoners, an Alabamian unknowingly spoke for numerous Johnny Rebs and Billy Yanks when he informed his wife that he would never desert his comrades, but he also wouldn't make any strenuous exertions to get out of the enemy's way, either. No doubt well aware of the culture's ethos regarding honor and manly courage, he urged his wife to let no one see that letter.[49]

At the other end of the Union command structure, Maj. Gen. William Rosecrans considered such an act to be "more base and cowardly" than desertion. Ohio's colonel Albert S. Hall, commanding the 33rd brigade, wrote to a friend alarmed to hear of some men who recently enlisted and collected a handsome cash bounty in the process but who never intended to follow through on their soldierly duties. Instead, according to Hall's informants, they planned to immediately be taken prisoner, paroled, and then sent home with both pay and bounty in hand. Even higher up the chain of command was Maj. Gen. John Pope, who was in command of the Union's Army of Virginia. Following the dismal August 1862 Second Bull Run campaign, Pope warned General-in-Chief Henry Halleck, "The straggling is awful . . . Unless something can be done to restore tone to this army it will melt away before you know it." Stanton also took the warnings to heart, admitting only a week later to Ohio governor David Tod, "There is reason to fear that many voluntarily surrender for the sake of getting home."[50]

In the first year of the war, a Union prisoner was allowed to return home after being paroled by his captors with the proviso that he would report his whereabouts to state authorities at the end of each month. Numerous paroled soldiers simply vanished, however, and with the Union armies desperate for men, federal authorities were forced to get a better handle on where exactly all those men were. As a result, the War Department issued General Orders No. 72 on June 28, 1862, which specified that a paroled Union soldier was now to be transferred to one of three new Northern parole camps set up to temporarily house those men until they were formally exchanged for Confederate prisoners of war. At that point, they would then be sent back to their regiments for further active duty.[51]

Joseph H. Geiger, a clerk for the US Circuit Court, was a bureaucrat assigned to monitor Camp Chase in Columbus, Ohio, which served as both a Confederate prisoner of war site and one of the three newly designated Union parole camps, which were also known as "camps of instruction." By late September 1862, Geiger had heard enough of the surrendering pranks from paroled Union prisoners such that he was compelled to send an urgent appeal to Secretary of War Stanton. The whole system, wrote Geiger, was "an inducement not only for cowards, but for men discontented with their officers, or even homesick to surrender." To make matters worse, Geiger relayed how too many men spoke of the kind treatment they received from the Rebels after their surrender and parole. According to Geiger, some paroled prisoners even became outlaws who refused to serve again in any capacity whatsoever.[52]

In the East, Lt. Col. George Sangster, the commander of the newly established "Camp Parole" in Annapolis, Maryland, reported a similar tale of frustration. Sangster was dismayed to conclude that apparently no more than five hundred of the several thousand paroled Union soldiers in his camp knew what army corps they belonged to. "I am convinced more and more every day that three-fourths of paroled men are stragglers and cowards," Sangster wrote to his superior. His concern was not surprising in retrospect, for those men who had intentionally surrendered to the enemy or who were captured while straggling had no desire to return to their units, where their comrades would probably know what they had done. Lying or creating a fictitious identity was deemed by many of these men to be the most expeditious short-term answer.[53]

Unfortunately for the Union men shepherded into these new parole camps, living conditions and sanitation were sometimes no better than what they may have experienced in a Rebel prisoner of war camp. Many men sent to Maryland's Camp Parole had arrived from Confederate prisoner of war camps with no shoes, having sold them to buy something to eat. Lying around and playing cards seemed to be the main daily focus. Life was tedious with the area residents strongly pro-Southern. "The country around the camp is very poor, owned and cultivated by men, who though minimally, are union men, yet at length are traitors and would rejoice at the success of the Rebellion," wrote a Camp Parole inmate to his brother. T. J. Carney of Illinois wrote to his friends at home stating that within the Annapolis camp "not a day goes by but there is fighting going on . . . evry day or two a man is brought to the hospital all cut or beat to peaces one morning three men was found dead on a brush heap with there throats cut from ear to ear and there pockets robed." Another paroled soldier recalled having plenty to eat at the Annapolis camp but that it seemed impossible to get clothing or blankets. He would have to manage with the vermin-infested clothing he arrived in. When a US Sanitary Commission member looked over Chicago's Camp Douglas in October 1862, he sadly reported how the paroled soldiers' barracks were hardly fit for respectable men and that the grounds were saturated with human bodily waste. Governors and influential citizens beseeched Washington politicians with warnings that such callous disregard for these honorable soldiers and former prisoners of war only served to discourage further home front volunteering.[54]

Following the August–September 1862 Second Bull Run and Maryland campaigns, Henry Halleck wrote to Edwin Stanton telling the secretary what he already knew: "Many thousand straggled away from their commands, and it is said that not a few voluntarily surrendered to the enemy, so as to be paroled as prisoners of war." Straggling and "skulking" had affected the Western armies as well. In December, William Sherman complained to his brother, Ohio senator John Sherman, that at the moment of marching, one-fourth of his army seemed to suddenly become sick and had to be left behind. However, according to Sherman, "The Great Evil is absenteeism, which is real Desertion, & Should be punished with Death." Gen. Ulysses Grant followed up in January 1863 by ordering the arrest and court-martial of any paroled soldier who was captured due to straggling from the army.[55]

Desperate wives and mothers were also not immune to suggesting similar courses of action. Some wives who had proudly encouraged their husbands to enlist in 1861 now had second thoughts as 1862 and the war dragged on. As a new mother in late July 1862, Margaret Cahill urged her husband—who was the colonel of the 9th Connecticut Infantry and fighting near Vicksburg, Mississippi—that "you must come home now . . . I cannot hold out much longer." Jane Standard likewise urged her husband, William, to think about being intentionally captured, but if that was his escape plan, he should first send all of his possessions to their home in Fulton County, Illinois. Stories abounded of how the supply-poor Confederates kept everything of value from their captured Union prisoners. "Then I would try to get 6 or 8 more of the boys in the same notion," Jane proposed. "Then I would go out and manage to be taken prisoner and then you would be paroled. Then you could come home and arrange for something else." Throughout a series of letters, Pvt. William Greene's widowed mother repeatedly urged her teenage son to desert and come home to Raymond, New Hampshire. She suggested that he "frame up a good story that you want to come home & see your widowed mother who is in poor health." Since William was only age seventeen and had entered the army without his mother's consent, she believed they could not force him back in and told her son as much. And in any event, Mrs. Greene supposed that if deceit was good for the goose, it was also good for the gander. "It's not wicked to use stratigy to get out of a place that there has been so much stratigem made use of to get one into it," she reasoned.[56]

Senior officers were often aware of the men's angst over their loved one's safety and security. They knew that soldiers whose primary focus was getting home rather than chasing the enemy were not good fighters. Maj. Gen. William Rosecrans even empathized with the privates' plight when he wrote to Secretary of War Stanton from Nashville by admitting, "Many have been led by lack of pay to temporarily desert, to look after their families. They are poor men, and much in need of money." As historians have pointed out, privates often saw a distinct difference between desertion and absent without leave. Even company-level officers occasionally saw that logic when it came to their own families. "I came to War to fight for the government and I will do it as long as I am able to," Capt. Henry Young of the 7th Wisconsin Infantry reminded his wife in January 1862. Young then hedged his remark by adding the proviso, "providing my Family don't suffer in my absence." These *volunteer* citizen-soldiers insisted they had the right to take leave when their family's welfare demanded it. If local and/or state governments would not see to their families' welfare, then they had to.[57]

Other women tried to chase away recruitment officers after seeing the hardships their now-alone female neighbors or family members had to endure. They pelted officers with rocks, and in one extreme example, one mother thrust a young child severely stricken with smallpox into the face of an enrollment officer. In other, more violent examples, such as in Pennsylvania's heavily Irish Anthracite coal regions, armed mobs ambushed enrolling agents while false names and addresses were routinely given by residents to enrolling agents. One Pennsylvanian warned Gov. Andrew Curtin that his working-class, antiwar neighbors had all secured guns, rifles, and plenty of ammunition to defend what they saw as their right to peaceably work their farms and be left alone by a distant federal government. These hardscrabble families believed that conscripting the husband and father during harvest season would destroy their family. "They dare any number to come and draft them before they have their work finished," he concluded. Conscription was an issue that centered on social class every bit as much as ethnicity and duty.[58]

The Reemergence of Partisan Politics

By the summer and fall of 1862, partisan politics was back on the rise in addition to the battlefield body counts. Frustrated with what they saw as the Lincoln administration's poor decisions and illegal policies, Democratic citizens on the street and politicians began to speak out sharply against the war. Antiwar hecklers in New York City obstructed recruiting efforts by surrounding enlistment offices and then regaling potential recruits with stories of horrific wounds and poor treatment in the army. Their success and numbers were sufficient enough for Mayor George Opdyke to ask police superintendent John Kennedy to station officers at each recruiting office in an effort to deter such acts. Democratic newspaper editors also began to loudly criticize the war effort. Those civilian men, in turn, who were loyal readers of those papers took notice and nodded their heads in silent agreement. The most vitriolic of antiwar newspapers were those that became known as the "Peace Democrat" or Copperhead press. As discussed in chapter 2, these were the Democratic Northern men and women who decried the war practically from the start as unwinnable and unjust, with the Lincoln administration and its abolitionist allies painted as the real aggressors. In addition, the administration's policies regarding the war's prosecution and attempts to stifle home front dissent were criticized as crimes against constitutional precepts. Their motto of "the Constitution as it is and the Union as it was" spoke to their belief in a strict interpretation of constitutional law. For these partisans, "the Constitution as it is" said what it meant and meant what it said. "The Union as it was" included the fact that slavery was legal in much of the United States and if that reality was going to be changed, it should be done so by Congress or at the ballot box, not at the cannon's mouth. There were approximately 360 Copperhead newspapers scattered throughout the Northern states during the war that stood firmly for peace at any price even at the cost of the Union. To reach their ends, they had little problem in trumpeting any Southern success while minimizing Union triumphs, which had a significant impact on staunch Democratic men deciding not to enlist. In his posthumously published memoirs, Union lieutenant general and US president Ulysses S. Grant reflected upon the strength of the North's Copperhead press, its mission, and its followers by referring to them as "an auxiliary of the Confederate army."[59]

The Copperhead/antiwar peace movement was not a fringe action, isolated to any given part of the North. Nor was it a top-down Democratic conspiracy. Rather, it was an organic, grassroots movement that presented a genuine, ongoing threat to the Lincoln administration's reunification-by-war efforts. The Democratic Copperheads seemingly questioned every act and policy position taken by the Republicans in a manner ritualized by a two-party system that routinely set party against party and citizen against citizen. Democratic Party leaders and the average Democrat in the street fed off of each other.[60]

The unrelenting Copperhead press criticism of the war coupled with a rising manpower shortfall due to the lack of enlistments became a marked danger to the Union war effort throughout the summer of 1862. To counter those baleful effects, Secretary of War Stanton unilaterally issued an order on August 8 decreeing that any printed or spoken public commentary that had the effect of discouraging enlistments or expressing hope for Union military failure would now be viewed as "implied treason." Since the US Constitution's definition of treason (Article 3, Section 3) included the sentence "Treason against the United States, shall consist only in levying War against them, or in adhering to their Enemies, *giving them Aid and Comfort*" [italics added], Stanton was now intentionally equating free speech to treason and in the process, all but gutted the Bill of Rights. Such speech was outlawed and would be dealt with accordingly by federal or local authorities. His order authorized any US marshal or town police chief to "arrest and imprison any person or persons who may be engaged, by act, speech, or writing, in discouraging volunteer enlistments, or in any way *giving aid and comfort to the enemy* [italics added], or in any other disloyal practice against the United States." What Stanton evidently chose to overlook was the Constitution's next sentence, which stated treason must also be an "overt Act," a crucial addition specifically intended to prevent politicians or judges from declaring that thoughts or mere words could be deemed treasonous. By so doing, the founding fathers sought to override centuries of thought that defined mere political opposition as a treasonous political crime against the state or monarchy. Stanton now returned to that perspective by broadening the definition of treason to include both overt acts of war and what the administration decided were disloyal or treasonous words. Delaware's governor William Cannon illuminated this Unionist rationale when he wrote, "The idea that the Government is bound to await the development of a conspiracy until the actors shall have perfected their plans and committed some overt act necessary to bring them within the technical definition of treason, is, to my mind, absurd. The object is not punishment, but prevention." The net effect was that the line separating traitorous acts and political speech narrowed greatly. A person could now be arrested for speaking or printing "traitorous" words or holding "seditious" viewpoints despite having committed no overt, physical acts of rebellion or subversion. The "wrong" type of political speech became criminalized. Even into our present day and regardless of which party holds power, the criminalization of political differences genie has yet to be put back into its lamp.[61]

In short order, US authorities began to carry out Stanton's edict from Maine to Kansas. Iowa's governor advised anyone who asked that openly discouraging enlistments or interfering with an officer in his line of duty were punishable offenses. The day after Stanton's edict, the district attorney for Wilkes Barre, Pennsylvania, was arrested solely for giving a speech in which he encouraged his listeners to stay home from the war and go to the polls instead, whereby they could elect men who would end the war without further bloodshed. In Urbana, Ohio, one man was arrested for purportedly discouraging enlistments on behalf of the Knights of the Golden Circle, alleged to be an anti-Lincoln "secret society." Another example was that of a Vermont man who was arrested for both discouraging enlistments and speaking "treasonable language." In all, from August 8 through September 8, at least 354 men were arrested under Stanton's August 8 edict. Of those arrested, 181 involved young men attempting to flee the draft, with another 10 arrested for aiding that first number.[62]

Yet within two and one-half months, the federal government reversed itself, perhaps seeing the civil rights nightmare it was creating. On November 22, Stanton ordered that anyone who was previously arrested and imprisoned for "discouraging volunteer enlistments, opposing the draft or for otherwise giving aid and comfort to the enemy in States where the draft has been made . . . shall be discharged from further military restraint." In the ongoing attempt to win the hearts and minds of all Northern citizens, the Lincoln administration went back to the starting line.[63]

In spite of Stanton's August 8 gag order, wives and family members who had earlier consented to their men going off to war now, in some cases, begged them to leave the army and come home however they could. Women who lived in remote rural areas or on farms without male protection felt especially vulnerable. Being left alone to tend to the family farm, business, and/or children for a brief period was a world away from the year or more that some wives were now expected to endure. Twenty-four-year-old Mary Wallace's 1862 diary, for example, abounds with her daily struggles in having to attend to two small children, sewing, boiling soap, keeping her pigs out of the corn, gathering and hauling wood, and other instances of what she routinely described as "choring around" after her husband enlisted into the 19th Michigan Infantry. Even during the initial ninety-day enlistments, dozens of southcentral and southeastern Pennsylvania women wrote pleading letters to their newly enlisted husbands. Written during the first half of July 1861, they never reached their intended recipients, for Gen. George Cadwalader intercepted and withheld them, believing their contents would be demoralizing to his troops' morale. The home front realities for women and their children often stood in stark contrast to the professions of patriotism and willing sacrifice their communities demanded. A result of this contradiction was that after the war commenced, some Northern women were often perceived by their communities, Northern newspapers, and even Union soldiers as not being properly committed to the war effort. Their indifference stood out when compared to their Southern female counterparts who were, after all, often dealing with the war's harsh realities right in their front yards. As a Union staff officer framed it, "Were the ladies of the North to imitate the South, they would make heroes of us all."[64]

The war also brought about stories of philandering soldier husbands far away from home along with similar tales of unfaithful wives. Time and distance strained traditional societal morals just as the rebellion itself tested the era's rules of civilized warfare. In particular was the cultural belief that a real man always exhibited self-control in the face of adversity. Loneliness and the natural desire for physical affection tested married men, many of whom failed the test. "O where are their marriage vows?" one faithful soldier asked in his diary after witnessing two ladies of the evening enter the tent occupied by his married captain and lieutenant. Another married man informed his wife that when groups of prostitutes visited his camp, it appeared that he was the only married man in the regiment. As may be expected, tales of marital infidelity were a two-way street. "Allmost all the married men that has been home on Furlough has come back with long faces," a Vermont private reported to a female friend back home in March 1863. "Some of them found their wives has cleared off with other fellows . . . Is it any wonder that the army is demoralized. Attaced as they are in the front by the rebels and by somebody else in the rear." Many of these salacious home front stories helped to keep some men rooted at home or perhaps serving in local home guard units. Though much of these rumors proved to be false, enough had merit, which contributed to a rise in the divorce rate during and after the war.[65]

Marital fidelity and physical safety were not the only concerns women faced concerning their soldier husbands. As with parents who feared for their sons' moral welfare, wives knew from repeated stories how the army could be a cesspool of gambling, drinking, and debauchery. Mothers and wives begged their men to avoid such temptations by remembering their religious training and adhering to the straight and narrow. Better yet, women often urged their men to come home for good by any means necessary.[66]

***

The new 1862 militia draft law prompted multitudes of draft-eligible men to abandon hearth and home in order to avoid the draft; a reality that would rear its head with each draft for the remainder of the war. In a Christmas Day 1862 letter to her husband, Washington socialite Elizabeth Blair Lee wrote how numerous Unionist acquaintances who had no desire to take part in the war had sailed off to Europe. Most draft-eligible men, however, who chose to flee their homes escaped into nearby Canada, beyond the reach of the federal government that, in the mind of pro-Lincoln newspapers, had provided countless benefits and blessings to them in the first place. In so doing, they became the nation's first "draft dodgers," a term later popularized during the twentieth century's contentious Vietnam War era. To counter the exodus, Secretary of State Seward issued an order on August 8 announcing that no passports would be issued to men liable to the draft until their respective states had filled their required quota. Pro-war Northern papers were biting and relentless in their condemnations of these men. Once in Canada, the skedaddlers would "ensconce themselves under the skirts of Mrs. Victoria," wrote the *Cleveland Plain Dealer*, "hoping that their ample folds will screen them from all harm." Michigan's *Grand Haven News* decried the "stampede" of "detestable poltroons" who were making their way into Canada. The paper proposed that the federal government should pass a law barring their return and then formally confiscate their personal property for the benefit of the state. Another Michigan observer documented how Detroit was the nozzle through which hundreds of men poured into an overtly hospitable Canada: "From Iowa, from Wisconsin, from Missouri, from Illinois, have the miserable wretches come . . . skedaddling for Canada." Crossing through any border town would do if it meant not having to serve in the Union army. "You can distinguish one of those characters almost the moment you place your eye upon him, from the sheepish, ashamed, hang dog look he invariably wears," declared one Ohio paper. To counteract the exodus, Union authorities made it a crime for any citizen to leave his state unless he first obtained a pass from his local provost marshal; an extraordinary intrusion into one's personal liberty that, temporarily at least, made a free White man's travel rights as no better than that of a paroled felon. In Indiana, for example, a draft-eligible man had to first prove his loyalty and that his desire to leave the state was not with any intent to evade the draft. No bond was required if his intended time out of state was less than two weeks, however, if longer than that, he then had to post a $1,000 bond.[67]

The year 1862 ended with Union morale and the want of battlefield success at its lowest point of the entire war. Unreliable army pay coupled with the failure of the home front's financial support systems promised to the initial volunteers led numerous stay-at-home men to do anything to remain in that category. Patriotic volunteering had evaporated, with men having to be bribed to enlist. The devastating Union defeat on December 13 at the battle of Fredericksburg represented the final nail in the coffin. To gain more men, the federal government had created the first-ever draft system via the Militia Act, yet the act's implementation was still erratic as the responsibility for sending forth men still rested with the various states. Lincoln and Congress realized that a more structured, national system was needed.

CHAPTER 6

"We Broke with Many Friends on Account of Politics"

Fall 1862's Emancipation Proclamation, Racial Animosity, and Home Front Ostracism

THE WAR WAS GOING POORLY FOR THE LINCOLN ADMINISTRATION AND the North throughout the late spring and into the early fall of 1862. The army needed more men as the battlefield losses and body counts rose ever higher. In Virginia, the Union military's premier Army of the Potomac suffered almost 40,000 casualties during the early April to July 1 Peninsula and Seven Days campaigns. Another 14,000 men fell during the ill-fated August 28–30 battle of Second Bull Run, which was followed by yet another 12,400 killed, wounded, or missing at the battle of Antietam Creek near Sharpsburg, Maryland, on September 17. In the Western theater, the Union suffered a ghastly 13,000 casualties at the April 6–7 battle of Shiloh, which was the largest casualty toll of any battle ever fought on the North American continent up to that day. At Richmond, Kentucky, on August 29–30, Iuka, Mississippi, on September 19, as well as at Perryville, Kentucky, on October 8, the North suffered close to another 10,000 casualties. All the while, civilians at home saw the casualty lists and read the letters from their loved ones at the front. This was not the quick, glorious war they had envisioned just a bit more than one year earlier. A result was that in the big picture, Northern men decided they wanted no part of such butchery and therefore stopped enlisting. All of which led to the enactment of the Militia Act and its consequences as discussed in the prior two chapters. Throughout the distressing late spring and summer of 1862, Lincoln knew he needed a way to galvanize the nation.

While the administration and Congress were debating the proper means to bring more men into the army, Lincoln had grappled with some type of slavery abolition measure as a potential means to those ends. It was imperative, however, that the North first obtain some manner of military victory before doing so, otherwise any new pronouncement could appear to be the last desperate gasp of a dying administration. Furthermore, the radical abolitionist faction in and out of Congress was constantly pressuring Lincoln to strike an overt anti-slavery blow.

Though somewhat of a tactical draw on the battlefield, that September 17 engagement at Antietam was viewed by the administration as the all-important strategic victory that Lincoln needed. After both sides remained within their lines the following day, when the sun rose on September 19, the Union army realized they held the field because Gen. Robert E. Lee had felt compelled to withdraw his Confederate Army of Northern Virginia back into its namesake state during the previous night. It was the window of opportunity that Lincoln had been searching for. Nonetheless, Antietam was a costly, gruesome victory that staggered the senses. More men were killed in the battle than in the entire Revolutionary War. More than 23,000 men wearing blue or gray were killed, wounded, or missing, with the battle of Antietam remaining up to the present as the single bloodiest day in American history.

Also for the first time in history, American civilians soon witnessed the Antietam carnage through the then still-novel invention of photography. Photographer Alexander Gardner and his assistant, James Gibson, had traveled to the battlefield to photograph the aftermath only two days after the clash had ended. Two weeks later, photographer Matthew Brady presented close to one hundred of Gardner's images at his New York gallery in an exhibit titled "The Dead of Antietam." Those first-ever images of rotting corpses and battlefield slaughter horrified many visitors, some of whom had stood in line for hours and later swore they wanted no part of such butchery. "If [Brady] has not brought bodies and

Antietam, Maryland—Gardner Photograph of Confederate Dead by a Fence on the Hagerstown Road (Library of Congress Prints and Photographs Division)

laid them in our dooryards and along the streets, he has done something very like it," wrote a reporter for the *New York Times* after seeing Brady's exhibit. The "glory and gallantry" of war was washed away by any who saw those photographs and served to quietly reinforce their decision to avoid the war.[1]

Nonetheless and in spite of the gore, that battlefield success, such as it was, gave Lincoln the political opening he needed. On September 22, five days after the battle ended, Lincoln announced his Preliminary Emancipation Proclamation, which would take effect just more than three months later on January 1, 1863. The proclamation declared that all slaves in any area still in rebellion against the United States on that date "shall be then, thenceforward, and forever free." Despite its lofty words, it was, in essence, strictly a military measure as it was only effective in those areas not already under Union military control. Lincoln had always felt that restoring the Union as well as regaining harmony between the

North and South were his main priorities. Emancipation was an unintended consequence, a timely military opportunity to use the latter to gain the former. From Lincoln's vantage, slaves were a valuable Southern resource assisting the Confederate war machine by tending to crops in Southern fields or by digging and building defensive works for the army. Under the long-standing rules of so-called civilized warfare, armies routinely seized or destroyed property valuable to the enemy's war-making efforts. Slaves in those areas loyal to the Union, however, such as the four border slave states, were not set free. By presenting the proclamation as a military strategy, Lincoln also hoped to dampen the inevitable constitutional criticisms. Nevertheless, from one end of the country to the other, emancipation now officially joined reunification as a formal war goal.[2]

Republicans generally cheered Lincoln's proclamation as did the abolitionists who had longed for this day. Numerous church bodies also heartily approved, and in the process, they reaffirmed their commitment to the belief that putting down the rebellion was a God-ordained holy war. Many conservative Democrats, undeniably, openly railed against Lincoln and what they saw as the proclamation's blatant unconstitutionality. They argued that God had certainly not approved nor inspired such an illegal decree. They reminded any who would listen that their party was all in when the war's initial and sole goal was restoring the Union. Now, however, they alleged the Republicans had pulled a bait and switch. As these Democrats saw it, the Emancipation Proclamation was the culmination of the abolitionist program, begun in the 1820s, to win control of the federal government. "All the support the war has ever received from Democrats was originally obtained by a base cheat, an infamous swindle, a damnable deception. The Democratic party trusted and was betrayed," railed the Sheboygan, Wisconsin, *Journal* in arguing their point. For many Democrats (but certainly not all), their willingness to support the war was fading fast. The Democrats argued that slavery was still legal in parts of the country and that such an important constitutional matter should be settled within the halls of Congress and not by presidential edict nor at the muzzle of a cannon. Now that Lincoln had opened the can of worms, constitutional questions abounded. For example, if the president had the constitutional power to free slaves with the stroke of his pen, did he also possess the authority to reenslave them in a similar manner? If his proclamation stood, were there any real limits then on presidential executive action?[3]

Lincoln's opponents abhorred the proclamation as well as the new militia draft law and their underlying mutual philosophy of risking White lives and property to free Black slaves. Taken together, these two acts represented a fundamental shift in the nature of the war on the battlefield as well as on the Northern home front. Countless Democrats who had proudly and openly supported the war when its sole goal was the restoration of the Union now crossed over into the Copperhead camp. Scores of men believed that given the fundamental switch in the war's focus, they were now absolved of any moral duty to die for their beloved Union if need be. Before the announcement, Pennsylvania's *Lancaster Daily Intelligencer* predicted such fallout. It quoted the staunchly Republican, New Haven, Connecticut, *Palladium*, which affirmed that the war was no longer one to restore the Union as it was. Rather, the *Palladium* declared it was now a war "to make the Union *what it never was,* but what *it ought to be.*" The Democratic-leaning *Intelligencer* deemed such speech to be unconstitutional and therefore treasonable, with the obvious net effect of further discouraging voluntary enlistments. "There are tens of thousands of brave and patriotic men ready to fight, and die if need be, in the effort to restore the Union," the *Intelligencer* asserted, "who would not raise a finger in support of such a war as is above indicated." In a letter to his well-known abolitionist brother, Henry Ward Beecher, written in late August 1862, Thomas Beecher reiterated this sentiment as far as rural New York was concerned: "The more emancipation you talk, the less recruits you can enlist." Other papers had been and still were far more blatant with their racist rationales, such as Pennsylvania's *Crawford Democrat,* which argued there were many men still at home who were willing to fight for Uncle Sam, "but they are not inclined to fight for Uncle Sambo." Characteristic of that mindset was a young Maine man, who, in writing to his uncle in November 1862, asked rhetorically why Lincoln's proclamation had not gone into effect immediately back in September. His answered assumption was that Lincoln knew the army would revolt. In any case, "I shall not enlist I tell you, not this winter certainly." Because of the proclamation, the young man was now convinced that "Old Abe and all his ghostly crew will feel like the boy that shit himself before they e'er get this through."[4]

Two days after issuing his proclamation, Lincoln threw more fuel on the fire by issuing Proclamation 94, which reiterated Stanton's August 8 prohibition against antiwar speech. The president also suspended the legal writ of habeas corpus for any person arrested on such a charge (see chapter 3). In this instance, the Constitution's wording appeared straightforward: "The privilege of the writ of habeas corpus shall not be suspended *unless when, in cases of rebellion or invasion, the public safety may require it.*" (Italics added) Moreover, the new order made them "subject to martial law and liable to trial and punishment by Courts Martial or Military Commission." The desired net effect of these two orders was that any civilian arrested for "discouraging enlistments" because of his speech could now be held indefinitely without charge in a military dungeon, rather than face trial in a civil court where a jury of the accused's peers might very well render an acquittal that would be highly embarrassing to the administration. Newspapers took note that since obtaining substitutes in anticipation of the draft was deemed to be discouraging enlistments, they were equally liable if they ran advertisements seeking substitutes.[5]

As with the Emancipation Proclamation, pro-Lincoln Republican papers applauded the new decrees while much of the Democratic press was aghast at what they felt was a new suppression of a civilian's fundamental free speech and civil rights. "It is palpably unjust that citizens should be taken from their homes and business and incarcerated in a prison for weeks and months for alleged political offenses, and denied the privileges granted the meanest criminals in the land," complained the *Indiana State Sentinel*. Furthermore, innumerable Democrats and strict constitutionalists saw a direct linkage between the two decrees. "It is a false philanthropy which seeks the good of four millions of negroes, at the expense of the peace and happiness of twenty-five millions of white people," wrote one staunch Democrat, typifying his party's antiwar faction. "We are not in favor of slavery, but we are in favor of the Union." An anti-abolition sheet known as the *New York Weekly Caucasian: The White Man's Paper* angrily decried the two acts, yet saw it as inevitable that "this attempted change in the *status* of the negro is accompanied by a corresponding change in the *status* of the white man." The belief that the country was sliding into dictatorial rule coupled with emancipation now as official war policy reconfirmed for many Northern White men that their previous decision not to enlist was as compelling as ever.[6]

While some argued against the proclamation's constitutionality, others opposed it (and therefore the war as well) because they sincerely believed that slavery was sanctioned by God in the Bible. For example, two frequently cited verses from the disciple Paul—Ephesians 6:5 and Colossians 3:22—called on slaves to be obedient to their earthly masters. Additionally, Southerners and many of their Northern well-wishers maintained that the average Southern slave was treated better than the typical Yankee "wage slave" toiling in some dirty and dangerous factory. An elderly Southern-sympathizing Ohio Democrat asked his nephew to consider what the word *slave* really meant. "When a man is so situated that he is forced to labour or starve, and when he does labor, must give over all what he eats and wears to some power beyond his control, he is then a slave," explained the older man. "There are more than 3 million of such slaves in the Northern states and crime is now rampant," he concluded, noting that crime was far more widespread in the North than in the South and directly relating that fact to the "wage slave's" condition. Other theologians believed it was God's providence that brought the Africans to America's shores. By so doing, their eternal souls could be saved through their acceptance of the Christian message. Now, however, the Emancipation Proclamation threatened to overturn, as the *New York Herald* opined, the rightful condition assigned to the Africans by God.[7]

Still more feared that such a presidential decree would only embolden the Confederacy. If the act was to be enforced to its letter, then it represented the "annihilation of the South, and the converse proposition to the restoration of the Union" claimed Illinois' *Ottawa Free Trader*. "The South will only fight the harder." One of the North's leading Copperhead newspapers, the *New York World*, argued that given human nature and the Southern mindset's reaction to insulting threats, the act would turn every ambivalent Southerner into a pro-war zealot. The resultant effect would be to strengthen the rebels' determination to fight to the last ditch.

That prediction was not entirely far-fetched. After learning of Lincoln's proclamation, one Confederate bureaucrat in Richmond recorded in his diary how, "some of the gravest of our senators favor the raising of the *black flag*, asking and giving no quarter hereafter." Others were more sanguine, knowing that such a controversial decree would sow Northern divisiveness, which could only help the Rebel cause.[8]

Simple economics also played a role in the widespread aversion to Lincoln's proclamation. Many poor, working-class Northerners envisioned hordes of freed Blacks streaming into their cities and competing with White men for the available manual labor jobs. For these working poor, it was a simple issue of bread on their family's table versus the possibility of none at all. This was especially the case in the larger urban areas such as New York City, where much of the immigrant Irish population settled. They had fled a system of caste oppression in Ireland that rendered them less than full citizens. Now in America and though they suffered ethnic discrimination, they learned in short order that their white skin afforded them a competitive advantage over Blacks that they meant to maintain. From their perspective, what self-respecting White man would voluntarily fight to bring about a scenario in which they would lose that privilege? The rhetorical answer for many was that they would not, with their anger resulting in considerable anti-Black rioting in New York City and various Midwestern cities throughout 1863 (discussed further in chapter 8). For numerous dirt-poor immigrants, there was the obvious employment competition, but on a deeper level, there was also the emotional gratification in knowing that no matter how low on the economic-social caste ladder they were, there was another ethnicity or race below them.[9]

Regardless of the lofty legal, theological, or political tenets put forth by those opposed to Lincoln's proclamation, other Northern men openly protested against fighting for abolition on blatantly racist grounds. Almost all mid-nineteenth-century White Americans, in the north or south, simply took it for granted that White racial supremacy was the natural biological order in the same matter-of-fact way that they knew the sun would rise in the East. Any differential treatment of Blacks by

Whites required no unique clarification, and when one was offered, it was presented as a reasoned thought explaining an obvious reality.

Despite the American Revolution's ideals of all men being created equal with full republican citizenship, Northern Blacks were assigned the lowest rungs on the societal caste ladder due solely to race and a growing belief in their diminished capacities compared to Whites. This growing racism that proposed that Blacks were biologically inferior to Whites gained further traction in the 1830s as a response to the rising abolitionist movement even though slavery was formally abandoned in the North by this time. As historian Patrick Rael pointed out, there was a wide gulf between total enslavement and full citizenship, let alone social equality. This was an era when Congress was dominated in large measure by the South and its "slave power," which was, of course, fully committed to slavery's preservation in their region. All manner of "scientific" theories were given credence to assert that White dominion and Black subservience were natural. The New England "Yankee" abolitionist, meanwhile, was viewed almost universally as a dangerous kook willing to tear down a blessed nation in order to elevate a degraded race. By the time the Civil War commenced in 1861, most of its participants and especially the younger rank and file had been born and raised in a culture that believed White supremacy to be God's and nature's ordained order.[10]

***

Innumerable Union soldiers already in the ranks completely agreed with the home front civilians who protested against Lincoln's new proclamation. They were those men who were staunch supporters of the war effort, who wanted to see the Union preserved, nevertheless blamed the whole mess on the New England radical abolitionist every bit as much as the antiwar Midwestern Copperhead. Typifying that viewpoint was the 76th Pennsylvania Volunteers' David Shoemaker. Writing from Hilton Head, South Carolina, Shoemaker informed his sister that the Yankee abolitionists did not fare well among his comrades. "There is some men here that would shoot [abolitionists] Horace Greely and Wendell Phillips as quick as they would Jeff Davis or [Confederate general P. T.] Beauregard." Those who had eagerly volunteered into the army when the war's sole purpose was to preserve the Union now felt betrayed and then livid when it appeared they were now fighting primarily for the Black man.[11]

In the case of the four slaveholding yet loyal border states, numerous Unionist slaveholders had proudly enlisted into the Union army believing they had done so to preserve the Union *and* slavery's legality within their states. Missouri diarist Elvira Scott wrote how no one should be surprised that Missouri's slave owners were among the most ardent opponents of secession. "They well knew that their own markets as well as the general commerce tied Missouri to the North," Scott explained. With Lincoln's new proclamation, however, they now saw the writing on the wall. Scores resigned, refusing to fight to free their own slaves and the immense wealth they represented. "We are all opposed to secession," nevertheless, "we who are in the army feel that we have been grossly deceived by the President and the party in power," wrote slave-owning Union major Benjamin Buckner of the 20th Kentucky Infantry to his fiancée. "If the issue had been the freeing of the Slaves instead of saving the Union as I sometimes think it has come to," wrote Pennsylvania private Adam Pickel to his parents, "I would not have mingled with the dirty job." Pickel's perspective was typical of numerous Union soldiers. Fighting to free the slaves was *not* the reason why the vast majority of Union men believed they had enlisted, even though from Lincoln's vantage, his new proclamation was purely a military strategy. After learning that several men from the Chicago Irish Legion (90th Illinois Infantry) had been arrested for failing to "hurrah for the Negro policies of the administration," the virulently anti-Lincoln *Chicago Times* then asked rhetorically, "Is it any wonder that volunteering has stopped?"[12]

While a civilian may have quietly decided he was not going to risk his life to fight for racial equality, many Union soldiers were far less reticent regarding their motives or lack thereof. Even for those soldiers who admitted to the logic of emancipation as a sound military strategy, accepting Blacks as their social equals or neighbors was unthinkable. They wanted no part of the economic and cultural implications of Black equality. In their letters home, they routinely used language that was widely accepted in their era but would now be considered abhorrent in the twenty-first century. "I shall be very glad when my time is out, they will not get me into it again," wrote Lt. Col. Henry Hubbell of the 3rd New York Infantry to his brother, because "I did not come out to fight for the nigger or abolition of slavery, much less to make the nigger *better* than white men, as they are every day becoming in the estimation and treatment of the powers at Washington." Sec. Lt. Richard Goldwaite of the 99th New York Infantry had proudly enlisted into the army for two years at age thirty-five immediately after the Confederates had fired upon Fort Sumter in April 1861. He was another of many who acknowledged he had enlisted for patriotic reasons but now admitted in a February 1863 letter to his wife that his feelings had changed dramatically since he believed the war was now one over emancipation. These were men who had proudly stepped forward when they thought the war was *solely* about stamping out treason, thereby saving the Union. "I tell you I did not come down here to do such dirty work as to fight to free the niggers. I enlisted to maintain the constitution of the United States," asserted an Illinois soldier in a February 1863 newspaper-published letter. With similar racial anger, Pennsylvanian Sam Croft informed his sister that any future attempts to integrate Blacks into the army as armed soldiers would cause a mutiny. Besides, "Loyal as I am, I would not serve my country with niggers for my companions," Croft insisted.[13]

As anti-draft and antiwar influence strengthened on the home front, that reality also strengthened the soldiers' resolve. Whereas most Union soldiers continued to support the war effort and understood the military logic of Lincoln's proclamation, stories nevertheless abounded of soldiers leaving the army, while some Republican soldiers who stayed opted to switch party allegiance. In fact, numerous soldiers started to liken their position in the military to that of a slave, assuring their families that, unlike a slave, they would leave at the first opportunity. More Illinois soldiers deserted in October 1862 than in any other month of the entire war. Indiana's military authorities reported arresting four hundred deserters per week in December 1862, with many more having escaped army pursuits. In the east, so many soldiers deserted the Army of the Potomac following the September 17 battle of Antietam and then the president's

September 22 Preliminary Emancipation Proclamation that an exasperated Lincoln is said to have remarked, "Sending men to that army is like shoveling fleas across a barnyard; not half of them get there." Furthermore, the lack of proper supplies still seemed omnipresent. After returning to his 10th Massachusetts Infantry encamped at Berlin, Maryland, Charles Brewster wrote to his mother on November 1 stating that the men in his regiment looked like "a crowd of beggars" as they were without clothes, blankets, or shoes. "If I could only get home, the Union might go to Hell," was their common refrain according to Brewster. Some deserted back to their small rural hometowns. Others sought to hide in the open in large cities, including many of the foreign immigrants who returned to their ethnic enclaves seeking anonymity. Some hitched rides with sutlers or civilians while others stole wagons for their journey. One popular ploy for deserters was to pose as part of a telegraph repair work detail. To stem the tide, the War Department issued general orders on September 24 creating its own departmental Provost Marshal General, an office that Congress would not formalize for another six months. That office would oversee each state's Special Provost Marshal, who was to be responsible for tracking down and arresting deserters, as well as uncovering disloyal persons and enemy spies. For a multitude of Northern citizens, it now seemed that the war's initial noble cause and the nation's long-standing tradition of the *voluntary* citizen-soldier had vanished. William Standard unintentionally spoke for many disgruntled soldiers when he wrote to his wife, Jane, "I am bound to get out of this Scrape as soon as possible and get home with my family. This war is the greatest humbug in the world."[14]

***

The growing antiwar sentiment coupled with resentment over Lincoln's Emancipation Proclamation galvanized Democrats and resulted in significant gains for their party in the House and Senate following the November 1862 elections, even though the Republicans held on to the majority in both chambers as well as the presidency. Five key states that Lincoln carried in the 1860 presidential election now sent a Democratic delegation to the House of Representatives. The largest victories were in

Indiana, Ohio, and Illinois, the Midwestern cauldron of antiwar dissent. Indiana's change was the largest, as its congressional delegation flipped from a Republican majority to an overwhelming Democratic majority. Overall, the Republicans saw their sixty-four-seat majority in the House of Representatives dwindle to twenty-seven seats, depending on how the border states were factored in.[15]

The battlefield situation was equally unsatisfactory. Dissatisfied with the Army of the Potomac's apparent slowness following the battle at Antietam in September, Lincoln replaced its commanding general, Maj. Gen. George McClellan, with star-crossed Maj. Gen. Ambrose Burnside on November 7. Burnside's clear orders were to move aggressively against the Rebel enemy. His southward march took the army to the banks of the Rappahannock River opposite Fredericksburg, Virginia, by early December. On December 13, 1862, one failed Union assault after another against the entrenched Rebels resulted in another disastrous Union defeat in that old colonial town. Northern morale and the prospect of a successful end to the war hit new lows. "If I ever live to get out of this they'll never fool me into it again," recounted a Union soldier who survived the Fredericksburg carnage. Civilians who may have romanticized the war at one time or at least sanitized it had by now learned the brutal realities from their friends and family toiling on the battlefield. Many soldiers had long known the real horror and wanted no more part of it, such as Capt. Martin Clark of the 23rd New York Infantry. Clark wrote after the Fredericksburg battle how it was all well and good to see two grand armies preparing to meet on the battlefield "always provided you are at a respectful safe distance to the rear."[16]

Dissatisfaction with Lincoln's Emancipation Proclamation, disappointing military results, harsh winter weather, and a lack of supplies led to desertion on a scale previously unseen in the Army of the Potomac, which was again encamped north of the Rappahannock River with the arrival of 1863. Ample rations, proper rest and medical care, mail, capable equipment, and appropriate welfare support for soldiers' families at home were and are the cornerstones for maintaining good morale for any army in the field. Armies can perform well for a limited time without possessing any of these factors, but never over the long term. In the case of Burnside's army, it seemed to be lacking in every one of those necessities.[17]

Furthermore, many men had not been paid in months, so they had no funds to send back to their families. Knowing that their loved ones were suffering with no money to buy life's necessities became a primary reason for soldier desertion (discussed further in chapter 9). In the same sense, no man not already in the service was going to voluntarily enlist and possibly leave his family to a similar fate as that now being experienced by various neighbors. Given that home front fear, Jane Standard of Fulton County, Illinois, wrote to her husband on February 19, 1863, claiming, "The Democrats won't let another man go to war from [here]." These fiscal realities were not lost on the army's general officers and frustrated them as much as the privates. "Great God! Why can we not have paymasters sent here?" an exasperated Brig. Gen. Robert H. Milroy wrote from Winchester, Virginia, to Maj. Gen. Robert H. Schenck on February 15, 1863, in an attempt to rectify this matter within his command. "The tales of anguish and misery that come to me from my poor soldiers, whose helpless families are dependent upon their scanty pay, which has been withheld six and eight months, is truly heartrending," Milroy wrote. He further warned Schenck how this mistreatment was damaging to army morale, hampered soldier confidence in the federal government, and resulted in the men wanting to get out of the army by any means so they could return home to their hurting families. In another egregious example, the 16th Connecticut Infantry had not received any pay since they left their training camp the prior August. "I think the reason they don't pay us off is that they know that half of the soldiers will run away," wrote one man from that regiment.[18]

Terrible winter weather along with another 13,000 casualties at the January 2, 1863, battle of Stones River near Murfreesboro, Tennessee, sapped army spirit in that Western region. The situation within the Army of the Potomac was hardly any better. That army—still encamped near Fredericksburg—attempted to cross the Rappahannock River in a movement that would draw Lee into the open, however, torrid rain and severe wintry elements resulted in the infamous and disastrous "Mud March" of January 20–22, 1863. That aborted offensive seemed to be the final straw for many within the Union's premier Eastern army as they watched countless wagons and horses bogged down in the mud. All the while, Confederate pickets laughed and jeered at the hapless Yanks from the other side of the river.[19]

A friend of recently retired Ohio senator Orville H. Browning returned from the Army of the Potomac's front lines in late January and reported to Browning how the soldiers' morale was in a grim condition. Multitudes of soldiers were dispirited and felt deceived; all of which, of course, wholly dampened any remaining thought of volunteering for those still at home. These men had volunteered to fight for flag and Union, according to Browning's friend, and would never have enlisted had they known the conflict would be transformed into an abolition war. Capt. Henry Young of the 7th Wisconsin Infantry reported similar news when he wrote to his wife on February 7 informing her that a fellow captain from the regiment was sent back to the state in search of recruits but had yet to secure the first man. "He says the war feeling is entirely played out in Wis." One week later, the Democratic *Daily Empire* in Dayton, Ohio, declared, "The People are tired of the war—are sick of it" and that if Republicans wanted to see more recruits, they could just as easily volunteer instead of disparaging Democrats for allegedly failing to do so. Overall, Union soldier morale had never been lower. In the east, army estimates showed 200 men a day were walking away from their posts, fed up with poor leadership, what seemed like endless defeats, and Old Man Winter's stinging cold and rainy weather.[20]

Shortly after Maj. Gen. Joseph Hooker replaced Ambrose Burnside and assumed command of the Army of the Potomac in late January 1863, army returns indicated that one man in ten had deserted; a figurative no-confidence vote in the army that was unmistakable to both federal officials and the folks back home. By February, General-in-Chief Henry Halleck informed Edwin Stanton that 282,000 soldiers were absent without leave, a staggering number that represented *36 percent* of overall army strength, with most of that number coming from desertions. Just a little more than one month later on March 10 and in an effort to stop the manpower hemorrhaging, Lincoln issued an executive order stating that any man who was unlawfully absent from his regiment would be restored without punishment if he voluntarily returned by April 1. Those who declined Lincoln's amnesty offer faced sterner punishments than heretofore if caught after that date. Maybe Hooker should have breathed a sigh of relief that the numbers were not worse. "If it were not treason to tell the truth," admitted one Pennsylvanian, "I would say that the whole army would run home if they had the chance, the universal sentiment among the men is 'I want to go home.'"[21]

GROWING SOCIAL OSTRACISM AND HOME FRONT SUSPICION

Twenty-two-year-old Beates Swift exemplified the man who underestimated war's realities and, after having "seen the elephant," decided he had experienced enough glory. Swift initially enlisted with ample cash bounty in hand for nine months into the 129th Pennsylvania Infantry in August 1862. A lawyer and staunch Republican abolitionist, Swift had a life-altering experience during the September 1862 Antietam campaign. Though not actively engaged, he suffered a serious foot injury as well as witnessing the horrific toll of battle on his friends and comrades. Within three months, he was sick of war and lying in a military hospital suffering from typhoid fever. With the New Year, Swift was looking to get out of the army by any means necessary, which he accomplished with a complete medical discharge in April 1863. He celebrated his newfound civilian status that first night out over a fine meal with friends, and within one week, his various ailments had miraculously disappeared. His pro-war Republicanism had also vanished and by mid-1863, Swift's diary revealed he had quietly become an antiwar Peace Democrat, tired of abolitionism and with little regard for Black people. On June 2, Swift wrote of a friendly discussion with a friend about Blacks serving in the army. Utilizing perverse logic along with the era's pervasive racism, Swift was all for it because "enough whites have been killed . . . Negroes could be subtracted easier and their loss would not be felt." Yet fearing the possibility of social ostracism over his changed perspective, Swift sensed his new sentiments were ones he should keep to himself, knowing that the vast majority of his friends, family, and community remained steadfast pro-Lincoln abolitionists. Moreover, as an ex-soldier, Swift most likely knew that the soldiers themselves were starting to demand that those stay-at-homes who would not fight or do nothing but complain should keep their mouths shut if they knew what was good for them. Clarence Johnson of the 1st New York Light Artillery boldly illustrated this demand when, in a letter to his parents, he declared that before any civilian started to "talk Copperheadism to a man in blue they must first find out if he is a soldier or a slink," or face the consequences of the wrong guess.[22]

Swift was hardly alone. As we see all too often in our modern era, political self-identification became the primary fault line for social divisiveness throughout the Civil War North and a key determinant as to whether a citizen would embrace or avoid the war effort. Then and now, such "attitude polarization" is driven by the internal sense of moral superiority often attached to partisan political beliefs combined with a disdain for the opposing perspectives and those who hold them. After Republican Marilla Leggett of Cleveland, Ohio, learned of a large Democratic rally in town, she illustrated that precept by snidely remarking to her diary how she assumed all of the local "shags and bobtails" were on hand to attend it. ("Shags and bobtails" was a nineteenth-century pejorative slang expression that referred to a shabby mob, low people, or the rabble.) Using demeaning terms or stereotypes to describe one's enemies is a standard tool of warfare. On the other side of that same coin were Democrats William and Jane Standard of Fulton County, Illinois. Even though William was serving in the 103rd Illinois Infantry—though rather unhappily—the attitude both spouses displayed within their letters to each other routinely assumed that all Republicans were wealthy, boisterous, yet hypocritical cowards who would frantically hire the first substitute they could find if a draft appeared imminent.[23]

Such bitter political prejudices and stereotypes lingered throughout the war and even after. Seneca Thrall, the surgeon for the 13th Iowa Infantry, wrote to his wife in late September 1863 remarking how he now realized that political party ties were older and stronger than family or church connections. With an identical perspective, Mrs. Rebekah Shunk of York, Pennsylvania, penned a post-war letter to the wife of former Confederate major general Howell Cobb, in which she explained how her husband was beaten at the war's beginning because of their antiwar beliefs. "We broke with many friends on account of politics," Shunk confessed, explaining how, like Seneca Thrall, "We felt political bonds to be the strongest on earth, for friendship and religion were trampled in the dust." Shunk further informed Mrs. Cobb that York had been "a splendid copperhead region" that held many friends of the South. She admitted that her one regret, with regards to her "Southern brethren," was that they were "too hard on *all* Northern people, making no distinction, between a low mischievous Yankee and an honest decent person from Pennsylvania." By the same token, Kentuckian Josie Underwood confided to her diary earlier in the war how those political bonds often drew people together who had never held any previous association. Then as now, politics made for strange bedfellows.[24]

Even today in our modern era, we hear of families and long-term friendships torn apart by contemporary politics and its attendant stereotypes. A 2017 Stanford University study by Political Science Professor Shanto Iyengar confirmed what our Civil War ancestors sensed: Political self-identities generate stronger interpersonal attachments than race, ethnicity, religion, or family ties. The study's core finding was that who or what one supports politically is a *choice* while immutable factors such as race or ethnicity are assigned at birth. Consequently, because political identity is a choice, the committed partisan will believe that it offers a lens into a person's humanity that most accurately reflects who that person truly is.[25]

One's opinion on the war's merits and how it was being fought dictated not only the likelihood of a man volunteering into the army, but eventually encompassed who civilian men and women would trust, socialize, or do business with. This attempted loathing of and ostracism toward the political other became the civilian weapon of choice in their public stance either for or against the war. In the case of antiwar dissidents (and as mentioned in the introduction), this home front social "warfare" was their personal statement that not only did they have no intention of volunteering (in the case of men), but they also had no intention of interacting with those who supported such a venture. For numerous civilian men and women, it was their way of protesting and avoiding the war.

In August 1861, a Union man in western Virginia wrote how the "Union people" and the secessionists would no longer allow the other

WINNING AND WEARING.

DOUBTFUL CITIZEN—*Sir, do you sell Copperhead Badges?* I want one. PATRIOTIC STOREKEEPER—*This is the only badge you Copperheads deserve.* (Doubtful citizen wears it for some days.)

"Winning and Wearing" "DOUBTFUL CITIZEN: 'Sir, do you sell Copperhead badges? I want one.' PATRIOTIC STOREKEEPER: 'This is the only badge you Copperheads deserve.' (Doubtful citizen wears it for some days.)" (Library of Congress Prints and Photographs Division)

to visit in their homes. When New York diarist George Strong wrote in early February 1863 of having visited one of his favorite clubs, "for the sole purpose of showing a cold shoulder to two or three of its habitués" so that he could manifest "my desire that we may be better strangers," Strong was firing a salvo in this mounting war of moral self-righteousness. People became highly suspicious of anyone they did not know well or who was not properly pronounced in his or her views. In a letter to Illinois governor Richard Yates written from Kendall County, Byron Shonts made precisely this point. "In times like this there can be no rideing the fence. A man must be on one side or the other," Shonts declared. Kentuckian Frances Peter added to the debate by remarking to her diary that in her contested town of Lexington, a person who claimed indifference or neutrality "has got to mean secesh, as it is generally the one given by secessionists or Copperheads when they are with Union people and do not wish or are afraid to own to their true sentiments." Then of course, there were always those who one St. Louis woman likened to weather vanes: staunch Unionists when in the company of Union people and full "Secesh" when surrounded by secessionists. In essence and as Missouri Supreme Court Justice William Napton expressed to his wife, "Neutrality is a dangerous and disgraceful position and gets Kicks and curses from both sides." Same as today, there often seemed to be very little middle ground.[26]

Lincoln's Emancipation Proclamation announcement in September 1862 and the new militia draft law became the double-barreled triggers for a previously hidden and internecine home front war of violence and communal retribution. It could be especially pronounced in those areas where a significant number of Unionist men were already in the army, leaving the Copperhead discontented behind. An Indiana man wrote to William Lloyd Garrison at 1862's year-end advising the famous abolitionist of just how short the powder keg's fuse had become within the Hoosier State's home front. "A war man here in Indiana can hardly speak or utter his patriotic heart in behalf of our government," lest he light the match. The man then further warned Garrison, "You could not believe the feeling of hatred there is springing up here in the west against New England states." Nor were women immune from engaging in physical violence. One man wrote how they would often meet at lonely crossroads to settle perceived political insults. "The air would be filled with mysterious articles of apparel, piercing, horrid yells would resound," he recalled, "and the sod would be torn up as if a Kansas tornado had visited the spot."

Later telegrams even reported of Copperheads firing random shots into the homes of Union soldiers. In southern Illinois, the wife of Union general John Logan vividly recalled how the middle-aged father of several Union soldiers was abducted, tied to a tree, and then horse-whipped for his family's political beliefs. Another officer's rural home was broken into by antiwar dissenters who destroyed its contents while numerous other Unionists found their farm animals butchered in the night. In some instances, the pillagers cut the hamstrings of horses, thereby rendering the animals useless for farm work.[27]

Even past neighborly courtesies were cast aside as the social friction accelerated. An Iowa housewife wrote to her husband relaying how their once-friendly but now Copperhead neighbor allegedly expressed her conviction that no Union soldier could ever get into heaven. "If she was not my nearest neighbor and I knew it was so, I would never have anything to do with her again," the wife asserted. Another comparable instance saw a Pennsylvania soldier's struggling wife write to him describing how an antiwar neighbor now demanded up-front payment before selling her any wheat. The husband was livid in his reply, reminding his wife how they once had to wait eighteen months to receive a forty-dollar repayment from the neighbor, who would now not advance her five dollars' worth of wheat. Such were the characteristics of Copperheads, wrote the husband. In a similar situation, Dr. James Hosea of Scott County, Indiana, wrote to Gov. Oliver Morton claiming to have attended a Copperhead meeting with fifty-four other men. According to the doctor, the attendees pledged not to help any families whose men had enlisted in the war and to shelter any army deserters who came their way. That scenario was not all that isolated. Thirteen officers from the 123rd Illinois Infantry petitioned President Lincoln to commute a fellow lieutenant's death sentence for desertion because his desperate wife repeatedly begged him to come home and relieve her poverty-stricken condition. "The community in which she lived was opposed to the war," wrote the officers, "and would do nothing to relieve her necessities because her husband was in the Army." Regardless of political beliefs, few Northerners suffered a greater hell on earth than the housewife left alone at home and whose political sympathies were viewed as out of step with the communal majority. For her, political rhetoric was replaced by the fire and brimstone of majority hate. She found herself engaged in a home front war that was not so much to be won or lost, but simply endured. Moreover, this type of collective dissent by antiwar and anti-draft dissidents was not uncommon, even going so far at times as to physically harass the families of Union soldiers so that the man might be forced to desert.[28]

The line between loyal dissent and treasonous activity became blurred for much of the Northern public, especially when considering that the young nation had no real precedent in dealing with internal opposition and dissent in wartime. There was no Department of Justice and in any event, non-military dissent was hardly criminal or cognizable by the federal court system. This discord was especially prevalent in the nation's four slaveholding yet loyal border states, where a contentious form of shadowy war emerged often pitting neighbor against neighbor in a quest for communal power and advantage. "This conflict of opinions and sympathies was nowhere more marked than in Western Maryland," wrote J. Thomas Scharf, who had served in the Confederate army and later wrote a history of western Maryland. Western Marylander and Unionist John Knode felt that antiwar and anti-draft dissent firsthand. He lost his barn, all of his farm tools, his crops, and much of his livestock to an act of arson. His family believed it was because he had married a Southern woman whose kin were quite vocal in their pro-Southern beliefs. The couple's nephew later noted how "It cost something in those days to be joined to a Southern woman in wedlock." Years later, the historian for western Maryland's Washington County wrote how no one-time friend or relation could be trusted anymore because "the son rose against the father, the daughter-in-law against the mother-in-law, and a man's enemies were often the men of his own house."[29]

Border state home guard units, which had supposedly been formed solely for defensive purposes, were alleged to be preying upon suspected dissidents. The matter had even worked its way up to Lincoln's desk. The president wrote to Union major general Samuel Curtis in Missouri expressing his concern that "arrests, banishments, and assessments are made more for private malice, revenge, and pecuniary interest than for the public good." It was not uncommon to see men attend public meetings or speeches with loaded revolvers strapped to their hips. Once dusk fell, many families locked their doors and windows and kept a loaded weapon nearby. Those who had two-story houses often sat upstairs with their downstairs locked and darkened. Innumerable families saw close relationships severed as kin took up arms for each side. "Secession has broken up the dearest social relations in every community of the border slave states," lamented the *Missouri Statesman* in October 1861, as it pitted "son against father, brother against brother, daughter against mother, friend against friend." St. Louis resident Leonard Matthews would have agreed with the paper, later writing how familial divisions often became so intense that "nearly all agreed among themselves not to mention the war at all." Rev. Alexander Cooper remembered how once the war started, the pleasant gatherings in his hometown of Camden, Delaware, became doomed for all time. "The boys, as well as the men, the grown-up women as well as the dear young girls of my boyhood days, arrayed themselves against each other in bitter hostility," Cooper recalled, "and it was sometimes said that one-half of the town did not speak or associate with the other half."[30]

Such sentiments became even more apparent by 1863 with the advent of a new national draft law (to be discussed in detail in chapter 7). In April of that year, Union captain Daniel O'Leary implored his Southern-sympathizing wife at home in Cincinnati to refrain from saying anything in public that would bring about trouble. "You cannot be too careful on that point," he added. In Kentucky, Unionist Josie Underwood told her diary how she was saddened that the war had strained a close friendship despite her attempts to keep politics at arm's length. "We have been such good friends all our lives," she lamented, "but there is restraint in our intercourse now . . . and so visiting together isn't so pleasant." Fellow Kentuckian Frances Peter surely understood how Underwood felt. Her prominent and Unionist Lexington family had been close friends and neighbors with the Morgan family well before the war, but with son John Hunt Morgan now a general in the Confederate cavalry, their mutual warm friendship had turned to antipathy.[31]

Throughout the North, the war not only physically separated family members as husbands, sons, and brothers went off to war, but it also psychologically alienated and split up those families whose members held differing opinions on the war's various political issues; a human trait that exists into the present day in the form of "unfriending" one another on social media over political differences. Typical of that was an Indiana woman who was also a stalwart Republican. She admitted to her army son how her once-loving relationship with her mother's Democratic family had become tense as the war progressed. "You can readily appreciate then when together how constantly guarded each has to be to avoid giving offence," she explained. The sad result, according to the mother, was that there was no longer any desire to seek out the others' company. An Ohio wife living with her resolutely Democratic in-laws begged her pro-Lincoln, soldier husband to never use the word "Copperhead" in his letters and even better, to keep his political comments separate from the rest of his correspondence. As she was obligated to read the letters aloud to his parents, "I know it would kindle strife if I read them as they are and it will also awaken suspicion if I don't read them." She admitted she had skipped over some of the more politically inflammatory passages in the past, especially those where she knew reading them aloud would do more harm than good, but in so doing inevitably aroused the suspicions and subsequent ill will of her in-laws. In Union Mills, Maryland, about thirty-eight miles northwest of Baltimore and four miles south of the Pennsylvania border, brothers Andrew and William Shriver had lived roughly 100 yards apart with their respective kin for decades. Yet the pro-Lincoln Unionism of Andrew's clan and the Confederate sympathies of William's family broke up the close familial bonds during the war years. In other sad instances, family farms that had existed for generations fell apart as the fathers and sons who did the heavy chores were no longer there, physically or in spirit due to differing political views.[32]

A pro-war Northern woman illuminated this overarching state of home front affairs when she wrote to a soldier friend, "The secesh and union do not associate together very much. I think the time will come when they will not speak to each other at all, and I think this will be perfectly right for my part," she explained and then firmly concluded, "I don't want to speak to a secessionist nor do I want one to speak to me." Another woman writing to the same soldier remarked that "peace and harmony" had vanished from her village because "society is broken up" over the war and the ensuing social divisions.[33]

As another means of psychologically avoiding the war, public accommodations such as saloons, hotels, and boardinghouses became identified as either Unionist or "Secesh" and therefore off-limits to the political infidel. Prior to the 1864 presidential election, poet Walt Whitman saw a "poor blear-eyed girl" serving beer in a Brooklyn saloon and wearing a Democratic, George McClellan-for-president badge on her chest. When Whitman asked her if all the girls working there were also for McClellan,

UP TO THE TIMES—BROOKLYN LOYALTY.

isement appeared a week or two since in a Brooklyn newspaper for " A Boarder,
'nion sentiments."

"Up to the Times—Brooklyn Loyalty" "An advertisement appeared a week or two since in a Brooklyn newspaper for 'A boarder, a gentleman of decided Union sentiments.'" (*Frank Leslie's Illustrated Newspaper*, February 6, 1864) she replied, yes, everyone. More importantly, she asserted they would not tolerate anyone working there who was not.[34]

Even the inviolability of the church fell victim to communal infighting. Some houses of religious worship transformed into houses of political allegiance while others were forced to close their doors for months if not years due to the bitterness. Just like their secular brethren, spiritually devout Republicans and Democrats alike portrayed the other as religious heretics. In Vincennes, Indiana, a member of the town's Presbyterian church quipped that its congregants "pray together in church and abuse each other out of church." Unionist Sarah Bovard recognized that lack of Christian charity as she told her diary on September 22, 1861, how her devout Democratic mother stopped by her house on the way to church "just long enough to wish old Lincoln dead." Meanwhile, she expressed her frustration with how numerous Democratic family friends "all look at me as they would look at a thief because I am not a seceder." Mary Sutton of Bethany, Indiana, took her religious fire and brimstone to the next level. She wrote to a friend in May 1863 vowing she would no longer teach known Copperheads in her Sunday school class. Such political heathens, she believed, should be quarantined within their own classrooms as if their political beliefs were a transmissible disease. In Sollarsville, Pennsylvania, Joseph Wise relayed to his cousin in Illinois how the acrimony had risen beyond social circles and was now extending into his town's church pews by writing, "Democrats and Abolitionists pass each other by almost as the ancient Israelites did the Leper." Wise then noted how one Democratic-led church in town had refused to pay its preacher because the man was regarded as a Republican abolitionist. In Greensville, Indiana, Joseph Sills took to the local newspaper in late November 1863 to announce that the congregation of the "Old Baptist" church he had been a proud member of for twenty-seven years had formally expelled him because his Unionist sympathies were no longer welcome in their apparently Copperhead enclave. In Reading, Pennsylvania, John Rhoads wrote to a physician friend relaying how a Democratic minister had hosted an open house party for the town's residents. Yet to the minister's dismay, only his Democratic friends showed up. Rhoads offered up an obvious observation: "the Copperheads were there, and the Union people stayed away."[35]

After anti-Lincoln Democrat Horatio Seymour won New York's governorship in November 1862, Ruth Whittemore of Owego told her brother that everyone might now as well hurrah for Confederate president "Jeff" Davis. Some antiwar neighbors had become so brazen, wrote Whittemore, that they publicly expressed hope that every Northern man who had enlisted to fight against the South would be shot dead. When their community learned of the death of one local soldier, Whittemore's Copperhead neighbors expressed joy at the news, further widening the social divide. In Philadelphia—a Northern city with considerable Southern sympathies—the animosity became so intense at its long-standing "Philadelphia Club" that its elite gentlemen members began to socialize in separate rooms based solely on their Republican or Democratic self-identities. A brawl nearly ensued after one Republican member proclaimed, "This place reeks of Copperheads!"[36]

Peace Democrat–Copperhead antiwar partisans and their immediate descendants left behind relatively few diaries, letters, or memoirs explaining their war and/or draft avoidance beliefs when compared to the post-war literary avalanche of those who held Unionist or pro-war positions. It is reasonable to assume today that they may have practiced some manner of self-censorship within their wartime commentary as a means of avoiding social ostracism as well as deflecting the threat of physical violence against themselves. Alexis de Tocqueville noticed this uniquely American trait approximately twenty-five years earlier when he observed in his classic *Democracy in America* how, "the majority raises formidable barriers around the liberty of opinion: within these barriers, an author may write what he pleases; but woe to him if he goes beyond them."[37]

These citizens recognized what modern psychological studies have confirmed; the act of ostracism is meant to deny the target a sense of communal family or belonging. As a consequence, such potential targets will often intentionally alter their public words and behaviors to avoid suspicion or public rejection. This fear of social excommunication is the rationale behind the current, twenty-first-century's "cancel culture" attack mindset. These modern studies have also shown that the absence of a communal feeling of belonging may even lead to physical or mental illness. Accordingly, the modern, public "virtue signaling" we see so much of today is essentially a proactive attempt by the signaler to avoid any potential social ostracism.[38]

Illustrating those social concerns was Charles Biddlecom, who wrote to his wife in November 1863 only two months after his enlistment explaining how he had already seen enough and intended to get out of the army one way or another. With regards to his actual letter, he urged his wife to not let anybody see it "because if I am found out it will make a devil of a rumpus." Lt. Richard Goldwaite of the 99th New York Infantry relayed to his wife in multiple January 1863 letters how he intended to resign because after serving for almost two years, he was now sick of fighting for Blacks. Yet like Biddlecom, Goldwaite recognized what would happen to him if others discovered his missives. He, therefore, added an addendum urging his wife to "burn all of these kind of letters" after she had read them. Throughout the North, citizens came to realize that they could speak freely if they lived in a like-minded community, though they also sensed they had better curb their tongue if they resided in a town in which they were part of the political minority. Those realizations generally increased as the war progressed. Those that did not often paid a social price. In one typical instance, Triphena Phillips wrote to her army brother from Naples, New York, relaying how she and her classmates ridiculed and had "considerable fun" with the only two girls in her school who dared to openly admit their Copperhead beliefs. "I suppose it is cruel," she confessed, "but we do not give them much peace." In Camden, Delaware, Alexander Cooper recalled how during the war, his Democrats completely silenced themselves as far as public demonstrations went. News of a Union battlefield triumph would generate a Republican street parade and victory bonfires, along with ample shouts and jeers directed at the Democrats. "We had to submit to it. We dared not resent it," wrote Cooper, "without visions of barred doors, prison cells and military dungeons, constantly floating before our eyes." A proud father and Ohio Republican wrote to his son prior to the 1864 presidential election as to how the local Peace Democrats had effectively muzzled themselves for the same reasons Cooper would later write about. "Treason cannot be uttered here, as in days gone by," the father explained, "for they know they will be punished."

It was not uncommon for Union provost marshals to arrest outspoken Democratic partisans for the flimsiest of reasons in the days leading up to an election, though they would only hold them in jail until the election was over. In the years following the war, ex-Union private John Billings wrote of his friends and neighbors who had held to such antiwar beliefs: "There is not one of them who, in the light of later experiences, is not heartily ashamed of his attitude at that time."[39]

Furthermore, many dissenters held a legitimate fear of physical harm carried out by pro-Lincoln partisans as a means of political retribution. Noted Copperhead Joseph Early of Lexington, Ohio, wrote to his brother in May 1863 stating that he was seriously considering relocating to New York for the summer "as the times are so very critical here that no man is safe who does not endorse the whole Negro program of the administration & of the last Congress." When the Republican *Peninsular Courier* in Ann Arbor, Michigan, urged citizens to "kill out treason at whatever cost," antiwar Democrats read between the lines and inferred that physical violence was now an appropriate means of doing so. Numerous Copperheads came to realize that they might be able to condemn the war and/or the draft in a printed manner such as through a newspaper, but to do so by himself out in public was to court physical danger. For innumerable Northerners—whether radical abolitionist or peace-at-any-price Copperhead—"he who is not with us is against us" became their conviction. For various pro-administration partisans, their antiwar neighbors or family members may have had the theoretical right to not enlist or support the North's war efforts, however, they made sure there would be a social price to pay.[40]

As always, the dissension cut both ways. Following Lincoln's election victory in November 1860, the wife of Democrat and then-Mississippi senator Jefferson Davis was heard to say publicly that she would no longer associate with Republicans. A pro-Southern Baltimore woman warned a newly arrived European visitor, "Be very careful about admitting that you are a Unionist in Baltimore" because "people won't like it. . . . It will close all doors to you." Whether radical abolitionist, antiwar Copperhead, or somewhere in between, countless Northern civilians were willing to discard past relationships, opting instead to believe that a person's entire humanity now could (and should) be boiled down into a rudimentary set of political stereotypes.[41]

If the North was going to win the contentious and escalating home front war, it first had to start winning the battlefield war. In order to do so, it became imperative that the Union armies had to slow desertions as well as obtain new soldiers by the tens of thousands. The federal government's answers lay in the regeneration of the Office of the Provost Marshal General in March 1863 and the passing of new federally run conscription measures. The Lincoln administration's assertion of its federal authority and power was about to supplant anything previously seen.

CHAPTER 7

"The People Here Are All of One Mind— That Is to Resist the Draft"

The 1863 Conscription Act, the Provost Marshal General's Bureau, and the Invalid Corps

As the 1863 New Year dawned, it was obvious to both Congress and the army that vast numbers of additional men would be required to fill the ranks up to their desired strength. Included in that calculus was the realization that all of the nine-month regiments raised the prior summer would be heading home later in the spring, as would dozens of the initial New York regiments who initially enlisted for only two years. After crunching all the numbers, federal authorities estimated that another 400,000 men would be required to bring the existing regiments up to their proper standards. Maj. Gen. William Sherman was especially vehement, arguing to his brother, Ohio senator John Sherman, that any man between eighteen and forty-five years of age who did not immediately enlist should be denied the right to vote until the war was over. "The army growls a good deal at the apathy of the nation," wrote Sherman, yet "the people at home quite comfortable and happy yet pushing them forward on all sorts of desperate expeditions." With volunteering having all but ground to a halt due to low civilian morale, rampant desertion from the ranks, a reemerging Democratic Party spirit that seemed to aggressively discourage enlisting, and the growing market demand for labor at pay rates that were outdistancing a soldier's $13 per month, the government recognized that a new national draft law was needed—one that would be run by the federal government rather than the ad hoc state-run systems of five months prior.[1]

Even President Lincoln admitted as much, later conceding in an unpublished letter that the country had obtained all the men it was going to get from purely patriotic motives. Nevertheless, the nation needed more if it was to survive. "You who do not wish to be soldiers, do not like this law. This is natural; nor does it imply want of patriotism," Lincoln acknowledged. "Nothing can be so just, and necessary, as to make us like it, if it is disagreeable to us."[2]

The resulting congressional legislation was known as the Conscription Act of 1863 (also termed the Enrollment Act of 1863), and it went into effect on March 3. The government's basis and rationale for the act was that the federal government had a duty to preserve a republican form of government for the states and its citizens, to preserve public tranquility, and to suppress insurrection if that threat endangered the first two responsibilities. To carry out those obligations, Congress asserted it had the right and duty to call citizens into national service. The act created two classes of potential draftees. Its principal edict stated that all unmarried male citizens—and any foreign immigrant who intended to become a citizen—between the ages of twenty and forty-five were deemed draft eligible as "Class 1." Though initial versions of the bill included eighteen- and nineteen-year-olds, the final law raised the minimum age to twenty, most likely so an adequate supply of ready substitutes could be had for those older, well-to-do men who wished to avoid service. "Class 1" would be the first to be called in any future national draft. Married men between the ages of twenty and thirty-five were deemed as "Class 2" and were also bound by the act's provisions. Younger Class 1 men were taken first, and the older, Class 2 married men were to be called last. New York's *Genesee Valley Free Press* humorously foretold one consequence. Since bachelors between the ages of thirty-five and forty-five were now subject to the draft before married men of the same age, the paper predicted how the country would soon be astounded by the number of recently married men in that demographic based on the number of weddings to occur during the present year. The *Free Press* rightly surmised

A RAY OF HOPE.

Sanguine Spinster.—" No more single men to be appointed to the Police; how fortunate! Wait till they come to draft the bachelors, and then!—"

"A Ray of Hope" "Sanguine Spinster.—'No more single men to be appointed to the Police; How fortunate! Wait till they come to draft the bachelors, and then!—'" (*Vanity Fair*, August 23, 1862)

that bachelors would soon be casting about and should be "prepared to pucker or shoulder arms." A nineteen-year-old New York woman wrote to her brother-in-law on April 15 of that new reality by stating she could not help but laugh upon learning of all the local marriages that had recently taken place.[3]

As with the 1862 Militia Act, there were reasonable family-based, non-medical exemptions available for those men otherwise subject to the draft; these were the exemptions that all of the North generally agreed with. For example, any man who was the lone son of a widow or of aged or infirm parents who depended upon him for their support would be granted an exemption. As would a widowed father who was the sole provider for his children who were under the age of twelve. Convicted felons or those subject to imprisonment in a penitentiary were also excluded. Those men older than age eighteen who already had two brothers in the service and those who were in the service on March 3, 1863, which was the effective date of the new draft law, were likewise exempted.[4]

The Enrollment Act and its provisions hardly came about in a cooperative spirit, however. Congressional debates and negotiations were acrimonious, and it ended up being passed on a highly partisan basis. Democrats relentlessly asserted that Lincoln's Emancipation Proclamation and his ongoing unconstitutional acts were the real reason men remained at home. If he would only reverse himself on such heinous policies, men would again flow into recruiting offices. For their part, Republicans accused the Democrats of doing everything they could to stymie recruitment efforts. "Radical Republican" congressman Thaddeus Stevens of Pennsylvania declared that the Democrats' real motive in urging their partisans to stay home was so they could carry state elections and regain federal power. In the end, all Republicans voted for the bill whereas 88 percent of Democrats opposed it. In just less than two years, the individual states and their governors had gone from holding all power over army recruitment to little more than recruiting agents for Lincoln and the War Department.[5]

To enforce the act, the government enhanced the powers and scope of the Office of the Provost Marshal General, which was originally created the prior year on September 24 and was now to be a separate agency under the auspices of the War Department. On March 17, thirty-six-year-old Col. James B. Fry was chosen to lead the new bureau with the title of Provost Marshal General. Fry then appointed an Acting Assistant Provost Marshal General (AAPMG) to oversee draft enrollment and operations within each state or territory. These men were

James B. Fry (Library of Congress Prints and Photographs Division)

generally honorable Union officers who were no longer fit for frontline duty due to a grievous battle wound, injury, or illness suffered in the course of their service. A provost marshal (with a cavalry captain's rank and pay) was then assigned to every congressional district within each state along with two other men—one being a physician or surgeon—who constituted each district's enrollment board. Two or more men were then assigned as enrollment officers within each district whose responsibilities were to canvass the towns and countryside to enroll all men between the ages of twenty and forty-five who were not otherwise exempt based on the act's provisions. These rolls were then corrected or enhanced by also consulting voter registrations, tax assessment books, and local company payrolls. Each provost marshal would also set up headquarter offices within his congressional district from which the new bureau's enrollment board and officers would operate.[6]

As an added duty, provost marshals were instructed to use hired detectives to seek out and arrest any deserters, stragglers, spies, or those civilians deemed to have committed "treasonable" acts or uttered similar "disloyal" speech. Most provost marshals were reliable Republicans, therefore their interpretations of the words treasonable or disloyal most likely carried significant partisan bias. These men were generally paid a monthly salary plus expenses and certain bonuses. There were obvious limits to their duties, however. Kansas provost marshal Alexander R. Banks explained to one of his detectives how it was essential that honorably discharged soldiers were not to be arrested as deserters merely because they did not have their paperwork on their person. "Sagacity and a prompt and close scrutiny of every case on the part of detectives must be exercised to prevent abuse or hardships of this nature," Banks advised, further explaining that no bonuses would be paid for deserters. In essence, these men became the era's equivalent of what would be known today as internal security or domestic intelligence, performing many functions similar to today's Federal Bureau of Investigation (F.B.I.).[7]

It is difficult to overstate the impact the Provost Marshal General's Bureau had on Northern internal security and draft enforcement from March 1863 through the end of the war in April 1865. For the first time in the nation's history, the federal government had created a bureaucracy designed and sanctioned to bring the full weight and power of federal authority into Northern communities on an almost daily basis. Indeed, the Lincoln administration's belief that it held such authority existed from the war's outset with internal security matters being initially handled by the State Department. That responsibility was then transferred to the War Department in February 1862. Such power was embodied by Secretary of State William Seward's alleged 1861 boast to the British ambassador, Lord Richard Lyons, on his newfound muscle. "I can touch a bell on my right hand and order the arrest of a citizen of Ohio," Seward asserted and then added, "I can touch a bell again, and order the imprisonment of a citizen of New York, and no power on earth, except that of the President of the United States, can release them. Can the Queen of England do as much?"[8]

For the remainder of the war, the fear, anger, and deep resentment the bureau's men generated within the anti-Lincoln, anti-draft, and/or antiwar communities was profound. As historian William Blair described them, "They were the men who pounded on a door in the middle of a night to roust a [purported] traitor out of bed and into a military prison." Pennsylvania Democrat and congressman Charles J. Biddle predicted this new bureau would lead to tyranny since the Keystone State's allotted twenty-five provost marshals could summarily arrest anyone on any pretext, all under the guise of preventing treason. Biddle noted that at the height of its military despotism, ancient Athens saw only thirty such men with that year now known in Grecian history as "the year of the tyrants."[9]

Throughout the North, these men shut down newspapers and arrested and detained citizens indefinitely without formal charges, the right of bail, or grand jury indictment. They restricted citizen travel by requiring passports and issued scores of loyalty oaths to citizens who were forced to sign their pledge of fidelity lest they be sent to or remain in a military dungeon. All without approval or oversight from the civil courts, whom Lincoln believed were wholly unable to mete out the arrests and convictions necessary to stop "disloyal persons" from "giving aid and comfort in various ways to the insurrection." When the anti-Lincoln editor of the Portsmouth, New Hampshire, *States and Union* bitterly predicted that "the rack and guillotines are next," he gave voice to the fear and resentment this new bureau generated throughout much of the North. They came to symbolize the despotic regime the antiwar community alleged was now in power.[10]

As Congress was debating and then passing this monumental piece of life-altering legislation in February 1863, the vast majority of American citizens had little knowledge of what was about to happen to them, for only the nation's largest urban newspapers maintained any type of Washington, DC, political reporting. When they learned of the new law, it hit the nation like a thunderbolt for it represented a seismic shift in the relationship between the federal and state governments as well as the country and its people. No event in prior American history had prepared its citizens to accept the level of nationalism and militarism implied in mandatory conscription. From the beginning, Northern citizens hated the draft, especially the working poor, those philosophically opposed to the war, or those who had decided not to enlist for one personal reason or another. Furthermore, a great chasm had developed between the Republicans and Democrats over the war's aims as well as how best to reunify the country. After all, in the spring of 1863 following the new draft law's enactment, the Union's premier army in the East—the Army of the Potomac—had yet to achieve a signal victory. On the contrary, it had suffered one dismal battlefield failure in Virginia after another. The May 1–6, 1863, defeat at the battle of Chancellorsville was the latest disaster. It followed the December 1862 debacle at Fredericksburg, which was the most lopsided Union defeat yet up to that time. As with the July 21, 1861, battle of First Bull Run, the August 28–30, 1862, battle of Second Bull Run saw the Union forces routed off the field near Manassas, Virginia, only twenty miles west of Washington, DC. Two months earlier, the Army of the Potomac retreated from its position at the gates of Richmond back to the safety of the Washington defenses following the June 25–July 1, 1862, Seven Days battles. Only the September 17, 1862, battle of Antietam in Sharpsburg, Maryland, could be viewed as a strategic victory, though a tactical draw on the battlefield. It was hardly a record that inspired confidence in potential new recruits.[11]

The new Conscription Act quickly became the all-consuming topic of discussion throughout the North. Countless Americans, especially those politically aligned with the antiwar wing of the Democratic Party, decried the act as unconstitutional and swore they would take no part in it. It was seen by many as the last desperate measure of a failed, autocratic regime. Writing from Pennsylvania on March 29, 1863, and only a few weeks after the act's passage, Henry Large wrote to his army brother relaying the news that the new draft was all anyone in their hometown was talking about. Everyone was alarmed, Henry noted, with some vowing that "if they are drafted they will skedaddle" because "unkle sam" was now too strong to resist. Provost Marshal Elijah Low from Maine's fourth district later recalled that while many men dutifully answered the initial draft call, scores of others "from all along the line skedaddled awfully." The widespread feeling of bipartisan cooperation that manifested itself in the war's opening months was broken as each side pointed fingers at the other. General-in-Chief Henry Halleck certainly felt the winds shifting. He complained in a private letter to Maj. Gen. Stephen Hurlbut how "The patriotism of some of our old Democratic friends seems to have been destroyed by the heat of party spirit." Whereas Democrats had argued for more than a year that there was an unequivocal difference between the nation's republican form of national government and any current administration, Republicans now maintained that amid an internal civil war with the nation's survival at stake, there was no difference, they had to be viewed as one and the same. "Loyal opposition" became an oxymoron. Party and state were now practically fused together as one.[12]

In Hamilton, Ohio, a Copperhead–Peace Democrat declared to a soldier friend following the act's passage, "The people here are all of one mind—that is to resist the draft. They all say that they will rebel against it . . . if they do I am in." His remark was hardly mere hyperbole for antiwar and anti-draft home front resistance did indeed intensify over the next eighteen months. Nevertheless, the soldier's reply to his civilian friend was typical of how toiling Union soldiers viewed such men who remained at home: "Your boast about resisting the draft is mere cowardly bombast. You and all of your stripe lack the courage to lift an arm to oppose the draft. You will, no doubt, purchase a revolver, and talk loudly about resistance, as all cowards do; but mark me for the expression, you will never use them." In fact, gun store owners in some communities did quickly sell out of revolvers, shotguns, and related ammunition following the act's commencement. Illinois' *Jacksonville Journal* reported only two weeks after the act's passage that the town's stores were "completely drained" of revolvers, knives, and buckshot. Indiana's *Richmond Palladium* likewise informed its Republican audience how "certain leading reptiles" of the Copperhead persuasion were buying up all available guns to resist the draft. Anti-draft and antiwar sentiment in the Hoosier State became so intense that Col. Henry Carrington warned Washington, "Southern Indiana is ripe for revolution." As a consequence, Carrington reported that Department of the Ohio commander Gen. Horatio Wright had ordered him to immediately stop the sale of arms within Indiana.[13]

What were usually words of protest in the first two years of the conflict now became mixed with physical violence. In Sullivan, Illinois, John Wilburn wrote to a cousin in the army asserting how "all the people here says that they wont go in this D——d war to free nigers that they won't stand the draft for it is contrary to the constitutuin." His cousin's reply was typical: Twenty armed men from his company could easily and happily enforce the new law throughout the entire county if they only had the chance.[14]

The new 1863 national draft law—like its 1862 state militia forerunner—was never intended to forcibly drag unwilling men into the army. Rather, it was designed to get more men to voluntarily enlist rather than suffer the era's social disgrace of having been conscripted. President Lincoln himself acknowledged this key point. It did not matter to the government—initially anyway—if those men were substitutes procured by the originally drafted man or the government.[15]

That communal shame of having been drafted was reinforced by the realization that the Office of the Provost Marshal General was tasked not only with administering and enforcing the draft, but also with arresting army deserters, bounty jumpers, and spies. This reality led to the unpleasant inference that a man caught up in the former category was considered a likely candidate for the latter. In other words, a drafted man was considered a de facto skulker who was unwilling to fight and ready to desert at the first opportunity.

As in 1862, the government utilized its carrot and stick approach; the carrot again being the ample cash bounties offered to men who would willingly enlist. To help facilitate recruiting, government authorities plastered buildings with posters touting the benefits of enlisting, placed patriotic appeals in newspapers, and wrote letters to prominent citizens urging them to assist the government in its current mission. Failing that, then came the stick in the form of threatened conscription via the drafts that would follow if towns failed to generate their enlistment quotas. That stick, according to Maryland's AAPMG, Capt. Henry C. Naill, was the most effective tool of all. Everyone knew no bounties were paid to men who were drafted.[16]

For those Americans who recalled the *voluntary* aspect of the citizen-soldier as well as the individualism bequeathed from their revolutionary forefathers, the federal government's new mandatory conscription policies were seen as tyrannical. It cut against the grain of American individualism that had dominated the nation's culture since colonial times. A free man's citizenship and the rights he held began with acts of individual choice. The government existed because of the free (White) man's consent, rather than authoritarian decrees that flowed downward from monarchs or governments to the individual. The level of nationalism, as well as militarism implied in the draft law, was without precedent in the young nation's history.[17]

For many men and their families—especially the wealthier or at least the more financially secure ones—no amount of cash bounty could induce them to enlist, despite the government's carrot-and-stick efforts. Only 2.7 percent of the Union armies' enlisted men came from well-off businessmen or the professional class. As a consequence, enlistment bounties became disproportionately attractive to the working class and irrelevant to the affluent. In one typical case, thirty-year-old Harvard Law School graduate and rising attorney Joseph Choate wrote to his wife in August 1862 as to how the new militia draft had created "some excitement and a little squirming." He declared the national government was entitled to the service of its people and even their lives if necessary, but then in his next letter mocked the absurd fear among various cowards who were trying to claim an exemption. Yet for all such bravado and criticism, Choate never volunteered his services and, by all accounts, never seriously contemplated the matter. For the secure or wealthy, their goal was to remain at home overseeing their farms, families, or businesses. They were prepared to pay anything to avoid being drafted and then sent to the front—another reminder of the "rich man's war, poor man's fight" dictum. To accomplish that goal, any man had several options in addition to the dependent support exemptions mentioned earlier.[18]

COMMUTATION

Avoiding the draft was initially quite legal and straightforward, and it resulted in some of the deepest home front polarization throughout the entire war. First, any drafted man could circumvent service simply by paying a $300 fee to the federal government through what was known as the "Commutation Clause." Paying that fee, however, bought its payer an exemption for the upcoming draft only, not for future levies, if any. It was a well-intentioned nod to the workingman as the intent was to hold down the prices paid for substitutes. The logic was that no man would pay an exorbitant price to hire one when he could simply pay $300 to the government and be done with it. The government, in turn, would then use those accumulated funds to pay bounties. Nevertheless, $300 was an immense sum of money for the time and was roughly equivalent to the *annual* wages of a man performing unskilled manual labor. Even so, the government would discover in little more than a year and to its dismay just how many men were willing to find $300 to avoid the war. In a typical instance, Mary Vermilion informed her soldier husband, William, on March 9, 1863—only six days after the act went into effect—how his thirty-five-year-old eldest brother already had his commutation money in hand in case he was drafted. Mary quoted her brother-in-law as saying he "would rather pay $1000 than be shot at one round." In addition, Mary also reported how William's twenty-five-year-old younger brother felt having to go into the service for three years would financially ruin him. From Mary's perspective, having to pay $300 would indeed *nearly* ruin him, but doing so was certainly the lesser of two evils. Commutation was especially problematic to the working-poor immigrant communities, which one study showed were two to ten times less likely to be able to buy their way out of the draft than native-born citizens. It was, however, a sum the well-off could easily afford and immediately brought about class warfare accusations, despite its objectives.[19]

Innumerable working-class citizens and soldiers came to loathe the moneyed man who never missed a public opportunity to pontificate in favor of the war yet didn't hesitate to come up with $300 to avoid putting on a blue uniform or that of his son(s). "Those men that are the most active at public meetings in favor of prosecuting the war will be the last to risk themselves," Joseph Dobbs assured his wife back home in Danbury, Connecticut, shortly after the Enrollment Act's passage. Dobbs then predicted, "They talk loudly . . . but you will find that when they are drafted they will to a man pay their 300 dollars. I have got the utmost contempt for that class of men." The well-known humorist "Artemus Ward" described these men as "willing to sacrifice all their wife's relations on the altar of liberty. They would fight from dawn to darkness, with wind for ammunition, provided the enemy was far enough distant; they would bleed, if the loss of blood was not too great, provided they could stay at home." Such hatred was especially bitter if the individual also happened to be an abolitionist, who many ambivalent Northerners blamed for the war in the first place. "If you could only be here and see them sneak when they thought the draft was coming you wouldn't blame me for being mad when I thought of them," Emily Harris angrily explained to her husband. Like untold other housewives opposed to the war, Harris believed that any man who approved of the war and its causes should be more than willing to go and fight. She resented that all they had to do was pay over a "paltry sum" to secure their safety while a poor man with a wife and children who did not have the available funds was forced to go against his will. "Is slavery any worse than this?" Harris asked rhetorically. "This is the freedom our Country has boasted so much of, is it?"[20]

Substitutes and Crimps

As in 1862, a drafted man could also legally skirt service by hiring a personal substitute to go in his place, with the fee to be theoretically negotiated between buyer and seller, though in reality the price was set by the age-old concept of supply and demand. Only a man who was not eligible for the draft, such as a foreign alien or a man older than the age of forty-five or younger than age twenty, could offer himself as a substitute. These were often men like forty-two-year-old Theodor Heinrich Brandes, who emigrated from Germany in 1853 and had worked as a day laborer ever since. With little regard for or understanding of the war's deeper issues or meaning, Brandes volunteered to serve as a nine-month substitute for a man twenty years his junior in September 1862, collecting $800 as his substitute's fee in the process. It was not his war, nonetheless, for Brandes and scores of other men like him, that sum of money represented the golden opportunity to gain his "American dream." In his case, Brandes rolled the dice and lost. He died from chronic diarrhea in a Union field hospital in mid-June 1863, only a few weeks from his discharge date. Procuring a substitute like Brandes exempted the man who paid for the substitute only as long as his replacement remained in the army and was serving honorably. If the substitute deserted or was otherwise dishonorably discharged, then the originally drafted man was obligated to take his place. It was also not unheard of for a man to sign up as a substitute, then immediately turn around and hire another for himself at a lesser fee, thereby pocketing the difference as a quick, tidy profit.[21]

Since an 1863 draftee's term of enrollment was for three years, hiring a substitute as a perceived once-and-done payment was the preferred option for those who could afford the going rates for a substitute. This logic was the twenty-twenty hindsight utilized by Justin Cozad in his unpublished memoir. Cozad wrote how he had actually hoped to be drafted early on, which he was in his hometown of Cleveland. He had no intention of serving in the army, however, so he easily bought a substitute for $300 "rather than make a fuss." This was far more preferable, Cozad explained, than having to pay $1,000 or more in 1864–1865 for a substitute. But again and regardless of one's logic, the fees were such that the average workingman could hardly afford them. In some sad instances, homefront wives reported to their husbands of cash-strapped neighbor families so desperate to keep the husband out of the war that they were forced to sell the family farm in order to raise the funds to buy a substitute.[22]

In short order, the growing business of procuring substitutes gave rise to recruitment or substitute brokers, who were known disparagingly in some quarters as "crimps." They acted as middlemen in finding substitutes for draft-eligible men and then providing those substitutes to the Union army, always taking a healthy commission from both the buyer and the substitute's paid bounty in the process. Some of the broker's tactics were reported as despicable, such as having his assistants drug or get drunk recently arrived immigrants or even unsuspecting, native-born young men. They would forge their enlistment papers and then turn these lads over to the army before they completely sobered up. New York provost marshal Theodore Bronson knew of such mistreatments, explaining how he had always tried his best to ensure that recruits first mustered in by him were treated fairly because Bronson knew that a swindled recruit "has neither the courage nor the disposition to face a battery." Other unsavory broker methods included bribing enrollment agents and provost guards to accept men wholly unfit for military service due to age, infirmities, or past felonious convictions. In one instance, a wounded veteran was rejected three times when he tried to reenlist on his own; however, the examining surgeon and mustering officer then told him on the sly that they would gladly accept him as an $1,100 substitute. Thirty-four-year-old and recently married Leonard Matthews was a successful St. Louis businessman who, like countless others, sought a substitute because he had no desire to disrupt his home and business by being forced to serve in the army. Yet he became frustrated with what he viewed as rampant collusion between the brokers and corrupt provost guards attempting to "corner" the market. Matthews decided to avoid the middleman and advertise for a substitute on his own. He was eventually able to find one for far less than the $1,300 the brokers were demanding.[23]

One enterprising ex-convict set up a substitute broker business with two offices in New York City. Knowing who all the thieves and rogues were from his past life, as well as their illegal deeds, he would routinely give them the option of enlisting into the army as one of his substitutes or having all of their activities reported to the police. In this dangerous

THE RECRUITING BUSINESS.

VOLUNTEER-BROKER (*to Barber*) "Look a-here—I want you to trim up this old chap with a flaxen wig and a light mustache, so as to make him look like twenty; and as I shall probably clear three hundred dollars on him, I sha'n't mind giving you fifty for the job."

"The Recruiting Business" "VOLUNTEER BROKER (*to Barber*) 'Look a-here—I want you to trim up this old chap with a flaxen wig and a light mustache, so as to make him look like twenty; and as I shall probably clear three hundred dollars on him, I sha'n't mind giving you fifty for the job.'" (Library of Congress Prints and Photographs Division) manner, he helped to fill the army's ranks with society's vermin while making quite a nice living, while it lasted. Others supplied the military with what one newspaper described as "children, idiots, cripples from birth, persons of disease of longstanding, and rebel deserters." Still others engaged in what was known as "doping," which meant finding an old or run-down human wreck, prettying the man up with a bath, haircut, and a shave, then perhaps dyeing his hair, adding some rouge to his cheeks, and dressing the man up in a decent suit before presenting him to the recruiting officer.[24]

The whole process became thoroughly organized. A broker's assistants or "runners" would stand ready at the Eastern docks prepared to round up uneducated and confused immigrants as they ambled off a just-arrived passenger ship's gangplank. In some instances, brokers were permitted to board the immigrant ships before anyone disembarked. Once aboard, they would cajole and reassure the nervous Europeans with all manner of promises. If his lies were ineffective, the broker would then resort to threats and intimidation, which often persuaded the confused and terrified foreigner to join the army. The net result was that many of these immigrants were legally bound to the broker and then shanghaied into the federal army before they ever set foot on American soil.[25]

The surviving record book of Detroit brokers Thomas Daley and John A. Mack gives insight into the brokers' activities and recordkeeping. These self-styled "military agents" were plying their trade right up to Robert E. Lee's surrender on April 9, 1865. In one transaction dated April 1, the entry shows Daniel W. Finch credited as a substitute for August A. Rasch within Detroit's third ward. Finch was paid $635, leaving a "net profit" of $15. Other entries show various expenses, such as how much was paid to their runner and paying off army provost guards and city constables. To further gather up business, brokers also placed ads in newspapers that targeted their services toward men of means desperate to avoid the next draft specifically and the front lines in general. A broker's runners were often placed in low-bounty areas ready to recruit eager men who were willing to be transported to a high-bounty town or state.[26]

As a down-on-his-luck Canadian, thirty-nine-year-old James McCoy was one such man who was recruited from his hometown and sent elsewhere. He was recruited in Quebec and then arrived in Massachusetts, where he enlisted on December 23, 1863, after collecting a $627 bounty, which was more than double the norm at the time. McCoy never bothered to discuss or even inform his wife of his actions until he wrote to her on January 17, 1864, from his regiment's camp at New Berne, North Carolina. Another small study on this topic revealed the depth of enlistment apathy. It showed that only about 20 percent of the substitutes hired in eastern Pennsylvania's eighth draft district officially resided in that district. Another 20 percent lived in other parts of Pennsylvania, however, the remaining 60 percent were recruited from outside of the Keystone State. Such schemes prompted one provost marshal to declare that the substitute brokerage business had become so efficient that new recruits were "shipped from one point of the United States to another as cattle are shipped and sold." Others noted how such tactics put Northern crimps in the same league as Southern slave traders.[27]

Any civilian working or living in a major urban area knew of the brokers' existence, and practically no one had anything good to say about them. "Whatever may be their proper name, it is difficult to speak positively; but one thing about them is certain—the greater number are consummate scoundrels," wrote an English visitor. Illinois' AAPMG, James Oakes, later opined, "The strong hand of the government should be laid upon the whole heartless crew of substitute brokers, whether principles or subordinates." Connecticut's AAPMG Charles C. Gilbert concurred with Oakes' assessment and then pointed out how the substitute himself was often of the lowest possible worth to the army. "There is no promotion for the substitute from the ranks, & he knows it," wrote Gilbert, "no 'Esprit de Corps' in him, & his only inducement is money with the expectation to embrace the first opportunity to desert the service & jump another bounty." Writing from Rappahannock Station, Virginia, on September 6, 1863, Pvt. Albert Wilder observed how great numbers of new recruits were arriving daily in the camps but none for his 39th Massachusetts Infantry so far. "And hope there will be none for it," he added, "if they make the trouble the rest do. They have to be guarded every night and day." Fred Lucas of the 19th Connecticut Infantry noted in August and early September 1863 how of the 137 men just arrived in his camp,

"Bounty Brokers Looking Out for Substitutes" (Library of Congress Prints and Photographs Division)

only 3 were drafted; the rest were substitutes anxious to desert at the first opportunity. In fact, he wrote that a handful had already been shot, with three mortally wounded while trying to escape. The last thing the army needed, Lucas opined, was "the addition of a crew of thieving, riot loving 'scape-graces as the majority N.Y. and Connecticut conscripts are."[28]

The men in the ranks quickly realized how the typical substitute was rarely a worthy soldier. They possessed few of the traits that governed real men, recalled Sgt. Austin Stearns of the 13th Massachusetts Infantry. Then with obvious annoyance toward those still at home, Stearns added,

"To think that men in town of the loyal north should send down such to be [our] companions . . . of all the worst specimens of humanity, here they were." Pvt. Alonzo Searing wrote to his sister from his camp near Beverly's Ford in northern Virginia on September 5, 1863, of having been assigned to guard and escort the newly arrived substitutes, draftees, and bounty men—the kind Austin Stearns referred to. After witnessing the execution of five Union deserters from the 118th Pennsylvania Infantry, Searing wrote that it was a hard sight to watch but that "I would rather have ten volunteers for service down here than fifty of these bounty jumpers and conscripts, for many of them are newly arrived foreigners, knowing little about our country . . . and simply enlist or take a bounty for what money they can make out of it. And thousands of them desert at the first opportunity." Thirty-nine-year-old Pvt. Aungier Dobbs concurred with that widely held opinion after seeing the latest army additions. It "would be better if one fourth who is now here was at home," he wrote to his wife in July 1863. The veteran soldiers sensed that for the majority of such men, enlistment cash bounties and then an opportunity to desert were what they sought most. It was maddening for the soldiers toiling away in the front lines to realize that other than boys who had recently turned eighteen years old, home front enlistment generated by a patriotic impulse was a long-dead motive in the aggregate. Between the high bounties offered to potential recruits and astronomical fees paid to substitutes, the war had become a profit-motivated business for the majority of those draft-exempt men now willing to put on a blue uniform.[29]

The frustration these Union soldiers felt regarding the quantity, quality, and demographic of the typical substitute was generally on the mark. When hundreds of substitutes started pouring into the 2nd New Hampshire Infantry in early December 1863, veteran Martin Haynes realized immediately that "most of them are foreigners, and many of them are just watching for an opportunity to desert." Watching over this "human vermin" was an unwelcome challenge to the regiment's veterans, who often had to send out company detachments scouring the countryside for deserters. In writing the regiment's history, Haynes later concluded that it was "no credit to New Hampshire that she turned such a mass of rubbish loose into her old veteran regiments." Haynes and the 2nd New Hampshire were hardly alone. In fact, 75 percent of the men who entered the Union army in 1863 as a result of that year's draft were substitutes. In addition, a study on substitute demographics revealed that substitutes were overwhelmingly foreign-born since foreign aliens were draft exempt, regardless of whether their substitution took place in an Eastern or Western urban or rural area.[30]

Despite such home front contention, paying a commutation fee to the government or hiring a substitute was not unique or uncommon in the nation's brief history. In an unpublished September 1863 memorandum, Lincoln acknowledged that point, writing how the substitute provision was "in accordance with an old and well known practice." Nor was this patriotism by proxy objected to by the public. To be sure, numerous Northern draftees who hired and paid for a substitute viewed their "representative recruit" as their own contribution to the Union cause that was every bit as patriotic as the farmer who stayed home to grow food for the army. In fact, starting with the 1863 draft, provost marshals occasionally used the term "representative recruits" in place of the word "substitutes" within their reports. In the larger picture, however, the downside of allowing a man to furnish a substitute inevitably reduced the available manpower pool with each successive draft. Furthermore, the president noted how there would have been a much greater outcry if those provisions were omitted. In reality, both long-standing options hailed from European traditions that went back a century or more. States used decentralized militia drafts during the eighteenth-century Indian wars as well as in the 1770s to maintain the Continental Army during the Revolutionary War. Several proposals were put forth by Congress during the War of 1812; however, that conflict ended before any could be utilized. State and local colonial governments routinely excluded men of power and fortune from the militia lists and replaced them with men from a lower social class. So while the practices were not uncommon, they still rubbed those the wrong way who could not afford either.[31]

THE INVALID CORPS

As previously discussed, various recruits realized shortly after beginning their enlistment that they were not cut out for the soldier life; that the day-to-day sobering realities were a far cry from the quick martial glory they had envisioned. Some immediately tried to extricate themselves from the army, such as seventeen-year-old Richard Jackson, who begged his father in June 1861 to get him discharged because of the poor food and treatment but by using the technical argument that he was underage. A year later, some soldiers were so emotionally or physically worn out that they urged their service-eligible friends and family members not to enlist, while others began contemplating how to get out, including allowing themselves to be captured by the Confederates and then paroled. As of April 1863, a new opportunity presented itself for desperate men to escape the front lines though they would not be sent home. This new opening was the creation of what was initially known as the Invalid Corps, which was placed entirely under the direction and jurisdiction of the Provost Marshal General's Bureau.[32]

The federal government's creation of the Invalid Corps in April 1863—later renamed the Veteran Reserve Corps (VRC) in March 1864—was meant to address the army's insatiable manpower needs and the growing shortfall in that area. The government's rationale for the corps' creation was to provide relatively light military tasks and the stable employment that went with them to those soldiers who were unfit for further frontline campaigning due to battle wounds, injury, or disease suffered in the course of their duty. By so doing, the army would not only honorably distinguish those worthy soldiers, it would free up the healthy and vibrant soldiers now performing those rearguard duties for hotter work at the front. Perhaps just as important, as the Elkton, Maryland, *Cecil Whig* pointed out to its readers, maimed or debilitated soldiers would now be provided for via service in the Invalid Corps. Therefore, this supposedly eliminated the deterrent of men not enlisting for fear that a war injury would deprive them of the means of supporting their families and thereby leaving them susceptible to the cold fate of charity.[33]

The responsibilities for what the government described as a "Corps of Honor" included policing duties such as escorting prisoners, serving as

HONORABLY DISCHARGED SOLDIERS!

ALL WHO DESIRE TO ENLIST IN THE

INVALID CORPS!

TO PERFORM
PROVOST AND GARRISON DUTY,

ARE REQUESTED TO CALL AT

North-East Cor. Broad & Spring Garden Sts.

And present their Discharges to the undersigned, who is authorized
to Enlist Men for the above Corps.

Lieut. GEORGE WAGNER,

RECRUITING OFFICER,

Late of the One Hundred and Tenth Regiment, Pennsylvania Volunteers.

Invalid Corps Recruiting Poster (Library Company of Philadelphia) a provost guard, or garrisoning Northern forts and prisoner of war camps for those healthy enough to shoulder a musket. Those men who were too weak for such duty or had lost limbs were tasked with responsibilities such as overseeing draft operations in Northern towns, working as hospital stewards, or perhaps serving as clerks, orderlies, and cooks. The government was generally correct in its assessment. "A number of the officers had but one arm and many were lame and the men as a general thing looked rather pale and not able to stand much fatigue," was how a Washington, DC, diarist described a review of some Invalid Corps men in November 1863. By the summer of 1865, more than 60,000 enlisted men and less than 1,100 officers had served in this new corps.[34]

In a somewhat similar fashion to those healthy, service-age civilian men who joined home guard units, and despite the government's laudable intentions, the Invalid Corps quickly acquired a reputation among the frontline soldiers as just another safe haven for the so-called cowards and shirkers. The corps became known as the "cripple brigade," with its men known as "Condemned Yanks." It further became the subject of laughs and ridicule when everyone realized that the Invalid Corps' initials—I.C.—was also the abbreviation used by the army to designate any worthless supplies that were "inspected—condemned." There was even a popular song from 1863 titled "The Invalid Corps" whose lyrics poked fun at the new organization. Such jeers and sarcasm were part of the reasons that led to the corps' name change less than a year after its creation.[35]

Brigade and regimental commanders in the field began to use the Invalid Corps as a convenient dumping ground for any wounded or ill junior officer who was considered useless or a troublemaker but whose field conduct was not yet sufficient to warrant dismissal from the service. Capt. John De Forest noted in his final report and history of the Veteran Reserve Corps that commanding officers "were apt to decide that anyone would do for an invalid corps who had incurred the necessary amount of physical disability, no matter what might be his character as a man or his history as a soldier." Moreover, any man who voluntarily enlisted into or sought a transfer into the corps had his manhood questioned *if* his debilitating condition was not physically obvious, such as a missing limb. To mid-nineteenth-century Americans, physical or mental disability was associated with dependency and emasculation, neither of which were hallmarks of martial masculinity. As for illness, army doctors were advised to view any soldier whose symptoms were not obvious as a shirker. Any man who did present any tangible sign of a mental trauma was usually treated only for his physical symptoms. If the physician could find nothing obviously wrong with the man, he was considered a malingerer who should be returned to the front lines post haste.[36]

The battle-hardened volunteers fighting, marching, and sleeping in Southern mud invariably felt bitterness toward *any* arm of the service whose express purpose was to keep its members away from the firing line, regardless of the reasons. For example, this scorn was also directed toward "the heavies," those heavy artillery units comfortably garrisoned in the many forts surrounding Washington, DC, and whose sole purpose was to protect the North's capital city from Rebel invasion. Such men were referred to by the frontline troops as "band box soldiers." From the perspective of numerous infantrymen down South, they were doing all of the hot work. All of those various rearguard units, such as the Invalid Corps, were just pomp and circumstance mostly filled with soft men unwilling to face hard duty. Sgt. Gustave Magnitsky summarized this feeling after he was medically transferred into the Invalid Corps in December 1863 against his wishes. "I hate to be in the Invalid Corps," he complained to his former commander, "because there are too many imposters in it. I do not like to be considered one of them." Capt. Henry Blake of the 11th Massachusetts Infantry echoed Magnitsky's opinion, later writing that the honorable soldiers he knew who were crippled in battle did not want to go into the Invalid Corps, believing their good name and whatever little fame they had earned would be tarnished by such an association.[37]

Dr. Joseph Tunnicliff, Michigan's state military agent at Washington, affirmed in his 1863 year-end official report what all soldiers knew; that there were those men who always became ill or injured just before the next battle or managed to drift back toward the field hospitals with various ailments once the shooting started. Accordingly, some of those "able-bodied shirks" and "malingerers" did indeed look for a transfer into the Invalid Corps after its creation, which led to its negative reputation among the good men. "This fact has become so patent," wrote Tunnicliff, "that a dread of being thus assigned to [Invalid Corps] duty is nearly universal with our [honorable] soldiers." In his post-war report, Illinois AAPMG James Oakes likewise bemoaned the "causeless and senseless jealousy and dislike manifested toward the corps by soldiers of active regiments in the field."[38]

Instead, those crippled men whose wounds or illnesses were not obvious often sought a full discharge on the grounds of total unfitness for any type of duty as a soldier. A typical example was twenty-year-old William Greene, who wrote to his mother on December 7, 1864, from his Washington, DC, hospital bed explaining how the authorities were examining hospitalized men for Invalid Corps duty on a daily basis. "Some get in, some get sent to the front, some get Discharged. I think I would like the latter very well," Greene admitted. This plea for a discharge stood in stark contrast to those men who had lost arms or legs. They often desired to somehow remain in the service because as one Invalid Corps veteran later recalled, "They began to appreciate the fact that a man minus one of the more important members of his body was lucky if he could get anything to do to earn a living."[39]

A correspondent for Maine's *Portland Daily Press* wrote to the paper from Washington, DC, in early May 1864 expressing satisfaction that the newly renamed Veteran Reserve Corps was to be restored to its original footing as a corps of honor but lamented that was necessary because "by culpable carelessness it had been allowed to degenerate into a refuge for cowards and shirks." The author admitted there were ample brave and deserving men in the corps; however, "so many of the other class had been smuggled in that few good soldiers were willing to be associated with them."[40]

Potential officers, on the other hand, were generally viewed in a different light due to the difficult hurdles necessary to obtain an officer's commission in the Invalid Corps. Those officers wounded in battle were given preference over those hindered by illness, and it soon became apparent that most of the candidates had indeed suffered grievous physical wounds in the line of duty. Yet as with the Regular or volunteer army, there were those men who had the necessary influence to secure comfortable positions within the corps, well away from the dangers of battle. Thirty-one-year-old Newton Colby, for example, wrote to his father in late September 1863 imploring him to secure the strongest possible disability certificate so that he could land a well-paying officer's position in the Invalid Corps. This plea followed his dismissal from the service due to illness earlier that month and his subsequent lack of current income. There were more than 1,400 applications for officer positions at that time, explaining Colby's sense of urgency. Colby must have missed the irony when he penned a January 1864 follow-up letter to his father. In it, he ridiculed the Invalid Corps commander of a nearby Washington, DC, barracks with who, Colby admitted, he was only somewhat acquainted. The commander also happened to be the son of Pennsylvanian George Woodward, the Democratic chief justice of the Keystone State's Supreme Court who once ruled against the draft's legality. "He is a great hearty looking young fellow—weighing about 200 and as robust looking an *Invalid* as you ever saw," Colby sarcastically noted regarding the barracks' commander. "How he got the place— except it was because his Father is a notorious Copperhead judge . . . I am sure I can't imagine."[41]

Post-war analysis of the Veteran Reserve Corps' officer ranks revealed that out of every one hundred of its officers, eighty-two were disabled by battle wounds, thirteen by disease, and five by accidental injuries. Officer applications required the applicant to provide his complete military history, evidence of good character and judgment, along with the recommendations of three officers he had previously served under. Due in part to these rigorous requirements that soon became public knowledge, Col. Charles Johnson was able to write to his wife from Indianapolis in March 1864, claiming that his Invalid Corps' sky-blue officer's coat was "a pass-port into society" and that it afforded him several public gestures of respect that were never offered to officers in any other branch of the service.[42]

Overall, the Invalid Corps/Veteran Reserve Corps succeeded in its mission of providing necessary military duties to honorable men who gave their bodies to preserve their country. On the few occasions when VRC men needed to use their muskets, John De Forest acknowledged they could do so "with as much alacrity and steadiness as other troops; it has shown that it could behave in battle as became a corps of veterans." While one could certainly find skulkers and shirkers hiding within its ranks, it would be unfair to make a sweeping generalization that such men were the rule and not the exception.[43]

CHAPTER 8

"The Fear of Being Drafted Makes One Almost Sick"

Resenting and Evading the Draft

As was the case with the 1862 militia draft, a common evasion tactic for the drafted man was to seek an official medical exemption on account of an illness or physical disability—perceived or otherwise. The financial incentive was huge, for a medical exemption meant that man would not have to pay the $300 commutation fee or buy a substitute. The excuses men came up with were amazing in some instances. The 9th Connecticut Infantry's colonel learned from his wife how one mutual acquaintance had obtained an exemption because he was supposedly suffering from an ingrown toenail. "There are very few enrolled or drafted men who do not claim disability of some kind, and of course demand exemption," stated Dr. Benjamin Morgan from Vermont's first congressional district. According to the doctor, these men invariably showed up "armed with certificates and testimonials" attesting to their chronic rheumatism, heart or lung disease, or anything else they had ever heard of for which any type of exposure to military duty would be life-threatening. New firms were created solely to attest to a drafted man's physical or mental disability. For a fee, an experienced attorney and an "elastic" country doctor would supply the required affidavits. Completely concurring with Morgan was Dr. Winston Somers from Illinois' seventh district. Somers observed how when his staff attempted to walk or move the men rapidly, "they generally pretend to be as stiff as a *foundered horse*. We feel as if we were among the lame, blind, dumb, and halt."[1]

After Wisconsin's forty-year-old Gilbert Claflin was drafted for nine months in November 1862, his wife, Esther, implored him to seek an exemption in a manner that played itself out in countless instances across the North. First, she urged him to try to borrow money to buy a substitute. If that was not possible, then he should go to the state capital in Madison to get his lungs examined by a sympathetic doctor in the hope that they might not be strong enough for further soldiering. If all went as anticipated, he could secure a medical discharge, preferably legitimately, but even by crossing the physician's palms with silver if necessary. For Esther, it was imperative that her husband stay out of the war by any means necessary. Another housewife wrote to her husband in early December 1863 doubting that their small hometown of Albion, New York, would generate its quota of 104 volunteers because so many were "rejected." By the end of the year, Illinois' *Ottawa Free Trader* declared, "The rush to Joliet from all parts of this congressional district to get exemption papers from the draft commissioner's amounts almost to a stampede."[2]

In some instances, angry and knowing neighbors may have outed an individual who was attempting to bamboozle the government in his draft exemption quest. One New Yorker had prepared an affidavit in conjunction with his father stating that the parents were wholly dependent on him for their sustenance. At least nine neighbors, however, signed a sworn counter affidavit claiming that nothing could be further from the truth. But in the main, this type of proactive community action was the exception. For instance, the provost marshal for the Eastern Division of Pennsylvania's second congressional district reported that his office's request that the citizenry report those names not on the eligible draft lists met with little success.[3]

Still others concocted family scenarios that surely must have generated laughs from military officials. One reluctant and blubbering young man swore to an enrollment officer that he was the only son of a widowed mother, that his two brothers were already serving in the army, and that his father was too ill to find any type of job—*all at the same time*. An equally confused draftee pleaded how he should be granted an exemption because he was entirely dependent upon his elderly mother for support. Seeking to relieve the aged woman of her apparent financial burden, enrollment officials promptly conscripted the man into the army, leaving him still in his bewildered state as he was marched away. In Philadelphia, a man told the enrolling officer that he was forty-four years old. He then went to visit his mother, who lived in a neighboring county, who told her son that he was actually forty-six. The man hurried back to the enrolling office seeking an exemption on account of his corrected age, while mentioning that he had not seen his mother in *ten years*. The smiling enrolling officers refused to exempt the man, no doubt thinking that if he could live so long without visiting a nearby elderly parent, he could easily leave his wife and family for the short nine months, if drafted.[4]

Draft evasion occurred throughout the North and was not limited to any particular locale or region. Any man who did not wish to don a blue uniform took advantage of whatever opportunity may have presented itself. That reality was illustrated by the historian of Greenfield, Massachusetts, who later wrote that of the eighty-eight men drafted from his village in July 1863, eight paid the $300 commutation fee, nine bought substitutes, and the remaining seventy-one all obtained some manner of exemption. Back in September 1862, roughly one-half of Marietta, Ohio's draft-eligible men had applied for exemption. Months later, another Buckeye State specimen sought an exemption by claiming, "My nose is too short, and my bowels wrong side up, unmentionables too short by one inch; troubled with worms, which keep up an awful gnawing" and finally conceding that his legs were "better on a retreat than on a forward march."[5]

If feigning illness or disability failed, some men resorted to flat-out bribery in an attempt to gain the desired exemption from the medical officer. Many of those men who were the most distraught over the prospect of being forced to leave their families came to believe that the army's medical officer quite literally held the power of life and death over a draft-eligible man and his loved ones, given his power to grant or deny a medical exemption. They were prepared to do anything to gain favor with those officers. On the other hand, some surgeons were personally

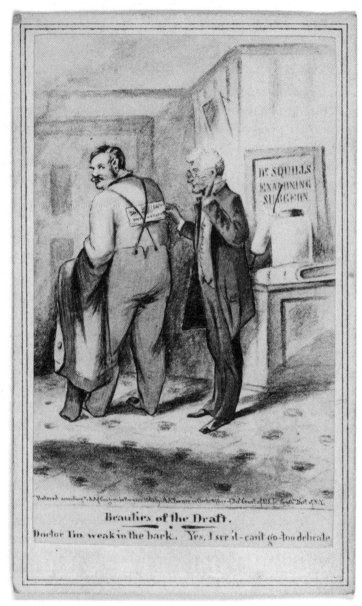

"Beauties of the Draft" "'Doctor I'm weak in the back.' 'Yes, I see it—can't go—too delicate.'" This satirical cartoon shows a man bribing a doctor to declare him as "too delicate" for the draft. (Library Company of Philadelphia)

so against the war that they quietly handed out hundreds of disability certificates as their means of protesting the draft. More than 160,000, or close to 31 percent, of *all* drafted men eventually obtained some type of medical exemption in order to avoid the front lines, whether legitimate or not. An Ohio newspaper editor was stunned at such numbers, lamenting how apparently not one-third of the remaining draft-eligible males were fit for military service. "It is one of the unspeakable shames of our country that the business of recruiting has degenerated, by the grossest mismanagement, into the vilest measures of venal corruption," complained an anonymous New York Republican. With the New Year, the government had seen enough of such frivolity and placed physicians under sterner scrutiny, including more extensive paperwork required with each exemption.[6]

Even examining board surgeons sometimes lamented their position. Thirty-one-year-old Dr. Joshua Nichols Speed admitted to his wife that he missed her and how he wished the "plagued [enrollment] law" had never passed. Speed knew his work was sometimes tedious and he did not like being away from his family, however, he was well aware that his current government employment exempted him from the draft while he was performing such duty. In Speed's personal calculus, serving the government as an examining board surgeon was clearly the lesser of two evils. It was preferable to the possibility of being drafted and then sent to the front lines to face Confederate shot and shell. "Everybody I have talked to about it advised me to stay by all means if by staying I am clear of the draft," Speed explained to his wife.[7]

Lying about one's age was also quite common and relatively easy. As previously mentioned regarding teen boys and ascertaining their real age, it was almost impossible to verify ages in the Civil War era. George Barns, the enrolling officer for Kansas's fifty-third subdistrict, admitted early on how he was stymied with this avoidance tactic. "Please inform me what I shall do in cases where persons say they are over 45 and are willing to swear to that fact," he asked his supervisor in early July 1863. Barns admitted how frustrating it was when his own judgment along with everyone else knew his subject was lying yet willing to swear to the veracity of his statement. In Michigan, English immigrant Aaron

Lockwood characterized the draft avoider who succeeded with that very scam. He was thirty-seven years old in 1863 when the enrollment agent came calling, nevertheless, he later proudly disclosed in a letter to his parents how he told them he was forty-seven so as to evade the draft.[8]

As in 1862, reluctant wives threw rocks at enrolling officers and poured bodily waste on them from second-story windows. Others, such as Iowa's Mary Watters, wrote letters to high-ranking army officials alleging their husbands had been illegally enlisted while rendered drunk by disreputable army recruiters; that they never would have enlisted if sober and leave a family to the whims of charity. Despite such aggressions, the most common methods for avoiding the draft were actually the easiest. Men routinely evaded the national draft and its enrollment provisions simply by ignoring them. Families refused to answer their doors when the enrolling officer came knocking. If they did open their door, they often declined to give the officer any information, and in some instances, even threatened to shoot the enrollment officer if he ever returned. Others simply gave out fictitious names and ages; a tactic that became so prevalent in 1863 that one Wisconsin enrolling officer decided to just copy his area's 1862 enrollment books verbatim. Another provost marshal reported how in other instances, a small community would post young children to act as scouts and sentinels on the lookout for the enrolling officer. If the alarm was sounded, all of the adults would flee, literally leaving no one who could give the officer any pertinent or legal information. In his final report, Minnesota provost marshal George Keith opined that a correct and proper enrollment simply could not be made in a time of war.[9]

As the weeks went by, in some quarters working-class men alleged that the wealthy had obtained the ear of those men conducting the draft and that they were seeking to rid their communities of "undesirables" by having them drafted. In addition, many Democrats became convinced that the enrolling agents were scrupulously obtaining the names of each and every Democrat, yet skipping over numerous Republicans. Such concerns were not without precedent. During the 1862 enrollment, ex–Ohio Democratic congressman Edson Olds warned that since the entire Ohio draft machinery was in the hands of Gov. David Tod and his Republicans, the whole process foretold inequity. "The supposition is a natural one," Olds surmised, "that the Governor would like to send the Democrats to the war, so as to keep them away from the polls, and retain Republicans at home, in order to save their votes for the party."[10]

When the draft was concluded, roughly 200,000 men who were conscripted simply decided not to report to their local enrollment office. Many went into hiding near their homes but only so long as they felt they were being sought out. One of the main complaints of those who were drafted and did show up for duty was that the government seemed unwilling to enforce the law against those who did not. In reality, the government often lacked the manpower to search out draft evaders. Provost Marshal General James Fry was well aware of these pitfalls. "Most of the embarrassments resulted," he later wrote, "from the opposition encountered *in almost every house* [italics added], if not to the act itself, at least to its application to the particular persons whose names were sought for enrolment." Fry then pointed out a crucial flaw in the act's verbiage: "The law made it the duty of this bureau to *take*, but did not make it the duty of any one to *give*, the names of those liable to draft."[11]

As in the summer and fall of 1862, the new national draft law had an immense psychological effect on those subject to its provisions but had no desire of going anywhere near Rebel shot and shell. "I have a perfect abhorrence to being drafted," wrote Edwin Fowler from Baltimore to his uncle in mid-August. Fowler's emotions on the matter were typical. He could not stand the thought of his wife and children being left to fend for themselves. "I can see nothing but starvation and I could never let this be," he vowed. Fowler surmised that if he was drafted, he could sell his furniture for one-half what he paid in order to buy a substitute.[12]

In September, an Ohio man wrote to his brother in Michigan with the news that about forty local men were about to stand trial in Cleveland for previously resisting the draft, all of which prompted others to leave the area "for regions unknown." After reading over the list of drafted men sent to him by his sister from their western New York hometown of Geneseo, army surgeon John Lauderdale replied, "How many I see among them who never would go or hire anybody to go in their places if there was not some means like drafting started to make things go." Two weeks later, Lauderdale's father wrote to him with the elder conveying his opinion that not one in five drafted men from their hometown's district would ever see service: "All would get exempted if they could & of those who are not exempted only those who cannot raise the $300 will go." The provost marshal for Michigan's fourth district reported in December 1863 that any man in his district was openly laughed at if he now spoke of enlisting. "They say they had rather stand the draft than enlist." For her part, Sarah Keen was one of many mothers who was relieved her son would not have to face the local draft wheel because he had already fled the area a year earlier. He had previously made his way to California in 1862 solely to avoid the war. Yet from Sarah's perspective, her son's exodus would have been just as necessary now in 1863, but far more difficult. Furthermore, she urged her son, "If you find they're going to draft there you had better leave for somewhere else. You must not wait until you are drafted before you run if you do you will be shot." Five days later, Keen wrote to her brother and crystallized her anxieties as well as those of countless other Northern civilians: "The fear of being drafted makes one almost sick."[13]

With voluntary enlistments having all but dried up, the Union propaganda war again gathered steam. To counter the ongoing concern that Northern women had become apathetic toward the war, well-known author Caroline M. Kirkland penned a widely distributed pamphlet titled *A Few Words in Behalf of the Loyal Women of the United States by One of Themselves*. The piece countered the allegation that Northern women lacked proper patriotic war support when compared to Southern women. "The feelings of Northern women are rather deep than violent," explained Kirkland. "Their sense of duty is a quiet and constant rather than a headlong or impetuous impulse." Nevertheless, an unmistakable point in Kirkland's essay was that a more boisterous outward display of support and loyalty from Northern women would be beneficial to the Union cause. This growing indifference also prompted new popular patriotic songs, including one titled "Take Your Gun & Go, John." It was a song designed to appeal to a woman's patriotic duty, many of whom had become war-weary, with its lyrics:

Don't stop a moment to think John, your country calls then go;

Don't think of me or the children John, I'll care for them
you know
But take your gun and go John, take your gun and go,
For Ruth can drive the oxen John and I can use the hoe

In the face of the new propaganda campaigns, many women felt their husbands had certainly done their duty and it was now time for them to come home and let some others go fight the war.[14]

OFF TO CANADA

Canada and its thousands of miles of shared border with the United States was an obvious destination for the so-called "skedaddlers." Newspaper reports told of men and their families fleeing across the border near Weston, Maine, and into the Canadian province of New Brunswick, where they had created a community known as "Skedaddlers' Ridge." In the northern New York village of Constable—only six miles from the Canadian border—apparently only one able-bodied man within the military age limits could be found. Every other draft-eligible resident not already in the army had fled to Canada. At the river border crossing between Detroit, Michigan, and Windsor, Ontario, armed Union soldiers posted on the docks and streets questioned any man carrying a large and suspicious-looking satchel. Despite such measures, scores of desperate men managed to slip past the Union sentinels. Augustus Yenner, for one, noted "how wonderful & strange" it was when he learned in early April 1863 that his brother, John, had eluded the authorities and safely reached Canadian soil.[15]

Overall, approximately 90,000 Northern men fled into Canada, well away from the federal government's authority and reach. Thirty thousand were army deserters, including one young man who fled into Canada after deserting from the 9th New York Infantry in April 1863. A May 1, 1863, letter from his father mentioned the family's relief that he was "safe & sound on Canada ground," but then warned him not to make any return attempts. "Don't you be enticed by no man or woman to cross back into the states," his father cautioned. "Some of these city officers that understand catching men tracked [a man] to Canady . . . and got him to cross over into the States, & then snapt him and if they find out where you are, they will play sharp in some way."[16]

The remaining sixty thousand skedaddlers fled from having to serve in the first place. The flood had been so widespread and obvious to the North's citizenry that composer John Molter penned a popular little ditty known as the "Skedaddle Quickstep," whose lyrics skewered those taking flight. So many army deserters and draft-dodging American men poured into Canada in 1863–1864 that Canadian farmers could find all the laborers they needed for their fields by offering only food and shelter. Meanwhile, enterprising Canadians in the Windsor area were able to cross the Detroit River and secure well-paying jobs in that eponymous town due to the labor shortages caused by so many men having either gone off to war or fleeing across the border. With regards to this new cross-border traffic, Canada's *Weekly Globe* felt that "the only thing to be regretted is that we have received skedaddling Americans, while the states are taking from us a great many solid and sturdy Britons, who are not liable to the draft, and consequently the most eligible employees in Yankeeland."[17]

Like Sarah Keen's son, some of the single or family men living in the East or Midwest decided they had seen or heard enough of war and drafts. Faced with the prospect of conscription and rather than escaping to Canada or any other foreign country, they packed up everything they owned and moved out to the far West with the hope of leaving the war behind and starting a new life. Regardless of the draft evader's destination, the reports from Midwestern provost marshals and politicians all read the same. In late June, Ohio's AAPMG informed James Fry that his district marshals in Toledo, Sandusky, and Cleveland were all reporting draft-eligible men fleeing their towns, with more than four hundred leaving Cleveland just since that city's enrollment had commenced. Later in the war, Wisconsin state authorities complained to their governor how thousands of men were escaping through Wisconsin and Minnesota to avoid the draft. "Are there no means for arresting the stampede from our State of the miserable, cowardly, copperhead scoundrels that are leaving by the thousands to avoid the draft?" asked Wisconsin's Surgeon General E. B. Wolcott. In a similar manner and upon learning that federal troops were being utilized to accompany "emigrant trains" into the West, an exasperated Brig. Gen. Alfred Sully, who was posted in the Dakotas Territory, rhetorically asked the Department of the Northwest commanding general John Pope, "Why will our Government continue to act so foolishly, sending out emigrant trains at a great expense? Do they know that most of the men that go are persons running away from the draft?" On another occasion, Iowa's governor issued a proclamation forbidding any draft-eligible man from leaving the state until the next draft was finished. Meanwhile, reports came in claiming that federal marshals were on the lookout for draft evaders by inspecting all ferries attempting to cross the Missouri River. Most authorities agreed that in 1864 alone, the total westward migration across the Missouri River, as well as through Kansas and Nebraska, totaled some 150,000 people, scores of whom were men of service-eligible age.[18]

This westward flight was especially the case for those who lived in hotly contested border areas where pillaging, revenge killings, and guerilla bands were a constant threat. Those who could not leave had to endure neighbors spying on each other, listening in on conversations and then having some report others to the authorities as disloyal. For those who undertook such a significant relocation, their families' welfare and the individualism it implied was deemed more important than any abstract notions of nationalistic duty, patriotism, or societal approval. Such was the case for twenty-seven-year-old Junius Wright and his wife, Elizabeth, who set out in a horse and buggy for Idaho in 1863 after leaving their southern Iowa home, which was only five miles north of the contentious Missouri border. For the draft-eligible Wright and his spouse, they reasoned it was the perfect time to take their long-delayed honeymoon and leave behind the omnipresent roving bands of bushwhackers and Confederate horse thieves.[19]

After President Lincoln signed the Homestead Act on May 20, 1862, which then went into effect on January 1, 1863, innumerable Americans began streaming westward. The act offered 160 acres of surveyed government land to any adult citizen who had never taken up arms in rebellion against the US government. The famous nineteenth-century phrase attributed to Horace Greely of "go west, young man" epitomized the belief that Western opportunity could alleviate many of the social and economic problems inherent in the East's major urban areas. A key caveat in the act was that claimants were required to build a personal dwelling and cultivate the land. Here was a golden ticket for those citizens who sought to avoid the war or the draft, though homesteading fell off in 1864–1865 due to good employment opportunities in the East at high wages. Meanwhile, technological advances in railroads and telegraph communications helped to facilitate this westward emigration.[20]

Ever since the initial California "gold rush" of 1848–1855, the possibility of finding gold in the Western hills and riverbeds also provided an incentive for many men and their families to head west. Corydon Ryan was one such man who succumbed to the gold fever, moving west in 1850 in search of riches. By 1853, he had quit the mining life and settled in western Wisconsin. With the onset of the rebellion, Ryan decided he held no desire for the war or its purposes. He had become a justice of the peace, yet despite his disdain for the war, Ryan feared he would still fall victim to the new draft law. Writing to his family back in northwestern Pennsylvania in the summer of 1863, he put forth the resentment held by many regarding the draft, as well as some toward his brother, Andrew, who was then serving in New Mexico with the Union army. "[Andrew] is a great Lincoln man as everyone is who has a good place in government employ," Ryan bitterly complained. "I am *not* so great as I am taxed heavy and will probably be drafted." Aspiring miner Robert Hawxhurst wrote to an Eastern friend from Virginia City, Nevada, explaining his moral quandary. At twenty-eight years old, single, with some savings but no dependents, Hawxhurst admitted he should probably be in the army helping out "with our noble cause." Yet he then reminded himself and his friend how, "with patriotism, ambition is combined and the idea of my going so far to enlist as a common soldier with but slight chance of promotion, is not a pleasant one." With the discovery of gold in Idaho in 1860, the lure of riches provided a new incentive for men looking to avoid the war. For many Northerners tired of war, patriotism had its limits.[21]

Of course, this westward migration presented a challenge to army recruiters. In his post-war report on his Illinois operations, AAPMG James Oakes wrote how this exodus became a serious problem in that "Many thousands of such persons left this state for the remote western territories, California, Oregon etc. on the eve of the late drafts, leaving their places to be filled by others, and thus adding to the burdens of those who remained at home." Union officers in the West found some but certainly not all of the skedaddlers. Maj. Patrick A. Gallagher of the 3rd California Infantry reported on June 26, 1863, of having stopped a train passing through the Nevada Territory containing sixty men, the majority of whom he ascertained were Eastern men fleeing west to avoid the draft.[22]

Even some war-weary soldiers saw the vast West as an escape opportunity filled with endless opportunities to achieve peace and personal gratification. They were emotionally and physically exhausted from the war and wanted out. A correspondent writing from the Port Neuf River in Idaho remarked on this in August 1863. He described the lovely new colony being settled there and of the Eastern emigres filtering in. Though the numbers were still rather small, he then lamented that "the majority of the emigrants, I fear, are Copperheads." In early September 1863, William Standard of the 103rd Illinois Infantry wrote to his wife from his regiment's Mississippi camp urging her to make some quiet inquiries into the possibility of selling their entire Illinois farm and some other property. If a sale was likely, William assured her he would "make one mighty effort to get out of this scrape [even] if I have to run out." They would then pay off their debts to her father and head west. "I think that I would prefer to go to California and get away from this infernal, unjust, unholy, and ungodly war."[23]

Rather than fleeing out West or to a foreign country, other draft-eligible men slipped into the South with the intent of hiding in the open in Union-occupied towns. Maj. Gen. William T. Sherman considered these men to be a nuisance and a constant source of trouble. He noticed them throughout Memphis, Vicksburg, or any other town occupied by his troops. Like any Union soldier, he resented their intention of avoiding the draft. Moreover, he knew their presence was partly an effort to profit from the war through trade or gambling. As far as Sherman was concerned, he had the right to round up these Northern runaways and impress them into military service.[24]

As much as the North's stay-at-home population disliked the new national draft law, the vast majority of Union soldiers risking life and limb at the front heartily cheered it, as did many civilians who already had loved ones serving in the military. Cora Benton of Albion, New York, for example, admitted in early August 1863 that she felt indifferent about the upcoming draft since her husband and brothers were already in the army. Concurrently, the soldiers disparaged those at home (other than close family members) who eagerly took advantage of any potential exemption to stay out of the war. Seventeen-year-old Leverett Bradley explained this perspective to his parents in a July 1863 letter, writing how the men in his company were pleased to see the stay-at-homes face the draft yet they also wished those men could not buy their way out for a mere $300. "But then," Bradley surmised, "this is a rich man's war; the poor man has to do the fighting." Like Bradley, Pvt. James T. Miller had earlier written to his parents on March 28, 1863, using language that typified this soldierly disdain. "If as you say that there's not a man in the town will come if they can raise the $300 it shows an amount of cowardice I did [not] think existed anywhere in the north much less in that township," Miller asserted. Countless Union soldiers wrote home expressing their delight with the new draft and even routinely mentioned specific civilian acquaintances by name who they hoped would now be forced to shoulder a musket and do their fair share of the hard work. For the soldiers, the draft was just because it forced all to help preserve the Union. From their viewpoint, the "stay-at-home patriots" and poltroons would finally be forced to shoulder a musket and pitch in, even though the veteran soldiers realized that drafted men, bounty men, and substitutes often possessed less than desirable martial qualities. With some self-satisfied jocularity, Chester Leach of the 2nd Vermont Infantry wrote to his wife how "I would like to be where I could see the flying around there has been since the draft." To Col. Marcus Spiegel of the 67th Ohio Infantry, the new draft would "bring out some of the cowards, who set at home [and] ridicule and everybody too cowardly to go themselves." Charles Tew of the 25th Massachusetts Infantry wrote how he loathed the "miserable cowards" who stayed at home. If only some of them came out, he surmised, the war would be over far quicker. Knowing that was not likely to happen, he mockingly complained to his wife, "let the cowards stay at home and nurse their sore toes."[25]

The boys in blue from the volunteer privates on up to regimental officers also drew a sharp distinction between their Confederate enemy and who they generally saw as the home front cowards, charlatans, or even traitors. The dominant belief from the war's opening weeks that the Rebs would run at the first sight of a well-trained Yankee was as dead as patriotic volunteering into the ranks. Every Union soldier who had "seen the elephant" a time or two was well aware that Johnny Reb could and would fight. Now, Union soldiers routinely wrote of possessing a warrior's respect for—and even some identity with—those men in gray who were willing to stand and oppose them on the field of battle, even though they viewed the cause for which those men fought as traitorous. "A Johnny we can respect—and regard as a brother soldier," Frederic Lockley wrote to his wife while also explaining his disdain for Union "dastards and traitors." (As the war progressed, the Confederate rank and file generally acquired the same martial respect toward Billy Yank.) Yet like Frederic Lockley, most Union soldiers held nothing but contempt for the healthy, home front skulkers who actively discouraged enlistments, complained endlessly about the war, or took advantage of the government or needy neighbors in business dealings. The soldiers' greatest scorn was for those who sympathized with the South and then worked against the Union war effort, as opposed to those men who publicly supported the war and the army yet declined to enlist because of familial obligations. A man could honorably choose to remain at home as long as he was not traitorous, hypocritical, or dishonest in his deeds and words.[26]

Wisconsin private Jabez L. Hutley, Ohioan George Brown, and Michigander Henry Truesdell all characterized this outlook when they wrote to their respective loved ones in June 1863 explaining how their Union comrades hated the Northern Copperheads more than the Southern Rebels. Ohio artillerist John Rieley told his mother and sister in April 1863 that if he had to choose, he would rather shoot a Northern Copperhead than Confederate president Jefferson Davis. Rieley's remark was not mere hyperbole, for he was hardly alone in his sentiments. A Maine soldier wrote to his brother in early August 1863, "If I could shoot a Copperhead I should feel more elated than to have the privilege of bayoneting a Rebel captain," while another Wisconsin man wrote how he could "shoot one of them copperheads with a good a heart as I could shoot a wolf." Writing to his mother from Washington in September, Walt Whitman told her that none of the men he cared for in the city's army hospitals ever spoke of Copperheads without a curse, which was followed with a vow that they would rather shoot them than the Rebels.[27]

The era's cultural and gendered ideal of bravery versus cowardice was also a key factor for these soldiers. While home on furlough in Bluffton, Indiana, Sgt. William Miller acknowledged this precept. He told his diary in early November 1863 that he was as strong a pro-war Democrat as ever and that obviously did not include being a rebel against the laws and government of the Union. He had no use for his Northern neighbors whose opinions on the war were no different from the Confederates. Miller, however, did observe one obvious difference between the two groups when he wrote, "The Rebs come out manfully and Sacrifice their lives for their opinions and Show themselves to be men while those I find here only talk and have not got the courage to take sides openly." Col. Orlando M. Poe of the 2nd Michigan Infantry also pulled no punches in describing such men while he and his regiment were on duty near Edward's Ferry, Maryland. "We have some little respect for the man who risks all, and taking up arms boldly confronts us," he explained to his wife, "but for the coward that swindles the country at such a time as this, above all others we despise, and I for one would gladly assist in hanging."[28]

The gallows seemed like the obvious solution to Union soldiers in dealing with home front malcontents fomenting insurrection. When Charles Smith of the 32nd Ohio Infantry learned that a neighbor had allegedly gathered several hundred armed men to resist the draft, he wrote in his diary that it "would be good policy to nip the bud in its infancy by suspending a few of the leaders up between the heavens and earth." Such gallows-related enthusiasm existed even as the war ended. Writing to his mother on April 17, 1865, from the 123rd New York Infantry's camp in Raleigh, North Carolina, Lt. George W. Baker noticed how secession sentiment had all but vanished from that Southern town. It was almost laughable, he explained, to now see his comrades casually mingling and smoking with the locals on their front porches while the soldiers played with their children. "As for me," wrote Baker, "I can take a Rebel that has fought me three years by the hand with a good stomach but I wish every Copperhead was hung."[29]

Pro-administration Northern civilians similarly concurred with the soldiers' sentiments. Growing up as a boy in Massachusetts during the rebellion, future US senator Henry Cabot Lodge could not recall ever hearing bitter words spoken about the Southern soldier who had acted out of loyalty to his community or state. On the other hand, Lodge clearly remembered the "extreme bitterness" felt toward the Northern man with Southern sympathies. These were the men, wrote Lodge, "who stayed at home, sheltered and protected by the arms and the laws of their State and their nation alike" yet "were loyal to nothing and risked nothing." New Yorker Thaddeus Carleton was a staunch Republican though too disabled by polio to join the army. "The poorest, meanest armed rebel in the insurgent army is a good man by the side of the best of [the Copperheads]," Carleton told his journal. After reading the antiwar speeches of Ohio congressman Clement Vallandigham—the North's most strident and well-known Copperhead—New York Union League co-founder George Templeton Strong wrote in his diary that compared to such men as Vallandigham, "The most barbarous, brutal Mississippian now in arms against us is a demigod." Strong wondered if the Northern people, with so large an apparent antiwar population, could be saved, ought to be saved, or if it was even worth the effort of trying to save them. It seemed evident to the boys in blue and ardent pro-war Northern citizens that there had to be a strong degree of political alignment and commitment between Northern civilians and their soldiers because victory would be achieved only if unity and loyalty existed between the army and the home front. Knowing that their efforts were supported by the folks at home was imperative for the soldiers' morale in the field.[30]

Southerners also seemingly held little respect for those vocal Northern dissidents. One soldier from the 31st New York Infantry encamped within Virginia's hills and hollows reported in an April 10, 1863, letter

RECEPTION OF THE COPPERHEADS AT RICHMOND.

COPPERHEAD SPOKESMAN. "Be so kind as to announce to PRESIDENT DAVIS that a few of his Northern Friends wish to see him."
POMPEY. "De PRESIDENT desire me to say dat you is mistaken, Gemmen. He haven't got no friends at de Norf; and when he wants any, he won't choose 'em among de *Peace Sneaks.*" (*Exeunt* COPPERHEADS *considerably abashed.*)—(*Vide* DAVIS's *Message.*)

"Reception of the Copperheads at Richmond" "COPPERHEAD SPOKESMAN: 'Be so kind as to announce to PRESIDENT DAVIS that a few of his Northern Friends wish to see him.' POMPEY: 'DE PRESIDENT desire me to say dat you is mistaken, Gemmen. He haven't got no friends at de Norf; and when he wants any, he won't choose 'em among de *Peace Sneaks.*'" (*Harper's Weekly*, January 31, 1863)
COURTESY OF HARPWEEK

to the New York *Sunday Mercury* that the delicate "chivalrous noses of our Secesh brethren cannot stand copperhead perfumery at all." At the high end of the Union military command structure, Maj. Gen. William T. Sherman also wrote how the average Southern Confederate had little use for the Northern Copperhead and scorned the idea of any alliance between the two groups. "They tell me to my face that they respect . . . our brave associates who fight manfully and well for a principle," Sherman wrote in a letter to Henry Halleck, "but despise the copperheads and sneaks who profess friendship for the South and opposition to the war as mere covers for their knavery and poltroonery." The tens of thousands of Southern men who sincerely believed they had picked up the musket to defend their homes and families from an invading army routinely viewed the average Northern Copperhead as all talk and no action.[31]

Nonetheless, for some veteran Union soldiers whose initial term of enlistment was about to end, no amount of money could entice them to reenlist, even as they derided those still at home. These men believed they had performed their honorable duty and now it was time for some of the "stay-at-home patriots" to step forward. German-born Gottfried Rentschler of the 6th Kentucky Infantry stressed this point in a letter to the editor of the German-language *Louisville Anzeiger*. Rentschler emphasized how the morale of the men in the Western Army of the Cumberland was good at present, however, the reason so many veterans were not reenlisting was because of what they calculated were the million-plus eighteen to twenty-two-year-olds still at home who had not yet lifted a finger for the cause. According to Rentschler, they were the ones who were quick to criticize entire divisions or armies, yet when the "call to arms" came toward them, "they crawl into their fathers' shirt pockets or hide under the counter." Eben Hale of the nine-month 45th Massachusetts Infantry had only a few weeks left in his term of service when he sarcastically told his mother what a great privilege it was to serve in the army. Not wanting to monopolize all the glory, however, "I shall stand aside and allow those immortal patriots who have been advocating a vigorous prosecution of the war . . . and joining home guards to try a little actual service and see how they like it." It may have been all fine and dandy for the stay-at-homes to create and join Northern home front organizations like union leagues or home guards, but to countless soldiers like Hale, all of that seemed rather absurd.[32]

***

The 1863 draft results revealed just how desperate the North's remaining draft-eligible population was to avoid military service. The enrollment began in May with 300,000 men called for soon thereafter. Provost marshal officials began pulling names out of their draft wheels in July and then continued throughout the summer. If the real intent of the draft was to first gain more men through enlistment, then the results were almost comical. Of the 292,441 names drawn in the 1863 draft, 52,288 paid the

$300 commutation fee while 164,395 (56 percent) obtained exemptions for various purported physical maladies. Only 9,881 drafted men directly entered the army straightaway; a ratio of only one in thirty. Another 26,002 furnished substitutes, which meant that *72 percent* of the men who donned a blue uniform as a result of the draft were substitutes. Meanwhile, 39,415 disregarded the law entirely by failing to report to the enrollment offices after their names were drawn. The numbers were alarming for both the administration and its professional soldiers. Writing from Washington, General-in-Chief Henry Halleck warned Maj. Gen. William T. Sherman on October 1 that his army encamped outside of Vicksburg, Mississippi, would never be properly refilled by the current draft. After reviewing the results, Halleck concluded that the current draft was practically a failure, "as nearly everybody is exempt. It takes more soldiers to enforce it than we get by it." Equally alarming to Halleck was his observation that the Northern Copperheads had seemingly done everything they could to stymie the North's draft efforts.[33]

No Northern state escaped the civilian stampede to avoid going into the army. Connecticut's AAPMG reported in late June that so many farm laborers had fled the town of Simsbury for parts unknown that numerous farmers no longer had any help in their fields. In Hingham, Massachusetts, one hundred names were drawn in July for the first draft, yet it appeared to the town leaders that only three of those one hundred men ever entered the army because of the draft. In central Michigan, the *Saginaw Valley Republican* reported that within its district, the fall draft had produced only one hundred men, whereas the government had collected $90,000 (three hundred men) in commutation money.[34]

Scores of men simply paid the $300 commutation fee; others purchased substitutes or were lawfully exempted based on the act's non-medical provisions. Yet the vast majority saved their money by claiming some manner of physical disability, thereby securing a medical exemption. A Vermont newspaper humorously reported on one of the "solid men" of Boston whose weight must have been between four and five hundred pounds. When he was asked if he intended to get an exemption from the examining surgeon, he replied, "No, I acknowledge I am a coward, but I don't want to pay two dollars to have it recorded."

Many still sought some manner of psychological refuge by joining local home guard units. By October 1863, Mary Vermilion had informed her husband, William, who was off fighting with the 36th Iowa Infantry, how "all the loyal young men in the county belong to the home guards."[35]

So many women eventually chastised men who shunned the draft that the *Waynesboro Village Record* quipped, "Many of our girls would like to be boys, that they might go to war; and more of our boys would like to be girls, that they might stay at home." The irony was not lost on many how in April and May 1861, young men rushed to the enlistment office seeking to demonstrate their physical prowess. Now only two years later, most remaining civilian men were trying to prove why they were physically unfit. Furthermore, and as the North was about to learn, those anti-draft efforts even included resorting to violence and physical retribution.[36]

Like the substitute, the average man who entered the army's ranks as a drafted conscript rarely turned out to be a solid, reliable soldier. Predictably, his martial enthusiasm was generally bottom of the barrel, and those grizzled veterans already fighting at the front sensed it immediately. Furthermore, the new regiments consisting almost entirely of drafted men and substitutes were soon deemed notoriously unreliable due to excessive desertions. "They are mostly old Soldiers, those that are not are as dumb as sticks," complained Orderly Sargent Ambrose Hayward. A frustrating example for Hayward were the two just-arrived Germans who were in the country barely eight days before they signed on as substitutes even though neither one spoke English while another two were described by Hayward as "Irishmen of the Pick & Spade school."[37]

An uncommon example in the other direction was that of forty-year-old Gilbert Claflin, who was drafted in September 1862 to serve for nine months in what became the 34th Wisconsin Infantry. A literate man and church deacon, Claflin appeared to be a drafted rarity. He went off to war leaving behind a wife and two young teen boys to run their forty-acre farm though his wife, initially at least, urged him to seek out a substitute. Despite his age, Claflin admitted he immediately took to drilling and the soldier life, such as it was. As Claflin acknowledged, the same could not be said for the majority of men in the unit who were

German immigrants with little interest in or knowledge of the war's goals or merits. "I have seen more anxiety depicted upon the faces of men during my short stay in camp than I ever saw in all my life before," Claflin relayed to his wife on December 21 from his Wisconsin training camp. As with most married men with families, the men Claflin referred to knew that being away from home would impose economic hardship and perhaps even poverty on their wives and small children. As discussed earlier, many Germans had left their homeland in the first place because they resented the idea of a distant government imposing mandatory conscription. Three weeks later on January 11, 1863, Claflin wrote how "The drafted men and substitutes are deserting all the while . . . There are about 800 drafted men here, and they are growing less every day." He relayed to his wife that of the thirty-three substitutes in one company, he was told that at least thirty had already deserted. By January 18, Claflin had seen enough to form a firm opinion: "I am satisfied that the 34th regiment of drafted men will be of little service to the government. There is a growing feeling of discontent among the men; not so much on account of their treatment, but on the account of the slackness of government in bringing in those who failed to report. And I do not believe if the drafted men here were at home and were called to report that 1 in 20 would go." The army soon agreed with Claflin's assessment. Army officers referred to the regiment as "a humbug"—plagued by poor discipline and desertion—and by the end of January 1863 the regiment was sent to Columbus, Kentucky, where it performed only garrison duty for the remainder of its nine-month enlistment.[38]

ANTI-DRAFT CIVILIAN VIOLENCE

As with the 1862 state militia drafts, the new Conscription Act was despised to such a degree by anti-draft citizens in various parts of the country that enrollment officers routinely faced physical harassment and violence. Every obvious and imaginative means thought of was utilized to deceive them. They were routinely pelted with rocks and eggs by angry wives or sisters while others turned their dogs loose on these men. Enrollment officers often received cryptic letters threatening their lives and property if they did not desist. Since any manner of federal security was lacking in many areas, especially rural ones, the enrollers quickly learned it was nearly impossible to complete their work without soldiers to protect them. In June 1863, a Palmyra, Ohio, officer found letters posted on his farm's gate post warning him to desist and of the consequences if he did not. An Indiana officer boldly shared a threatening letter he had received with the local paper. Its warning was typical:

> We the undersigned will give you our advice for your own good and if you don't lay aside the enrolling, your life will be taken tomorrow night, and you had better take our advice as friends; we don't expect to interrupt you; but we have heard men with vengeance against you say that you had better stay at home, and you had better take our advice and stay at home.
> From YOUR FRIEND[39]

Sometimes those threats were even carried out because as one anti-draft Pennsylvania newspaper framed it, the act was as popular as a smallpox epidemic and enrolling officers as welcome in most towns as a pack of rabid dogs. As a consequence, in some locales it was difficult if not impossible to find qualified enrollment officers at the pay being offered. Moreover, the officer was expected to pay his own expenses. As it turned out in some instances, the costs of maintaining a horse and buggy along with room and board often equaled his salary. Eastern Pennsylvania's AAPMG William B. Lane later reported that finding qualified enrolling officers was one of his most serious challenges from day 1 because honorable men already engaged in business or professional pursuits would not leave such work for the pay offered to enrollment officers. This fiscal concern was in line with why many gainfully employed men opted not to enlist in the first place. The result, according to Lane, was that enrollment boards were often compelled to hire unemployed men whose primary qualities seemed to be physical courage and indifference to verbal insults, rather than thoroughness or fidelity to their duties.[40]

Such courage was indeed a job requirement once violent opposition to the draft became a growing concern. One woman informed her soldier husband in late June 1863 how one enrolling officer in Fulton County,

Indiana, had been beaten almost to death by anti-draft men who then burned all of his papers. In Berks County, Pennsylvania, J. S. Richards wrote to the Judge-Advocate warning that secret organizations had been formed by men pledged to resisting the draft and fomenting armed resistance to conscription if need be. They met at taverns, members' houses, schools, and in barns. Richards further stated that more than 170 men had been sworn in at one such gathering and that their numbers were continuously increasing. Detroit provost marshal John Newberry notified Michigan's AAPMG that he believed there were up to 1,500 disaffected men in the city who would instantly join any attempted draft disruption. "A spark here would explode the whole and bring it into the most violent action," Newberry warned. In another instance, Greencastle resident Matilda Cavins wrote to her husband relaying the persistent rumors that anti-draft men were threatening to burn the town to the ground as part of their resistance. In Peoria, Illinois, the state's fifth district provost marshal reported to his superior in mid-July that all of the town's magistrates, judges, and police officers were opposed to the draft and owed their positions to the government's enemies. In the event of anti-draft violence, he warned there was "not a policeman that would lift a finger to quell a riot." The provost marshal in Brown County, Wisconsin, reported that anti-draft men in his territory "had publicly announced that no enrolling officer could go through the towns alive." None of his men were killed, but none successfully enrolled any men, either. In a similar manner, Esther Gilbert of Oconomowoc, Wisconsin, wrote to her soldier husband on June 18 about how one enrollment officer in Ixonia "don't dare to do it" while another was shot in the town of Ashippun and was not expected to live. In Milwaukee, Esther concluded, "They have been attacked by the Irish women and stoned." Over the final two years of the war, thirty-eight provost marshal officers were murdered, sixty were wounded, and another twelve suffered extensive personal property damage as a direct result of performing their lawful duty; and those numbers included only bureau employees, not any soldiers or civilians who may have lost their lives or became wounded suppressing armed and violent dissent.[41]

Draft Riots

The North was racked with both rural and urban anti-draft violence from the late fall of 1862 through the late summer of 1863. In the small village of Sycamore, Ohio, Sarah Lundy wrote to a friend describing how the "Butternuts" in neighboring Crawford County had burned down one church and partially tore down another because the ministers preached "good Union sermons" rather than ones in favor of the Copperhead position. In most instances, it was working-class Whites who revolted against the draft and its perceived inequities.[42]

Six Wisconsin counties experienced severe disturbances in November 1862, primarily instigated by anti-draft Catholics. The most serious incident occurred in Port Washington on draft day, November 10, when a crowd beat up the draft commissioner and threw him down the courthouse steps. They seized and burned the draft rolls and then began running amok through the streets. Wisconsin governor Edward Salomon ordered troops into the town who succeeded in quelling the riot. On March 6, 1863, in Detroit, Michigan, rampaging Whites burned that city's small Black neighborhood to the ground after Union provost and militia troops blocked a mob from lynching a Black man named William Faulkner who had just been convicted of raping two young White girls and sentenced to life in prison despite his vigorous claims of innocence. For many of the rioters, their anti-Black rage was driven by the conviction that Blacks were to blame for both the new draft law and the war; a conflict the rioters believed they had no real stake in nor any desire to be part of. Faulkner's conviction was overturned six and a half years later after the girls admitted they made the whole story up.[43]

The most historically famous anti-draft riot occurred in New York City as the draft lottery was commencing. For four days from July 13 to 16, 1863, hundreds of young "rough fellows & some equally rough women" primarily from New York's working Irish underclass battled in the streets against the city's police officers. In the process, New York City was effectively shut down as countless peaceful citizens were forced to take shelter in their homes. The rioting was finally suppressed only after Army of the Potomac troops arrived from the recent Gettysburg battle with orders to shoot to kill. The casualty totals can only be estimated at somewhere between 100 and 150 deaths; the majority of those most likely being rioters and bystanders shot dead by Union troops, which made the New York draft riots the most violent and deadly in the United States throughout the nineteenth century. Similar events occurred in the days to follow in Boston; Troy, New York; Portsmouth, New Hampshire; and Rutland, Vermont.[44]

Union army authorities across the North similarly responded to their territory's riots. From Concord, New Hampshire, the AAPMG's office informed Capt. John S. Godfrey that he should use force "without hesitancy" if he deemed it necessary to properly carry out the draft in his district's towns of Conway, Jackson, and Bartlett. Moreover, any man who stood in opposition to the draft act's provisions must be arrested and dealt with as the law directed. It soon became apparent that these civil disturbances had one common denominator: The perpetrators were almost exclusively anti-draft and/or anti-Black immigrant populations residing in Democratic stronghold areas. After witnessing the interparty strife firsthand in Pennsylvania, Washingtonian Mary Henry told her diary, "In my humble opinion we have every reason now to fear civil war between the Republican & the Democrats our country is in a terrible state."[45]

Other antiwar and anti-draft dissidents, with generally strong Democratic leanings, bandied together into loosely organized "secret societies" for self-protection. The most famous of these furtive, oath-bound groups was the Knights of the Golden Circle, an organization that dated its creation back to 1854 as a means of advancing American expansionism into their idealized "golden circle" region of Central America, the Caribbean, and especially Mexico. Once civil war became a reality, the Knights discarded their expansionist aims, opting instead to support Southern secession and anti-abolitionism. With the rise of what they viewed as the administration's tyrannical behavior and unconstitutional arrests of Democratic partisans, the group became a figurative haven for Democrats seeking safety, comradery, and a means of striking back. While the legitimacy and actual influence of these secretive organizations have been debated over the last century and then always with the benefit of twenty-twenty hindsight, there is little doubt that at the time,

THE NAUGHTY BOY GOTHAM, WHO WOULD NOT TAKE THE DRAFT.

MAMMY LINCOLN—"*There now, you bad boy, acting that way, when your little sister Penn takes hers like a lady!*"

"The Naughty Boy Gotham, Who Would Not Take the Draft" "Mammy Lincoln—'There now, you bad boy, acting that way, when your little sister Penn takes hers like a lady!'" (*Frank Leslie's Illustrated Newspaper*, August 29, 1863) state and local politicians, Union army authorities, and Unionist civilians had every reason to believe in their existence and react accordingly.[46]

DRAFT INSURANCE SOCIETIES

Notwithstanding the government's well-meant intention of holding down the prices paid for substitutes, the commutation clause and its $300 fee became the most contentious aspect of the 1863 draft law. Many working-class men simply did not have an extra $300 they could readily part with. Later that year, the satirical magazine *Yankee Notions* published a parody of the popular song "We Are Coming Father Abraham" to drive home the point of the new draft law's unfairness.

> We're coming, Ancient Abram, several hundred strong,
> We hadn't no $300, and so we come along;
> We hadn't no rich parents to pony up the tin,
> So we went unto the Provost, and there were mustered in.[47]

One potential solution was the creation of "draft insurance societies" in which working- or middle-class individuals, as well as numerous municipalities, banded together to collectively protect themselves against the hated draft and its clauses. Based on the concepts of insurance, civilian members pooled their premium dollars into the society with the understanding that if any one (or more) of the members were drafted, the pooled funds would be used to pay that member's $300 commutation fee to the government. The fee any man had to pay was based on the society's number of members versus the number of its men who were drafted. The *Cincinnati Enquirer* reported back on August 2, 1862, how the town's main street merchants were forming themselves into just such an organization. Sarah Keen of Acushnet, Massachusetts, wrote in July 1863 how a family member had joined an "insurance club" so that if he was drafted "he shan't have to pay so much to get clear." A month later in mid-August, Sam Lauderdale wrote to his sister from St. Louis explaining, "The way we do here is to form ourselves in to a company— say ten—signing an agreement that each one will pay his equal share in buying the exemption of any or more that have signed the agreement that may be drafted." Therefore, Lauderdale calculated that with a proportion of only one in ten, "the percent to pay [is] comparatively small for each of us." Sam's position on his desire to avoid the war was unequivocal: "I consider myself just as well off out of the Army as I would be in." Yet despite the relatively low expense, many working-class poor lived a hardscrabble, hand-to-mouth existence. They simply did not have any discretionary cash to pay premiums into a draft insurance society and so were forced to take their chances with the draft wheel or resort to other means.[48]

Municipalities, especially those controlled by antiwar or anti-draft Democrats, were sometimes willing to access their coffers and use the various public funds to pay commutation fees for poorer, working-class citizens. Their rationales were often not merely a philosophical opposition to the war or an altruistic gift to a local citizen. Rather, there was a practical concern that the wife and children of a poor man sent into the army might become a ward of the town. Better to pay his commutation fee than being forced to house and feed his family indefinitely. Employers also created their own collectives by withholding a small amount of each employee's pay with the understanding that the funds would be used to pay commutation or obtain a substitute if any employee was drafted. Accordingly, newspaper ads for draft insurance increased and touted how the funds would be used to buy substitutes in the event members were drafted. The size of these groups varied from a few dozen members to much larger collectives, such as the banker-managed Chicago Draft Insurance Company, which was initially capitalized with $100,000 and whose stated mission was to provide substitutes for its drafted members.[49]

In some cases, men may have been coerced into joining these organizations, or at a minimum, turned a blind eye to their existence. A Pennsylvania deputy alleged that some men's homes were threatened with the torch if they did not join the local "mutual protection club."[50]

Union soldiers were generally disdainful of anything home front men did to evade service. These men followed the news closely, and through letters with loved ones and friends, they knew exactly which townsfolk had enlisted, who had not, and to what lengths the latter group was going to avoid conscription. When James Miller of the 111th Pennsylvania

Infantry learned that his three stay-at-home brothers had joined the recently created "Farmington Mutual Insurance Society," which was simply a draft insurance collective, he became incensed that they had subscribed to such a "white livered cowardly piece of poltroonery." Miller referred to it in his letters home as the "Farmington Cowards Mutual Insurance Society," describing it as filled with those men who spoke of the war as a just one and wanted to see it properly finished but who would then do anything to avoid their fair share of the dirty work.[51]

In another instance, Joseph Crowell recalled how he had enlisted into the 13th New Jersey Infantry as an eighteen-year-old lad in August 1862 after listening to some of his town's most prominent men exhorting teen boys like him to enlist. Yet he never forgot how those same leading citizens later formed a draft insurance society in his New Jersey town because they were fearful of being drafted. What stuck in Crowell's craw years later, however, was not that they had invested in such a scheme during the war, but how decades after the rebellion ended, those same, now elderly men would boast at various political meetings as to "how *we* saved the Union!" With their non-enlistee's selective memory at work, only the hero remained.[52]

Yet as discussed previously, this soldierly scorn often did not apply to their close friends or relatives. This was especially the case if a family had one or more members already serving in the army. These men and their kin viewed their service as representing not merely themselves, but their families as well. From their perspective, such a household should not be subjected to further military duty until those families with no one serving stepped up and contributed a member to army service. This conviction even applied to army chaplains. Father Peter Paul Cooney was the chaplain of the 35th Indiana Infantry and in the past was tasked with helping to recruit men into the army. Yet in September 1863 he advised his brother on how to avoid the draft. His carefully worded instructions were for his brother to first seek a medical exemption. If that did not work, then he was to claim that he was the only support for their aged mother. As a last resort, Cooney advised his brother to just pay the $300 commutation fee. After all, Cooney reasoned, the $300 fee was much less than his brother's business would lose if he was forced into the army.[53]

This new, ratcheted-upward war avoidance was highlighted in Pennsylvania during the summer 1863 Confederate invasion that culminated in the epic July 1–3 battle of Gettysburg. Innumerable southcentral Pennsylvanians who had previously and publicly professed dedicated support for the war now seemed unwilling to step forward to enlist or even serve in the hastily assembled, ninety-day state militia. Many were of the "Pennsylvania Dutch" community; the Democratic-leaning, ethnic German farmers who had little to no interest in the war or its goals and who primarily wished to be left alone. They certainly had no desire to abandon their fields as their crops were maturing. Better to let someone else go, someone more suited to war-making. A young woman in central Pennsylvania wrote to her cousin on June 28 touching on how the local initial urgency vanished into apparent indifference. "I don't know where it went, but there were no men to go after that, at least not many," she concluded. When a member of the New York militia arrived at Harrisburg, whose units were sent to Pennsylvania to assist in its defense, he expected to find civilian men toiling everywhere with picks and spades preparing for the defense of their state capital. Instead, he witnessed, "Hundreds of strong men in the prime of life loitered in the public thoroughfares," all of whom "gaped at our passing columns as indifferently as if we had come as conquerors, to take possession of the city, they cravenly submitting to the yoke." From the Confederate perspective, the Pennsylvanians' reluctance revealed more than a lack of patriotism, but a lack of courage and character. In addition, witnessing such amazing numbers of able-bodied men not yet in uniform had a deleterious effect on the invaders, who now sensed that from a manpower perspective, the Yankees could fight on as long as they wanted.[54]

More importantly, this regionalized refusal of the locals to fight back was noted by Northern newspapers. In New York, diarist George Strong described Pennsylvania as "the meanest state in the Union" and that a bit of suffering at the Rebels' hands would do wonders for the area's well-to-do farmers. After the Rebels captured a large wagon train within a mere ten miles of Washington on June 28, a patent office bureaucrat stated in his diary that a people who refused to turn out en masse to

A PRUDENT PROCEEDING.

EXCITED NEW YORKER—" *Look here ! your State's invaded—its soil polluted. What are you going to do ?*"

OLD EPHRAIM (to his Son)—" *Son Ephraim, send for the New Yorkers and the Jerseymen, to fight for us, while I and thou mark up the prices.*"

"A Prudent Proceeding" "EXCITED NEW YORKER—'Look here! Your State's invaded—its soil polluted. What are you going to do?' OLD EPHRAIM (to his Son)—'Son, Ephraim, send for the New Yorkers and the Jerseymen, to fight for us, while I and thou mark up the prices.'" (*Frank Leslie's Illustrated Newspaper*, July 25, 1863)

COURTESY OF HOUSE DIVIDED: THE CIVIL WAR RESEARCH ENGINE AT DICKINSON COLLEGE

resist an invader probably deserved to have their capital taken and the surrounding countryside laid waste.[55]

As always, the Union boys in blue also took notice of the civilian apathy. Sgt. David Craft wrote to his sister four days after the Gettysburg battle admitting, "I am almost ashamed of Penn. Thousands of great cowardly louts who should have rushed to arms at the first prospect of invasion are found skulking while the Rebs are at their very doors." Another bluecoat opined that "if there ever was a miserable, low-lived set of people it is the Pennsylvanians" because "all they seem to care for it is to make all the money they can out of us . . . as for their having any idea of fighting for themselves they have none." These stay-at-home civilians then further illustrated their wartime indifference by seeking to charge wounded Union soldiers—the same soldiers who had just defended their homes—the then outrageous sum of $40 for nineteen loaves of bread. Other reports told of residents charging soldiers for water while one man purportedly presented a bill for twenty-five cents to a Union general for four bricks that had been knocked off his chimney. Pennsylvania was hardly alone, however. When the government learned in June 1863 that the Confederates were marching northward, the administration called for 100,000 men across the four-state area of Pennsylvania, Maryland, Ohio, and West Virginia to enlist for six months in the state militias. After the danger had receded and the headcounts were tallied, they realized that barely 12,000 had stepped forward and of that number, nearly one-third came from Indiana, which was not even part of the initial plea.[56]

What was especially galling to the Union privates were the civilian complaints about how the army was conducting itself on the battlefield; all voiced from the warm comforts of their living rooms and parlors. "It is a mighty easy thing for them to tell us to shed the last drop of our blood in this glorious cause," groused one private, "but I notice the fellers who make that kind of talk never enlist." "And if they are drafted," chimed in another, "they either have a cramp in the stomach, or an old mother dependent upon them for her support. I wish they had to face the music." As for the dependency issue, another recently discharged Ohioan added in December, "If you would have told them that they would have to depend on [their children] two years ago, you would have insulted them but now they are very dependent." To the Union armies' rank and file, staying at home was one thing, but then to be criticized and carped at by those same "fireside rangers" was beyond the pale.[57]

"Come Home if You Have to Desert, You Will Be Protected"

Deserting the Army to Get Home, Good Jobs and Inflation as Reasons to Stay Home

DESERTION'S EFFECTS ON THE ARMY AND ENLISTMENTS

Desertion from the ranks had been a thorn in the Union army's side ever since the summer of 1862, however, as 1864 dawned and throughout that year, it reached near epidemic proportions. Any man who was conscripted or who had enlisted for any reason other than a personal sense of duty was more likely to desert than one whose patriotic impulses were still paramount. Studies show that those workingmen who enlisted in early 1861 and came from pro-Republican communities were the least likely to desert. Wealthier men, who rarely enlisted in the first place but sought out officer's commissions when they did, also tended to desert at lower rates. The men most likely to desert were those who enlisted primarily for pay, glory, or some other reason that had little to do with the core political issues being debated on the field of battle.[1]

The act of desertion proved to have a baleful impact on the army in two areas. Not only did it decrease the number of men present in the ranks, but it also served to hinder recruiting efforts back home. Deserters told their tales of woe to any who would sympathetically listen. They spoke of family poverty, their repeated campaign hardships, and the alleged inhumane treatment suffered at the hands of officers, no doubt with the intent of rationalizing their actions. Most salacious, according to Col. James Fry, was how deserters would tell of "being tied up by the thumbs." Though not a severe punishment, according to Fry, he acknowledged the listener probably inferred that it meant the soldier was "hung up by the thumbs," which Fry admitted was "a most barbarous proceeding." These generally exaggerated stories circulated from one Northerner to the next and eventually gained credence, resulting in what Fry considered to be one of the most serious obstacles to recruiting during the war's second half. This diminished willingness to enlist was especially felt in those areas where antiwar sentiment was high to begin with.[2]

Whereas desertion had always occurred in the Union armies for one reason or another, the deed skyrocketed in 1864, averaging 7,333 per month compared to 4,647 per month in 1863. October 1864 saw 10,692 desertions, the highest monthly number for the entire war and indicative of Northern war weariness. Congress became so frustrated with such numbers that it passed legislation near the rebellion's end stipulating that any man who had previously deserted the army or navy and did not voluntarily return within sixty days "relinquished and forfeited their rights of citizenship and their rights to become citizens." Moreover, deserters would be forever banned from holding any office of public trust.[3]

Desertion was also a potentially deadly business for those caught by Union authorities. The official sentence for desertion was death though, in the aggregate, that punishment was rarely imposed. Instead, deserters were sometimes branded with the letter "D" on the cheek, arm, or hip. A "D" on the left side meant drunkard; a "D" on the right meant deserter. Sometimes a soldier was branded with a "W," which stood for "worthless." In most cases, however, forcing deserters back into the army's depleted ranks was deemed a better choice than maiming or shooting them. Furthermore, there was a legitimate concern that such capital punishment would deter enlistments. Volunteers might willingly accept the risk of battlefield death, however, enlistments were sure to fall if potential recruits viewed the military as a brutally tyrannical entity that routinely executed its own men. While the historical numbers are somewhat

"Death of Johnson—Fryday [sic] Dec. 13th, 1861" By Alfred Wordsworth Thompson (Virginia Museum of History and Culture 2000.165.3.R)

imprecise, approximately 200,000 men deserted the Union armies during the Civil War. Of that number, roughly 80,000 were caught and arrested, which meant that a deserter had an approximate 60 percent chance of never being apprehended. Of those caught, roughly 150 were convicted and executed for the crime of desertion—which included bounty jumping—during the war's last two years as an example to others.[4]

Numerous high-ranking officers believed that potential deserters would be swayed into staying if they witnessed the consequences administered to those who were caught. A Vermont officer who sat on a court-martial board wholly agreed with that rationale, explaining to his wife how, "There ought to be a few of them shot as examples and perhaps it would frighten others to remain who will now desert . . . it seems rather hard, but to secure discipline in our army some such measures must be adopted." Yet it was not always so quick and clean for officers sitting on such boards, or any officer for that matter who the soldiers believed had abused them. Those officers who handed down death sentences faced potential battlefield retribution from the friends of a man executed for desertion. Another Vermont soldier wrote in January 1864 how strange it was that the authorities would let desertion go unpunished for two years but now seemed to be shooting every deserter they caught. "Some of those officers that sit on courts martials will be very apt to die suddenly during next summer's campaign," predicted the Vermonter, "for the friends of those men that have been shot has got them marked, and there is always opportunitys anough during a battle to put an end to their miserable existence." Nonetheless, the threat of such extreme discipline in no way stemmed the tide. The most common method of desertion was actually the easiest. Men on furlough or sick leave back home simply failed to report back for duty. Henry Halleck wrote as early as July 19, 1862, that of the thousands sent home on sick leave, hardly any ever returned.[5]

Once in the field, marches between one point and another or on advance picket duty afforded ample desertion opportunities, including fleeing over to the Rebels. Most who abandoned their posts were foreigners who had first enlisted as a substitute and then only after collecting their hefty substitute or bounty money. Such cowardly acts were especially egregious to Maj. Gen. George Meade, who angrily lectured his wife's brother-in-law on the sorry state of his new Union recruits, most of whom Meade felt were "worthless foreigners, who are daily deserting to the enemy." One old veteran later wrote of the 5th New Hampshire Infantry, which had earned a solid fighting reputation in the war's early years. By mid-1864, however, the man recalled that so many new conscripts and substitutes had deserted to the "Johnnies" that the Confederate pickets would joke with their Union counterparts about the Yanks relinquishing and sending over the 5th's regimental colors. The Rebels then erected a sign on their entrenchments that read, "Headquarters 5th New Hampshire vols. Recruits wanted." In the main, the man who enlisted for the first time in late 1863 through the war's end and primarily for the bounty was essentially useless, having never learned the lesson of submission to military authority.[6]

Charles Biddlecom (first mentioned in chapter 1) typified the useless recruit. He reenlisted in late 1863 solely to avoid the draft and collect a bounty and then looked to desert at the first chance. Biddlecom first volunteered when the war began solely as a way to prove his manhood, having admitted he cared nothing for the Union. When the quick and easy war he expected did not materialize, Biddlecom finagled a medical discharge in early August 1861. As he was not in the service on March 3, 1863, when the new enrollment law took effect, he was therefore deemed eligible for the new draft. His brother-in-law, David Lapham, upon being told that Charles may be drafted, wrote how he hoped Charles would not obey the law. "The Republicans and Abolitionists made no bones about saying the war should be carried on for abolition, not for the restoration of the Old Union," Lapham wrote. Like innumerable others, a deeply embedded, cultural racism lay at the heart of his complaint. "I believe the masses of the slaves are much better off in slavery than out of it," Lapham admitted, "especially in the manner the abolitionists would take them out, if they could." Lapham need not have worried for his brother-in-law had no intention of obeying either the spirit or the letter of the new law. Biddlecom had always considered himself the "black sheep" of his family, yet within two months of his new induction, he was looking for a means of escape. "I do not mean to winter in one of these dog holes . . . I can play off enough to get out of this and I mean to do it," he avowed to his wife, then conceding, "Now you see I'm going in for getting out of this just as soon as is possible."[7]

After having enlisted and netted a handsome bounty only five months earlier in late summer 1863, James Horrocks (first mentioned in chapter 1) was another who was soon searching for a way out. Despite his well-educated British upbringing, Horrocks exemplified the recently immigrated hireling for whom the war was solely an opportunity for financial gain. Writing from his Washington, DC, camp to his parents in England on February 21, 1864, Horrocks revealed that if and when his artillery unit started for the Virginia front, he would skedaddle to Philadelphia with his well-laid plan to hide in the open within the city's teeming masses. He explained that if he was quickly caught, he would only be charged with being absent without leave, for a soldier had to be absent at least ten days before being formally accused of the far more serious charge of desertion. By that time, he planned on being on a ship headed back to England. "If I was in England or in the English service I should consider that it was a shame and a sin to desert but—you know the old adage—When you are in Rome you do as the Romans do," he clarified to his parents after having seen numerous Union soldiers looking to flee the army. With his hopes of gaining promotion to the relatively safe rear-guard position of quartermaster sergeant watching over baggage trains having all but vanished, Horrocks knew he would have to take part in any upcoming battle as a cannoneer or driver given his current role as a company clerk. Seeking to rationalize his decision, Horrocks wrote, "I assure you that what would be considered in England and what I would consider myself as a disgraceful action is here regarded universally as a *Smart thing* and the person who does it is a *dem'd smart fellow.*" Horrocks had learned that by early 1864 and unless one was a naive teenage boy who had just turned eighteen years old, any notions of enlisting for patriotic glory were long gone. His inner calculation was simple: to serve as a private meant he may die without honor or glory and with no benefit to his parents. To achieve promotion to quartermaster sergeant meant a good chance of then gaining an officer's commission and returning home safe and sound. Unlike many native-born 1861 and 1862 enlistees, the war's loftier purposes played no part in his reasoning.[8]

AVOIDING CONFEDERATE PRISONER OF WAR CAMPS

If witnessing the suffering of a soldier-neighbor's wife and children contributed toward keeping service-eligible men rooted at home—as well as seeing the rampant desertion that resulted from that suffering—then new accounts of captured Union men languishing in fetid Confederate prisoner of war sites further prompted Northern men to double down on their war-avoidance decision. This was due in part to the prisoner exchange system's parole feature (first discussed in chapter 5), which was effectively terminated by Union authorities in the summer of 1863. Federal officials came to realize that every Confederate exchanged immediately or soon thereafter ended up back in Rebel service and therefore, the war could go on indefinitely.

Furthermore, federal authorities had fully expected in 1862 that any captured Black Union soldier would be treated the same as any White one when it came to prisoner exchanges. That December, however, Confederate president Jefferson Davis proclaimed that no Black soldiers nor their White officers would be subject to the exchange agreements. That edict became law the following May when the Confederate Congress passed a joint resolution reiterating Davis's earlier pronouncement. On July 31, 1863, the Union countered by publishing Lincoln's General Orders No. 252, declaring in essence, an eye for an eye when it came to the South's treatment of Black prisoners and how the North would respond. It essentially suspended the prior prisoner exchange pact until the South was willing to treat Black prisoners no different than White prisoners.[9]

Thus began in earnest the misery and suffering of each side's prisoners of war due to the lack of resources available to properly feed and house tens of thousands of such men. Prison camps sprang up all over the North and South, and they quickly became known as god-forsaken places to be avoided at all costs. The most notorious Southern prisoner of war camp was officially known as Camp Sumter, located in southwest Georgia. Better known as "Andersonville," the infamous twenty-six-acre, open-air stockade opened in late 1863 and was designed to hold 10,000 prisoners of war. It featured one small muddy stream running through it that served as both a water supply and latrine. At its peak, however, 32,000 men were imprisoned there, all with minimal food, clothing, and shelter. One of those men was Pennsylvanian Samuel Gibson, who recorded in his pocket diary on June 9, 1864, that he was "Still in this Hell-upon-earth of a Prison" with his comrades' health conditions deteriorating by the day. Almost three weeks later on June 28, Gibson spoke for every captive when he wrote, "If this is not Hell itself, it must be pandemonium; which is only Hell Gate. Heaven forbid I should ever see a worse place." By the time the war ended, more than 45,000 Union prisoners had passed through Andersonville's gates. During its existence, almost 13,000 Union soldiers died there, in other words, at least one in four men who entered never left, all victims of slow starvation, foul water, disease, and exposure to both brutally hot summers and cold winters.[10]

Word of these new and miserable prison camps reached each side's civilian public and had an indelible impact on those still at home. A Vermont newspaper described Andersonville's stockade as "a sort of pig pen" with the Union prisoners "restricted to a scanty swinish fare of soured corn meal." From St. Louis, Mrs. Sarah Hill heard of the prisons' "horrible brutalities" and wrote to her army husband declaring that she would rather see him honorably killed in battle rather than learn of him taken prisoner and then sent to one of those "hell holes."[11]

Nearly as infamous as Andersonville was the three-story, one-time tobacco warehouse known as Libby Prison, located within the Confederacy's capital of Richmond, Virginia, and which housed captured Union officers in eight low-ceilinged rooms on the top two floors. Its windows were barred yet remained open to the elements, which resulted in Libby's captives baking in the brutal summers and freezing in the cold winters. Reports surfaced of diseased, emaciated prisoners so cramped together that they were likened to sardines in a can. Army engineer Orlando Poe spoke for scores of Northern soldiers when he admitted to his wife in late November 1863 that the mere thought of languishing in a filthy prison like Libby was enough to make one fight desperately. As with Andersonville, such overcrowding, unsanitary conditions and a lack of proper food led to horrific tales of death and disease.[12]

On the south side of Richmond was Belle Isle, a fifty-four-acre open-air prison located on an island in the middle of the James River. The

Libby Prison, Richmond, Virginia, April 1865 (Library of Congress Prints and Photographs Division)

river's swirling, speedy rapids around the island served to deter escape attempts while a footbridge connecting the island to Richmond facilitated the movement of guards and prisoners, the latter group consisting of noncommissioned Union officers and privates. Similar to Andersonville, the open-air Belle Isle camp contained no barracks for its inmates, only a relatively few tents, which resulted in the prisoners suffering as the seasons changed. Reports from escaped Union officers, previously exchanged Union prisoners, and Rebel deserters allowed Northern civilians to become well aware of the horrid conditions in what one Northern paper termed "these Black Holes of the Confederacy," especially after the Lincoln administration decided to stop the prisoner exchange system in the summer of 1863. That decision was controversial in the North and hardly enjoyed bipartisan support. "What could possibly be more discouraging to enlisting than the fact that our men taken prisoners by the enemy, can see no end to their captivity and their sufferings in rebel prisons, because of the policy adopted by the administration in regard to exchange," asked the Democratic-leaning *Star of the North* in Columbia County, Pennsylvania. From that paper's perspective, the predictable sad result henceforth was that Union soldiers unfortunate enough to fall into the enemy's hands were most likely going to starve and rot in Rebel prisons; a prediction that had ample prescience in it. That new policy along with the steady newspaper reports of those prisons' conditions and the soldiers suffering within them served as yet another reminder to the Northern stay-at-homes that they should steer clear of army service.[13]

The Home Front Assisting Desertion

By early 1864, the Northern home front was painfully aware of the horrors found on the battlefield, in disease-ridden encampments, in Union hospitals, and in Confederate prisoner of war camps. The one-time holy war of three years prior had transformed into a for-profit business for some, while for others it was an insatiable, unholy monster to be avoided at all costs. Like numerous Union soldiers, so much of the Northern civilian public was fed up with the war and the reasons for it that they repeatedly urged their kin in uniform to get out any way they could and had done so ever since the fall of 1862 following Lincoln's Emancipation

Proclamation. "Richard, take a fools advice and come home if you have to desert, you will be protected" an Illinois man assured his nephew in the 16th Illinois Infantry. "The people are so enraged that you need not be alarmed if you hear of the whole of the Northwest killing off the abolitionists." By the same token, a young Michigan man writing to his father from Grand Rapids was disheartened to read all the various letters urging soldiers to desert or resign and to "do no more for the 'nigger.'" An Ohio soldier received a more subtle letter from "an old democratic friend" imploring him to "quit murdering his southern brethren." After reading similar accounts, an Iowa recruit informed his parents how "Sometimes I see letters to the boys in this Regiment so full of Secesh notions that if the writers were exposed they would be severely punished, letters encouraging desertion &c." The issue of antiwar or anti-draft civilians encouraging desertion was every bit as severe as discouraging enlistments from earlier in the war. Even more disconcerting to the Lincoln administration were the professional antiwar speakers, newspaper editors, or other perceived rabble-rousers who encouraged family members to induce their army kin to desert. This type of antiwar speech was considered part and parcel of the Peace Democrats' "fire in the rear" threat that the Lincoln administration had come to fear more than the Confederate armies.[14]

For most pro-war Unionists, there was a distinct line between privately arguing against the war's merits compared to publicly encouraging those acts—such as desertion or not enlisting—that would have a tangible impact on the army's ability to put down the rebellion. It was especially grating when the "free speech" issue was raised by war opponents. Given what they viewed as the clear-cut language in the Constitution's first amendment, antiwar partisans held that they should have an unlimited right to publicly speak their mind on the war with no political consequences from the federal government. With regards to promoting desertion, these protestors reasoned that they were not in the army, not subject to its disciplinary requirements, nor had they done anything that gave aid and comfort to the enemy. The issue gave rise to one of Lincoln's most famous wartime quotes that was in the form of a rhetorical question; one which he asked in a June 1863 letter to a group of federal lawmakers: "Must I shoot a simple-minded soldier boy who deserts, while I must not touch a hair of a wily agitator who induces him to desert?" Lincoln's missive was in regards to ex-Ohio congressman and prominent Copperhead Clement Vallandigham, who was arrested by Union authorities on May 5, 1863, after giving an anti-administration speech that was deemed treasonous as it allegedly gave aid and comfort to the enemy. By utilizing the "doctrine of necessity," Lincoln maintained that Vallandigham was not arrested because he was merely giving a speech that may have been damaging to the administration's political prospects, "but because he was damaging the army, upon the existence, and vigor of which, the life of the nation depends," wrote the president. In Lincoln's lawyerly opinion, Vallandigham was "warring upon the military; and this gave the military constitutional jurisdiction to lay hands upon him." In the larger picture, Lincoln believed dealing with the cunning dissenter provided the greater good. "I think that in such a case, to silence the agitator, and save the boy, is not only constitutional, but, withal, a great mercy." Here concisely, were the hallmark ingredients of the Lincoln administration's efforts to combat desertion and the underlying essence of disloyalty nestled within it: the full power of the government leveled against organized subversion coupled with "great mercy" toward the sometimes hapless boy who understood little of what he did.[15]

While those still at home had no intention of enlisting, families and friends of soldiers seeking to desert continued to concoct all manner of ways to help them escape. Some families persisted in smuggling civilian clothes to their soldier relatives to make it easier for them to desert their posts. In western New York, Ann Smith told her husband in late March 1864 of the reports that there were new soldiers' uniforms strung all along the fences around nearby Elmira, left there by deserters after replacing them with civilian attire. One resident reported finding three uniforms just in his garden. Others waited along the way home with wagons or provided canoes to help a deserter cross over rivers. In West Jefferson, Ohio, six clothing merchants were arrested by orders of the local provost marshal for selling "skedaddling suits" to deserters. They were released only after posting a $5,000 bail each.[16]

As with the bounty jumper, deserting soldiers cut or dyed their hair or shaved off their mustaches in an attempt to alter their appearance. In one instance, every soldier in one man's company knew he received a suit of clothes from home yet no one seemed to care. At the next morning's roll call, he wore the civilian suit under his army uniform. Later that morning, he went off into the woods to supposedly chop wood for the camp and, predictably, never returned. Once army authorities learned of the practice, commanding officers ordered that all future packages sent from the home front must show an invoice of their contents. Any contraband clothing was to be confiscated. The word of such exploits soon reached all the way to the army's highest level. "So anxious were parents, wives, brothers and sisters to relieve their kindred, that they filled the express trains to the army with packages of citizen clothing to assist them in escaping," Maj. Gen. Joseph Hooker later testified.[17]

Once home, deserters hid out in their own houses or in that of a sympathetic neighbor, rarely venturing outside. If a deserter with no struggling family came from a town or village that was resolutely pro-war, he often traveled elsewhere, choosing to settle in areas where support for the war was weak. Those who deserted sometimes decided to keep wearing their uniform when they arrived unknown in a Northern town; brazenly hiding in the open under the pretense that they were merely on furlough. Civilian men who sought to avoid the draft did so as well, acquiring used uniforms as a means of presenting an appearance that they were already in the service. The *Valley Spirit* in Franklin County, Pennsylvania, responded by urging that no man not on active duty should be allowed to wear a US army uniform. "These stay-at-home patriots who are so fond of aping the soldier, would have their vanity brought down a peg by such a wholesome regulation." Even innocent acts offended some soldiers. "I hope father won't wear my coat," wrote a Wisconsin lad after having served a year in the army because "I hate to see a civilian in soldier's dress." Dedicated soldiers sensed that because of their travails and hardships, they had become somehow different from their civilian friends, home guard members, family, and most deserters. A figurative wall now existed between those who shared the ordeals of campaigning and trial by fire and those who had not.[18]

Antiwar and deserter-friendly communities devised early warning systems such as placing horns or bells in houses. If word of an approaching provost marshal and his squadron reached the community, a resident would sound the alarm. That signal allowed deserters to flee into nearby woods with ample provisions for a few days or until the danger had passed. Moreover, sympathetic neighbors routinely gave the arresting authorities faulty information as to the deserter's whereabouts. A deserter was not always a coward looking for a way out but a dedicated family man who realized his wife and children were suffering and needed his presence back home. These were men who were born and raised in a culture that had no experience with war or military service for the previous forty years, other than the far-away, brief, and paltry Mexican War. When they abandoned their posts to tend to dire familial needs, they often did so with no feeling of misconduct.[19]

Time and again, soldiers who abandoned their posts to attend to desperate circumstances at home were adamant that they had every intention of returning to the army and were therefore not guilty of desertion. Those soldiers stressed that such temporary unauthorized absences, known colloquially in the army as "French leave," should have garnered the much lesser charge of absent without leave rather than desertion, especially if the soldier had indeed returned to his unit voluntarily rather than being arrested at his home. As the war dragged on, few Union privates looked down upon any fellow soldier who took some temporary French leave in order to tend to his hurting family. These men sensed that self-preservation is mankind's most natural impulse and that urge extended to a man's loved ones. While desertion may have been considered cowardly in the abstract, in reality, most privates considered a comrade's motives before assigning that dreaded label. Since most soldiers served in locally organized units, many a man's comrades may have been neighbors back home and knew of his home front challenges. "No blame was attached to anyone who was smart enough to get away," wrote a soldier in the 4th Rhode Island Infantry because, as discussed earlier, their culture's individualism ethos acknowledged that a man's tangible responsibilities to his family and the local community took precedence over any theoretical national duty. Furthermore, his right to make that decision for himself was foundational to what it meant to be a free White man in mid-nineteenth-century America.[20]

CHAPTER 9

By 1864, relieving a desperate family was the primary reason men fled the army. Unreliable army pay and the effect that had on struggling Northern households prompted husbands and fathers to desert by the tens of thousands. If the federal government could not hold up its end of the social contract, then many men felt they had the moral right—and obligation—to leave and attend to their families, or so their conviction went. The era's gendered and social ideal dictated that while a man had a duty to serve his country, his first obligation was to his family. Consequently, compassionate home front civilians routinely kept silent or looked the other way when deserters appeared. This was especially the case if the civilians were personally opposed to the war or if they lived in a community that was overwhelmingly against the war, such as in the lower Midwest. Within these communities, the provost marshal and his deserter-hunting party were often viewed as a type of fugitive slave hunter and were treated with a similar contempt. This war antipathy allowed thousands of deserters to escape to and survive in towns all across the North. In addition, those civilians who had never considered enlisting because they were indifferent to the far-off war or completely absorbed in their own affairs were not likely to contact the authorities and get involved in what might become a dangerous neighbor-versus-neighbor conflict, especially when the civilian award for doing so was a relatively mere thirty dollars. The authors of the Cumberland County, Illinois, history published in 1884 wrote that there was no evidence of residents encouraging their soldiers to desert during the war but on the other hand, there was also no effort made to turn over deserters to the authorities. Since the deserters were not likely to submit meekly to any arrest, "the people had not the courage of their convictions sufficiently to feel prepared to shoot old acquaintances, or be shot by them." Minnesota provost marshal George H. Keith capsulated this feeling in his end-of-war report. Since, according to Keith, the deserter was able to keep away from the hired detectives, much of the local intelligence fell to the civilian population. However, "very few civilians are willing to arrest deserters for the reward of thirty dollars," Keith noted, since the informant "gets the ill will of the deserter and his friends for life." Capt. B. F. Westlake of Illinois' ninth district would have echoed Keith, and then added, "But to induce citizens generally to engage in this dangerous work the reward would require to be much higher."[21]

Then there were the antiwar townsfolk who were prepared for violence in their desire to assist deserters who were being sought out by federal officials. From their viewpoint, armed resistance in keeping friends and relations out of an army engaged in an unconstitutional and unjust war was every bit as legitimate as the anti-draft violence that first reared its head in the fall of 1862 and remained present ever since. On March 11, 1863, in the small hamlet of Hoskinsville, Ohio, approximately one hundred armed residents turned away—and even threatened to shoot—five Union soldiers and a US deputy marshal who had arrived to arrest a young man charged with desertion. After learning what had transpired from the empty-handed soldiers, Union authorities in Cincinnati dispatched two companies of troops from the 115th Ohio Volunteer Infantry to arrest those involved. Meanwhile, the local and state press quickly weighed in on what was described as "a small speck of war in Ohio," praising the patriots and denouncing the traitors. Who exactly were the former and the latter depended on the newspaper's partisan political leanings.[22]

In Charleston, Illinois, on March 28, 1864, armed Copperheads hiding in the open and purportedly hell-bent on "cleaning out" any Union military presence in the town ambushed a group of mostly unarmed soldiers from the 54th Illinois Infantry as they mingled with the locals while waiting for the next train that would return them to their regiment. It was a brief, murderous affair as any man wearing a blue Union coat with brass buttons was shot at. In his later report based on eyewitness depositions, Illinois' AAPMG James Oakes stated that more than one hundred shots were fired and nearly every soldier present was either killed or wounded. In sum, six Union soldiers were slain and twenty more injured in a manner that might be rightly compared to a twenty-first-century terrorist attack. After the firing stopped, a frantic dispatch was sent to the town of Mattoon, about twelve miles away, asking for soldiers to come at once. About three hundred arrived by evening, putting an end to the day's bloodshed. Yet after hearing reliable reports that the Copperheads were gathering in force and planning another attack, James Oakes sent word on March 30 requesting that another five hundred men be sent to Charleston with all haste by special train. The feared Copperhead follow-up attack never materialized and, with hundreds of armed Union soldiers now in Charleston, peace returned to the town.[23]

One of the more famous alleged acts of resistance became known as the "Fishing Creek Confederacy" and took place in Pennsylvania's strongly Democratic Columbia County, situated within the Appalachian Mountains. In the early evening of July 30, 1864, several veteran Union soldiers and two civilians led by Lt. and Asst. Provost Marshal James S. Robinson rode into Benton Township in northern Columbia County to search for specific deserters. Word of the deserter-hunting party spread quickly, resulting in a confrontation between Robinson's men and, unbeknownst to them at the time, a number of the deserters. Shots rang out, including one that mortally wounded Lieutenant Robinson.[24]

The federal authorities were outraged, their anger heightened in the days to follow by persistent reports that several hundred antiwar deserters had bandied together and fled into the Fishing Creek valley. Their purported hideout was a newly constructed "fort" on North Mountain that allegedly included four artillery pieces. Throughout August, hundreds of Union troops marched into the area, scouring the countryside for the rumored fort and the deserters, but finding nothing other than a few small-scale, abandoned camps. On August 31 and in a face-saving act, one hundred local citizens were arrested in their homes by Union soldiers and charged with disloyal activities. Forty-four were sent off to dank, dark Fort Mifflin, located on Mud Island, just below Philadelphia in the Delaware River. There they were held for several months in a bombproof cell. One man died in the overcrowded prison, another went insane, and five more contracted serious illnesses. Only a small handful of the initial one hundred arrested were ever convicted, and those sentences were later pardoned by Presidents Abraham Lincoln and then Andrew Johnson. Most Democrats and even some Republicans decried the trials as a travesty. Gen. George Cadwalader, who was in command of the Union soldiers looking for the deserters and their purported fort, remarked, "The whole thing is a grand farce." Coupled with the fact that no large-scale armed resistance was ever uncovered, the heavy-handed presence and arrests by the Union military only added to the locals' dominant antiwar perspective.[25]

Such acts of overt, armed resistance were carried out and rationalized by those Northern dissenters who believed that the Lincoln administration's new draft laws and chipping away at an individual's constitutional civil rights were destroying the country. These generally working-class people may not have comprehended the war's overarching economics, but they certainly knew that paying exorbitant fees for commutation or substitutes was beyond the reach of most of them. They were keenly aware of the grave financial and physical dangers their families would face if they were taken from their homes and forced into the army. They realized how their dissent had its roots in class divisions every bit as much as any political theory. Suspending the right of habeas corpus, secret trial by military commission rather than by a jury of one's civilian peers, free speech now labeled as treasonous, forcing men against their will into the army, and the Emancipation Proclamation convinced many that their belief in "the Constitution as it is and the Union as it was" required them to now pick up the musket just as their revolutionary forefathers had done. As historian John H. Schaar put forth, an analysis of the Declaration of Independence, the Constitution, and its preamble would reveal that a citizen's only legitimate loyalty should be to a free society and its government. In the minds and opinions of these dissenters, refusing to obey an administration that itself had betrayed the constitutional trusts given to it by the citizenry was not disloyal or treasonous, but actually the duty of the conscientious citizen. It was nigh impossible for some staunch antiwar communities such as the few just discussed to accept that what they regarded as a political lunatic fringe was now in command of the nation's reins of power.[26]

A Strengthening Economy as Another Reason to Ignore the War

After three years of war, serving as a soldier in the Union army was viewed simply as a business by innumerable newer recruits who were mostly substitutes. The immense bounties and supposedly steady monthly pay represented both a long-term nest egg and current income. Even more potential recruits chose not to enlist because the war had created numerous lucrative employment opportunities for those who enjoyed decent health, though the draft still hung over the head of many like the sword of Damocles. "I am just here on heavy expenses for nothing," bemoaned one enrolling officer in early 1864 after spending days on end without signing up any new recruits. Missouri's prominent St. Louis businessman Judson Bemis succinctly illustrated that avoid-the-war civilian mindset. After learning in early April that another 300,000 men were called for, the thirty-one-year-old Bemis wondered where they would all come from. In any event, he was adamant in a letter to his brother, "I do not want to go—I have our man in the army for three years or the war, and would rather put in two or three more than go myself." Besides, Bemis further rationalized that any man who could be had for $300 would probably be of more service to the army than himself. "Therefore," he concluded, "my conscience feels at ease on that point."[27]

Meanwhile, the prospect of finding gold in the Western mountains still spurred many to head west. By so doing, a man garnered the possibility of finding great riches while also giving the slip to the draft wheel back home. That reality prompted Iowa's governor, William M. Stone, to write to Union general Samuel R. Curtis at his Department of Kansas headquarters in February 1864, begging the general to prevent Iowans from fleeing the draft. Stone surmised that the Iowans' excuse was that they were traveling to the new Idaho mines where gold was discovered only a few years earlier. Curtis replied by sympathizing with Stone's plight and urged him to remind Iowa's citizens of their patriotic duty, which by March 1864 was like asking Don Quixote to keep tilting at his famous windmills. He warned Stone of his reports claiming that a human tide was on its way from as far east as Ohio. With regards to the gold stories, "The news from Idaho is almost fabulous," Curtis wrote, "and it is hard to tell whether love of gold or fear of the draft has the longest end of the singletree."[28]

To compete with the private sector, the federal government had begun to offer reenlistment sweeteners the prior summer to those veterans and their regiments whose three-year terms of service were ending soon. Given the terms of the March 1863 Enrollment Act, these men could not be drafted once mustered out nor compelled to serve in any other manner. Therefore, on June 25, 1863, the War Department began authorizing so-called "veteran" regiments. Men who had served for a minimum of nine months could now reenlist for three years or the duration of the war. The sweetener was an immediate thirty-day furlough, one month's pay in advance, and a $400 bounty to be paid out in installments. Upon reenlistment, he would immediately receive $25 of his bounty, a one-time $2 "premium," and his first month's pay of $13. Another $50 of his bounty would be paid out on his next payday with the next $50 at the six-month point and each six months thereafter. The final $75 would follow at the end of the three years. Considering the monthly pay of $13, the $400 bounty for a man already in the service meant that his monthly income would be almost doubled over the three-year term.[29]

Such inducements were necessary to keep men in the service because everyone from administration officials down to the lowliest private knew that good employment and wages back home served to discourage enlistments. Factory work was brisk as the demand from the North's war machine continued unabated. As early as March 1863, then eighteen-year-old Martin Reiss, who was working as a happy-go-lucky itinerate harness maker in St. Louis, wrote to his brother of how he had heard the constant rumors of the war's imminent end for almost two years. Not only did Reiss seemingly give no thought to enlisting, he then explained that he did *not* want the war to end, "because as soon as this war is over, times are going to be rough." The war was distant to young workingmen like Reiss who did not yet have to worry about the draft. Reiss had all the good-paying work he wanted and did not want the gravy to stop flowing. Many, of course, were frustrated by such realities. "What the devil do they pay so much wages for at home," complained Charles Tew to his wife in November 1863. Tew's solution regarding high wages was simple: "Cut them down and then they will enlist fast enough to end the war." Union engineer John Westervelt even saw such inequity at the front. He witnessed two hundred to three hundred government-employed civilian men dragging lumber off of Charleston sandbars that had broken loose from harbor obstructions. It was hard work, and while their toils spared the soldiers from doing such laborious duty, the $30 plus rations the civilians received was far more than a soldier's pay. "Why should these men get more pay than our soldiers," Westervelt wondered, "and escape the draft in the bargain?"[30]

While jobs remained plentiful for any who sought one, home front price inflation had risen so fast and far that workingmen and their families routinely faced monthly budget shortfalls. A sad reality was that the purchasing power of those earlier bounties was being reduced on literally a monthly basis. Those stay-at-home men with jobs paying more than the army pay of $13 per month knew their families would suffer if they volunteered, therefore home front price inflation served as a recruiting deterrent. Much of that fiscal pain was the result of the North's new paper money.

Initially, the US government financed the war with its gold reserves. As those reserves fell, the federal government needed an alternative means of paying for the war. It began by selling bonds that could be redeemed with interest upon maturity. In August 1861, which was only four months after the war commenced, Congress passed the "Revenue Act," which initiated the nation's first-ever federal income tax. The act stipulated that citizens would now have to pay a 3 percent tax on income of more than $800 per year, however, it would be twelve months before those funds were collected. The government then turned to the printing press in February 1862, when it began to issue legal tender paper money known colloquially as "greenbacks" because the backs of the notes were printed in green ink. Far easier and less onerous on the public in the short term than taxation or confiscation, the vast increase in the printed supply of money in the economy predictably leads to inflation, which is an increase in prices and a concurrent cheapening of the value of the paper money.[31]

Inflation began to take hold almost immediately and had a profound negative effect on working- and middle-class households. Rising prices only worsened as the war progressed and, at their worst, were 80 percent higher than pre-war levels. No region of the North was immune. "War prices are terrible. I paid $3.50 to-day for a hoop skirt," twenty-year-old Caroline Richards of upstate New York complained to her diary in

January 1863. In Detroit, German immigrant Johann Look was stunned at the rising prices, noting in a May 1863 letter to his children how "everything has become so expensive all of a sudden." Less than a year later in March 1864, Detroit's *Free Press* reported how coffee prices had more than doubled since the war's commencement, rising from 20¢ to 45¢ a pound. Meanwhile, eggs had doubled from 10¢ to 20¢ a dozen. At the same time, potatoes that had sold for 25¢ a bushel in 1861 were now commanding the same price for only one-fourth that amount. In New York, the price for home heating coal had doubled to $10.50 per ton from the $5.25 per ton it had averaged in the fifteen years prior to 1863. By August 1864, Judge Thomas Anderson wrote to his son from Marion, Ohio, that prices were exorbitant. "Laborers get $3.00 per day," wrote the elder Anderson. "Farming and wool-growing are the best occupations now." In New York, the cost of food, shoes, and clothing had mostly doubled within a year, far outpacing home front wages and that of a Union private. One newspaper urged tenants to move to the suburbs, which was not a practical solution for most working-class renters.[32]

The price of gold spiked; its rise reflecting a corresponding decline in the public's faith in the war effort. By the middle of summer 1864, greenbacks, which were initially issued on a one-to-one basis with a gold dollar, were down to forty cents worth of gold. Meanwhile, the price of gold seemed to rise or fall with every morsel of news or rumor from the front. The attendant uncertainty and fear generated by both rising prices and rising body counts, coupled with the need for steady family income served as a recruiting deterrent. "How any can deliberately make up their minds to go I cannot understand," wrote Almyra Barker to a male friend after reading all the latest news. With the possibility of another draft looming in September, innumerable working-class men with families to feed and not already wearing a blue uniform sought any means to keep it that way. An added war-avoidance incentive for family men living in mostly urban areas was the pitiful sight of "war widows"; women whose husbands had been killed in the war and with little to no experience in earning a living on their own were now forced into labor such as commercial sewing, which often paid near-starvation wages.[33]

While monetary inflation created the illusion of prosperity for many, it wreaked havoc on the working class. Real wages declined for farmers, laborers, factory workers, and the soldiers themselves. These issues had been predicted in the congressional debates, nevertheless, the public's concern for a stable monetary policy was subordinated to the administration's need in obtaining funds to carry on the war. Still, in response to the public's cry, Congress increased a private's pay from $13 to $16 a month; however, that was small comfort because price inflation had been so severe that $16 in June 1864 represented only $6.40 in 1861 dollars. When the war ended in 1865, it required $216.80 to purchase what could have been obtained for $100 in 1861.[34]

By the summer of 1864, the war was not going well for the Union. More men were required to fill the ranks, the war was as bloody as ever, and war weariness had surged. Meanwhile, home front morale had plummeted to levels not seen since the winter of 1862–1863. Not until the fall of that year and some sweeping battlefield victories would matters start to reverse themselves.

"The Apathy of Our People Is Our Stumbling Block"

Avoiding the War Intensifies for Civilian and Soldier Alike

A SOLDIER FOR ONE HUNDRED DAYS OR A SAILOR FOR THREE YEARS

Growing desertions, a strong home front economy, along with rising civilian war weariness all combined to give Union authorities continued uneasiness over their manpower dilemma. The supply of stay-at-home men who had yet to serve seemed like a bottomless well, therefore, how to get more of them into a blue uniform remained a constant concern at the Union's highest governmental levels.

Spring 1864 brought one partial solution with the creation of what became known as "hundred days' men." With the war's end seeming closer than ever and after some backroom negotiation with Lincoln in a manner similar to what transpired in 1862, the governors of Illinois, Indiana, Wisconsin, Iowa, and Ohio formally offered the president 100,000 men on April 21 to serve a mere one hundred days. The desired goal was conceptually similar to what spurred the Invalid Corps' 1863 creation. These green "hundred days' men" would garrison various Northern forts and prisoner of war camps, guard bridges, and the like so that any healthy veteran troops now performing that rearguard work could be freed up for frontline work. This duty also extended to guarding supply camps in one-time Confederate territory now under Union control. As a result, Union authorities hoped this new and sudden infusion of veteran troops at the front would provide the final, overwhelming death blow against secession and the Confederacy.[1]

As with many of the original 1861 ninety-day men, here was a chance for the remaining multitude of stay-at-home rangers to dip their toes into the war for what would be a short season, performing relatively safe duty, as well as the opportunity to rid themselves of any allegations of cowardice that may have been whispered behind their backs. An added incentive was that they would not be subject to the then-pending draft and its three-year service requirement. Most had refused to consider enlistment earlier when the term was two or three years, so if they survived these one hundred days at some easy garrison, they would then head home with the self-satisfaction of having contributed their honorable duty to the war effort. Each state's recruiting efforts were intense; in Indianapolis, Charles Wilson told his diary on April 26 how the call for the hundred days' men had created "quite a stir." Yet in the end, none of the five states met their quotas, each realizing that their calls were made at the height of the spring planting season. In the case of Ohio, Gov. John Brough simply called out the newly reorganized Ohio National Guard, which had been created the year before. Most men who signed on the year before were led to believe they would never serve outside of Ohio but were now distraught when orders came for duty at the front.[2]

Barzilla Shaw was an example of one man who faced this unexpected change of events. Married with two young children, twenty-eight-year-old Shaw left his Coshocton, Ohio, family farm in 1864 to join the one-hundred-day 143rd Ohio Infantry after having declined earlier enlistment opportunities. He was initially appointed to the rearguard position of quartermaster sergeant. Though his regiment saw action during the Petersburg campaign, like many soldiers, Shaw's diary revealed his biggest worries were acquiring enough to eat and not becoming grievously ill. As his one hundred days neared their end, Shaw's most pressing concern was to simply get home in one piece.[3]

The historian for one of these one-hundred-day regiments later wrote that these volunteers were generally older and "of the more substantial class of citizens." They were the men who had helped to orga-nize and equip the early regiments and were now generally in charge of their hometown's businesses. For this reason, they considered themselves irreplaceable at home for any commitment longer than a season, if that. Even a few of those men who did volunteer soon had second thoughts. After experiencing buyer's remorse, one Ohioan managed to finagle a military doctor's exemption after signing up. Yet when he reported to the regiment's colonel for formal approval, he foolishly admitted, "Colonel, I have no doubt I could stand the service as well as any of the men, but the fact is my family cannot get along without me, and my business will suffer, this is why I got excused." The colonel promptly rejected his exemption and sent him back into the ranks.[4]

Some civilians sensed these new one-hundred-day soldiers would be laughed at and resented by the veterans. Demia Butler of Indianapolis, Indiana, wrote to her brother fearful that the town ladies were going to make their new, local 100-day regiment "a perfect laughing stock" with their grandiose plans for supplying the unit. "The Veterans love them none to[o] much now," she wrote, recognizing that any new recruit would quickly become an object of scorn if he could not brave for three months what others had endured for three years. Other new units saw no fanfare upon their departure. In Cedar County, Iowa, a historian recalled that when their new 100-day regiment set out on May 30, there was little to no demonstration because war "had become a serious business, and no one was certain of the end."[5]

Demia Butler was right as to how numerous grizzled veterans in the frontline trenches were less than impressed with the concept behind these latest short-term volunteers. "I suppose all those 100 day men think they are doing great things and will take a great deal of credit to themselves for being willing to go for 100 days with the understanding that they will not be placed where there is any danger of their seeing a rebel!" complained Capt. Jacob Ritner to his wife, knowing these men were supposedly only going to perform rearguard duty. With some sar-casm mixed with anger, Ritner concluded, "We are all glad the cowardly rascals are willing to do even that much to help us end the war." Maj. Henry Dalton wrote home also convinced these new men would not be worth anything of consequence and further resenting that they were to be paid more for garrisoning forts around Washington than those veterans serving at the front.[6]

Veteran soldiers like Ritner and Dalton knew from hard-won experience that no man could become a good soldier in only one hundred days, especially when every veteran knew these new volunteers would be focusing on the calendar every bit as much as their duties. What they wanted were committed men willing to serve for the long term. Capt. Henry Young wrote to his wife explaining that such short-term men did the veterans no good and furthermore, the administration's policy of sending short-term holiday soldiers had become "very obnoxious" to the veterans on the firing line. Pvt. Andrew Linscott of the 39th Massachusetts Infantry considered the one-hundred-day men "a humbug" who cost the government more than they were worth, while Lt. Charles Morse of the 2nd Massachusetts Infantry wrote home complaining that these green volunteers would have no idea how to properly care for themselves or their rations in the tented field. Such recruiting, Morse reasoned, was little more than a political farce. Once in battle, some quickly acquired the reputation of running after the first Rebel volley was fired in their direction though most served honorably. They returned home after their one-hundred-day service with the self-satisfaction and public acclaim they sought in the first place.[7]

As the war dragged on, various Northern men who had decided to stay away from army life sought to reclaim their potential loss of civic manliness by enlisting into the navy since that military branch was believed to offer easier and safer duty. Army soldiers who were weary of endless hot marches and sleeping on the ground also sought transfers into the navy. After all, no one actively sought out martyrdom. "You need not worry for me," wrote Union sailor George Geer to his wife in January 1863, "as I am always looking out for No. 1 and am not going to get killed or Drowned in this War." Knowing that the Confederacy possessed no formidable navy, these men rightly reasoned their service on a Union warship would likely be little more than coastal blockade duty that guaranteed three square meals a day and a dry hammock to sleep in. By the late summer of 1864, navy rendezvous stations were overflowing

Civil War Navy Recruiting Poster (Library of Congress Prints and Photographs Division)

with men seeking to avoid the draft, the front lines, or both, often to the consternation of naval officers. According to one commander who witnessed dozens of new seamen coming on board his vessel, a ragtag few were "desperate nautical characters," however, most had obviously never seen a ship before. To the officer's dismay, they shuffled on board with nothing but the poorest clothes on their back and included "God-forsaken-looking ex-ministers, schoolmasters, and lawyers." The stampede to avoid the army by enlisting in the navy had even reached the highest levels of the Lincoln administration. "A desire to enter the Navy to avoid the draft is extensive," wrote Secretary of the Navy Gideon Welles in his diary on August 26, "and the local authorities encourage it, so that our recruiting rendezvous are, for the time being, overrun."[8]

BLACK SOLDIERS NOW ACCEPTABLE

With the White body count constantly rising and no martial enthusiasm to replace those dead men by enlisting, Northern civilians by the bushel reversed themselves and now saw the logic of allowing Black men to fight in the war. With the same reasoning that drove the creation of the hundred days' men, many Unionists simply wanted more armed men at the front, believing that would end the war sooner. Blacks were allowed to serve since 1862 but only in menial manual labor roles and not as armed soldiers. When the war began, both sides seemed to agree that this would be a White man's fight. In the case of the Union, the thought of a Black man in a blue uniform shouldering a weapon next to an identically attired White man presented an image of equality that much of the North would not accept. That formally changed on May 22, 1863, when the federal government created the Bureau for Colored Troops, which was charged with recruiting and organizing Black regiments. As of February 1864, all able-bodied Black men between the ages of twenty and forty-five were deemed eligible for the draft. Concurrently, Union authorities began to aggressively recruit Black men for service in the "United States Colored Troops," or USCT.[9]

The North's abolitionist and reform-minded communities cheered the idea of Black men fighting for the Union for it represented a level of equality previously denied to them. Others also approved but not in the altruistic manner put forth by the reformers. Much of the civilian North's racist biases and stereotypes against Black men under arms began to dim with the realization that every Black man volunteering into the army was one less reluctant White man that may have to be drafted. Northern business interests in much of the industrialized North also cheered the idea, because if Blacks were not allowed, then Northern quotas would have to be filled in part by well-trained White factory workers. As the *Chicago Tribune* had earlier framed it, "Every white man drafted into the army, while a negro volunteer is rejected, or exempted, *goes to the war as that negro's substitute, without bounty.*" Many reasoned that if the war was transformed from one primarily about union into one now over emancipation, then there was no reason why Blacks should not have the privilege of facing Rebel artillery and musketry. Not only Northern free Blacks but Southern freed slaves could be enlisted as allies against their previous Southern White overlords. In the same racist manner that Beates Swift approved of Blacks serving in the army because their loss would not be felt as much as Whites (see chapter 6), a Union officer wrote following the Enrollment Act's commencement how he wanted to arm Blacks only so that they and their Rebel masters could fight it out. "In so doing, some will get killed," he acknowledged, and then with those who were left standing, "give them a country somewhere in the Southern domain, and make them go to it." In that same vein, a Northern army chaplain wrote with delight how "the Negro can now be made to carry on this war" solely because "we need *our* boys at home." (Italics added) Taken all together, many reasoned that a Black man could stop a Rebel bullet just as well as a White man.[10]

THE OVERLAND CAMPAIGN

At the same time Union authorities were frantically searching for more men from an ever increasingly reluctant populace, the military chessboard and the tactics used to fight the war were about to change. The North had a new military field leader in the form of one Lt. Gen. Ulysses S. Grant, who arrived in Washington in spring 1864 having been promoted to general-in-chief of all Union armies. After analyzing the battlefield scenario across the country, Grant determined that for the first time ever, all federal armies would act in concert with one another. If Grant was right, his simultaneous, multiple-front strategy would deny the Confederates the ability to hastily move troops from one point to the other to meet an isolated threat. He placed his field headquarters with the Army of the Potomac, which was now commanded by Maj. Gen. George Meade. That army set out in May to begin what became known as the Overland campaign, which took place in Virginia from May 4–June 12, 1864. In the Western theater and at the same time as Grant's Eastern offensive, Maj. Gen. William T. Sherman would lead three federal armies from Chattanooga, Tennessee, down through Georgia with orders from Grant to move against Confederate major general Joseph E. Johnston's Army of Tennessee, "to break it up and to get into the interior of the enemy's country as far as you can, inflicting all the damage you can against their war resources." Sherman's Atlanta campaign commenced on May 7.[11]

As with Sherman's orders, Grant no longer desired to capture and hold territory. Instead, his immediate objective was to seek out Robert E. Lee's Confederate Army of Northern Virginia with the intent of using his vastly superior numbers of men and material to grind his foe down. Grant's orders to Meade were clear-cut: "Lee's army will be your objective point. Wherever Lee goes, there you will go also." Lincoln, at last, had found a general who understood what the president had earlier described as "the awful arithmetic." According to Lincoln's secretary, the president realized after the Fredericksburg disaster in December 1862 that if the same bloody battle were fought every day for a week and with the same relative results, the Confederate army would be wiped out, but the Army of the Potomac would remain a mighty host.[12]

The campaign became a nonstop bloodbath for both sides. The first engagement occurred from May 5–7 in a seventy-square-mile tangled thicket seventeen miles west of Fredericksburg known as the Wilderness. In three days of brutal fighting, the Union's Army of the Potomac suffered about 17,000 casualties in what was generally regarded as a drawn battle. The May 8–21 battle of Spotsylvania Court House saw another 18,000 Union men killed, wounded, or missing in what would become the third-bloodiest engagement of the entire war. Yet Grant and his army still pressed on, confident that, unlike the North, Lee could not replace his own immense casualties. Equally heavy fighting occurred at the North Anna River, Totopotomoy Creek, and Bethesda Church in the days to follow. On the Confederate side, Lee fully understood Grant's intent. As a trained engineer familiar with the art of the military siege, Lee knew he had to destroy Grant's army in the open before it could cross the James River. As Confederate lieutenant general Jubal Early later explained, Lee had warned him that if Grant's army was able to cross the James, "it will become a siege, and then it will be a mere question of time." Then on June 3, at a crossroads just northeast of Richmond known as Cold Harbor, more than 4,500 Union soldiers fell in a matter of hours in one failed charge after another. "It was not war; it was murder," wrote Brig. Gen. Evander Law after recalling the carnage his well-entrenched Confederates had delivered to their blue-clad foe. In his post-war posthumous memoirs, Grant himself regretted he had ever ordered the last charge at Cold Harbor. Yet despite that defeat, Union forces were able to cross the James River using pontoon bridges, and by mid-June, the Army of the Potomac settled into their newly dug trenches around the Petersburg, Virginia, area for what would become ten months of siege warfare, just as Robert E. Lee had rightly feared.[13]

Total Union casualties for the six weeks were roughly 55,000; an appalling number previously unheard of in the North. A tsunami of wounded men flooded into Washington's hospitals in such numbers that surgeons and nurses were both aghast and overwhelmed. Walt Whitman was helping in those hospitals and though he was well accustomed to the sight of shot-up and mangled men, he now witnessed something he had previously not seen: men who had literally gone insane because of the nonstop slaughter they saw and experienced during the preceding weeks. "They have suffered too much, & it is perhaps a privilege that they are out of their senses," Whitman wrote to his mother. Such losses rendered Grant "a butcher" within the Copperhead press, which, as previously mentioned, was a minority yet vocal faction within the Democratic Party. With the presidential election less than five months away, the partisan newspaper assault had more to do with discrediting the Republican administration than vilifying Grant. Nevertheless, the immense casualties weakened Northern soldier and civilian morale, which led to desertion and home front apathy previously unseen. The Lincoln administration realized more men needed to be called for and, depending on one's political perspective, the need was either to see the job through properly or gather up more cannon fodder to appease a despotic regime.[14]

Though skulking may have initially been associated with green enlistees, bounty men, or conscripts, by the summer of 1864 that habit became equally prevalent with Grant's veterans, especially those nearing the end of their three-year enlistment terms. The traditional standards of martial ardor were losing out as veterans sought to stay alive by any means required, especially for those having survived the grisly Overland campaign. Courage, perhaps once defined by heroic battlefield exploits, now became simply surviving on a day-to-day basis. By this stage of the war, both armies had learned the hard way how rifled musket technology had rendered the massed frontal assault against strong defensive works a generally futile endeavor. West Point military doctrine taught that an attacking force assaulting a solid, well-entrenched defensive position needed at least a three-to-one manpower advantage to have a reasonable chance of success. Both armies now realized there was nothing wrong with that guideline. Brutal trench warfare was now the order of the day, with any veteran realizing that the best way to survive was laying low, being in the rear, or even finagling passage onto a hospital transport ship headed to Washington under the guise of being wounded. Pragmatism supplanted idealism as a key emotional weapon in a soldier's quest for survival. That last tactic became so pervasive by summer that military surgeons were immediately sent aboard the ships as soon as they docked in order to examine every man before he was allowed ashore, thereby separating the truly wounded from the skulkers.[15]

The warnings about the realities of war that some Union soldiers had started to send home in the summer of 1862 never really stopped as the rebellion dragged on. The body counts and butchery they witnessed throughout 1864's Overland campaign, Sherman's march through Georgia to Atlanta, and the trans-Mississippi only added to that chorus. After enlisting two years earlier in July 1862 and expecting a short stint in the army, Frederic Lockley now confessed to his wife in a July 8, 1864, letter how, "My patriotism is about given out . . . I would not enlist again to save the country from perdurable ruin." Writing in mid-August from City Point, Virginia, Charles Tripp admonished his parents to never let his brothers enlist. From what he had experienced, Tripp wrote for countless Union privates when he concluded it was far better for a man to risk the draft than face Rebel cannon and musketry in some woebegone swamp or forest. Writing from the Chattahoochee River twelve miles west of Atlanta in late October, a war-weary William Standard swore to his wife in Illinois, "If I was out of the scrape and knew as much as I know at this time, it would take one million of dollars to get me in again & not then." After learning that his father and surviving brothers were contemplating enlistment, Pvt. John Sheahan also spoke for many when he felt compelled to ask his father, "Have you not done enough already? Is it not enough for a father to lose one son in battle and have another at the disposal of the fortunes of war, without coming himself or even letting any more of his family?"[16]

***

Union authorities concluded by the late spring of 1864 that the draft process generated ample commutation money but far fewer soldiers. Throughout the first two 1863–1864 drafts, 133,000 men were conscripted, however, 85,000, or close to two-thirds simply paid the $300 commutation fee rather than don a blue uniform and head off to war. At war's end, Union authorities calculated that more than $26 million had been paid in commutation money. As a microcosm of that reality, Minnesota provost marshal George Keith noted in his 1865 final report that commutation was "decidedly injurious" to his efforts. With but few exceptions, he admitted that his district could obtain very few men via the draft while commutation was an option. Col. James Fry reviewed the numbers and saw the writing on the wall: The army would never get to its desired strength as long as a reluctant man could pay $300 and avoid service. Nor did Fry have any confidence that the army could find a willing substitute or volunteer to serve instead of a drafted man who paid the commutation fee. Bounties, Fry believed, were the better option. In a June 6, 1864, letter to Edwin Stanton, Fry urged the secretary to repeal the commutation clause. As Congress debated the matter, many

Democratic papers and even some Republican ones protested, believing the clause was the only way that a workingman might legally avoid service. Despite the pushback, Stanton concurred as did Congress and on July 6, the commutation clause ended as a means of avoiding the draft and the war, thereby bringing renewed allegations that the North's conscription system discriminated against the working classes.[17]

After the commutation option was repealed, substitute prices predictably soared, resulting in a corresponding increase in the cash bounties offered by state and local municipalities. Men who refused to enlist when the cash bounties were "only" several hundred dollars now reconsidered as they climbed toward one thousand dollars. After learning of those incredible numbers, the *North Carolina Presbyterian* had earlier reminded its readers that such Northern bounties now "approximate in ordinary times what would purchase an able-bodied slave in the South." Even some veterans who were counting down the days to their discharge became seduced by the possibility of reenlisting so as to collect the immense windfall, often to the complete consternation of their wives. David Smith, then stationed at a fort in New York harbor, told his wife that like others, he might be persuaded to take the large bounty. She told him to keep right on if he did, that his family wanted and needed him at home, bounty or not. Following Lincoln's call in July 1864 for another 500,000 men to serve one, two, or three years, the people from Illinois' seventh congressional district paid an average bounty of $1,056 per man, surpassed only by a New York district that paid $1,060 per man. Concurrently, substitute prices soared to the point that only the wealthy could afford them. A worried New Yorker named James Lyman bemoaned this very fact to his brother, Ben, who had already skedaddled and was now safely ensconced in Nova Scotia. Inevitably, with the elimination of the commutation clause, shrewd draft-exempt men refused to enlist so they could hold out and receive substitute pay, which in many urban locales still outpaced bounties in rural areas. Moreover, scores of men still sought to enlist wherever they could obtain the largest bounties. The result was that large cities and wealthy counties siphoned off men from the surrounding country and received credit for volunteers who actually resided elsewhere. Then when the draft was ordered, the rural districts and less affluent counties were compelled to furnish men in place of those for whom credit should have been received in the first place. Nineteen-year-old Martin Reiss was working in a St. Louis harness shop when that profit-oriented notion entered his mind in the summer of 1864. In a June 18 letter to his brother, Franz, he admitted "the wish to stay away from death as long as possible" was paramount; however, by late August, Reiss had a change of heart. If a draft appeared imminent, he would offer himself as a substitute solely to profit from the rebellion. Those men now willing to serve knew that when the draft occurred, panicked draft-eligible men would pay handsomely to avoid service.[18]

***

The spring/summer 1864 military bloodbaths in Virginia and elsewhere led to a decline in Northern morale and an increase in war apathy not seen since the winter of 1862–1863. A Connecticut diarist wrote how "The war drags hard and heavily; nobody seems to have any feeling of interest for the armies and they are seldom spoken of." With no end to the war in sight, the ongoing draft processes and the fear it generated within working families only added to the weariness and a desire to get away from it all. The number of draft-eligible men fleeing the next draft in New York's nineteenth district was so enormous that its provost marshal urgently telegraphed his superior on August 5 asking what means he had at his disposal to stem the tide. "A stampede is going on that threatens to be serious unless checked. I know of no remedy," he warned. After reviewing the daily reports from the September 1864 draft in Pennsylvania's tenth district, Col. James Fry wrote that "nearly all the men fail to report." Writing from Mt. Pleasant, Michigan, in August and September 1864, housewife Ellen Woodworth told her husband how, "The talk is now all about the draft . . . Everyone is anxious to avoid it" but in the end "several enlisted, for fear of being drafted." A man in Salem, Indiana, wrote to a friend in the army on September 4—the very day of his town's scheduled draft—informing his friend that thirty-five men from the town would be chosen and equally aware that only one hundred remained to choose from; the young man silently calculating his odds while expressing a sense of dread not unlike that in Shirley Jackson's classic 1948 tale titled *The Lottery*.[19]

Rural farmers felt especially trapped. Paying the $300 commutation fee was no longer an option and many could not afford the prices that substitutes now commanded. Yet as their fall harvests were ripening in the fields, they also knew that now was the time to begin preparing their farm and family's winter supplies. "Oh this cruel war dragging men from their homes and for what," an anti-Lincoln Ohio farm wife complained to her reluctant soldier husband posted in Nashville. With sarcastic bitterness, she added, "But I must not ask that else I will be called a traitor." Her husband had dug deep into the family savings in order to pay the $300 commutation fee earlier that summer before that option was terminated, but now with fewer willing men remaining at home and sensing the inevitability of being drafted for up to three years with no recompense, he enlisted for one year in September. Like innumerable others, his motive had nothing to do with patriotic fervor, but only as a calculated strategy so his family could gain the $480 bounty that, he trusted, would see them through his hopefully safe return. For countless farm families all across the North, the thought of the husband having to abandon his farm and family because he was being dragged off by a distant national government to fight in an even farther-off war was a dreaded nightmare. These peaceful, rural people reasoned they did not start the war and wanted no part of it. Family and local obligations came first.[20]

A young woman living in the southern Wisconsin town of Pardeeville felt part of that nightmare. She wrote to a soldier friend in late September 1864 remarking how a great many of her town's men had recently fled south in the hope of landing federal government jobs, thereby making themselves exempt from the draft. Others, she observed, were planning to move north to Minnesota later that fall. Her predicted result was that the town would soon be completely evacuated, leaving no men at home to protect the women and children in the event of any emergency. "Truly a patriotic town," she lamented with ample cynicism.[21]

Public dispiritedness coupled with individual attempts to avoid the draft became so widespread that one New York paper bitterly remarked in early September, "If it were possible, our next army would be entirely composed of the sweepings of emigrant ships, of negro slaves, and of any other refuse we could pick up." A fair assessment and one that contradicted the North's preferred vision of the manly citizen-soldier rushing to his nation's defense. In reality, had it not been for the waves of immigrants desperately seeking to escape their homelands as well as tall boys turning eighteen or even seventeen years old, far more reluctant men who sought to avoid the war would have been forced into the army.[22]

Despite the multitude of men who had left their hometowns to fight for their own personal reasons, everyone at home as well as most soldiers realized that there were still plenty of able-bodied men who had simply refused to enlist. In Washington, DC, Polish-born translator Adam Gurowski made precisely this point in his diary on October 2. He wrote with no little amazement of the crowds of young civilian men everywhere, "as if for the last three years no war was raging." Yet with the $300 commutation fee option off the table, the draft-avoidance options for workingmen were dwindling. One man joined the New York state militia, which his soldier friend viewed as "a very good dodge, that is, if he is as patriotic as he was the Saturday night before I enlisted." Joining a draft insurance society was one possibility, another was for draft-eligible men to switch their residence to a community that had always exhibited no trouble in meeting their enlistment quotas if they had previously lived in one that had shown difficulty in getting enough men to enlist. Others opted for having no permanent address at all, a tactic that first took hold in the fall of 1862. A Union soldier convalescing in a New York hospital wrote to a friend expressing some surprise after learning that the latter was apparently going to abandon his Eastern farm and move out to the prairie lands. The soldier and his pen wondered if this was all about avoiding the draft. "Women are living with their mothers, siblings and furniture stays in the house while the man is moving around, here today, there tomorrow, but lives nowhere?" the soldier asked rhetorically in describing the typical scenario. "What kind of politics are you going for?" was his more direct admonition.[23]

At the other end of the financial spectrum were those draft-eligible men with ample wealth and assets. They were still seeking someone, anyone, to go instead of them even though substitute prices had skyrocketed from one end of the North to the other. Unlike for workingmen, those rising prices were still not a factor for the well-off, as witnessed by the Veteran Reserve Corps' Dennison Griffing, who was posted at Camp Burnside guarding Confederate prisoners just outside of Indianapolis, Indiana. Griffing wrote to a friend in Illinois on September 24 remarking how substitute prices in some instances had now reached $2,500 and were hard to find even at that astronomical number. The draft was currently underway there, Griffing explained, and as a consequence, "those that have been drafted look as if they had lost their last friend." When Union general Grenville Dodge learned that his stay-at-home brother might be drafted, his advice was short and simple: "get a substitute." Price was apparently not an issue. That was also the case in Delaware, from where Alexander Cooper wrote of knowing one frantic acquaintance who paid $1,500 for his replacement. In Detroit, twenty-eight-year-old attorney Henry Billings Brown paid $850 for one in late August after doing "some hard thinking about this confounded draft." New York's wealthy, forty-one-year-old George Templeton Strong recorded in his diary on August 29 how he had visited his local provost marshal's office that morning and after waiting an hour, "I purveyed myself a substitute, a big 'Dutch' boy of twenty or thereabouts, for the moderate consideration of $1,100." Strong wrote of his substitute as being his "alter ego," a perspective wholly in line with the culture's "representative recruit" ethos discussed in chapter 7. Four days later, Strong learned there would be no upcoming draft, nevertheless, he added, "I do not regret the $1,100 I paid for that substitute." The same concept applied to thirty-seven-year-old Benjamin Hedrick, a North Carolina anti-slavery man who had fled his state for the North in the late 1850s. Hedrick never volunteered for federal service, and in a letter dated July 20, 1864, from his wife, she relayed her anxiousness that he quickly find a substitute given the president's recent call for 500,000 more men. If he quickly did so, she believed his example might be followed by others for the betterment of the country.[24]

Marion, Ohio's Thomas Anderson wrote to his son explaining that men who did not want to go off to war were compelled to pay such hefty prices for substitutes, which could only be those men who were draft

AN EXEMPT.

OFFICER. "You're a Foreigner, you say?"
APPLICANT. "Born in Tipperary, yer honor.'"
OFFICER. "Did you never get Naturalized?"
APPLICANT. "Ne'er a time."
OFFICER. "Did you never Vote?"
APPLICANT. "Oh! for the matter of votin', yer honor, I
allus Votes. Many's the Vote I've guv FERNANDY WOOD;
an' av' he were Mayor now———(is marched off.)

"An Exempt" "OFFICER. 'You're a Foreigner, you say?' APPLICANT.
'Born in Tipperary, yer honor.' OFFICER. 'Did you never get Naturalized?'
APPLICANT. 'Ne'er a time.' OFFICER. 'Did you never Vote?' APPLICANT.
'Oh! For the matter of votin', yer honor, I allus Votes. Many's the Vote
I've guv Fernandy Wood; an' av' he were Mayor now—(*is marched
off.*)" (Library of Congress Prints and Photographs Division)

exempt, such as foreign aliens, healthy men older than age forty-five, or teen boys between eighteen and twenty years of age. With each successive draft, however, the supply of willing substitutes went down as those from the past had already been marched off to war. One solution was to increase the ready pool of available cannon fodder. As evidence of that occurring, Anderson told his son of newspaper reports claiming how shiploads of Germans were arriving in Boston ready to serve as substitutes for three years at bargain prices. In some instances, they were not even allowed to disembark before sailing off to Virginia's killing fields. Such news prompted another man to remark in his diary how it all reminded him of the transatlantic slave trade but with White men instead of Negroes as the trafficked subjects. These were accurate reports, as H. Alexander Jr. of the Boston mayor's office had informed Massachusetts governor John Andrew that a large portion of his city's draft-eligible population were unmarried men already working for or with the federal government. "More or less of these men are now leaving the city daily to avoid the draft," Alexander warned. He felt that number was sure to increase as the September 5 draft approached and by then, Alexander predicted that more than five hundred of Boston's ablest-bodied young men would have skedaddled. His solution was to keep importing foreign mercenaries to serve as volunteer hirelings rather than draft native-born sons. "I have, I think, a reasonable prospect of procuring 300 men (foreigners) to apply on our quota" he informed Andrew, however, Alexander knew it would take six or seven weeks for the men to arrive, thereby necessitating a temporary suspension of the draft.[25]

Confederate diplomats and spies across Europe were certainly not blind to the North's European recruitment efforts. They took a contemptuous view of the matter, with their dispatches scornfully reporting how the Yankees were now filling up their armies with the scum of European society since they had apparently emptied all of the Northern prisons and poorhouses. For their part, Union politicians reasoned that many of these poor immigrants may have felt as if they had just hit the jackpot since they purportedly received their substitute fee (less the broker's commission), a $100 government bounty, $16 per month pay, plus their food and clothing from the government. Almost one thousand German mercenaries arrived in Boston in the manner previously described throughout 1864 with barely a word of English understood or spoken among them; all to serve instead of the innumerable American citizens who were frantically trying to avoid the war. Adding to the confusion was that once they arrived at the front, none of the officers nor the privates in the ranks had any idea where these non-English-speaking foreigners had come from in the first place.[26]

From one end of the North to the other, towns and villages of all sizes were caught up in draft quotas and calculations. As in 1863, there seemed to be little home front regard as to whether the recruits they were sending forth were efficient men or peripatetic vagrants. Nor did they seem to care if the country was getting good value for the huge sums of money being spent. Rising substitute prices and the bounties offered by municipalities often became inversely proportional to the recruit's quality. The higher the former, the lower the latter. For the statistical majority of the North's remaining healthy, service-eligible men, their main concern was avoiding the war in general and the draft in particular, and the veterans in the field knew it. "The apathy of our people is our stumbling block," Maj. Gen. George Meade groused to his wife in a July 1864 letter. Another soldier wrote to his wife from Chattanooga, Tennessee, on July 24 complaining of the same war weariness he had heard from the home front, especially regarding the conflict's financial costs. Capt. George Anthony later wrote to his brother back home in New York, angrily noting how "There has been one grand scramble to get *our* quota filled and *us* exempt from the draft!" Anthony was bitter over what he saw as the North's apparent indifference to what the army should be and the home front convictions needed to make that happen. This sad situation was obvious at the highest levels of the army. In a letter to Secretary of State William Seward dated August 19, 1864, Lt. Gen. Ulysses S. Grant remarked that he did not get one good recruit for every eight bounties paid. Such was the sorry state of affairs regarding substitutes and bounty jumpers.[27]

When Confederate lieutenant general Jubal Early led a raid into Maryland in July 1864 that culminated in the July 9 battle of Monocacy, many Union soldiers viewed Early's offensive as a good thing. These men believed that such attacks on Northern soil would shake the North out of their draft-numbers, money-focused apathy and remind them that there was still a war going on. As always, the ultimate goal was that more men would voluntarily enlist. Union colonel Robert McAllister was especially bitter over that current state of affairs for he knew the army needed more men rather than money. Writing to his family from outside of Petersburg, Virginia, on July 16, McAllister complained how such men "would rather pay their $300 and let us do all the fighting here and also defend Washington . . . The mass of the people [have] turned their attention to making money, regardless of our national safety."[28]

From the Iowa home front, Louisa Reed referred to those stay-at-homes as "cowardly sneaks," which she defined as those men who railed against the horrors of war and its carnage, yet were profiting from the war to a degree they never dreamed possible before the blood started to spill. Across the country in New Hampshire, Maria Sargent acknowledged to her Union army husband in July how the soldiers probably felt wronged that volunteering had slowed to a crawl. From their New London hometown, Maria wrote how the local men who had yet to enlist now hated more than ever the thought of being dragged into the war due to 1864's staggering death tolls. "Even Republicans say they will go to Canada before they will go to war," wrote Sargent. Two months later, Sargent admitted to her husband that if he was home now, she would not let him enlist again "for all the money in the world." For women at home like Reed and Sargent, any one-time honor in the war had vanished.[29]

THE WAR'S SILENT DIARIES

In spite of the new carnage occurring on Southern soil, the rebellion still seemed distant and unobtrusive to innumerable Northerners just as it had in the war's earlier years. Despite maintaining detailed diaries of their daily comings and goings, avoiding the draft seemed to be the only real dent the war made in their consciousness from the time conscription became a concern in the late summer of 1862 on through the end of the war. Even amid the July 1863 New York draft riots, visiting British army officer Arthur Fremantle made that very point. He recorded in his diary of the vast luxury, ease, and comfort he saw in New York and Philadelphia when compared to what he had witnessed in Charleston, South Carolina, or Richmond, Virginia. "The streets are as full as possible of well-dressed people, and are crowded with able-bodied civilians capable of bearing arms, who have evidently no intention of doing so," he wrote with no little amazement. "They apparently *don't feel the war at all* here."[30]

Letter writers were certainly no different concerning war indifference or apathy. Epitomizing that reality was the wife of a wealthy lawyer who shipped her adult son off to Europe at the first hint of war, then later wrote to him in 1863 stating there were so many young men lounging around in their hometown of Hartford, Connecticut, that it seemed like there was no war. In March 1863, industrialist William E. Dodge wrote to a friend in England explaining how "but for the daily news from the War in the papers and the crowds of soldiers you see about the streets you would have no idea of any war." Two months later in late May, the well-educated, Russian-born wife of Union general John Turchin expressed in her diary how "In the present circumstances the most shameful, the most dangerous, and the most harmful flaw of American nature is the immeasurable complacency of its people." The radical abolitionist and women's rights advocate Parker Pillsbury wrote to a friend in July 1864 while visiting his brother in rural New Hampshire as to how the local population "could not apparently care less" about the war. "Trade & manufacturers are now graded to the war plane," Pillsbury further remarked, "and so peddling prospers." This indifference seemed to amplify itself the farther one was from the front. Housewife Cora Benton admitted the existence of similar emotions to her husband, who had enlisted into the 17th New York Light Artillery in August 1862. "I did not *feel* there was a war," she wrote, "till you went—till it broke up my dear home-circle," while in Cleveland, a wife rhetorically asked her husband in November 1863, "Can it be we are to live through this rebellion, and see nothing of it! living as peacefully in our own times as ever." Even as late as December 1864, a young woman in upstate New York wrote to her army brother remarking how, "We would not know that war existed in this quiet little town were it not for the absence of loved ones or the occasional newspaper."[31]

That same month, German émigré Julius Wesslau wrote to his parents from New York informing them how that city seemed more heavily populated than ever. It seemed to Wesslau as if New York had become one large festive event based on all of the balls, operas, and theater events that were occurring constantly. He further observed that making big money and avoiding the draft were the primary reasons for the influx, with the result that "the main streets are clogged with fine and glittering ladies and gentlemen, and sometimes there are so many carriages it's dangerous to cross the street." Even Curtis Burke, a Confederate prisoner of war languishing in Chicago's Camp Douglas, sensed how the war appeared to have little effect on the Northern civilians. Burke recorded in his journal on June 9, 1864, how he was part of a work detail repairing his barrack's roof. From his lofty vantage, he was able to gaze over the prison stockade and see the lush, clean land for miles, "the people walking about as if there was no war going on."[32]

Ever since the war began and in a broad sense, the veteran Union soldiers toiling on Southern battlefields largely felt disgusted toward those hale and hearty civilian men who, from the soldier's perspective, refused to enlist and join them in preserving the Union. As the war progressed, however, and especially once the carnage from the spring/summer of 1864 became well known throughout the North, those soldiers began to realize that home front war or draft avoidance did not carry the same social stigma as it once did. The people had grown callous and weary of war. In modern jargon, by mid-1864 the Northern public now uttered a collective "whatever" with regards to paying commutation fees or hiring a substitute. They were merely business transactions involving advertising, possibly a broker, maybe some negotiating, and the inevitable transfer of large sums of money. "Soljerin'" was viewed by potential enlistees solely from the business perspective. Any notion of patriotic rallying 'round the flag was long gone.[33]

***

Meanwhile, staunch antiwar partisans had no intention of disappearing from the ongoing home front debates over the war's merits. The public and private attacks against Democratic citizens and newspapers—both figurative and literal—that labeled any dissent as treasonous sympathy for the Rebels led to the creation of a new "secret society." The latest Democratic entry was known as the Order of the Sons of Liberty, which appeared in early 1864. It followed 1863's short-lived Order of American Knights, which, in turn, had followed the Knights of the Golden Circle (discussed in chapter 8). They changed their names to suit the needs of the times, wrote an early historian of these societies, in the same manner that a fugitive from the law assumed an alias.[34]

Just as numerous Unionists had witnessed or even experienced Copperhead-initiated violence against them during the preceding year and a half, Democrats saw their newspaper offices burned to the ground on occasion and their outspoken partisans harassed by Union military and civil authorities. At the war front, Democratic-leaning soldiers often found themselves punished for their views while their Republican comrades could voice or even publish their opinions with impunity. In the Northern home front version of civil war, the concept of an eye for an eye had reached deadly proportions, especially in the Midwestern states of Illinois, Indiana, and Ohio. "The law of retaliation is doubtless a barbarous code, but is justifiable according to the stern rules of war," wrote one Democrat, who then stressed that his party would never resort to it except in self-defense. Yet according to Clement Vallandigham, who admitted he was a founding member of the Sons of Liberty, his new organization was a nonthreatening one designed solely to help protect Democrats from such violent acts. Moreover, it stood ready to assist Democrats whose civil rights were being trampled on by the administration, as well as to provide an organized means for electing Democrats to office, thereby making the group a forerunner of the modern political action committee. Joining a clandestine group like the Sons of Liberty offered the anti-draft and/or antiwar citizen a means of collective dissent against the Lincoln administration, comradery, and protection in much the same way as joining a local Union League council offered a proud Unionist (who was often too old for the military) the means of countering his belief that the North was riddled with pro-Southern traitors. To those who supported the Lincoln administration's war efforts, the Sons of Liberty meant to carry out by force that which Democrats could not control through the ballot box. It was just another nefarious cabal whose intent was to generate violent unrest against lawful authority. "Every Democrat may not be a traitor, but every traitor is a Democrat," became a new Republican catchphrase.[35]

THE 1864 PRESIDENTIAL ELECTION

Northern war weariness and antiwar sentiment reached their zenith with the arrival of the summer of 1864 and its concurrent presidential canvass. At their August 29–31 national convention in Chicago, the Democrats nominated former Union general and "War Democrat" George B. "Little Mac" McClellan as their party's presidential candidate, which was no surprise. Everyone had known for months that McClellan would be the nominee. As a concession to the party's antiwar faction, McClellan's running mate was Ohio congressman and loyal Copperhead George H. Pendleton. Furthermore, the Copperheads were able to control the committee responsible for writing the party's official platform. The result read like a Copperhead manifesto.

The convention presented the war as an unmitigated failure that had accomplished nothing other than to butcher men and drain the public treasury. Lincoln's curtailing of the citizenry's fundamental civil rights such as suspending the right of habeas corpus was proof positive of the Republicans' desire to have an autocratic regime. Democrats demanded an immediate effort be made to stop hostilities with a negotiated settlement to follow. What, precisely, the North could offer that would bring the South back into the Union was left unsaid. After all, while he was willing to negotiate with the Rebels, Lincoln publicly required reunification of the Union and slavery's abolition as mutually agreed-upon goals before any formal negotiations. For his part, Confederate president Jefferson Davis insisted upon the exact opposite. Nevertheless, for the antiwar wing of the Democratic Party, their overarching rhetorical question was self-evident: What self-respecting citizen would willingly take part in such a crusade?[36]

Though numerous Democratic newspapers supported the war early on, that backing began to shift dramatically in 1863. By the time of the 1864 presidential campaign, no Democratic paper maintained its earlier pro-war position. An Ohio woman wrote to a New Jersey friend claiming that the Copperheads in her town seemed more concerned with the election than the draft and were putting all of their efforts to that end. She found their opinions "provoking" and could hardly believe that "Jeff Davis himself would consent to stand on a platform so full of treason as the one on which they intend to elect McClellan." An openly Copperhead editor named Franklin Weirick likewise argued for McClellan in his Selinsgrove, Pennsylvania, paper one week before the election, convinced that such a victory would stop the hated draft. Farther south, the 1864 presidential election stirred as much interest in the army camps as on the home front. Lincoln and his Republican allies—who had dubbed themselves the National Union Party back in May—were confident of their majority support within the army though they knew it was close. An Iowa surgeon had written earlier of a suspicion that was now widespread. "It is a common saying here that if we are whipped," he predicted, "it will be by Northern votes, not by Southern bullets." To that end, Henry Miner of the 4th US Regular Infantry encamped at City Point, Virginia, wrote to his father on October 11, 1864, stating that the election and whether or not the soldiers would be allowed to vote was the talk of the camp. If they were able to cast their votes, "it will go pretty hard against little 'Mac,'" Miner predicted.[37]

Nonetheless, the Democrats were fighting tooth and nail to save the country as they perceived it. After having arrived back in Washington, an Ohioan wrote in October about how surprised he was to see so much support for George McClellan among the new recruits. But then he realized that most had enlisted solely for the bounty, thereby avoiding the draft. A few weeks later and in the trenches outside Petersburg, Virginia, a Michigan soldier wrote home describing how the majority of the privates in his company were "hurrahing for McClellan." In both instances as well as countless others, their McClellan vote rested on the hope that his victory would end the war immediately and they could all go home.[38]

Despite the numerous issues that the Democrats could have been debating, such as the war's staggering costs in men and material coupled with home front inflation, what really united the Democrats behind

McClellan was his refusal to support Lincoln's emancipation policies. Race became their hot-button topic along with the issue of "miscegenation," which was a new word created to describe the feared blending of the races. As historian Arnold Shankman fittingly portrayed it, McClellan was shrewd enough not to say anything that would cost him the widespread racist vote.[39]

The 1864 campaign was as bitter and contentious as any in our modern era. One Democratic newspaper editor advocated assassination if Lincoln was reelected. In a typical attempt to avoid the home front political maelstrom, Union captain and Ohioan Orlando M. Poe reminded his young wife, Eleanor, not to talk about either candidate in public. "You must understand," Poe explained, "that what is loyalty in case of Mr. Lincoln's re-election may not be so construed if his opponent is successful." Since Poe considered his and his wife's primary duty to the country and not to either candidate, better to quietly let the people decide where that duty would lie based on their votes. As is always the case, each side's partisans viewed a potential victory by the other party as a calamity that the nation would never recover from. An Indiana Democrat writing to her friend in New Hampshire just days after the election but before all the votes were tallied spoke for countless Democrats everywhere when she wrote, "The country is ruined forever . . . if Mr. Lincoln is elected." On the other side of the political aisle, an Indiana Republican told her diary, "We look for a speedy permanent peace if Lincoln is reelected, but disaster and defeat if the Copperheads are to rule."[40]

**

The Northern electorate knew how crucial the 1864 election was to the nation's future. Far more voters went to the polls than they had four years earlier in 1860, with much of that increase going to George McClellan. For example, in the Middle Atlantic states of New York, Pennsylvania, and New Jersey, Lincoln's totals as a whole fell from 54 percent in 1860 to 50.6 percent four years later. In five other states—Connecticut, Maine, Minnesota, New Hampshire, and Vermont—his percentage of the vote also shrank from 1860. In the upper Midwest cauldron of Illinois, Indiana, Ohio, Michigan, and Wisconsin, however, Lincoln scored an impressive increase with his aggregate totals in those states rising from 52.7 percent to 55 percent. When all the votes were counted, the final tally revealed an Electoral College landslide victory for Lincoln. His margin of victory was 212 to 21—as he scored a win in twenty-two of the twenty-five Northern and loyal border states. Only Kentucky, Delaware, and McClellan's home state of New Jersey landed in the general's column. The popular vote, however, told a far different story. Lincoln won 55 percent of the ballots cast, totaling 2,213,665 votes to McClellan's 1,802,237, a respectable though not overwhelming 400,000-vote margin that was indicative of the divisiveness throughout the North. Within his mind, a McClellan voter may have quietly decided that his vote was genuinely *for* McClellan or perhaps more specifically, *against* Lincoln. Either way, it was a vote against the ongoing war, what it represented politically and culturally, and his ongoing desire to personally avoid it.[41]

Lincoln garnered only 350,000 more votes than he had four years earlier when there were four candidates. A shift of eighty thousand key votes in certain states would have resulted in McClellan carrying the day; this deeper analysis revealed that Lincoln's win was hardly the rout that a cursory look at the Electoral College numbers would indicate. A few of Lincoln's confidants admitted as much. "The size of his majority did not come up to the expectation of Lincoln's friends," Union major general Carl Schurz later wrote in his memoirs. Much if not most of the country still seemed to lean Democratic, yet in the end, a sufficient number had voted to preserve the Union rather than tossing in the towel on the republic. They refused to believe that the suffering and public cost in blood and treasure had been in vain.[42]

Perhaps most rewarding to the president were the votes cast by his Union citizen-soldiers. Seventy-eight percent of the boys in blue who voted (4 percent of the overall total Northern vote) went for Lincoln, a slightly more than three to one margin. In fact, in New York and Connecticut, this so-called "bayonet vote" may have provided Lincoln with his margin of victory. It is also important to note that at least 20 percent of the soldiers—one in five—who could have voted chose *not* to. Almost all of those were Democrats who could not bring themselves to vote for a defeatist platform that considered their efforts a failure as well as one that their Confederate enemy was publicly hoping would win. Perhaps they were also intimidated into silence by a military that would have viewed their publicly cast Democratic vote as a betrayal to the army and its mission. Stories abounded of overtly vocal, pro-McClellan soldiers suddenly finding themselves on the front lines. The soldier vote was certainly most gratifying to Lincoln and surely the biggest personal blow to McClellan. "I would rather be defeated with the soldier vote behind me than to be elected without it," Lincoln had earlier remarked to a friend. No other demographic of the Northern electorate voted against the Democratic ticket so unequivocally. George "Little Mac" McClellan might have taken some solace in the fact that it wasn't him personally the soldiers voted against, but rather the Copperhead tribe he had aligned himself with.[43]

Much of the immediate post-election and distant future Civil War history proclaimed Lincoln's 1864 win as a landslide; a sweeping mandate from the people that could be agreed with if one looked only at the electoral results rather than the much closer popular vote. This viewpoint came about in much the same way that the North strove to remember the war during the remainder of the nineteenth century as one of valorous collective unity, rather than an unpopular struggle that held significant dissent and resentment. Yet the Civil War, the reasons for it, and how it was fought were detested throughout much of the North within a few months of the war's commencement with that discontent becoming crystallized during the 1864 presidential canvass. Furthermore, one could argue that during his four years in office, Abraham Lincoln was despised by a sizeable portion of the Northern populace as much if not more so than any modern, twenty-first-century president. Immediately after his assassination on Good Friday, April 14, 1865, however, Lincoln began the transformation from a controversial president into the hallowed martyr we remember to this day. "Mr. Lincoln is to be hereafter regarded as a saint," Iowa senator James Grimes predicted the day after Lincoln's assassination. "All his foibles, and faults, and shortcomings, will be forgotten, and he will be looked upon as the Moses who led the nation through a four years' bloody war, and died in sight of peace." Throughout the remainder of the nineteenth century, the sanctified and then mythologized Lincoln began to take shape.[44]

Lincoln's victory in the November 1864 presidential election conveyed an unmistakable message to the Copperhead press and public, effectively ending their time as a formidable political foe to the Republican administration. Yet despite Lincoln's reelection, some Copperhead dissent remained, and it was vilified as much as ever. "There is no young men here except Copperheads and they are beneath our notice," wrote one young Nebraskan to her friend. The disdain, of course, still worked both ways. Rachel Hunt and Ohio's Almeda Bennett had managed to remain friends throughout the war despite political differences. A week after Lincoln's reelection, Rachel replied to Almeda's earlier Christmas visit request by writing that Almeda was more than welcome to visit but with a cautionary reminder, "We are all Copperheads out here." For most of the indifferent Northern public, however, avoiding the draft was still the major concern.[45]

CHAPTER 11

"There Is No Patriotism Left.
Tis All for Money Now"

One More Draft to Avoid

As 1864 rolled into 1865 and with the presidential election settled, avoiding the draft and the front lines were more of an imperative than ever for those still at home. An immense number of healthy, service-eligible men remained who still supported the war in theory yet had no intention of stepping forward when considering the possible real costs to themselves, their families, or their businesses. After digesting the butcher's bill from the previous year, many reasoned that a huge enlistment bounty was of little value to a dead man. Given Maj. Gen. William Sherman's 1864 capture of Atlanta and subsequent march through Georgia in December, along with a string of victories in the Shenandoah Valley that fall, much of the North sensed that the Confederacy was at last in its death throes. Yet, on the other hand, no one could predict a precise end. Accordingly, no one wanted to be drafted into the army, especially when the war's conclusion seemed reasonably close.

Within the army's ranks, there were plenty of conscripted men who had never wanted in and still wanted out. Most were not willing to run the potentially deadly risk of desertion, so they tried to "play off" (faking an illness or injury) in order to obtain a medical release. The "playing off" ruse had always been a popular method for a reluctant warrior to avoid the front lines and had started to manifest itself with those 1861 men who mistook their enthusiasm for the cause with a capacity for military life. Hospital steward Spencer Bonsall had described these malingerers in his diary as "old good-for-nothing fellows who have been sick ever since they entered the service; others enlisted for the bounty and are now shamming sick in hopes they may get their discharge and go home." Some of the more common faking techniques were to swallow tobacco, which soon produced nausea and vomiting. Constant limb or back pain was another popular complaint. Others coated their tongues with ashes, chalk, clay, soap, or several other common items to appear ill and, as discussed previously, desperate men sometimes resorted to a self-inflicted wound to obtain a discharge. Capt. Daniel O'Leary of the 15th Kentucky Infantry explained this reality to his wife when he wrote that he might have to get sick and play off on the doctors because "It is the quickest way of getting a leave of absence." The authorities could do nothing if a soldier succeeded in obtaining a medical discharge and then miraculously recovered. Such scenarios were hardly uncommon. "The percentage of men discharged for incurable disorders, from which they soon after surprisingly recover, is not small," an army surgeon admitted in an official manual given in 1863 to the army's medical officers. Furthermore, he was convinced that "in every village there are one or more instances of the expertness or perseverance of the malingerer."[1]

Though most Union soldiers served their full terms with honor, the "playing off" ploy certainly worsened as the war became longer and more brutal. In the Western theater and as Sherman was preparing for his famous "March to the Sea" in November 1864, he ordered that all men not in top health should be sent back to Union-occupied Nashville or furloughed and sent home. Like numerous others and in a subsequent letter to his wife back in Indiana, recently drafted "Sime" Freeman admitted that if he had learned of the general's plans earlier, "I should have played off a week or two and then I would have got to go." In the East, a New York cavalryman with a good service record and only three weeks left on his enlistment had earlier admitted to his wife that he was playing off by pretending he had not yet recovered from an illness. His case was hardly unique. Though his unit had sent for him numerous times, he had managed to remain in the hospital. "I am in hopes that it may last until my time is out," he concluded. Writing in late February 1865 from a Union army hospital in Nashville, Jacob Row compared being in the hospital to languishing in jail as he and the other patients were constantly surrounded by armed guards. As for returning to the front, Row was adamant. "If they send me to the regiment, I will try and play off if I can so I can be sent back to the rear again."[2]

An examination of Union reenlistment numbers from November 1863 to November 1864 also reveals the depth of the growing soldier disenchantment. Of the approximately 922,155 soldiers who were eligible to reenlist during that one-year time frame, only 136,507 elected to do so, or slightly less than 15 percent. Many certainly felt they had proudly done their duty and were ready to go home; however, an ample number were disillusioned with what the war had become. It was no longer their war.[3]

***

Notwithstanding the hundreds of thousands of new men who were fed into the army's ranks in 1864, the need for more bodies continued apace since so many opted not to reenlist when their service terms expired. Another 300,000 men were called for by Lincoln on December 19, 1864, with any needed drafts scheduled for February 1865. Bounty offerings and substitute fees soared higher than ever as that next draft became the all-consuming issue throughout the North. As one result, Maj. Gen. William Sherman complained from Savannah, Georgia, how profit-driven Northern recruiting agents had arrived with the intent of inducing Black freedmen to serve as substitutes for deep-pocketed White draftees. Sherman could not tell what was more difficult, saving these freedmen from their past Southern masters, or the recruiting agent "that threatens him with a new species of slavery." A fifty-year-old German immigrant named Kaspar Herbst living in Fairview, Pennsylvania, wrote to his parents soon after the war's close describing how the last men drafted and "scared to death" paid anywhere from $1,200 to $1,500 for a substitute. In some instances, Herbst reported how desperate draftees with little cash sometimes turned over their home and farm ownership to whoever was willing to go in their place. In Marion County, Ohio, Rice Harper wrote to his brother-in-law regarding February's upcoming draft and how, "Everyone appears to have made up their mind that they are not going." Harper also noted how local townships were trying to raise money to buy substitutes but were having little success. From the western New York village of Albion, Cora Benton wrote to her soldier husband casually remarking how a mutual acquaintance paid $1,500 for a substitute after he was drafted. Other townsmen headed west, she continued, either to find substitutes or to flee the draft. "In fact it's almost impossible to get a man to go," Benton explained. "Neither patriotism or money can induce them."[4]

That sentiment appeared to be universal. Writing to his father in Vermont on January 8, 1865, from Little Rock, Arkansas, twenty-four-year-old Albert Harris wrote that he was all in favor of the upcoming draft. It was imperative, Harris reasoned, that the North not stop now but do everything in its power to crush the rebellion even if it took "every able-bodied man in the whole North." Harris boldly declared he was not afraid to stand *by* them, though not necessarily *with* them. Yet three weeks later on January 29, Harris avowed in another letter that if the Vermont authorities drafted him in February, he would get out of it using any possible exemption he could think of. If that gambit proved unsuccessful, his last resort would be to buy a substitute "if it costs me one thousand dollars." Like Albert Harris and just days before the war ended in April 1865, James Bamon wrote to a friend of his resolve to pay $1,000 for a substitute if necessary to avoid the front lines.[5]

It is worth pointing out that $1,000 in 1865 was the equivalent of approximately $18,500 in 2023 when factoring in inflation. As with countless others, men such as Harris and Bamon rationalized that what was good for the country was not necessarily good for them. Whether paying the $300 commutation fee when still an option or buying a substitute, the generally well-off members of Congress had made it quite easy for financially secure men to spend money rather than having to serve in the army. It was an opportunity the affluent almost always took advantage of—at whatever the cost. Such choices were often not affordable for the poor.

Twenty-three-year-old Pvt. Adelbert Baughman of Plymouth, Ohio, told his diary of the collective fear generated by the upcoming draft.

Baughman had enlisted into the 1st Ohio Independent Battery back in September 1864, though with the New Year he was assigned to the local provost marshal's office in Harpers Ferry, West Virginia, where the battery was currently stationed. Baughman ran into one of his captains who had just returned from a recruiting trip back home to Plymouth where, with regards to substitutes, he encountered little supply to meet the ample demand. Baughman noted in his diary on January 14 that, according to the captain, "The Plymouth folks were very much scared about the coming draft. They have the money but can't find the men." From Holland, Michigan's Dutch community, Frederick J. Van Lente wrote to his son in the 25th Michigan Infantry on February 20 of the various laments heard throughout their village "because everyone trembles for the draft." This was now especially the case with married men and their wives with small children who had previously avoided being conscripted. Van Lente followed up with another letter four days later with the news that his other son had decided to enlist and collect the bounty rather than take his chances with the draft; a 180-degree change from the family's original plans. His decision, according to Van Lente, had triggered "despairing screams" from the man's wife throughout the day. Twenty-nine-year-old Charles Cleveland of Adrian, Michigan, made a similar observation. He told his diary in early February that the upcoming draft was "the absorbing topic" in Detroit following a day trip to that city. It was the same everywhere. Like every taxpayer in every village across the North, Cleveland lamented the quantity of money his town would have to raise or borrow to buy substitutes but then acknowledged that doing so was still a far better option than personally having to face the draft wheel.[6]

Yet like innumerable others, Ohio's John Giffen had no intention of facing the draft lottery, having already skedaddled to Ontario, Canada, with the apparent full knowledge and support of his family. Giffen lamented to his father on February 20 how "awful" it was that an acquaintance back home had to pay $800 for a substitute and how he intended to get on with his Canadian schooling, war or no war. Two months later on April 18, Giffen again wrote to his father, relaying how he had just heard the "great news" of Lincoln's assassination four days earlier on April 14 and now hoped to be home soon.[7]

For every drafted man desperate to avoid the war and willing to pay almost anything to secure that safety, there was usually another, generally younger draft-exempt man willing to take his money and serve as a substitute. Writing from Baltimore on March 30, William Wilkins Glenn observed in his journal how no one was stepping forward to voluntarily serve unless they were first paid an exorbitant amount of money to do so. According to Glenn, Baltimore's city council was offering $200 to assist any drafted man looking for a substitute. Then the state of Maryland was offering another $300 on top of that. Using those numbers and assuming a substitute now commanded $1,000, Glenn calculated how the 300,000 men called for would cost $300 million, half paid by city and state governments and all funded in debt-bearing interest to be paid for by general taxation. "Was there ever so costly a war since the invention of currency," Glenn wondered.[8]

If the substitute who grabbed that cash intended to serve honorably and to the best of his ability, he was also willing to roll the dice that he would make it home unscathed. Twenty-one-year-old Canadian William Doherty was one such young man who entered the 5th Michigan Cavalry as a one-year substitute in February 1865 with that very mindset. In an April 10 letter written from Virginia to his family back home, Doherty clarified that the reason he had not told anyone of his actions was because he first wanted to see if he liked American army life or not, an explanation that suggests he may have been willing to desert had he not. He was happy to state, however, that he thoroughly enjoyed his new employment and, in any event, he expected to be home soon now that Confederate general Robert E. Lee had surrendered the ragged remnants of his once-mighty Army of Northern Virginia the day before at Appomattox, Virginia. Should nothing change, Doherty explained how he fully expected to be home in ten months "with a pocket full of greenbacks."[9]

The Union's collective psyche seemed at a manpower crossroads. The North's civilian home front was frustrated because they consistently heard and read how the Rebels were always on the verge of collapse, yet on the other hand, the calls for hundreds of thousands of more men continued unabated. After learning of the latest call in December, a doubtful

Union private asked his wife simply, "Will the people always submit to this?" To others, it seemed like the general populace was still more than able to ignore the whole matter. Philadelphian Franklin Dick told his journal in March 1865 that the locals went on about their lives as normal. "They continue their giddy amusements—the errands go on with business as usual," Dick wrote, while the war was merely an interesting topic of conversation.[10]

Yet as the Northern stay-at-homes' desire to avoid military service intensified, soldier resentment toward them increased proportionally. Michigan cavalryman Edward Warner stated to his mother how he hoped some of the "cowardly sneaks" still at home would finally come to their country's aid. Warner stressed that not all who stayed away were cowards, for he admitted that some simply could not leave. However, there were plenty who could go if they would only find their backbone. Tom McManus wrote to his sister on February 1, 1865, mocking the "many stout able-bodied young men at home" who were "trembling in their boots for fear of the Draft" yet were about to learn the meaning of reveille and roll call. Numerically speaking, McManus did have a point. William Barton of the 5th New York Cavalry wrote from his Winchester, Virginia, camp to his recently discharged brother back home in New York with some humor as he predicted how a mutual acquaintance was about to reacquire his heart palpitations now that another draft was on the horizon. Barton further noted several more men whose names he hoped would be called. By the time the February–March 1865 drafts were scheduled to take place, Union veterans like McManus and Barton had acquired a few years of experience in seeing the lengths that various Northerners would go through to avoid serving in the army.[11]

The final aggregate tally of conscription numbers was telling and revealed the depth of Northern draft-avoidance sentiment. Between July 1863 and April 1865, four national drafts took place resulting in a call of more than 1.5 million men. The North had a base of 4,449,872 military-age men upon which it could draw. Of the 776,829 men drafted, only 46,347 (just less than 6 percent) were actually held to service in the Union army. More than 160,000 men—or roughly 21 percent of those drafted—simply refused to report to their draft boards for examination. These men were illegal draft evaders by choice and deserters by law, according to Provost Marshal General James Fry.[12]

The onus that the draft placed on countless Northern households coupled with emotional war weariness had slowly led to a revised judgment by both civilians and Union soldiers regarding those who opted to stay home. What was viewed as shameful, cowardly behavior in the summer of 1861 became acceptable in a shrug-of-the-shoulders manner by late 1864. As discussed earlier, numerous civilians and soldiers alike now agreed that no family should be obligated to send more than one member into the service while scores of others had yet to provide any. Nothing had changed as the calendar rolled over into 1865.

Draft insurance societies were another example of how the North's collective mindset was evolving. They often earned the ire of many as just another means for the poltroons and skulkers to avoid serving when they were first created in 1862 following the Militia Act's passage. Now more than two years later in March 1865, the government accorded them legal status and they were even officially recognized by the War Department. As a Maryland newspaperman with strong Southern sympathies, William Glenn characterized this change though with a twist. He told his journal on March 15 that he could never understand how a courageous man could ever contribute money to buy men who would then make war on his own Southern brethren. Yet sensing that the draft was closing in on him, Glenn revised his thinking. "I may do it—and very soon," he admitted. "But if I do, it will be because I am whipped—which I am not yet." After Lincoln suspended any further drafts following Lee's surrender, Glenn admitted on April 14 of the "great relief" he now felt.

He prided himself on the fact that he had "never yet given any aid or comfort in any form to the [federal] Govt." whether by paying a commutation fee or subscribing to any draft insurance society. Therefore, he did not yet consider himself a "subjugated subject." Glenn spoke for millions of Northern men when he wrote, "It is a relief to me to know that I am no longer in danger of being drafted."[13]

Draft, Draft! Draft!!

THE
Davenport Draft Insurance Co.

Capital, $50,000.

THE Davenport Draft Insurance Company incorporated under the laws of the state of Iowa, is prepared to insure, for a premium of *Two Hundred Dollars*, against the impending draft a

Limited Number of Enrolled Men

in the various districts and sub-districts of the state of Illinois, and guarantee to furnish to such of the insured as may be drafted, an accepted substitute, or instead thereof the sum of $1,000 at the option of the company.

A. J. PRESTON, President,
JNO. L. DAVIES, Vice President.
IRA M. GIFFORD, Treasurer.
W. F. KIDDER, Secretary.

For policies apply to

Jno. L. Swits & Co.,

General Agents, Nickolls Block, (up stairs) Davenport, Iowa, or to

SWANDER & CO.,
or M. S. HERRICK,
Rock Island, Ill.

feb'y1dw2w.

Draft Insurance Advertisement (*Evening Argus*, Rock Island, Illinois, February 9, 1865)

BOUNTY BONDS

As far back as summer 1862, the Northern states had authorized small townships to levy extra property taxes or issue "bounty bonds" in order to raise the funds required to pay the handsome bounties necessary to entice men to volunteer. In either case, local residents were going to end up footing the bill. As 1865 began, small communities across the North realized it was time to pay the piper. The typical procedure saw a citizens' meeting authorizing the local town council to impose a bounty tax and float bonds in anticipation of the expected revenue. Predictably, that issue became a source of mounting aggravation for civic leaders and citizens alike. Those local families who had proudly volunteered a husband, son, or brother in April–May 1861 with no bounty now faced the additional slap of seeing their property taxes increased to pay off the bounties for those who had needed a financial inducement to enlist a year or more later. The anger felt by Capt. George Anthony of the 17th New York Independent Battery epitomized this outlook. He lectured his stay-at-home brother that he had no problem with substitution or generous bounties as long as the bill was paid solely by those who were exempted. But to pay those debts by general taxation was "an outrage" upon the families whose men had voluntarily entered the service earlier. Jane Standard of Illinois would certainly have agreed with Anthony. An ardent Democrat, Standard wrote to her husband on February 2, 1865, describing how she was livid to learn their township was considering a broad-based property tax in order to buy substitutes so that the stay-at-home patriots could remain in that category. With obvious anger, Jane wrote, "I think any of them might as well go as you." Furthermore, "I will never give one red cent to keep any of them from the war." In Marion, Ohio, the town placed a new levy on all homes while incomes of more than $600 per year now had to pay a 5 percent income tax to help raise bounty money. A Vermont farmer wrote to his son recounting how he had calculated that their hometown would have to pay bounties between four and six hundred dollars to compete with neighboring towns. "And few want to go for that," he noted, because, "There is no patriotism left. Tis all for money now & those towns that pay the most soonest fill their quota."[14]

To minimize the financial pain, counties and towns often formed bounty committees that went door-to-door begging residents for donations, especially from the wealthy, who everyone realized were the most likely to sit out the war. Others visited shops and businesses seeking voluntary subscriptions to the local bounty fund. Of course, not everyone was eager to dig deep into their pockets. "The standing difficulty in these operations," opined the *Pittsburgh Gazette* was that "there are many mean, close-fisted fellows who will not pay a cent to a bounty fund because they happen to be over age or otherwise exempt." In some predominantly antiwar communities, such as in Iowa's Copperhead-controlled Boone County, supervisors voted not to offer bounties at all as their means of keeping men out of the war. Across the North, each successive draft along with growing war weariness brought about evermore civilian groans of "not again." To combat such miserliness, the names and dollar amounts of those who subscribed were trumpeted in the local press while a shaming notice was also printed of those who refused to contribute or had reneged on previous pledges.[15]

After the war ended in April 1865, those small towns that had dipped into their public coffers to keep private citizens out of the war now had to face their balance sheet realities. The town of Pelham, Massachusetts, was a typical example. With the war over, an emergency meeting on May 27, 1865, allocated an additional four thousand dollars to reimburse individuals who had lavishly contributed to bounty funds. Two weeks later and with some sober reflection, the town council reconsidered what they admitted was a hasty act. Pelham's rate of taxation amounted to $25 or more for every thousand borrowed and remained elevated for at least seven years after the war ended. Quite the fiscal burden for a town whose valuation and population were both slowly shrinking.[16]

Unique Military Challenges

Though the Confederacy's end seemed near, no one knew for certain when that day would arrive. In the East, the Army of the Potomac was still dug in around Petersburg, Virginia, and engaged in boring yet deadly trench warfare as 1864 ended. In the Western theater, Sherman's army had finished its march through Georgia and was now encamped around

Savannah as it prepared for its northward thrust through the Carolinas. There were other and smaller unique military concerns that needed to be addressed by those in state or federal power. The state of Michigan offered one such example and served as a microcosm of the home front's war weariness. In late 1864 and fearing Rebel raids emanating from neighboring Canada, the state made plans to create the twelve-month, 30th Michigan Volunteer Infantry solely for home front border duty, that is, nowhere near Confederate cannon or musketry. This arrangement was designed to give any volunteer the peace of mind in knowing he was always reasonably close to home should any family emergency arise. To entice recruits, volunteers for the new regiment were promised full army pay, a cash bounty, and exemption from any future draft. Within the never-ending game of partisan politics, the ardently Democratic *Detroit Free Press* took a derisive view toward Michigan's new "home guard" regiment, sarcastically pointing out how the new regiment "presents many attractions for those having a fancy for the milder experience of military life," especially since volunteers were promised both regular pay and bounties.[17]

Yet to the surprise of practically everyone, recruiting officers found their work to be slow going because prospective recruits, especially older married ones, simply refused to believe the regiment would truly remain in the state. In Hillsdale, a frustrated George Douglas informed Michigan adjutant general John Robertson on November 26 how his recruiting efforts were meeting with little success. "I exhaust my powers of eloquence every day in this direction," Douglas reported, "and still they are not convinced, thinking it is an underhanded game to get them to the front." After Capt. William Atwood wrote a few days later of similar frustrations, the regiment's new colonel, Grover S. Wormer, instructed his recruiting officers to give his personal assurances that the new regiment would not leave the state. Moreover, Wormer advised his officers to remind potential recruits that close-to-home, in-state service was preferable to facing the draft, where any man might then end up at the front. Yet, such home front mistrust was not unwarranted, considering how civilians had learned how numerous one-hundred--day Ohio regiments supposedly recruited solely for home front duty actually ended up at the

Virginia meat grinder back in the summer of 1864. In the case of the 30th Michigan, the new 1,000-man regiment was indeed fully recruited by early 1865, but overwhelmingly with unmarried eighteen- and nineteen-year-old boys who were too young to serve until then.[18]

If gaining solid recruits was difficult enough, the never-ending bounty-jumping scam continued to frustrate army recruiters and provost marshals. When asked for his plea to the charge of bounty jumping and then desertion, one soldier smugly asked, "Which one? I have deserted thirteen times." New York's sixth district provost marshal Theodore Bronson turned in his resignation convinced that his efforts were having little if any positive effect. In a letter to New York senator Edwin Morgan, Bronson bemoaned how deserters and bounty jumpers knew that any maximum penalty (death) would most likely be set aside by the president. According to Bronson, a New York cavalry lieutenant informed him that three hundred recruits were sent to Bronson for mustering; however, one hundred had already deserted between their camp and Bronson's office. Bronson's final straw was learning of one man named Peter Glenn whom he had personally recruited but had deserted on his way to his new regiment. Glenn was soon arrested and sent to Governor's Island under desertion charges personally prepared by Bronson. The man easily escaped and, according to Bronson, was now in jail at White Plains, New York, facing charges of having since murdered his wife. Glenn was a typical specimen of the bounty jumper criminal class and those new recruits now filling up the Union armies' ranks.[19]

Frank Wilkeson was one green and headstrong recruit who experienced the Peter Glenn's of the army firsthand. Like many inexperienced teen boys before him, Wilkeson ran away from home at age sixteen yearning to acquire the martial manhood he believed military service would bestow upon him. He made his way from his father's Hudson River valley farm to Albany, New York, where he managed to enlist into the 11th New York Battery, then fighting at the Virginia front. To his utter amazement, he soon found himself surrounded by hundreds of far older "ruffian" recruits, all looking to desert at the first opportunity and therefore guarded constantly by armed sentinels. Wilkeson described how he was completely belittled by the older men after admitting he had enlisted solely for patriotic motives, whereupon he was robbed of all his meager possessions. He learned that like a prison, a social pecking order was established by these men. "A recruit's social standing in the barracks was determined by the acts of villainy he had performed," Wilkeson explained, "supplemented by the number of times he had jumped the bounty." Those at the top of the order commanded the others' respect and were entitled to such rights as choosing the most desirable bunk or standing at the head of the chow line. "If there was a man in all that shameless crew who had enlisted from patriotic motives, I did not see him," Wilkeson concluded. "There was not a man of them who was not eager to run away. Not a man who did not quake when he thought of the front. Almost to a man they were bullies and cowards, and almost to a man they belonged to the criminal classes."[20]

Those criminal elements often had ample reason to enlist because as briefly mentioned in chapter 1, such men deemed the court-offered option of going into the army as preferable to being tossed into jail. A junior officer with the 176th New York Infantry surmised in 1863 that was because those criminals possessed either an eagerness for adventure or felt confident they could desert before being placed into the ranks. As a result, the officer recalled that the new volunteers being sent to his regiment "included a good deal of rubbish and worse than rubbish." In the case of the 11th New Hampshire Infantry, 625 such men were sent to fill the regiment's depleted ranks, however only 240 of them ever reached the regiment. The remainder deserted in route. O. Leland Barlow of the 16th Connecticut Infantry similarly decried those shenanigans after witnessing the human refuse being sent to the front under such terms. "If a man commits any crime except murder," he wrote to his sister, "it pardons him to go into the Army." A post-war report even noted that numerous veteran criminals had sought out the army "not only for refuge but as a field for fresh depredations."[21]

President Grover Cleveland later confirmed this court-offered opportunity during his first term of office from 1885 to 1889. After Cleveland was drafted in July 1863, he secured a Polish substitute for the mere fee of $150. Writing in 1887, Cleveland recalled that as the then assistant district attorney for New York's Erie County, "I had abundant opportunity to secure without expense a substitute from discharged convicts and from friendless persons accused of crime if I had wished to do so."[22]

One newspaper reported that an inspection of an unnamed city's police records over a three-month period revealed that with only a handful of exceptions, no man charged with theft, arson, or drunkenness was ever brought to trial without first being given the enlistment option. The reporter noticed with some disgust that the number of men who had enlisted to avoid the state prison outnumbered all other reasons, and to rub some final salt into the public wound, those men had all received their enlistment bounty. Illustrating that reality was a captain in the 83rd Pennsylvania Infantry who cynically wrote in August 1863 how many of his regiment's first conscripts were the "cream and flower, the very head and front" of the preceding July's New York draft rioters. They were now in the army to avoid facing charges of arson, robbery, and even homicide. The captain decided that most of them "were the grandest scoundrels that ever went unhung." Army demoralization would surely follow when this "mercenary horde" lacking in any martial spirit or moral pride arrived to take the place of the proud three-year veterans who had purportedly enlisted solely from patriotic motives. Since word of this sad state of affairs would inevitably filter back to the home front, its net effect would be to further discourage enlistments.[23]

By 1865, many a man who chose to remain at home—as well as his family—saw little substantive difference between languishing in jail or being drafted and then forcibly marched off to the front lines at the point of a bayonet. Numerous reluctant boys in blue even compared that reality to Southern slavery. The widespread martial ardor that dominated the April and May 1861 training camps was a long-ago memory. Those newspaper- and letter-reading, law-abiding citizens who had not enlisted for their personal reasons had no intention of volunteering themselves, their husbands, sons, or brothers to serve alongside such ne'er-do-wells as those described by Theodore Bronson and Frank Wilkeson.

Yet given the ongoing threat of being drafted coupled with the ever-increasing bounties, any man and his family might reconsider if he could first gain a substantial amount of bounty money that would greatly enhance the family's financial security. John W. Harry of Watertown,

Ohio, certainly felt that way in a September 3, 1864, letter to his brother. "I won't advise eny one to go to ware in such a caus as this," he wrote, "but I expect it wood bee beter too inlist then to bee drafted." Sarah Lundy also personally witnessed that calculation, noting how plenty of men in her Ohio hometown were enlisting only because of the lucrative bounties coupled with the fear of being drafted. From the time the $300 commutation option ended in July 1864, bounties became so immense that men who had never considered enlisting before—whether aging fathers or young sons and brothers—now viewed a $1,200 bounty or more as the windfall that would offer financial security well into the future. Veteran soldiers stunned at this turn of events again felt compelled to caution their parents and siblings about war's realities and not to see just the financial payoff. "The large bounties all look very nice and the bright side appears for a moment," a New York veteran wrote to his parents in September 1864. "But there is a dark side to it and no one knows much of it until he finds himself deprived of the comforts of home and amid the deadly shells and bullets of the rebels." John Voltz likewise lamented to his brother, Felix, "I have cursed the day I have enlisted for what benefit will I ever derive from being a soldier." At the other end of the spectrum were those single men who had no good home to return to, so they opted to reenlist, take the lucrative bounty, and resume "soljerin.'" When all was said and done, the bounties paid throughout the Union—which included those offered by state and local governments—were estimated to have totaled around $750 million (or just less than $14 billion in 2022 when factoring in inflation). That staggering sum—which became necessary to entice men to fight for their country—was more than all Quartermaster Department expenditures for the entire war. To describe it another way, it was roughly as much as the regular salaries paid to the troops after their enlistment and five times as much as all ordnance expenses.[24]

***

The Union's military and civil authorities were painfully aware that desertion continued to plague the Northern armies, and of the deleterious effect desertion had on army morale and manpower. In order to get some of those men back into the ranks, Lincoln issued a carrot and stick proclamation on March 11, 1865, that targeted current deserters. His offer highlighted how the war's end seemed closer than ever with an emotionally exhausted federal government looking to deliver a coup de grâce to the rebellion rather than spending resources seeking out deserters hiding in dark places. The president's carrot offered a full pardon and amnesty to any deserter who voluntarily returned to his unit or turned himself in to any provost marshal within the next sixty days. The lone stipulation was that those men then had to serve honorably for the remainder of their enlistment term, plus a period equal to that which the army had lost by their desertion. Failing that, Lincoln's stick came into play. Any man who remained a deserter after the sixty-day grace period was considered to have voluntarily relinquished and forfeited his citizenship rights, or the right to become a citizen in the case of enlisted immigrants. In addition, any deserter would no longer be allowed to hold any public office once the rebellion ended.[25]

The results of Lincoln's offer were hardly what anyone hoped for and spoke to the depth of Northern war weariness. After tabulating the numbers, Col. James Fry reported to the secretary of war that of the 119,000 men who were currently recorded as having deserted from the ranks, a paltry 1,755, or approximately 1.5 percent, took advantage of Lincoln's amnesty offer. To make matters worse, Fry informed the secretary that those numbers did not include the approximately 161,000 civilian men who were drafted but failed to report for duty at their local provost marshal's office. By law, they were also considered to be deserters. Fry admitted that up to 30 percent of the men in that latter category may have had a valid excuse; nevertheless, taking that 30 percent into consideration still left about 230,000 men officially labeled as deserters. According to historian Fred Shannon, the sad reality was that the total effective force of the army at no time during the war exceeded one million men, and as many as 40 percent were listed as deserters at war's end. In essence, one man out of every seven enlisted or drafted during the war was a deserter. They decided it was not their war.[26]

***

Following the two principal Confederate surrenders in April 1865, the tens of thousands of deserters, draft dodgers, and bounty jumpers who had fled to Canada and elsewhere began to return home throughout the upcoming summer. Where "home" now was could be a tricky proposition. Considering that Northern communities were generally well aware of their local soldiers' actions, the skedaddlers and deserters knew they most likely faced shaming and ostracism if they came from a staunchly pro-war community. Conversely, those men who lived in a predominantly antiwar and/or anti-draft town knew they would most likely face no unpleasant consequences. In numerous instances, returning deserters with little or no family often reinvented themselves and settled in locales that had little to no support for the war.

New York congressman Calvin T. Hulburd, whose district bordered Canada, wanted to make sure the shirkers faced the appropriate consequences. He wrote to Secretary of War Stanton soon after the war ended expressing a desire to see the skedaddlers arrested as they attempted to recross the border and then fully prosecuted as deserters. In Hulburd's opinion, such a course of action would give proper satisfaction to the loyal citizenry in general and the returning, honorable veterans in particular. Yet no such action was ever initiated. Those deserters who chose not to accept Lincoln's amnesty provisions suffered only a loss of any back pay and the ignominy of being dishonorably discharged, which was hardly a concern for any of them. More importantly, they knew they could return home without fear of arrest. Within six months after the war's end, any draft evasion or war resistance was forgiven by the federal government.[27]

The government's inaction was due in large part to the simple fact that there were no longer sufficient military authorities in place to arrest and detain those men. Once the war was over, Col. James Fry's Provost Marshal Bureau was ordered by the War Department to begin discharging excess employees so that in many districts, only a provost marshal and one clerk remained in place. Other districts were consolidated, which meant that one provost marshal was left to administer what was once two or more districts. If the War Department truly wanted to punish the army deserters and civilian skedaddlers, then this order was reminiscent of Stanton's gaffe in closing down the North's recruiting offices in April

1862. The net effect, according to Fry, was that his bureau was no longer capable of arresting and detaining deserters unless the War Department allowed provost marshals to employ and pay suitable individuals to carry out the task. Fry also suggested a second option, which was to offer a cash bounty large enough to induce civilians to arrest deserters and then deliver them to the local provost marshal; a suggestion appearing as a forerunner to the Wild West's "bounty hunter" of the then not too distant future.[28]

Realizing the apparent lack of consequence for their earlier actions, many deserters and bounty jumpers returned to their hometowns and then acted with brazen impudence in public. Throughout the North during the 1865 summer, Fry received numerous dispatches from his remaining provost marshals that all reported essentially the same concern: Their towns were becoming infested with returning deserters who openly flouted their prior behavior. Law-abiding citizens feared for their safety and property with the provost marshal having no manpower to deal with the threats. In one such case, Provost Marshal Capt. Elijah Low of Maine's fourth district reported how his territory was overrun with army deserters, bounty jumpers, and draft dodgers. Even worse, they openly taunted any returned soldiers they encountered who were crippled by wounds or diseases suffered during the war.[29]

Yet despite the purported quick riches, bounty jumping was not a ticket to long-term leisure for the class of men who engaged in it. An old veteran of the 209th Pennsylvania Infantry wrote in the early twentieth century that not one man still living could be found throughout the land who was willing to stand up and admit "I was a bounty jumper." Moreover, the veteran claimed that he never knew nor heard of a bounty jumper who was not a bum or a deadbeat for the remainder of his life.[30]

Those Northern dissidents who spoke out against the war or who were suspected of disloyalty were also released from their prison cells after the war ended and with having to endure nothing more onerous than taking a loyalty oath. Roughly 13,500 American citizens accused of disloyal activity had been held indefinitely without formal charge in military prisons and denied the writ of habeas corpus following Lincoln's suspension of the writ in August 1862. In many instances across the

North, their imprisonment was set forth by local officials acting solely on their own. Even in the far western state of California, alleged Confederate sympathizers had languished in wooden stockades pending their oath of loyalty to the federal Union. Another 213, mostly from Missouri, were housed at the Union's Mississippi River–based Rock Island Prison until the war's end.[31]

FORGET THE DISSENT, REMEMBER THE GLORY

The economics-driven joy that much of the North quietly felt as it watched countless unemployed men march off to war in April and May 1861 turned to angst as those veteran soldiers began to return home. If the sight of threatening, obnoxious deserters returning home was cause for fear, the thought of hundreds of thousands of hardened and unemployed citizen-soldiers pouring into the North's urban and rural communities only added to the anxiety. "Our gallant soldiers" were now viewed by the stay-at-homes as unwanted and potentially dangerous labor competition. Concurrently, those factories and industries that had fed the North's war machine now saw demand for their goods sputter to a halt. The economy fell while inflation soared. At the same time, any veteran who was not a farmer had to wonder where he would find work in a country that was now on the verge of being swamped by two million men returning home, about three-fourths of whom were under the age of thirty. Scores of recently arrived immigrants competed with returning soldiers for jobs. As a result, unemployment rose noticeably between the last three months of 1865 on through the beginning of 1868, contributing to a five-year crime wave that lasted from 1865 to 1870. For the returning veterans, many of whom were physically or psychologically battle-scarred, their confidence in having a stable fiscal future was hazy at best. Scores of boys in blue returned home to no jobs, no incomes, and no sense of belonging. It was a volatile combination and hardly spoke to the collective glory soon to be manifested in the nation's memory.[32]

With the rebellion over, those Northern civilians who were touched by the war now wanted to forget the past four years and get on with their lives. Families who had lost a loved one certainly grieved their loss, but they also knew they, too, needed to move on. The North wanted to experience a return to normalcy and not face the bitter reminders of the war. Illustrating that viewpoint was how more than 99 percent of the million-plus war-related photographs taken during the rebellion were eventually thrown away or destroyed due to a lack of interest. Moreover, as Brian Matthew Jordan argued, the dearth of battlefield and soldier monuments erected in the fifteen years after the war ended compared to the last two decades of the nineteenth century also illustrated the North's post-war desire to forget and move on. For many more Northern residents, however, that sense of normalcy had never really gone away. The statistical majority of the North's population had not felt the hard hand of war yet they, too, also wanted to forget. The North's solution on how best to accomplish that was to remember the collective glory, not the bitter dissent.[33]

To a large degree, Northern citizens sought to remember only the glory because they were not yet ready to confront the true horrors that the war had wrought. Veteran soldiers-turned-authors—as well as civilians—wrote their reminiscences by the thousands and in the process gave readers the idealized "sentimental romanticism" of war they still desired because the Civil War was still deemed an ennobling venture that filled its participants' lives with special meaning. Any author who felt otherwise knew best to remain quiet. As one scholar observed, "dissension in the era of the Civil War equaled failure in the literary marketplace." Moreover, a form of "spiritual censorship" blanketed the land. The war's unseemly aspects were still judged untouchable by America's cultural guardians. "We do not like to read such narratives," claimed one literary critic in 1867 with regards to the tales of suffering and captivity written by ex-Union prisoners of war. "They are too remindful of the late sorrow, and we would for our own taste discourage their publication," the critic advised. Tales of war or draft avoidance, desertion, disease, sordid behavior, public corruption, private hypocrisy, or criminality might only be hinted at but never bestowed in full to a mostly female reading public that was deemed too delicate for such themes. Not until the twentieth century were such topics accepted by the nation.[34]

***

In his recollections of Civil War–era Chicago, Frederick Cook wrote that with the passage of time, the war was now "apt to be regarded as one of heroisms only." Yet for Cook, it was the "seamy and sordid side" of the war that he could never forget. In the decades after the war, Northern towns of every size and in every state placed monuments in public spaces to honor those who had served in what was then known to some as "The War of the Rebellion." Decoration Day, later known as Memorial Day, was an official holiday in every Northern state by 1890 and was often celebrated with speeches and festivities honoring the Union's fallen heroes. These patriotic commemorations during the last quarter of the nineteenth century reflected Northern White society's desire to remember their victory through the communal spirit of willingly shared sacrifice devoid of any class or ethnic distinctions. Like those memorials, leading publications of the day, such as *Harper's Weekly* and *Century*, published numerous articles that praised the manliness and courage of those Union soldiers. Political candidates knew they needed to identify themselves with the Civil War if they hoped to win an election. The rebellion was (and still is) viewed as a "good war" similar to how later generations looked back upon World War II. This outpouring of righteousness portrayed the North's citizen-soldier as the ultimate warrior—a man who left his home for purely defensive purposes—and in the process vindicated the legitimacy of the Union war effort.[35]

Perhaps not surprisingly then, this "treasury of virtue" focused on tales of heroic grandeur and noble sacrifice. Yet simultaneously, the public's memory also chose to forget the stories of cowardice, indifference, racial hostility, overall war avoidance, and home front violence that included the murders of military officials and communities bitterly divided over the war's aims, costs, and legitimacy. As for deserters, no man ever seemed to acknowledge himself as such. That same forgetfulness applied to many one-time dedicated Copperheads.[36]

Such civil dissent was largely ignored, as compared to the public opposition to the Vietnam War, which was well-remembered afterward and to this day. In addition and for some men, their actual wartime experiences did not coincide with their desired recollections. John Hilton offers one not-so-unusual example. Hilton requested and received a medical discharge for rheumatism from a sympathetic army surgeon in January 1863, only three months after his enlistment into the 111th Pennsylvania Infantry. He wanted out and his letters to his wife reveal his inability to cope with the battle mayhem he had witnessed. Years later, though, Hilton would tell people he had resigned in January 1865, not 1863, and that a heart attack reluctantly forced him out of the army just after the paperwork for his promotion to captain had been processed. After the war, Hilton joined veterans' organizations and attended regimental reunions, and when he passed away, his obituary identified him as Capt. John Hilton.[37]

Like Hilton, innumerable men who apathetically remained at home or were even zealous Copperheads began to reimagine themselves as steadfast pro-war patriots in a manner that modern jargon might describe as "gaslighting." In one example, New York diarist George Strong wrote of how men who were once prominent Copperheads were now eagerly applying for membership in the staunchly pro-Republican and elite Union League Club he co-founded in late 1862. Strong wrote with some amusement how all of those men seemed to forget their past words and deeds and were now recasting themselves as unwavering Unionists from the war's very beginning. "What a pity we had not known this a year ago," Strong told his diary with some subtle sarcasm. "We should have been saved much uneasiness." In that same manner, a Union veteran later prophesied, "Future historians may be more kind to them than we who suffered because of them, but it is not likely that the descendants of any Copperhead will claim public honors for their anti-Union forbears." At the same time, Union veterans whose wartime service was that of battle-field flight or a rearguard shirker worked to reimagine their experiences as a patriotic sacrifice rather than cowardly shame. Only after many years were they able to fashion a war whose recollections meshed with their idealized expectations and ideals.[38]

Moreover, as the war was ending with Union victory in hand—and especially after Lincoln's assassination—community vigilance committees demanded that those citizens whose loyalties were considered dubious now publicly demonstrate their patriotic bona fides. Those who refused risked a physical punishment designed to send a clear message to others: Patriotism and its concurrent public displays were not optional but mandatory. Even such public repentance did not always erase the bitterness. Secretary of the Navy Gideon Welles noted in September 1866 how "There is a kinder feeling among Republicans toward beaten Rebels than towards Copperheads." More than three years after the war ended, Josiah Tatman sat down on August 7, 1868, and penned a "To whom it may concern" letter that spoke directly to that lingering hostility. In his missive, Tatman claimed to have been a Union loyalist surreptitiously playing the part of a Southern sympathizer for parties unmentioned, nevertheless, he was still—three years later—unable to reveal his true motives, employer, and innocence. Yet because of his overt, wartime Copperhead actions, all of his past friends still scorned him. "My name is anathema, I am shunned by all; my life is a living hell," Tatman confessed.[39]

***

This sense of the stay-at-home male civilian feeling some manner of "survivor's guilt" or private shame in his post-war relations with soldiers cut across the generations. In one instance, psychologist Silas Mitchell recalled how it was a family decision that he would stay at home caring for his mother while his three younger brothers went off to war. His manly duty to his family was clear, yet Mitchell's pathos was such that he always regretted that he, too, was not engaged in putting down the great rebellion. Nor did it take long for a prominent Connecticut man to feel those same pangs of regret, once the war was over and the potential danger to himself had passed. According to Bernard Blakeslee of the 16th Connecticut Infantry, that unnamed man looked him in the eye on the very day of the regiment's return home in 1865 and said, "I would give fifty thousand dollars to have seen and been through what you have." Those nonveterans sensed in the decades after Appomattox that they remained passively at home figuratively gazing at those men who were now part of the manly cult of Homeric heroes.[40]

In public, only that hero remained. In private, however, the majority of the North's civilian population knew the four years of civil war had only grazed their lives. The North had fought the war with one hand behind its back, as writer Shelby Foote so aptly described it in Ken Burns's documentary film *The Civil War*. In the overarching collective sense, the hardships the North endured had been tolerable because, for most, they strove to isolate themselves from the rebellion and its home front consequences. The statistical majority of the North's population knew it had not really been their war.[41]

CONCLUSION

"What's Past Is Prologue"

THIS BOOK HAS ATTEMPTED TO REMIND THE READER THAT THE AMERican Civil War—as observed and experienced by the Northern home front—was hardly the widely popular moral crusade portrayed within much of our collective historical memory. From the poor immigrant laborer on up to the well-bred, upper-class elite, many in the North were opposed to its rationales and methods, sometimes violently so. From the day the war began, innumerable Northern men—along with their families—quietly decided they had no intention of volunteering into the Union armies. This desire to stay as far away as possible from the front lines became so widespread that the federal government was compelled to threaten conscription only fifteen months after the rebellion commenced if more men did not immediately volunteer. As the body counts continued to rise and conscription was implemented, avoiding the war in general and the draft, in particular, became a constant focus in their civilian lives. Of the more than 776,000 men drafted by the federal government during the war's final two and a half years, a mere 6 percent were actually held to service, the remainder paying the commutation fee, hiring a substitute, or gaining some manner of medical exemption, or they technically deserted by simply refusing to show up at their assigned mustering station. Their reasons were varied and ranged from the perceived primacy of familial obligations trumping any manner of so-called national duty to a philosophical disagreement over the war's deeper questions.

Most, but certainly not all of these dissidents were Democrats, who were at the time the opposition party both at the presidential and congressional levels. Partisan politics certainly played a role in their opposition; however, for many, there was a sincere aversion to what they viewed as the Lincoln administration's unconstitutional acts in the manner the war was prosecuted both on the battlefield and on the home front. While most Democrats initially supported the war when the sole, publicly stated goal was to reunite the Union, their backing changed to opposition dramatically in the fall of 1862 with the advent of the Militia Act and Lincoln's Emancipation Proclamation. Democratic support for the war never returned to its spring 1861 level. As Nathan Kalmoe illustrated in his recent study on Civil War partisanship and violence, Democratic dissenters did indeed hinder the Union's war efforts by persuading enough of their loyalists not to contribute to the cause and by fielding candidates and a party platform in 1864 that would have readily given up any military advantage at that point to an immediate peace.[1]

In the heated partisan politics of the era, steadfast Republicans became the ones most likely to enlist in the military. Democratic aversion toward the war and Lincoln culminated in the 1864 presidential election where 4.5 out of every 10 voters—nearly half—cast a vote against the war policies of Abraham Lincoln and his Republican administration. Despite that level of opposition, Lincoln's modest popular vote win (though electoral landslide) and then the Union's military victory in the Civil War itself foretold a number of important precedents. Perhaps most important was the principle that the federal government can legally force its citizens into military service. By the mid-twentieth century, it would have been a challenge to find many Americans who disagreed with that principle. Never again would the states be responsible for raising an army nor would the federal government allow commutation or substitutes. Furthermore, the Provost Marshal's Bureau and its internal security responsibilities presaged the vast domestic surveillance and law enforcement bureaucracies twenty-first-century Americans are well aware of.[2]

Post-war Republicans generally succeeded in portraying themselves as the party of the martyred Lincoln that saved the nation, whereas the Democrats and their peace-at-any-price wing were depicted as little more than traitors. By "waving the bloody shirt" and with few exceptions, the Republican Party would dominate the national political landscape for the next twenty years. Modern-day readers, however, would do well to realize how in our modern era, the two parties have somewhat reversed their Civil War–era perspectives. Conservative Republicans today who view themselves as strict constitutional originalists who believe that document says what it means and means what it says would quite likely have considered themselves a Democrat in the Civil War North. At the same time, the Radical Republicans of the Civil War era who were agitating for slavery's abolition and a measure of equality between the races were considered the "progressives" of their era, even as many if not most Northerners and practically all Southerners viewed their position as reckless and even dangerous.[3]

The level of dissent throughout the North and its concurrent desire to avoid the war was hardly unique to the American character, either from before the war or since. Unchallenged national unity was hardly the political culture of the mid-nineteenth century and has remained so up to the present day. One could even argue that open opposition to government policy was tolerated far more freely prior to World War I than since. Moreover, we must remember that dissent in war is the rule within our republican form of government rather than a rare exception. Furthermore, it is often partisan politics and the legal supremacy of those in power who conflate the issues of loyal versus treasonous activity. As we the people look backward, we should also realize how historians may reevaluate the past through their own personal lens of pro- or antiwar sentiment.

In an analysis of Oliver Wendell Holmes Jr.'s Civil War service, historian Peter Carmichael wrote how Holmes concluded that a man's conscience becomes the supreme arbiter of his duty. Yet we must ask if there is a point when that conscience—in the form of protest and dissent—crosses over into disloyal activity. Modern Americans must realize that no war is supported by everyone. Dissent is a cornerstone foundational to the American experiment, and its propriety in times of war is an issue that has divided Americans throughout our history. Speaking out does not automatically render one a traitor. It is not uncommon in our modern era for opponents of America's military conflicts to face home front charges of cowardice or betrayal—and the social ostracism that often goes with it—in a manner very similar to the Democratic Party's Copperhead faction during the Civil War.[4]

The United States has been involved in twelve major wars starting in 1776 when the founding fathers declared independence from Great Britain up through the present day. Yet not one of those conflicts garnered the wholehearted approval of *all* of the nation's citizenry, for there has always been an often broad and diverse, yet vocal faction of the populace vehemently opposed to the conflict. The "Tories" who were still loyal to the British crown during the War for Independence were considered traitorous by some revolutionaries. World Wars I and II both saw a noticeable and vocal pacifist contingent within the United States. Aversion and protest in this country against the Vietnam War is well documented and remains fresh in the minds of many living Americans. Like the Civil War of more than a century earlier, that conflict featured countless stories of young American men burning their draft cards and/or fleeing to Canada. Indeed, many believe the United States won that war on the battlefield but lost it in the end due to what Lincoln knew as "the fire in the rear." In the various Middle East wars occurring in our twenty-first century, the Iraqi War's Code Pink protesters could be viewed as spiritual descendants of the Civil War's Copperhead movement. Even more recently and at the time of this writing, a new Quinnipiac University poll revealed that 52 percent of Democrats would flee the United States rather than stand and fight if the country was invaded in a manner similar to Russia's current invasion of Ukraine. Many citizens today as in all times view their primary loyalty and obligation to their personal and families' welfare, not a distant national government.[5]

Many Americans today see little reason for the country to be engaged in nation-building in overseas countries such as Iraq or Afghanistan in much the same way as innumerable Civil War–era Northern citizens had no desire to participate in such experiments down South. The Russian and Marxist revolutionary Leon Trotsky captured this age-old struggle when he purportedly wrote in the early twentieth century, "You may not be interested in war, but war is interested in you." Even though our country and the world have "shrunk" due to incredible technological advancements in transportation and communications during the past 160+ years, much of the localized existence and individualism concepts discussed in this work remain valid. Perhaps much of that is simply human nature. In that regard, we may ask ourselves if the Civil War's local versus national debates ever really ended, or do they rear their head from time to time in a different form? When it comes to American war and its inevitable strains of avoidance, dissent, and opposition reaction, Shakespeare's famous phrase "What's Past Is Prologue" rings true.

Notes

Introduction

1. The American Battlefield Trust estimates 38.6 percent of eligible Northern men as having served in the Union military. 1,532,278 Northern men served while another 2,430,924 men were eligible but did not serve. "Civil War Service by Population" listed under "Civil War Casualties" at https://www.battlefields.org/learn/articles/civil-war -casualties, accessed Aug. 2, 2020; also see Schindler, "Dismantling the Dichotomy of Cowardice and Courage during the American Civil War," 21. Using the 1860 federal census in conjunction with National Park Service data, Schindler calculated that just more than one in four Northern men of military age either volunteered or were drafted into the Union armies. Also see Gallman, *Defining Duty*, 7–8; "1860 Census: Population of the United States," US Census Bureau, https://www.census.gov/library/publications /1864/dec/1860a.html, accessed Feb. 13, 2020.

2. Linderman, *Embattled Courage*, 12, 31–32; Orlando M. Poe to Eleanor Poe, Nov. 30, 1863, Orlando M. Poe Papers, Library of Congress (hereafter referred to as LOC).

3. Haidt, *The Righteous Mind*, 225; Linderman, *Embattled Courage*, 12; Walsh, *Cowardice: A Brief History*, 1, 7–8.

4. A key goal within this work is to explain the war's evolving objectives, the growing dissent to those aims, and the era's social and cultural norms that shaped the average civilian's and soldier's perspectives. To achieve those ends, I strove to avoid the use of "presentism," which is to judge, comment on, or recast the past based on the morals and values of the present. For instance, commonly used and accepted racial epithets of the Civil War era are deemed abhorrent today. Therefore, such language and attitudes are used in this work solely within historical quotes to accurately portray the era's varied perspectives.

5. Geary, *We Need Men*, ix; Hess, *Liberty, Virtue, and Progress*, 47, 63; Davenport and Lloyd, *Rugged Individualism: Dead or Alive?* 5–21; Kettner, *Development of American Citizenship, 1608–1870*, 173–76.

6. Fry, "Final Report Made to the Secretary of War by the Provost Marshal General," 12. Hereafter referred to as "Final Report PMG." The Office of the Provost Marshal General was created in March 1863 primarily to oversee and enforce the national draft.

7. Linderman, *Embattled Courage*, 1; Carmichael, *War for the Common Soldier*, 12; Jones, "Violence on the Home Front," 60; Frank, *With Ballot and Bayonet*, 172–73.

8. Clarke, "'Let All Nations See': Civil War Nationalism and the Memorialization of Wartime Voluntarism," 67; Blight, *Race and Reunion*, 138–39, 238; Blanchard, *Counties of Morgan, Monroe, and Brown*, 72; Sterling, "Civil War Draft Resistance in the Middle West," xv.

9. Boynton, *Dedication of the Chickamauga and Chattanooga National Military Park*, 275; Michie, "Reminiscences of Cadet and Army Service," 183; Marvel, *Mr. Lincoln Goes to War*, 59; Whitman, *Specimen Days*, 80.

10. Hess, *Liberty, Virtue, and Progress*, 69–70; Cimbala and Miller, *The Northern Home Front during the Civil War*, 67–68.

11. Hess, *Liberty, Virtue, and Progress*, 69–70.

12. Sala, *My Diary in America in the Midst of War*, vol. 1, 151–52; Parish, *The North and the Nation in the Era of the Civil War*, 151, 154.

13. Haidt, *The Righteous Mind*, 84–89, 258. Glaucon (Plato's brother) argued that man acts virtuous primarily because he fears the consequences of getting caught engaging in bad behavior, especially the damage to his public reputation; Holmes Jr., *The Common Law*, 110.

CHAPTER 1

1. McPherson, *Ordeal by Fire*, 164.

2. McKay, *The Civil War and New York City*, 73. For localized examples of initial, widespread war support, see Bratt, "A Great Revolution in Feeling: The American Civil War in Niles and Grand Rapids, Michigan" and Raus, *Banners South*, 6–20; Hamilton, *Reminiscences of a Veteran*, 129; also Smith, *No Party Now*, 34–37; Gallagher, *The Union War*, 1–6.

3. Fahs, *The Imagined Civil War*, 11–12; Stout, *Upon the Altar of the Nation*, 28; *London Illustrated News*, June 15, 1861; Bellefonte, Pennsylvania *Centre Democrat*, Apr. 26, 1861; quoted in Mahoney, *From Hometown to Battlefield in the Civil War Era*, 205; Nelia Moler to "Dear Sister," Apr. 23, 1861, Anderson Family Papers 1854–1931, LOC; Mitchell, *The Vacant Chair*, xii, 4.

4. Fry, "Final Report PMG," 6; Kahan, *Amiable Scoundrel*, 165–67; Robertson Jr., *Soldiers Blue and Gray*, 4–5; Stone, "Washington on the Eve of War," 8–9; Shannon, *Organization and Administration of the Union Army*, vol. 1, 27; Newell and Shrader, *Of Duty Well and Faithfully Done*, 1–3, 49.

5. Newell and Shrader, *Of Duty Well and Faithfully Done*, 1; Frank, *With Ballot and Bayonet*, 19; Hsieh, *West Pointers and the Civil War*, 2–3; Frank, *Martial Metaphors*, 207.

6. Cunliffe, *Soldiers and Civilians*, 17.

7. Basler, *Collected Works of Abraham Lincoln*, vol. 4, 331–32.

8. Chamberlain, "Military Affairs in Maine," in *The Union Army*, vol. 1, 21; O'Connor, *Civil War Boston*, 57; Eddy, *The Patriotism of Illinois*, vol. 1, 90; Robertson, *Michigan in the War*, 10–11; *Annual Report of the Adjutant and Q. M. General of the State of Michigan for the Year 1858*, 17; Hall, *Cayuga in the Field*, 17; Burt, *My Memoirs of the Military History of the State of New York*, 9.

9. Goodheart, *1861: The Civil War Awakening*, 191–92; Whisker, *The Rise and Decline of the American Militia System*, 335; Cunliffe, *Soldiers and Civilians*, 185.

10. Shannon, *Organization and Administration of the Union Army*, vol. 1, 32, 259; for examples of appeals to Cameron, see Galusha A. Grow to Cameron, May 5, 1861, *The War of the Rebellion: A Compilation of the Official Records of the Union and Confederate Armies*, ser. 3, vol. 1, 160 (hereafter referred to as *O.R.*); Erastus Fairbanks to Cameron, May 7, 1861, *O.R.*, ser. 3, vol. 1, 121; William Dennison to Cameron, Apr. 22, 1861, *O.R.*, ser. 3, vol. 1, 101–02; Charles S. Olden to Cameron, May 1, 1861, *O.R.*, ser. 3, vol. 1, 142–43; Fritsch, *The Untried Life*, 15.

11. Matteson, *A Worse Place than Hell*, 122; *American Presbyterian*, June 6, 1861. For other newspaper examples, see *Union and Journal [Maine]*, May 3, 1861, and *Burlington [Iowa] Weekly Hawk-Eye*, May 11, 1861; Union League Club, *In Memoriam, Henry Whitney Bellows*, 12–13; Adams quote in Fritsch, *The Untried Life*, 15; Rable, *God's Almost Chosen Peoples*, 3, 51–68; Stout, *Upon the Altar of the Nation*, 103; Frank, *With Ballot and Bayonet*, 60–61; Warren, *The Legacy of the Civil War*, 20.

12. White, *A Philadelphia Perspective*, 86; Nevins, *Diary of the Civil War*, 122; Censer, *Papers of Frederick Law Olmsted, vol. IV*, 459; Giesberg, *Civil War Sisterhood*, 15–16, 29.

13. Blair, "We Are Coming, Father Abraham—Eventually," 188; Watson B. Smith to "Dear Father," Apr. 25, 1861, "Civil War Voices: Soldier Studies" at http://www.soldierstudies.org/index.php?action=view_letter&Letter=221, accessed May 20, 2020; Silber and Sievens, *Yankee Correspondence*, 130–31. Scholarly Northern home guard studies remain scarce. See Foster, "Defenders of the Home Front," for a contemporary and thorough analysis. Also see Bahde, "Our Cause Is a Common One."

14. Sandow, "Limits of Northern Patriotism," 190.

15. Letter from Samuel J. Reader to his sister, copied into his diary, Oct. 21, 1861, Samuel J. Reader diaries, vol. 5, Kansas Historical Society; Wister and Wister, "Sarah Butler Wister's Civil War Diary," 279; Orr, *Last to Leave the Field*, 13; Ward, *Letters of Artemus Ward to Charles E. Wilson 1858–1861*, 69–71.

16. Bahde, "Our Cause Is a Common One," 72; Clark, *Border Defense in Iowa during the Civil War*, 2, 12; Richard Yates to Edwin Stanton, Aug. 11, 1862, *O.R.*, ser. 3, vol. 2, 351; Edwin Stanton to Richard Yates, July 15, 1863, *O.R.*, ser. 3, vol. 3, 494.

17. George W. Denig, "Memoirs," 139, Ohio History Center Archives & Library.

18. Brandt, *From Home Guards to Heroes*, 32; Mahoney, *From Hometown to Battlefield*, 198, 343; No author stated, "Wisconsin Home Guards during the Civil War," 213.

19. Sandow, *Deserter Country*, 57–58; Donohoe, *The Printer's Kiss*, 180; Lare and Hartzell, *Rebellion Record of Allegheny County*, 13.

20. *Rockland County Messenger*, Aug. 22, 1861; *Joliet Signal*, Aug. 27, 1861; Holmes, *Poems of Oliver Wendell Holmes*, 393–95.

21. *Rockland County Messenger*, Oct. 31, 1861; *Lancaster Daily Intelligencer*, Aug. 19, 1862; *Cleveland Plain Dealer*, Dec. 13, 1861.

22. See https://artsandculture.google.com/asset/the-home-guard-thomas-hicks/qgGHHXtSKZAGnA?hl=en.

23. Church, *Civil War Letters*, 14; Lyman Blackington to "Dear Sister," Jan. 19, 1862, "Private Voices," https://altchive.org/private-voices/node/12786, accessed Apr. 25, 2020; *Franklin Visitor*, Jan. 21, 1862; Schulman, "The Pleasure of the Parlor," 106; James Wade to "Dear Mother," June 7, 1862, Benjamin Wade Papers, LOC.

24. Daniel Perry to Mary Perry, Feb. 13, 1862, Daniel Perry Papers, Oneida County Historical Society; Walton, *A Civil War Courtship*, 30; *Butler American Citizen*, July 13, 1864; Burrows and Keating, *Yours Affectionately, Osgood*, 221.

25. Fry, *Republic in the Ranks*, 7; Wiley, *Life of Billy Yank*, 38–39; McCaffrey, *Army of Manifest Destiny*, 31, cited in McPherson, *For Cause & Comrades*, 28.

26. Huston, *The Panic of 1857 and the Coming of the Civil War*, 3–6.

27. "U.S. Business Cycle Expansions and Contractions," 1, https://www.nber.org/cycles /, accessed Jan. 24, 2020; Smith, *No Party Now*, 25; Holzer, *Lincoln President-Elect*, 55–56; Marvel, *Lincoln's Mercenaries*, 16–18; Guelzo, *Fateful Lightning*, 127; Huston, *The Panic of 1857 and the Coming of the Civil War*, 222–25; Burrows and Wallace, *Gotham: A History of New York City*, 865.

28. Gallman, *The North Fights the Civil War*, 100; Laas, *Wartime Washington*, 32; *The Crisis*, Feb. 21, 1861; *Clearfield Republican*, Mar. 27, 1861; Marlatt, *Stuart Letters*, vol. 2, 940–41.

29. Kohl, *Irish Green and Union Blue*, 20.

30. Reardon, "We Are All in This War," 11; Bingham, *History of Connecticut*, vol. 2, 586; quoted in Johnson, "A Debt Justly Due," 216–17; Miller, "Catholic Religion, Irish Ethnicity, and the Civil War," 280.

31. Edward Hawley to Eugene Hawley, June 1, 1861, Eugene F. Hawley Civil War Letters @ https://collections.ctdigitalarchive.org/islandora/object/150002%3A9405, accessed Nov. 23, 2021; Sauers, *Civil War Journal of Colonel William J. Bolton*, 13–14; McCabe Jr., *The Civil War: A Soldier's Letters Home*, 19–20; for Union officer's pay, see Boatner, *The Civil War Dictionary*, 624.

32. Longacre, *From Antietam to Fort Fisher*, 23; Hallock, "The Role of the Community in Civil War Desertion," 123–34; Larz Anderson to "My Dear Nelson," May 5, 1861, *O.R.*, ser. 1, vol. 52, pt. 1, 162.

33. *St. Louis Republican* cited in *Rutland Herald*, Aug. 15, 1861; Bruen and Fitzgibbons, *Through Ordinary Eyes*, 52; Samuel Dickerman to Brother, Aug. 25, 1861, Bamber Family Papers, Archives & Historical Collections, Michigan State University, Lansing; *Daily Green Mountain Freeman*, Aug. 30, 1861.

34. Shannon, *Organization and Administration of the Union Army*, vol. 1, 260; quoted in Wiley, *Life of Billy Yank*, 38.

35. Marvel, *Mr. Lincoln Goes to War*, 45; Frank, *Martial Metaphors*, xv; Grant letter in Simpson, Sears, and Sheehan-Dean, *The Civil War: The First Year*, 348; Collier, *Letters of a Civil War Soldier*, 14; Thomas Evans diary, Feb. 23, 1862, LOC; Frank Rieley to "Dear Mother," Sept. 5, 1861, Francis and John Rieley Papers, Western Reserve Historical Society; Verter, "Disconsolations of a Jersey Muskrat," 236.

36. Snell, "If They Would Know What I Know," 81; Wallace, *Life & Letters of General W. H. L. Wallace*, 116–17; Wister and Wister, "Sarah Butler Wister's Civil War Diary," 306.

37. Stevenson, *The Victorian Homefront*, xxxiii, 23; Rose, *Victorian America and the Civil War*, 166; Castel, *Tom Taylor's Civil War*, 6.

38. Sarah Forrer to Augusta Bruen, Oct. 14, 1861, Catharine Mitchill Family Letters, Wellesley College Library; B. F. Smart to his father, Aug. 4, 1861, Manassas National Battlefield Park Library; McCabe Jr., *The Civil War: A Soldier's Letters Home*, 13; Blight,

When This Cruel War Is Over, 65. The belief that war service would be beneficial in later life was not unfounded. As but one extreme example, with the exception of Grover Cleveland, each of the seven post-war US presidents from Ulysses Grant to William McKinley served as an officer in the Union army.

39. Connecticut newspaper quoted in Guelzo, *Fateful Lightning*, 241; *Cedar Falls Gazette*, October 18, 1861; Flotow, *In Their Letters*, 26; also see Hart, "The White Feather Campaign," http://www.inquiriesjournal.com/articles/151/the-white-feather-campaign-a-struggle-with-masculinity-during-world-war-i, accessed Feb. 29, 2020.

40. Skinner, *Little Incidents*, 3; *Gallipolis Journal*, Apr. 3, 1862; Fahs, *The Imagined Civil War*, 124–28. Also for the ideals of republican motherhood and women's participation in the war, 120–24; Silber, *Daughters of the Union*, 18–19.

41. Aldridge, *No Freedom Shrieker*, 34, 40–41, 193.

42. Spar, *Civil War Hospital Newspapers*, 229; Marrin, *Unconditional Surrender*, 60–61; Edmonds, *The Female Spy of the Union Army*, 331–32; Crist, *The Papers of Jefferson Davis*, vol. 10, 52.

43. Linderman, *Embattled Courage*, 87–88; Mitchell, *The Vacant Chair*, 12; Donohoe, *The Printer's Kiss*, 72; *Holmes County Republican*, Nov. 7, 1861; quoted in Massey, *Bonnet Brigades*, 30; Rhoades and Bailey, *Wanted—Correspondence*, 119–20; Davis, *Affectionately Yours*, 47.

44. Winther, *With Sherman to the Sea: The Journal of Theodore F. Upson*, 19.

45. Blair, "We Are Coming Father Abraham—Eventually," 189; Ai Baker Thompson to father, Apr. 18, 1861, Ai Baker Thompson letters, Manassas National Battlefield Park; Mushkat, *A Citizen Soldier's Civil War*, 6.

46. Rodgers, "Hoosier Women and the Civil War Home Front," 110–11; Henry L. Brown to Dear Friends, Apr. 27, 1861, Henry L. Brown Papers, Burton Historical Collection; George C. Burmeister diary, April 29, 1861, Iowa Digital Library at https://diyhistory.lib.uiowa.edu/transcribe/3402/86585, accessed Oct. 10, 2020; Foroughi, *Go If You Think It Your Duty*, 28. For modern studies pertaining to the definitions of manhood and masculinity during the Civil War and Reconstruction eras, see Foote, *The Gentlemen and the Roughs: Violence, Honor, and Manhood in the Union Army*, Smith, "Abraham Lincoln, Manhood, and Nineteenth-Century American Political Culture," and Marten, *Sing Not War: The Lives of Union and Confederate Veterans in Gilded Age America*.

47. *Putnam's Monthly* quoted in Greenberg, *Manifest Manhood and the Antebellum American Empire*, 135; Carmichael, *War for the Common Soldier*, 229, 253; Dubbert, *A Man's Place*, 32; Linderman, *Embattled Courage*, 18.

48. Silliker, *The Rebel Yell & the Yankee Hurrah*, 23; Billings, *Hardtack & Coffee*, 25–26; Stillwell, *The Story of a Common Soldier*, 10; Hicks, "Personal Recollections of the War of the Rebellion," 520–21; Hard, *History of the Eighth Cavalry Regiment, Illinois Volunteers*, 39; Davis, *Dear Wife*, 13; Hinkley, *A Narrative of Service with the Third Wisconsin Infantry*, 2.

49. Lande, *Psychological Consequences of the American Civil War*, 6–8; Davis, *Dear Wife*, 5; Volwiler, "Letters from a Civil War Officer," 510.

50. Andrews, *Civil War Brockport*, 40.

51. Goss, "Going to the Front," 149; Billings, *Hardtack & Coffee*, 101; L. S. Shorton to D. B. Sterret, Aug. 29, 1861, Lewis Leigh Collection, Box 23, US Army Heritage and Education Center; Love, *Wisconsin in the War of the Rebellion*, 153; Rood, *Story of the Service of Company E and the Twelfth Wisconsin Regiment*, 50.

52. Parish, *The North and the Nation in the Era of the Civil War*, 2; Flotow, *In Their Letters*, 25; Wistar, *Autobiography*, vol. 2, 14–15; Billings, *Hardtack & Coffee*, 38–41; also Carmichael, *War for the Common Soldier*, 19–20.

53. Sherman, "A New England Boy in the Civil War," 314–15; Smith, *Brother of Mine*, 25–26; Kreiser, *Marketing the Blue and Gray*, 91.

54. Sears, *For Country, Cause & Leader*, 4.

55. Mitchell, *The Vacant Chair*, 7, 90; Harper, *Women during the Civil War*, 308; Greenberg, *Manifest Manhood and the Antebellum American Empire*, 113; Wilkie, *Pen and Powder*, 198; Throne, *Civil War Diary of Cyrus F. Boyd*, 125.

56. Shannon, *Organization and Administration of Union Army*, vol. 1, 48; Nagler, "Loyalty and Dissent," 331, 335.

57. Carmichael, *War for the Common Soldier*, 123; Dubbert, *A Man's Place*, 34–35; Frank, *Martial Metaphors*, 1–2.

58. Bond, *Under the Flag of the Nation*, 13; Favill, *Diary of a Young Officer*, 14; Wiley, *Life of Billy Yank*, 36.

59. Kettleborough, "Moratory and Stay Laws," 458; Fish, "Social Relief in the Northwest during the Civil War," 312.

60. Alfred J. Bloor diary, May 21, 1861; Kohl, *Irish Green and Union Blue*, 4, 17.

61. Lewis, *My Dear Parents*, 23.

62. Frank, *With Ballot and Bayonet*, 18; Cunliffe, *Soldiers and Civilians*, 113, 116–17; Bartholow, *A Manual of Instructions for Enlisting and Discharging Soldiers*, 23.

63. Brandt, *From Home Guards to Heroes*, 46.

64. Parish, *The North and the Nation in the Era of the Civil War*, 63.

65. Keating, *Shades of Green*, 4.

66. *Illustrated London News*, vol. 39, no. 1103, 151–52; Sala, *My Diary in America in the Midst of War*, vol. 1, 399; Keppler and Strohsahl quoted in Kamphoefner and Helbich, *Germans in the Civil War*, 26–27.

67. Guelzo, *Fateful Lightning*, 235; Hess, *Liberty, Virtue, and Progress*, 81–82; Wiley, *Life of Billy Yank*, 41; Frank, *With Ballot and Bayonet*, 58; Chandra Manning's *What This Cruel War Was Over: Soldiers, Slavery, and the Civil War* remains a standard work on slavery's centrality as the underlying cause of the war. "Fire-eaters" were pro-slavery Southern Democrats who, for years, had eagerly pushed for secession.

68. Du Bois, *Black Reconstruction*, 716; Jimerson, *Private Civil War*, 41; Brandt, *From Home Guards to Heroes*, 40; Luebke, "To Transmit and Perpetuate the Fruits of This Victory," 198–99; Gallagher, *The Union War*, 4, 65–66.

69. Livingstone, *Charlie's Civil War*, 18; Bliss, *Letters Home to Rehoboth*, 102; O. W. Norton to Dear Sister L., Jan. 16, 1862, "Civil War Voices: Soldier Studies" @ http://www.soldierstudies.org/index.php?action=view_letter&Letter=724, accessed May 20, 2020.

70. Lowenfels, *Walt Whitman's Civil War*, 227; Basler, *Collected Works of Abraham Lincoln*, vol. 5, 388; Kalmoe, *With Ballots and Bullets*, 71–72.

71. Ayers, *In the Presence of Mine Enemies*, 218–19; Foner, *Free Soil, Free Labor, Free Men*, 45; Jimerson, *Private Civil War*, 98–99; Engs and Brooks, *Their Patriotic Duty*, 287–88; Adelbert Bly to Anna, Nov. 9, 1862, Adelbert Bly Papers, Wisconsin Historical Society; Letter from Samuel J. Reader to his sister, copied into his diary, August 18, 1862, Samuel J. Reader diaries, vol. 5, Kansas Historical Society. The American Colonization Society, founded in 1816, was one such organization created to encourage and support free African American migration to Africa. Black Americans, however, were overwhelmingly opposed to the idea.

72. Frederickson, *Inner Civil War*, 173–76; Bohrnstedt, *Soldiering with Sherman*, 4; Kiper, *Dear Catharine, Dear Taylor*, 27–28; quoted in Robertson Jr., *Soldiers Blue and Gray*, 10–11.

CHAPTER 2

1. Schlosser and Robortella, *Writing Home*, 18; O. R. Gross diary, Apr. 15, 1861, Manuscripts and Archives Division, New York Public Library; Robert McClelland to "Dear Augusta," Apr. 19, 1861, Robert McClelland Papers, Bentley Historical Library; Baird, *Josie Underwood's Civil War Diary*, 84; Krug, *Mrs. Hill's Journal*, 14.

2. Margaret Rieley to "Mr. Graham," Sept. 4, 1861, Francis and John Rieley Papers, Western Reserve Historical Society.

3. Cox, "War Preparations in the North," 93; Greenberg, "Charles Ingersoll: The Aristocrat as Copperhead," 196; White, *A Philadelphia Perspective*, 85; Ruehlen, "The Specter of Subversion," 66–68; Bulla, *Lincoln's Censor*, 112; George Farr autobiography, Michigan State University Archives & Historical Collections, 16.

4. "War Democrats" were those Democrats who initially supported the Lincoln administration's war efforts when the publicly stated goal was solely to reunite and restore the Union; McDougall quoted in Fry, *New York and the Conscription of 1863*, 10–11; *Daily News* quoted in Blondheim, *Copperhead Gore*, 13–14.

5. Newton Chandler to Jane Chandler, June 8, 1861, N. A. Chandler Gold Rush Era Letters; Briggs, "The Enlistment of Iowa Troops during the Civil War," 336; Harlow Orton to John Jay Orton, April [no date], 1861, in Gregory, "The John Jay Orton Papers," 183; Brown, *Baltimore and the Nineteenth of April 1861*, 114; Henry Billings Brown diary, Apr. 25, 1861, Burton Historical Collection.

6. Thomas B. McFarland to "Friend Yonnie," Aug. 10, 1861, McFarland-Hall-Beck Families Papers, Archives and Special Collections, University of Pittsburgh; Throne, *Civil War Diary of Cyrus F. Boyd*, 10; see Noe, *The Howling Storm: Weather, Climate, and the American Civil War*; Justus F. Gale to his father, Nov. 7, 1862, in Silber and Sievens, *Yankee Correspondence*, 140–41; Tatum, "Please Send Stamps," 297; Fritsch, *The Untried Life*, 11.

7. Snow and Drew, *From Lexington to Baghdad and Beyond*, 54; *Boston Post*, Sept. 13, 1861, quoting *New York World*; Bingham, *History of Connecticut*, vol. 2, 581; Richard Yates to Simon Cameron, Sept. 12, 1861, *O.R.*, ser. 3, vol. 1, 500.

8. Skinner, *Little Incidents*, 4; Unknown to Pargellis, Sept. 30, 1861, Bertha M. Carter Papers—Hood/Pargellis Families, box 5, folder 32, Center for Archival Collections, Bowling Green State University; William Heyser diary, Oct. 4, 1861, "The Valley of the

Shadow" at https://valley.lib.virginia.edu/papers/FD1004, accessed Nov. 30, 2020; Boston quoted in Gallman, *The North Fights the Civil War*, 84.

9. *New York Times*, Aug. 4, 1861; *New York Daily Tribune*, Aug. 18, 1861.

10. Warshauer, "Copperheads in Connecticut," 67; Buck, "A Contest in Which Blood Must Flow like Water," 4.

11. Weber, "Lincoln's Critics," 33; for book-length analyses of the Copperheads, see Weber, *Copperheads: The Rise and Fall of Lincoln's Opponents in the North* and Gray, *The Hidden Civil War: The Story of the Copperheads*.

12. *Detroit Free Press*, Jan. 26, 1861.

13. Sedgwick quoted in Ruehlen, "The Specter of Subversion," 26.

14. Tyler, *Recollections of the Civil War*, 26; Croner, *A Sergeant's Story*, 18; "Mary" to Edward Dickerman, Aug. 25, 1861, Bamber Family Papers, Archives & Historical Collections, Michigan State University, Civil War Collections at https://civilwar.archives.msu.edu/Object/7-1D-593/bamber-family-letter-august-25-1861/, accessed Sept. 13, 2020; Gates, *The Colton Letters*, 59.

15. *Cass County Republican*, Aug. 1, 1861; Murdock, *Ohio's Bounty System in the Civil War*, 10; Dayton, "The Raising of Union Forces in Illinois during the Civil War," 408.

16. Walls, *Individualism in the United States*, 4–5; Kohl, *The Politics of Individualism*, 4–6; Davenport and Lloyd, *Rugged Individualism*, 9; Gallman, *Defining Duty*, 251; Arieli, *Individualism and Nationalism in American Ideology*, 106.

17. Davenport and Lloyd, *Rugged Individualism*, 5–6, 9–10; Arieli, *Individualism and Nationalism in American Ideology*, 189; Nagler, "Loyalty and Dissent," 334–35; Tocqueville, *Democracy in America*, vol. 2, 119, 121; Kohl, *The Politics of Individualism*, 11.

18. Ford, *A Cycle of Adams Letters, 1861–1865*, vol. 1, 17; O'Connor, *Mellon's Millions, the Biography of a Fortune*, 23–24; Basler, *Collected Works of Abraham Lincoln*, vol. 8, 223–24.

19. Ross quoted in Wiley, *Life of Billy Yank*, 281–82; Curti, *The Roots of American Loyalty*, 162; Lawson, *Patriot Fires*, 8–9.

20. Shannon, *Organization and Administration of the Union Army*, vol. 1, 15–22; Snow and Drew, *From Lexington to Baghdad and Beyond*, 54, 57; Jimerson, *Private Civil War*, 181–82; Dayton, "The Raising of Union Forces in Illinois during the Civil War," 426; Murphy, *The Kimberlins Go to War*, 9.

21. Jimerson, *Private Civil War*, 181–82; Prokopowicz, *All for the Regiment: The Army of the Ohio, 1861–1862*, 4–5; Rose, *Victorian America and the Civil War*, 7, 91–92; Parish, *The North and the Nation in the Era of the Civil War*, 155.

22. Cashin, "Deserters, Civilians, and Draft Resistance in the North," 264; Sandow, *Deserter Country*, 2; Gallman, *Defining Duty*, 66, 253–54; Blair, "We Are Coming, Father Abraham—Eventually," 190.

23. Frank, *With Ballot and Bayonet*, 11; Wiley, *Life of Billy Yank*, 24.

24. Kent, *Three Years with Company K*, 12; *Chicago Daily Tribune*, July 19, 1861.

25. Burt, *My Memoirs of the Military History of the State of New York*, 31; George McClellan to Edwin Morgan, July 15, 1862, *O.R.*, ser. 3, vol. 2, 225–26.

26. Smith, *No Party Now*, 79; Orr, "Cities at War," 7–8; Kohl, *The Politics of Individualism*, 14; Kalmoe, *With Ballots and Bullets*, 31, 54.

27. Fahs, *The Imagined Civil War*, 1, 124–26.

28. Stanley, "The Volunteer's Wife," 256–59.

29. Sutherland, "The Laggard Recruit," 12; Linderman, *Embattled Courage*, 87–88.

30. Publisher's promotional announcement for the novel in *Philadelphia Press*, July 19, 1864.

31. Gallman, *Defining Duty*, 30–31.

32. See Blondheim, *Copperhead Gore*, for the complete novel, two of Wood's congressional speeches, and a full, modern analysis of Wood and *Fort Lafayette*.

33. *Grand Haven News*, Oct. 30, 1861.

CHAPTER 3

1. Stillwell, *The Story of a Common Soldier*, 9; Buckingham, *All's for the Best*, 9–10; Sandow, "Limits of Northern Patriotism," 181–82.

2. Simpson and Berlin, *Sherman's Civil War*, 78; Farquhar, *The First Million the Hardest*, 67–68.

3. Joshua Chamberlain Jr. to Joshua L. Chamberlain, undated [1862], Chamberlain-Adams Family Papers, Schlesinger Library; Smith, *Fanny & Joshua*, 120–21; Longacre, *Joshua Chamberlain: The Soldier and the Man*, 16, 49–51.

4. For a book-length treatment of the War Department's woeful condition at the start of the rebellion, see Meneely, "The War Department, 1861"; Kelley, "Fossildom, Old Fogeyism, and Red Tape," 104–05.

5. *Cambridge Guernsey Jeffersonian*, June 7, 1861; Wilkie, *The Iowa First*, 24.

6. Patterson telegrams, *O.R.*, ser. 1, vol. 2, 168–70.

7. Wilson, *The Business of Civil War*, 24, 149–50; Hinkley, *A Narrative of Service with the Third Wisconsin Infantry*, 6–7; *Defiance Democrat*, May 11, 1861; Olcott, "The War's Carnival of Fraud," 706–07; Larson and Smith, *Dear Delia*, 39–40.

8. Smith, *The Enemy Within*, 15–16.

9. Kelley, "Fossildom, Old Fogeyism, and Red Tape," 109–10; George H. Thomas to William Patterson, Nov. 4, 1861, William Franklin Patterson Papers, LOC; Prokopowicz, *All for the Regiment: The Army of the Ohio, 1861–1862*, 4; Cox, "War Preparations in the North," 90.

10. Cox, "War Preparations in the North," 96; Billings, *Hardtack & Coffee*, 110; Sears, *For Country, Cause & Leader*, 5–6; Wilkie, *The Iowa First*, 7; H. D. Smith to Mother & Father, May 30, 1861, "Civil War Letters of Hubert Dwight Smith," https://www.hillsdalehistoricalsociety.org/smith-civil-war-letters, accessed Apr. 25, 2020.

11. J. Carlile to Simon Cameron, *O.R.*, ser. 3, vol. 1, 280; S. Kirkwood to Simon Cameron, *O.R.*, ser. 3, vol. 1, 498–99; M. Meigs to Simon Cameron, *O.R.*, ser. 3, vol. 1, 582–83; Orr, "Cities at War," 209–10.

12. James Wade to "Dear Mother," June 7, 1862, Benjamin F. Wade Papers, LOC.

13. Meier, *Nature's Civil War*, 12; Shannon, *Organization and Administration of Union Army*, vol. 1, 225; Larson and Smith, *Dear Delia*, 51, 55; Wills, *Army Life of an Illinois Soldier*, 8.

14. *Daily Pittsburgh Gazette*, Dec. 23, 1861; *Morgan County Gazette*, Dec. 18, 1861; *Cedar Falls Gazette*, Jan. 10, 1862. In theory, a company contained 100 men. Ten companies then formed a regiment.

15. E. B. Quiner Scrapbooks, "Correspondence of the Wisconsin Volunteers, 1861–1865," vol. 5, Wisconsin Historical Society, 155.

16. Snell, "If They Would Know What I Know," 82.

17. Sandow, "Limits of Northern Patriotism," 180; *Logansport Journal*, Oct. 12, 1861.

18. Quoted in Lee, *Discontent in New York City*, 65.

19. *Pennsylvania Daily Telegraph*, May 15, 1861.

20. *Brooksville Republican* quoted in Sandow, "Limits of Northern Patriotism," 177, 186–87.

21. Raus, *Banners South*, 11–12; Gallman, *Defining Duty*, 8.

22. Isaac Beers letter, September 27, 1861, Bentley Historical Library, University of Michigan; Albert Wilder to "Sister Sarah," Nov. 15, 1862, Albert Wilder Papers, William Clements Library; Heidelbaugh and Paone, *Between Home and the Front*, 24.

23. Gray quoted in Miller, *Harvard's Civil War*, 31.

24. Baker, *Affectionately Yours*, 20.

25. Gordon, "The Attitude of the Women of the North and South during and Since the War of the Rebellion," 235–36; George Kryder to "My Dear Wife," Mar. 23, Apr. 7 and 15, 1863, George Kryder Papers, Center for Archival Collections, Bowling Green State University; Marilla W. Leggett diary, Jan. 1, 1862, Marilla Wells Leggett Papers, Western Reserve Historical Society.

26. Foroughi, *Go If You Think It Your Duty*, 6–7; Lensink, *"A Secret to Be Burried,"* 98; Hammond, *Diary of a Union Lady*, 143; Castel, *Tom Taylor's Civil War*, 48; Giesberg, *Army at Home*, 19–20; Gates, *Agriculture and the Civil War*, 234–36, 242.

27. William B. Mitchell to "Dear Coz," Aug. 3, 1862, William B. Mitchell Papers, Ohio History Center Archives & Library; Croner, *A Sergeant's Story*, v, 17.

28. *The Agitator*, Oct. 16, 1861.

29. Kreiser, *Marketing the Blue and Gray*, 3; Frank, *Martial Metaphors*, 5; Cohen, "You Have No Flag Out Yet?" 380; Moers, *The Dandy: Brummell to Beerbohm*, 13; Tynan and Godson, *Uniform: Clothing and Discipline in the Modern World*, 1.

30. Shannon, "Refashioning Men," 606; "Home Guards," *Vanity Fair*, May 25, 1861, 249; *Star of the North*, Feb. 26, 1862; Sheldon, *Sibyl's Influence; Or, the Missing Link*, 147.

31. Gallman, *Defining Duty*, 69–71, 75–76.

32. Mujic, "We Are Setting the Terms Now," 115–17.

33. Yale historian quoted in Aaron, *The Unwritten War*, 354; Hamilton College student quoted in Cohen, *Reconstructing the Campus*, 49; Redsecker Young diaries, Historical Society of Dauphin County, Harrisburg, Pennsylvania; Mujic, "We Are Setting the Terms Now," 109; White and Glenn, *Untouched by the Conflict*, 15, 25–26; Cohen, *Reconstructing the Campus*, 20, 46–47.

34. Mujic, "Ours Is the Harder Lot," 35, 40, 41.

35. Wiley, *Life of Billy Yank*, 19; Mujic, "Ours Is the Harder Lot," 37; George D. Robinson letter, June 12, 1861, Bentley Historical Library; Charles Kroff diary, July 10, 1861, Western History Collections.

36. Karamanski and McMahon, *Civil War Chicago*, 60–62; Cunliffe, *Soldiers and Civilians*, 203.

37. Frassanito, *Grant and Lee: The Virginia Campaigns 1864–1865*, 26; Mayberry and Bakken, "The Civil War Home Front: Diary of a Young Girl, 1862–1863," 24; Josyph, *The Wounded River*, 4; Masters quoted in Cimbala and Miller, *The Northern Home Front during the Civil War*, xi.

38. Mannis and Wilson, *Bound to Be a Soldier*, 4; Glaza-Herrington, *Dear Brother and Sister*, 7; letter from Samuel J. Reader to his father, copied into his diary, July 25, 1861, Samuel J. Reader diaries, vol. 5, Kansas Historical Society; Wiley, *Life of Billy Yank*, 247–50.

39. C. B. Thompson to Ai Thompson, Apr. 18, 1861, Ai. B. Thompson Letters, Manassas National Battlefield Park Library; Richard, *Busy Hands*, 3.

40. Charles C. Brown to his sister, July 19, 1861, Charles C. Brown Letters, Manassas National Battlefield Park Library; Frank Badger to his mother, Sept. 21, 1862, Alfred M. Badger Papers, LOC; Alfred C. Woods to Dear Aunt, May 23, 1861, "Civil War Voices: Soldier Studies" @ http://www.soldierstudies.org/index.php?action=view_letter &Letter=368, accessed May 21, 2020.

41. Bernt Olmanson to family, Nov. 25, 1861, "Letters of Bernt Olmanson," http:// www.olmanson.org/BerntO/index.html, accessed Nov. 5, 2020; Wiley, *Life of Billy Yank*, 257; Robertson Jr., *Soldiers Blue and Gray*, 120.

42. McClellan Gen. Orders No. 7, Sept. 6, 1861, *O.R.*, ser. 1, vol. 51, pt. 1, 472–73; *Christian Messenger* quoted in *Daily Green Mountain Freeman*, Sept. 20, 1861.

43. William Hammond to Edwin Stanton, Nov. 10, 1862, *O.R.*, ser. 3, vol. 2, 753; Abernethy, *Private Elisha Stockwell, Jr. Sees the Civil War*, 1–6.

44. U.S Constitution, Article 1, Sec. 9; Reed, *America's Two Constitutions*, 61, 63; Clarke and Plant, "No Minor Matter," 882; Neff, *Justice in Blue and Gray*, 152–54.

45. Kurtz, "The Union as It Was," 91–92, 96; Kautz, "Fodder for Cannon," 61–68.

46. Gilbert, *Freddy's War*, 32–33.

47. Barrett, *The Irish Way*, 3–4; "It Was Not For To Be Soldiers We Came Out" @ https: //irishamericancivilwar.com/2019/01/12/it-was-not-for-to-be-soldiers-we-came-out -recruited-straight-off-the-boat-some-new-evidence/, accessed Mar. 17, 2020; quoted in Miller, *Emigrants and Exiles*, 359.

48. Kurtz, *Excommunicated from the Union*, 110; Kurtz, "The Union as It Was," 91–113; *Chatfield Democrat*, Dec. 21, 1861; also see Wade, "Irish Apes: Tactics of De-Humanization," https://thesocietypages.org/socimages/2011/01/28/irish-apes -tactics-of-de-humanization/, accessed June 4, 2022.

49. Col. Silas Burt to Edwin Morgan, Aug. 21, 1862, Edwin D. Morgan Papers, New York State Library; Wesslau quoted in Kamphoefner and Helbich, *Germans in the Civil War*, 63; Current, *The Civil War Era, 1848–1873: History of Wisconsin, vol. II*, 314–15; Kautz, "Fodder for Cannon," 111–12.

50. Kautz, "Fodder for Cannon," 93, 113–14; Blied, *Catholics and the Civil War*, 129.

51. Reardon, "We Are All in This War," 13; Rawley, *The Politics of Union*, 71–73; see Gallagher, *The Union War*.

52. *New York Daily Tribune*, Nov. 9, 1860; *Boston Post*, Dec. 13, 1860.

53. Polner and Woods, *We Who Dared to Say No to War*, 78–82; Moody, *Life of D. L. Moody by His Son*, 82; For further reading on conscientious objection during the Civil

War, see Wright, *Conscientious Objectors in the Civil War*; Lehman and Nolt, *Mennonites, Amish, and the American Civil War*; Kashatus, *Abraham Lincoln, the Quakers, and the Civil War: "A Trial of Principle & Faith"*; Brock, "When Seventh-day Adventists First Faced the Draft: Civil War America."

54. Geary, *We Need Men*, 36; Wright, *Conscientious Objectors in the Civil War*, 39–40, 121.

55. Croner, *A Sergeant's Story*, 23; Wright, *Conscientious Objectors in the Civil War*, 151–53; Marshall, *A War of the People: Vermont Civil War Letters*, 13–14.

56. Circular No. 61, *O.R.*, ser. 3, vol. 3, 606–07; John Dix to Henry Halleck, Oct. 24, 1863, *O.R.*, ser. 3, vol. 3, 922; George Ruggles to various provost marshals, Dec. 15, 1863, *O.R.*, ser. 3, vol. 3, 1173.

57. Clarke, "'Let All Nations See': Civil War Nationalism and the Memorialization of Wartime Voluntarism," 74; Cirillo, "Waiting for the Perfect Moment," 9–38; Maas, *Marching to the Drumbeat of Abolitionism*, 100. The "border states" were slaveholding states that did not secede from the Union.

58. Child, *Letters of Lydia Marie Child*, 150–51.

59. *The Crisis*, Jan. 29, 1862; Hammond, *Diary of a Union Lady*, 165–66.

60. Sandow, *Deserter Country*, 4.

61. Howells quoted in Goodman and Dawson, *William Dean Howells: A Writer's Life*, 68; Edel, *Henry James: The Untried Years*, 170–79; William James quoted in Greenslet, *The Lowells and Their Seven Worlds*, 289; also see Menand, *The Metaphysical Club*, 73–75; Aaron, *The Unwritten War*, 91–92.

62. Henry W. Baker to his sister, Oct. 12, 1861, in Silber and Sievens, *Yankee Correspondence*, 131–32; Samuel Storrow to his father, Oct. 12, 1862, in Silber and Sievens, *Yankee Correspondence*, 70–73; Robinson, *My Brother Theodore Roosevelt*, 23. See Taylor, *"The Most Complete Political Machine Ever Known"* for a history of the Union Leagues and their kindred Publication Societies.

63. *Cincinnati Daily Commercial*, Feb. 3, 1862; Shannon, *Organization and Administration of the Union Army*, vol. 2, 175–243.

Chapter 4

1. Cox, *Eight Years in Congress*, 235; Carter, *Troubled State*, 45–46; Thomas Lowe to William Lowe, Apr. 6, 1862, Lowe Family Papers, Dayton Metro Library.

2. Beale, *The Diary of Edward Bates*, 239.

3. Goodrich, "Civil War Letters of Bethiah Pyatt McKown," 245; McClintock, *Lincoln and the Decision for War*, 266; Hubbart, "'Pro-Southern' Influences in the Free West," 46; George Brown to Leander Brown, Apr. 22, 1862, George M. Brown Family Correspondence, Clarke Historical Library; Benton, *The Movement for Peace without a Victory during the Civil War*, 12; Schneider, *Old Man River*, 272–73, 279.

4. Gen. Orders No. 105, Dec. 3, 1861, *O.R.*, ser. 3, vol. 1, 722–23; Gen. Orders No. 33, Apr. 3, 1862, *O.R.*, ser. 3, vol. 2, 2–3.

5. Kelley, "Fossildom, Old Fogeyism, and Red Tape," 104; Marvel, *Lincoln's Autocrat*, 356; Simpson and Berlin, *Sherman's Civil War*, 217; Terrell, *Indiana in the War of the Rebellion*, vol. 1, 21–22; Belmont, *A Few Letters and Speeches of the Late Civil War*, 66–67.

6. *New York Times*, Apr. 5, 1862; *Detroit Free Press*, Apr. 5, 1862.

7. Edwin Stanton to Henry Halleck, May 1, 1862, *O.R.*, ser. 3, vol. 2, 29; Gen. Orders No. 60, June 6, 1862, *O.R.*, ser. 3, vol. 2, 109.

8. For studies on the 1862 Peninsula campaign, see Sears, *To the Gates of Richmond: The Peninsula Campaign*, and Gallagher, *The Richmond Campaign of 1862: The Peninsula & the Seven Days*; McCabe Jr., *The Civil War: A Soldier's Letters Home*, 40–41.

9. Gurowski, *Diary, from March 4, 1861 to November 12, 1862*, 247; Priest, *Turn Them Out to Die Like a Mule*, 104; Sanitary Commission Executive Committee to Abraham Lincoln, August 5, 1862, *O.R.*, ser. 3, vol. 2, 297–300; also see Meier, *Nature's Civil War: Common Soldiers and the Environment in 1862 Virginia* for a complete examination of this issue.

10. John Miller to George Miller, Aug. 4, 1862, George Miller Papers, York County History Center Library & Archives; Burt, *My Memoirs of the Military History of the State of New York*, 111.

11. Floyd, *"Dear Friends at Home . . . ,"* 19.

12. Greene, *Letters from a Sharpshooter*, 126; Hoffman, *A Vermont Cavalryman in War and Love*, 130; DeRosier, *Through the South with a Union Soldier*, 95; Bruen and Fitzgibbons, *Through Ordinary Eyes*, 159; Bonner, *The Soldier's Pen*, 114–15.

13. Henry J. Johnson to Clara Johnson, Aug. 18, 1862, Henry J. Johnson Papers, William Clements Library; Greene, *Letters from a Sharpshooter*, 137; Hess, *Liberty, Virtue, and Progress*, 48.

14. Bliss, *Letters Home to Rehoboth*, 30, 123–24.

15. Melville, *Battle-Pieces and Aspects of the War*, 63.

16. Murphy, *The Civil War Letters of Joseph K. Taylor*, 75; Henry Walker to wife, Sep. 3, 1862, Henry Walker Correspondence, LOC; Castel, *Tom Taylor's Civil War*, 48.

17. Francis Barlow to Edward Barlow, July 8, 1862, "Massachusetts in the Civil War" @ https://www.masshist.org/database/2203?ft=Massachusetts%20in%20the%20Civil %20War,%201861-1862&from=/features/massachusetts-in-the-civil-war-1861-1862/ peninsula-campaign, accessed Aug. 3, 2020; McCabe Jr., *The Civil War: A Soldier's Letters Home*, 42; anonymous author letter dated Apr. 22, 1862, "Civil War Letters," Delaware County NY Genealogy and History Site at https://www.dcnyhistory.org/ milcwlettersbloomvillemirror.html#taylornote, accessed May 10, 2020; George Daggett to Willard Daggett, July 21, 1862, Folder 1, Eaegle Family Papers, Michigan State University Archives & Historical Collections; Matthews and Wecter, *Our Soldiers Speak*, 143.

18. Shannon, *Organization and Administration of Union Army*, vol. 1, 292; *Cedar Falls Gazette*, July 25, 1862.

19. Baynes, *Morale*, 99–100.

20. A. H. Marsh to Dear Parents, June 25, (no year but probably 1862) and A. H. Marsh to Dear Brother, July 25, (no year but probably 1862), "A. H. Marsh Civil War Letters," https://fentonhistsoc.tripod.com/id119.html, accessed July 22, 2020.

21. Risse, *Mending Bodies, Saving Souls*, 5.

22. Albinus R. Fell to wife, Jan. 19, 1862, Civil War Document Collection, US Army Heritage and Education Center, Carlisle, Pennsylvania; Priest, *Turn Them Out to Die Like a Mule*, 34.

23. Feeney, "Manifestations of the Maimed," 37–38.

24. Riley M. Hoskinson to his wife, Oct. 27, 1863, Riley M. Hoskinson papers, Special Collections, University of Washington Libraries; Roberts, *This Infernal War*, 72; Carmichael, *War for the Common Soldier*, 145; Flotow, *In Their Letters*, 181–82. During the Civil War, two Union soldiers died of disease for every one killed in combat.

25. Schultz, *Women at the Front*, 80–81; Alcott, *Hospital Sketches*, 70.

26. Henry Clay Long to "Dear Wife," Apr. 24, 1862, "Civil War Letters of Henry Clay Long" @ https://henrylong687641266.wordpress.com/i-am-glad-i-am-not-a-soldier/24-april-1862/, accessed Dec. 7, 2020.

27. William Fullerton to "Dear Sister," Mar. 13, 1863, William B. Fullerton Civil War Letters, Special Collections and Archives, University of California; John W. De Forest report, *O.R.*, ser. 3, vol. 5, 543–44.

28. Carmichael, *War for the Common Soldier*, 186; Beatty, *The Citizen-Soldier*, 217; Fiske, *Mr. Dunn Browne's Experiences in the Army*, 282–83.

29. John E. Ryder to Alfred G. Ryder, Mar. 25, 1862, Ryder Family Papers, Bentley Historical Lib.; Charles Tripler to R. B. Marcy, May 29, 1862, *O.R.*, ser. 1, vol. 11, pt. 1, 206–07.

30. Goodell and Taylor, "A German Immigrant in the Union Army," 158, 160.

31. *Annual Report of the Quartermaster General of the State of Michigan for the Year 1862*, 16; Burt, *My Memoirs of the Military History of the State of New York*, 110. Maj. Gen. John Pope commanded the Union's Army of Virginia, which was created on June 26, 1862, from four smaller commands operating within that state. Pope's command along with several corps from Maj. Gen. George McClellan's Army of the Potomac were soundly defeated at the battle of Second Bull Run.

32. Murdock, *Patriotism Limited*, 5; US 1860 Census, introduction, xvii at https://www.census.gov/library/publications/1864/dec/1860a.html, accessed Feb. 19, 2021.

33. Furniss, "To Save the Union 'in Behalf of Conservative Men,'" 73–74.

34. Lincoln to Union governors, July 1, 1862, *O.R.*, ser. 3, vol. 2, 187–88.

35. Vallandigham, *Record of Hon. C. L. Vallandigham*, 126–27.

36. Charles Rowland to Richard Yates, July 9, 1862, Richard Yates Family Papers, Abraham Lincoln Presidential Library and Museum; Samuel Reader diary, Aug. 18, 1862; Helen Aplin to George Aplin, July 20, 1862, Aplin Family Papers, William Clements Library; *Cleveland Plain Dealer*, July 14, 1862; *Daily Ohio Statesman*, July 29, 1862.

37. *New Albany Daily Ledger*, July 16, 1862; Hamand, *Coles County in the Civil War*, 17; *New York Herald*, Aug. 2, 1862.

38. *Grand Haven News*, Aug. 6, 1862; *Frank Leslie's Illustrated Newspaper*, Sept. 7, 1861, 262.

39. Johnson, "A Debt Justly Due," 210, 212, 217, 223.

40. Seward, *Seward at Washington as Senator and Secretary of State*, 115; Oliver Morton and others to Abraham Lincoln, July 9, 1862, *O.R.*, ser. 3, vol. 2, 212–13; Barnes, *Memoir of Thurlow Weed*, vol. 2, 420–21.

41. Weber, "Conscription and the Consolidation of Federal Power," 11; Geary, *We Need Men*, 24, 33–34; Quigley, "Civil War Conscription and the International Boundaries of Citizenship," 384; Edwin Stanton to Rufus Saxton, Aug. 25, 1862, *O.R.*, ser. 1, vol. 14, 377–78.

42. Gen. Orders No. 94, *O.R.*, ser. 3, vol. 2, 291–92, 333–35; Duggan, *Legislative and Statutory Development of the Federal Concept for Military Service*, 22–23; Weber, *Copperheads*, 52.

CHAPTER 5

1. Gates, *The Colton Letters*, 144; Elizabeth H. Pierce to Augusta Bruen, Aug. 24, 1862, Catharine Mitchill Family Letters, Wellesley College Library; Johns, *Life with the Forty-ninth Massachusetts Volunteers*, 12.

2. Cunliffe, *Soldiers and Civilians*, 185–86; Leach, *Conscription in the United States*, 169; Mitchell, "From Volunteer to Soldier," 355; Nevins, *A Diary of Battle*, 117.

3. Terrell, *Indiana in the War of the Rebellion: Report of the Adjutant General*, 78–79; VandeCreek, "Economic Development and Labor in Civil War Illinois," Northern Illinois University Digital Library @ https://digital.lib.niu.edu/illinois/civilwar/economic #footnote1_pynkcws, accessed July 22, 2022.

4. "Order Respecting Volunteers and Militia," *O.R.* ser. 3, vol. 2, 380–81; Houston, *Keep Up Good Courage*, 6; Rundell Jr., "Despotism of Traitors," 345; McMurtry, "Everybody is afraid of being drafted . . . ," 4.

5. Ward, *Army Life in Virginia*, 2–3; Johns, *Life with the Forty-ninth Massachusetts Volunteers*, 12; E. S. Calderwood to wife, Apr. 15, 1863, Eben S. Calderwood Correspondence, Maine Historical Society.

6. Bartholow, *A Manual of Instructions for Enlisting and Discharging Soldiers*, 86–87; Baxter, *Statistics, Medical and Anthropological*, vol. 1, 446; Newton Kirk to Robert Crouse, Oct. 24, 1862, Robert Crouse Papers, Bentley Historical Library.

7. Campbell, *"A Grand Terrible Dramma,"* 10–14; Barton et al, *Noble Sentiments of the Soul*, 14, 24; Mayhue, *A Civil War Journey: The Letters of John W. Brendel*, 7, 12; Mary Smith to William J. Smith, Nov. 30, 1862, William Jay Smith Papers, Ohio History Center Archives & Library.

8. Boggs, *Patriotism by Proxy*, 11; Murdock, *Ohio's Bounty System in the Civil War*, 9, 13.

9. *Cedar Falls Gazette*, Aug. 1, 1862; Benedict, *Vermont in the Civil War*, vol. 2, 277; *Ottawa Free Trader*, Aug. 2, 1862; Marvel, *Lincoln's Darkest Year*, 110.

10. Seward dispatch, Aug. 8, 1862, *O.R.*, ser. 3, vol. 2, 359.

11. Anderson, *Life and Letters of Judge Thomas J. Anderson and Wife*, 254.

12. Sarah Keen to William Keen, Sept. 10, 1862, Keen Family Letters, William Clements Library; Henry Billings Brown diary, Sept. 1, 1862 & 1862 year-end (though undated), Burton Historical Collection.

13. Mohr, *Cormany Diaries*, 233–34.

14. Christian H. Isely to Marie Isely, Oct. 22, 1862, Isely Family Papers, Special Collections and University Archives, Wichita State University; J. Gerry Smith to "Dear Brother Luke," Sept. 12, 1862, American Civil War Documents, Manuscripts, Letters and Diaries Collections, Series 29, Special Collections, Chicago Public Library.

15. *Woburn Weekly Budget* quoted in Greenleaf, *Letters to Eliza from a Union Soldier*, 8–9; *Lamoille Newsdealer*, Aug. 29, 1862; *Bedford Gazette*, Nov. 20, 1863; *O.R.*, ser. 1, vol. 4, 304; *American Volunteer*, Sept. 4, 1862.

16. Andrew Curtin to Edwin Stanton, Oct. 25, 1862, *O.R.*, ser. 1, vol. 19, pt. 2, 468, 489–90; Edward Salomon to Edwin Stanton, Nov. 12, 1862, *O.R.*, ser. 3, vol. 2, 761, 765; *Journal of the House of Representatives of the State of Ohio*, vol. 59, 13; John Wool to Edwin Stanton, Sept. 3, 1862, *O.R.*, ser. 3, vol. 2, 509.

17. Kimmel, *Mr. Lincoln's Washington*, 101; *American and Commercial Advertiser*, Aug. 9, 1862; Bernard, "Lincoln and the Civil War as Viewed by a Dissenting Yankee of Connecticut," 211; Skipper and Taylor, *A Handful of Providence*, 143.

18. "Order to Prevent Evasion of Military Duty," *O.R.*, ser. 2, vol. 4, 358–59; *Cleveland Plain Dealer*, Sept. 11, 1862.

19. The concept of substitution and substitutes will be discussed in more detail in chapter 8.

20. *Iowa Daily Gazette*, Aug. 29, 1862; *Daily Democrat and News*, Sept. 4, 5, and 8, 1862; *Hartford Daily Times*, Aug. 14, 1862, quoted in Gordon, *"I Never Was a Coward,"* 10.

21. Van Alstyne, *Diary of an Enlisted Man*, 1–2.

22. George Patch to "Dear Father and Mother," July 25, 1862, George H. Patch Papers, Virginia Historical Society; Mohr, *Cormany Diaries*, 229; Fry, "Final Report PMG," 11; Lapham, *My Recollections of the War of the Rebellion*, 195.

23. Crowell, *The Young Volunteer*, 10.

24. John Ames to "My Dear Mother," July 21, 1862, John W. Ames Papers, US Army Heritage and Education Center; Col. Silas Burt to Edwin Morgan, Aug. 23, 1862, Edwin D. Morgan Papers, New York State Library.

25. De Trobriand, *Four Years with the Army of the Potomac*, 72, 330–31; John Burrill letter, Sept. 15, 1862, Burrill Letters, Manassas National Battlefield Park Library; Silber and Sievens, *Yankee Correspondence*, 40–41; Throne, "Iowa Doctor in Blue," 115.

26. Greiner, Coryell, and Smither, *A Surgeon's Civil War*, 13; Winfield Perry to "Dear Mother," Jan. 8, 1863, Winfield M. Perry Papers, Oneida County Historical Society.

27. Peck, *How Private George W. Peck Put Down the Rebellion*, 13–14.

28. Rankin, *Toward a More Perfect Union*, 4–5.

29. Ira B. Conine to "Dearest Jennie," Aug. 3, 1863, Ira B. Conine Correspondence, Center for Archival Collections, Bowling Green State University.

30. Hamlin, *Report of the United States Provost Marshal of Rhode Island*, 5; Fry, "Final Report PMG," 153.

31. Margaret Harris to Leander Harris, Dec. 14, 1862, Leander Harris Letters, Milne Special Collections and Archives, University of New Hampshire Library, Durham.

32. James, *To See the Elephant*, 47; Mitchell, *Civil War Soldiers*, 85; Charles F. Weller to Kate McElwain, July 7, 1862, "Civil War Letters and Journal of Charles F. Weller," New York Heritage Digital Collections at https://cdm16694.contentdm.oclc.org/digital/collection/srr_ocpl/id/2683/rec/3, accessed Oct. 11, 2020.

33. Byron Churchill to "My Dear Mother," Nov. 13, 1862, Gilder Lehrman Collection; Coles and Engle, *A Yankee Horseman in the Shenandoah Valley*, 21; *Indianapolis Daily Journal*, Aug. 16, 1862; Glaza-Herrington, *Dear Brother and Sister*, 346.

34. *Dubuque Herald*, Aug. 10, 1862; Garrity, "We Respect the Flag but . . . ," 37; George Hupman to "Dear Parents," Aug. 30, 1863, George S. Hupman Letters, Library

of Virginia; W. H. Faxon to Henry A. Potter, Aug. 7, 1862, Henry Albert Potter Papers, Bentley Historical Library.

35. *Lamoille Newsdealer*, Aug. 29, 1862; Phelan, *Who Only Stand and Wait*, 19.

36. Butterfield, *The History of Waukesha County, Wisconsin*, 521.

37. Sterling, "Civil War Draft Resistance in the Middle West," 84; Murdock, *One Million Men*, 70; Wickman, *Letters to Vermont, vol. 1*, 47–48; Helmreich, *To Petersburg with the Army of the Potomac*, 79.

38. *Cincinnati Daily Press*, Nov. 12, 1861.

39. Hogan, *General Reub Williams's Memories*, 53.

40. Croner, *A Sergeant's Story*, 20; *New York Daily Tribune*, Aug. 7, 1862.

41. *Grand Haven News*, Sept. 3, 1862.

42. Miller, *Collected Writings of Walt Whitman*, vol. 1, 223; Gen. Orders, No. 14, May 26, 1864, *O.R.*, ser. 1, vol. 36, pt. 3, 240–41.

43. Goodell and Taylor, "A German Immigrant in the Union Army," 162; Roberts, *This Infernal War*, 25, 231; Logothetis, "A Question of Life or Death," 27–28.

44. Carmichael, *War for the Common Soldier*, 313.

45. Ewing, *From Home to Trench*, 56.

46. Dow Webster to Amanda Webster, Oct. 22, 1864, Papers, 1864–1865, Library of Virginia; David Keiholtz to "Dear Brother," Jan. 8, 1863, David Keiholtz Papers, Library of Virginia.

47. Albert, *History of the Forty-fifth Regiment Pennsylvania Veteran Volunteer Infantry*, 50.

48. McElroy, *Andersonville: A Story of Rebel Military Prisons*, 98; Silkenat, *Raising the White Flag*, 132–33.

49. McMahon, "The Battle of Horseshoe Ridge," William J. Sullivan Collection, Center for Archival Collections, Bowling Green State University; J. D. Paull to "Sir," Oct. 7, 1862, and Abraham Bope to "Dear sister," May 21, 1863, Gilder Lehrman Collection; Blomquist and Taylor, *This Cruel War*, 268–69.

50. Rosecrans Gen. Orders No. 15, Nov. 14, 1862, *O.R.*, ser. 1, vol. 20, pt. 2, 49; *Western Reserve Chronicle*, Dec. 3, 1862; John Pope to Henry Halleck, Sept. 2, 1862, *O.R.*, ser. 1, vol. 12, pt. 3, 796–97; Edwin Stanton to David Tod, Sept. 9, 182, *O.R.*, ser. 2, vol. 4, 499.

51. General Orders No. 72, June 28, 1862, *O.R.*, ser. 2, vol. 4, 94.

52. Styple, *Writing and Fighting the Civil War*, 119; Joseph Geiger to Edwin Stanton, Sept. 29, 1862, *O.R.*, ser. 2, vol. 4, 576.

53. George Sangster to William Hoffman, Jan. 19, 1863, *O.R.*, ser. 2, vol. 5, 194.

54. Styple, *Writing and Fighting the Civil War*, 119, 121–22; George Weddell to "Dear Brother," June 17, 1864, Weddell Family Papers, Center for Archival Collections, Bowling Green State University; T. J. Carney to "Highly Esteemed Friends," Feb. 10, 1863, Yates Family Papers, Abraham Lincoln Presidential Library and Museum; Nash, *History of the Forty-fourth Regiment, New York Volunteer Infantry*, 273–74; *Chicago Daily Tribune*, Oct. 10, 1862; Geary, *We Need Men*, 45–46.

55. Henry Halleck to Edwin Stanton, Nov. 25, 1862, *O.R.*, ser. 3, vol. 2, 872; Simpson and Berlin, *Sherman's Civil War*, 348–49; Ulysses Grant Gen. Order No. 10, Jan. 26, 1863, *O.R.*, ser. 2, vol. 5, 216.

56. Keating, *The Greatest Trials I Ever Had*, 103; Roberts, *This Infernal War*, 73; William Rosecrans to Edwin Stanton, Nov. 23, 1862, *O.R.*, ser. 1, vol. 20, pt. 2, 91; Greene, *Letters from a Sharpshooter*, 52, 60.

57. Carmichael, *War for the Common Soldier*, 178–79; Reid and White, "A Mob of Stragglers and Cowards," 64; Larson and Smith, *Dear Delia*, 37; Cashin, "Deserters, Civilians, and Draft Resistance in the North," 266.

58. Palladino, *Another Civil War*, 96–100.

59. McKay, *The Civil War and New York City*, 149–50; Skidmore, "The Copperhead Press and the Civil War," 347–48; Grant, *Personal Memoirs*, vol. 2, 502.

60. Warshauer, "Copperheads in Connecticut," 80; Weber, *Copperheads*, 11–12.

61. War Department order dated Aug. 8, 1862, *O.R.* ser. 3, vol. 2, 321–22; US Constitution, Article 3, Section 3; Marvel, *Lincoln's Autocrat*, 220–21; Blair, *With Malice toward Some*, 37–39; Cannon quoted in White, "To Aid Their Rebel Friends," 78. Professor White's doctoral dissertation offers an in-depth analysis of the Civil War North's evolving perspectives on treason.

62. Wubben, *Civil War Iowa and the Copperhead Movement*, 64; A. Ricketts to Maj. Levi C. Turner, Aug. 30, 1862, Case Files of Investigations by Levi C. Turner and Lafayette C. Baker, RG 94, National Archives, Washington, DC; *Highland Weekly News*, Aug. 28, 1862; *Daily Green Mountain Freeman*, Sept. 2, 1862; Neely Jr., *The Fate of Liberty*, 60–62.

63. General Orders No. 193, Nov. 22, 1862, *O.R.*, ser. 2, vol. 4, 176–77.

64. Massey, *Bonnet Brigades*, 198; McCune, *Mary Austin Wallace: Her Diary, 1862*, 5–9; Longacre, "Come Home Soon and Don't Delay," 395–406. These letters from Pennsylvania women remained unopened until October 1939 when they were discovered among the George Cadwalader papers at the Historical Society of Pennsylvania. Historian Edward Longacre concluded that taken as a whole, these letters "present a deeply disturbing picture of northern home front morale in dissolution at a period preceding the days when the hardships and discomforts of war were manifest on a national scale." Janney, *Remembering the Civil War*, 24; staff officer quoted in Rable, *Fredericksburg!* 85.

65. Mohr, *Cormany Diaries*, 246; Hammond to Eliza Quilty, Mar. 16, 1863, Quilty Family Civil War letters, Special Collections and Archives, Middlebury College Library; Cimbala and Miller, *The Northern Home Front during the Civil War*, 58–60.

66. Massey, *Bonnet Brigades*, 213.

67. Laas, *Wartime Washington*, 220; Burt, *My Memoirs of the Military History of the State of New York*, 123; *Cleveland Plain Dealer*, Aug. 7, 1862; *Grand Haven News*, Aug. 13, 1862; Michigan letter quoted in *Saint Johnsbury Caledonian*, Aug. 22, 1862; *Cincinnati Daily Commercial*, Aug. 11, 1862; *Daily State Sentinel*, Aug. 25, 1862.

CHAPTER 6

1. *New York Times*, Oct. 20, 1862.

2. Text of Preliminary Emancipation Proclamation dated Sept. 22, 1862, in Masur, *Lincoln's Hundred Days*, 290–93; Escott, *"What Shall We Do with the Negro?"* xvii; for a discussion of Lincoln's justification in using the Emancipation Proclamation as a legal tool of war, see Carnahan, *Act of Justice: Lincoln's Emancipation Proclamation and the Law of War*.

3. Scott, *A Visitation of God*, 98–99; Wood, *Black Scare*, 20; Sheboygan *Journal* quoted in Klement, *Wisconsin in the Civil War*, 41.

4. *Lancaster Daily Intelligencer*, Sept. 02, 1862; Rugoff, *The Beechers*, 447; *Crawford Democrat* quoted in Shankman, *Pennsylvania Antiwar Movement*, 143; George P. Paul to Aaron Jones Fletcher, Nov. 13, 1862, "Civil War Letters of Aaron Jones Fletcher," https://www.actonmemoriallibrary.org/civilwar/fletcher/fletcher-intro.html, accessed Feb. 8, 2022.

5. Lincoln Proclamation dated Sept. 25, 1862, *O.R.* ser. 3, vol. 2, 587–88; Neely Jr., *The Fate of Liberty*, xiii–xiv, 62; *Lancaster Daily Intelligencer*, Sept. 02, 1862.

6. *Indiana State Sentinel*, Oct. 27, 1862; Winan Allen to Annie Cox, Feb. 10, 1863, Allen Family Papers, Newberry Library; *New York Weekly Caucasian*, Oct. 4, 1862, quoted in Masur, *Lincoln's Hundred Days*, 29.

7. *New York Herald*, Aug. 7 and 17, 1862; Daly, *When Slavery Was Called Freedom*, 57–72; Folmar, "Pre–Civil War Sentiment from Belmont County: Correspondence of Hugh Anderson," 204–05; also see Noll, *The Civil War as a Theological Crisis*.

8. *Ottawa Free Trader*, Sept. 27, 1862; *Dayton Daily Empire* quoting *New York World*, Oct. 4, 1862; Jones, *A Rebel War Clerk's Diary*, vol. 1, 159.

9. Spann, *Gotham at War*, 126–27; Ignatiev, *How the Irish Became White*, 2–4; Wood, *Black Scare*, 20–21.

10. Rael, *Eighty-Eight Years*, 128–29; Fredrickson, *Racism: A Short History*, 79–80; Saxton, *The Rise and Fall of the White Republic*, 2–4.

11. David Shoemaker to Mary Shoemaker, June 17, 1862, Shoemaker Family Papers, Detre Library & Archives; see White, *Emancipation, the Union Army, and the Reelection of Abraham Lincoln*, 69–97 for a detailed examination of the Emancipation Proclamation's damaging effects on Union army morale, resignations, and desertions following its enactment.

12. Elvira A. W. Scott diary, State Historical Society of Missouri, 63; Buckner quoted in Phillips, *The Rivers Ran Backward*, 210; Adam H. Pickel to his parents, Feb. 22, 1863, Adam H. Pickel Papers, Rubenstein Library; *Chicago Times* quoted in *Miami County Sentinel*, Aug. 6, 1863.

13. Newman, "A Democrat in Lincoln's Army," 163; Skipper and Taylor, *A Handful of Providence*, 191–92; Roberts, *This Infernal War*, 286; Samuel W. Croft to his sister, Feb. 12, 1863, Learned T. Bulman '48 Historic Archives and Museum, Washington & Jefferson College.

14. Girardi, "I Am for the President's Proclamation Teeth and Toe Nails," 406; Towne, *Surveillance and Spies in the Civil War*, 48; Nicolay and Hay, *Abraham Lincoln: A History*, vol. 6, 142; Blight, *When This Cruel War Is Over*, 187; Lonn, *Desertion during the Civil War*, 161; O'Brien and Diefendorf, General Orders No. 140, Sept. 24, 1862, *General Orders of the War Department*, vol. 1, 394; Roberts, *This Infernal War*, 21.

15. Randall and Donald, *The Civil War and Reconstruction*, 458–59.

16. Carmichael, *War for the Common Soldier*, 230–31; Raus, *Banners South*, 242.

17. Baynes, *Morale*, 101.

18. Roberts, *This Infernal War*, 75; Gen. Robert H. Milroy to Gen. Robert H. Schenck, Feb. 15, 1863, *O.R.*, ser. 1, vol. 25, pt. 2, 82–83; Gordon, *"I Never Was a Coward,"* 19.

19. Noe, *The Howling Storm*, 220–26, 256.

20. Pease and Randall, *Diary of Orville Hickman Browning*, vol. 1, Jan. 29, 1863, 620–21; Larson and Smith, *Dear Delia*, 140; *Dayton Daily Empire*, Feb. 14, 1863; Hooker testimony, *Report of the Joint Committee on the Conduct of the War*, vol. 4, 112.

21. Towne, *Surveillance and Spies in the Civil War*, 48; Basler, *Collected Works of Abraham Lincoln*, vol. 6, 132–33; Adam H. Pickel to his father, Feb. 8, 1863, Adam H. Pickel Papers, Rubenstein Library.

22. Heindel, *The 1863 Diary of Beates R. Swift*, 4, 14–16, 20, 29, 31; Frank, *With Ballot and Bayonet*, 168–74; Clarence H. Johnson to "Dear Father and Mother," Nov. 1, 1864, Letters, 1864 Sept. 21–1865 May 21, Library of Virginia.

23. Haidt, *The Righteous Mind*, 100; Tappin and McKay, "The Illusion of Moral Superiority," Social Psychology and Personality Science at https://journals.sagepub.com/doi/full/ 10.1177/ 1948550616673878?papetoc=, accessed Nov. 19. 2021; Marilla W. Leggett diary, Aug. 26, 1863, Marilla Wells Leggett Papers, Western Reserve Historical Society; Roberts, *This Infernal War*, 5, 183.

24. Throne, "Iowa Doctor in Blue," 168–69; Brooks, "Howell Cobb Papers," 384–86; Baird, *Josie Underwood's Civil War Diary*, 89.

25. Martinovich, "Americans' Partisan Identities Are Stronger than Race and Ethnicity," *Stanford News*, Aug. 31, 2017, https://news.stanford.edu/2017/08/31/political-party -identities-stronger-race-religion/.

26. Thomas B. McFarland to "Friend Yonnie," Aug. 10, 1861, McFarland-Hall-Beck Families Papers; Nevins, *Diary of the Civil War*, 295–96; Byron Shonts to Richard Yates, Mar. 1, 1863, Yates Family Papers, Abraham Lincoln Presidential Library and Museum; Justus L. Cozad autobiography, 84, Western Reserve Historical Society; Smith and Cooper Jr., *A Union Woman in Civil War Kentucky*, 155; Goodrich, "Civil War Letters of Bethiah Pyatt McKown," 358; Phillips and Pendleton, *The Union on Trial*, 1.

27. A. G. Gardner to William Lloyd Garrison, Dec. 31, 1862, Anti-Slavery Collection, Boston Public Library; Goodspeed, "History of Warren County," 132; Elder, *Love amid the Turmoil*, 107; Logan, *Reminiscences of a Soldier's Wife*, 145.

28. Larimer, *Love and Valor*, 295; Mary Ann Arnold to John C. Arnold, May 19, 1864, and John C. Arnold to Mary Ann Arnold, June 5, 1864, John Carvel Arnold Papers, LOC; Murphy, *The Kimberlins Go to War*, 72; Plante, "The Shady Side of the Family Tree," National Archives at https://www.archives.gov/publications/prologue/1998/winter /union-court-martials, accessed Oct. 10, 2021; Massey, *Bonnet Brigades*, 216.

29. Dunning, "Disloyalty in Two Wars," 625; quoted in Ernst, *Too Afraid to Cry*, 6, 9, 22.

30. Phillips, *The Rivers Ran Backward*, 188, 242; Abraham Lincoln to Samuel Curtis, Jan. 5, 1863, *O.R.*, ser. 1, vol. 22, pt. 2, 17–18; *Missouri Statesman* quoted in Taylor, *The Divided Family in Civil War America*, 3, 83–84; Harris, *A Most Unsettled State*, 62; Hancock, "Alexander B. Cooper's Civil War Memories of Camden," 53.

31. O'Leary and Jackson, "The Civil War Letters of Captain Daniel O'Leary," 159–60; Baird, *Josie Underwood's Civil War Diary*, 112; Smith and Cooper Jr., *A Union Woman in Civil War Kentucky*, xix–xx.

32. Davis, *Affectionately Yours*, 56; Marie Isely to Christian H. Isely, July 16 and Aug. 2, 1863, Isely Family Papers, Special Collections and University Archives, Wichita State

University; Macsherry, *Pastime: Life & Love on the Homefront*, vii–ix, 170; Whiteaker and Dickinson, *Civil War Letters of the Tenure Family*, x–xi.

33. Rhoades and Bailey, *Wanted—Correspondence*, 140–41, 171.

34. Phillips, *The Rivers Ran Backward*, 175–76; Miller, *Collected Writings of Walt Whitman*, vol. 1, 242.

35. Scott, *A Visitation of God*, 4–5, 111; Sarah Waldsmith Bovard diary, July 28 and Sept. 22, 1861, http://freepages.rootsweb.com/~haefner/genealogy/Bovard/sarahbovard2.html, accessed May 6, 2022; Mary Sutton to Rufus Dooley, May 19, 1863, Rufus Dooley Papers, Indiana Historical Society; Joseph Wise to "Cousin Tillie," June 14, 1863, Wise-Clark Family Papers, Special Collections & University Archives, University of Iowa Library; *Putnam Republican Banner*, Nov. 26, 1863; Welsko, "Copperheads and Blacksnakes," 61.

36. Rundell Jr., "Despotism of Traitors," 349; Philadelphia Club, *The Philadelphia Club, 1834–1934*, 41.

37. Sandow, *Deserter Country*, 13; Towne, *Surveillance and Spies in the Civil War*, 310–11; Tocqueville, *Democracy in America*, vol. 1, 337–38.

38. Williams, *Ostracism*, 3–4, 175; also see Williams and Nida, *Ostracism, Exclusion, and Rejection*.

39. Aldridge, *No Freedom Shrieker*, 58–59; Skipper and Taylor, *A Handful of Providence*, 185–86; Phillips and Parsegian, *Richard and Rhoda*, 52–53; Hancock, "Alexander B. Cooper's Civil War Memories of Camden," 66; Engs and Brooks, *Their Patriotic Duty*, 303; Billings, *Hardtack & Coffee*, 20.

40. Joseph Early to "Dear Brother & Sister," May 10, 1863, Joseph Early Letters, Lewis Leigh Collection, Box 50, US Army Heritage and Education Center; *Peninsular Courier* quoted in Olsen, "We Come Not to War On Opinions," 43.

41. Laas, *Wartime Washington*, 14; Hauranne, *A Frenchman in Lincoln's America*, vol. 2, 482–83.

CHAPTER 7

1. Fry, "Final Report PMG," 1; Simpson and Berlin, *Sherman's Civil War*, 373; Raymond, *History of the Administration of President Lincoln*, 331.

2. Basler, *Collected Works of Abraham Lincoln*, vol. 6, 445.

3. Marvel, *Lincoln's Autocrat*, 275; *Genesee Valley Free Press*, Feb. 25, 1863; Taber, *Hard Breathing Days*, 154.

4. Public Resolution No. 54, Mar. 24, 1863, *O.R.*, ser. 3, vol. 3, 88–89.

5. Duggan, *Legislative and Statutory Development of the Federal Concept for Military Service*, 45; US Congress, *Congressional Globe*, 37th Cong., 3rd Sess., 1262; Parish, *The North and the Nation in the Era of the Civil War*, 101–02.

6. Gen. Orders No. 140, Sept. 24, 1862, *O.R.*, ser. 3, vol. 2, 586; Randall, *Constitutional Problems under Lincoln*, 249.

7. Alexander R. Banks to Hugh A. Cook, July 6, 1863, Letters Sent, RG 110, Records of the Provost Marshal General's Bureau, National Archives, Kansas City, Missouri.

8. Miller; "To Stop These Wolves' Forays," 204; Sanborn, *Reminiscences of Richard Lathers*, 229. Seward's comment to Lyons, though often quoted, does not appear in any of

Seward's published correspondence or papers. Also see Hyman, *To Try Men's Souls: Loyalty Tests in American History*, 141–43.

9. Blair, *With Malice toward Some*, 100; Baker, *Affairs of Party*, 155–56; US Congress, *Congressional Globe*, 37th Cong., 3rd Sess., 1215.

10. Reed, *America's Two Constitutions*, 92; Basler, *Collected Works of Abraham Lincoln*, vol. 5, 436–37; *States and Union* quoted in Ruehlen, "The Specter of Subversion," 111–12.

11. Shannon, *Organization and Administration of Union Army*, vol. 1, 323; Weber, "Conscription and the Consolidation of Federal Power," 9; Leach, *Conscription in the United States*, 217–18; Ekirch, *The Civilian and the Military*, 103.

12. Furniss, "To Save the Union 'in Behalf of Conservative Men,'" 73–74; Gunn, *One Man's War*, 180; Stanley and Hall, *Eastern Maine and the Rebellion*, 175; Henry Halleck to Stephen Hurlbut, July 30, 1863, *O.R.*, ser. 1, vol. 24, pt. 3, 563–64; Taylor, *"The Most Complete Political Machine Ever Known,"* 11; Neely, *The Union Divided*, 193–94; Bensel, *Yankee Leviathan*, x.

13. *Daily Green Mountain Freeman*, Apr. 25, 1863, quoting *Cincinnati Daily Commercial*; *Jacksonville Journal* (Illinois), Mar. 19, 1863, quoted in Sterling, "Civil War Draft Resistance in the Middle West," 193–94; *Richmond Palladium*, Mar. 13, 1863; Henry Carrington to Lorenzo Thomas, Mar. 19, 1863, *O.R.*, ser. 3, vol. 3, 75–76.

14. Wilburn quoted in Sterling, "Civil War Draft Resistance in Illinois," 260.

15. Basler, *Collected Works of Abraham Lincoln*, vol. 6, 445–49.

16. Henry C. Naill report, "Historical Reports of the State Acting Assistant Provost Marshal General and District Provost Marshals," 1865, RG 110, Records of the Provost Marshal General's Bureau, M1163, National Archives, 25–26 (hereafter referred to as "Historical Reports").

17. Ekirch, *The Civilian and the Military*, 103; Bledsoe, *Citizen-Officers*, 6.

18. McPherson, *For Cause & Comrades*, 182; Martin, *The Life of Joseph Hodges Choate*, vol. 1, 240–42.

19. Elder, *Love amid the Turmoil*, 67–68; Anbinder, "Which Poor Man's Fight?" 350–51.

20. Barton et al, *Noble Sentiments of the Soul*, 153; Cranmer, *History of the Upper Ohio Valley*, vol. 1, 479; Emily Harris to Leander Harris, Aug. 6, 1863, Leander Harris Letters, Milne Special Collections and Archives.

21. Anbinder, "Which Poor Man's Fight?" 353; Holtmann, *A Lost American Dream*, 44–51.

22. Justus L. Cozad autobiography, 86, Western Reserve Historical Society; Ellen Woodworth to Samuel Woodworth, Nov. 10, 1863, Ellen Woodworth Letterbook, Clarke Historical Library.

23. Theodore Bronson to Maj. Felix Agnus, March 19, 1864, Theodore B. Bronson Letterbook, LOC; Kiefer, *History of the One Hundred and Fifty-third Regiment*, 254–55; Harris, *A Most Unsettled State*, 62–63.

24. Ford, "Letter to the Little Folks," 390–91; Dayton, "The Raising of Union Forces in Illinois during the Civil War," 436; Murdock, "New York's Civil War Bounty Brokers," 267.

25. Murdock, "New York's Civil War Bounty Brokers," 264–65.

26. Thomas Daley Company book, March–April 1865, Clarke Historical Library.

NOTES

27. McCoy marriage certificate and John McCoy to Martha McCoy, Jan. 17, 1864, McCoy Family Papers, Rauner Special Collections Library; Anbinder, "Which Poor Man's Fight?" 370; Dayton, "The Raising of Union Forces in Illinois during the Civil War," 435–36.

28. Sala, *My Diary in America in the Midst of War*, vol. 2, 372; James Oakes report, "Historical Reports," 45; Charles Gilbert report, "Historical Reports," 32; Albert Wilder to "Brother William," Sept. 6, 1863, Albert Wilder Papers, William Clements Library; Barker, *Dear Mother from Your Dutiful Son*, 134, 141.

29. Kent, *Three Years with Company K*, 214–15; O'Shaughnessy, *Alonzo's War*, 104–05; Haas, *Dear Esther*, 167.

30. Haynes, *A Minor War History*, 140–42; Haynes, *A History of the Second Regiment*, 206; Anbinder, "Which Poor Man's Fight?" 368–69.

31. Basler, *Collected Works of Abraham Lincoln*, vol. 6, 447–48; Boggs, *Patriotism by Proxy*, 31; Perri, "The Evolution of Military Conscription in the United States," 429–30; McPherson, *Battle Cry of Freedom*, 603.

32. Richard H. Jackson to Father, June 17 and 22, 1861, Gilder Lehrman Collection; General Orders No. 105, *O.R.*, ser. 3, vol. 3, 170–72.

33. Fry, "Final Report PMG," 91–92; Circular No. 12 from Ohio AAPMG dated July 13, 1863, Darius Cadwell Papers, Western Reserve Historical Society; *Elkton Cecil Whig*, Dec. 5, 1863.

34. "Washington during the Civil War: The Diary of Horatio Nelson Taft," Nov. 18, 1863, https://www.loc.gov/collections/diary-of-horatio-taft/about-this-collection/, accessed July 21, 2020; for contemporary analyses of the Invalid Corps/Veteran Reserve Corps, see Paul Cimbala, "Federal Manpower Needs and the U.S. Army's Veteran Reserve Corps" and "Soldiering on the Home Front: The Veteran Reserve Corps and the Northern People." Also, Stinson, "The Invalid Corps"; De Forest report dated November 30, 1865, *O.R.*, ser. 3, vol. 5, 543–67.

35. De Forest report dated Nov. 30, 1865, *O.R.*, ser. 3, vol. 5, 552; Donald, *Gone for a Soldier*, 238; Billings, *Hardtack & Coffee*, 79; also see Wilder, "The Invalid Corps."

36. Handley-Cousins, *Bodies in Blue*, 12, 43; De Forest report dated Nov. 30, 1865, *O.R.*, ser. 3, vol. 5, 547.

37. Pelka, *Civil War Letters of Colonel Charles F. Johnson*, 13–14; Magnitsky quoted in Cimbala, "Soldiering on the Home Front: The Veteran Reserve Corps and the Northern People," 186; Blake, *Three Years in the Army of the Potomac*, 304.

38. Wiley, *Life of Billy Yank*, 342; State of Michigan, *Annual Report of the Adjutant General, 1863*, 484–85; James Oakes report, "Historical Reports," 39.

39. Greene, *Letters from a Sharpshooter*, 272; Crowell, *The Young Volunteer*, 457.

40. *Portland Daily Press*, May 6, 1864.

41. Cimbala, "Federal Manpower Needs and the U.S. Army's Veteran Reserve Corps," 11–12; Hughes, *Civil War Papers of Lt. Col. Newton T. Colby*, 242–44.

42. Fry, "Final Report PMG," 93; also see US War Department, *Field Record of the Officers of the Veteran Reserve Corps*. Fully 85 percent of VRC officers had suffered debilitating war wounds; Cimbala, "Federal Manpower Needs and the U.S. Army's Veteran Reserve Corps," 11–12; Pelka, *Civil War Letters of Colonel Charles F. Johnson*, 221.

43. De Forest report dated Nov. 30, 1865, *O.R.*, ser. 3, vol. 5, 553.

CHAPTER 8

1. Keating, *The Greatest Trials I Ever Had*, 173; Morgan and Somers quoted in Baxter, *Statistics, Medical and Anthropological*, vol. 1, 191–92, 446; Randall, *Constitutional Problems under Lincoln*, 251.

2. Cook, *A Quiet Corner of the War*, 24–25; Taber, *Hard Breathing Days*, 267; *Ottawa (IL) Free Trader*, Dec. 19, 1863.

3. Phelan, *Who Only Stand and Wait*, 108; Edwin Palmer report, "Historical Reports," 7.

4. Murdock, *Patriotism Limited*, 58; *Frank Leslie's Illustrated Newspaper*, Dec. 6, 1862.

5. Thompson, *History of Greenfield, vol. 1*, 343; Murdock, *Ohio's Bounty System in the Civil War*, 19–20.

6. Levine, "Draft Evasion in the North during the Civil War," 818; Murdock, *Ohio's Bounty System in the Civil War*, 20; "The Wrong Way to Get Soldiers," in *The Round Table: A Weekly Record of the Notable, the Useful and the Tasteful*, Jan. 16, 1864.

7. Hanchett and Speed, "An Illinois Physician and the Civil War Draft," 157.

8. George W. Barns to Capt. A. R. Banks, July 8, 1863, Letters Received, Northern District of Kansas, National Archives, Kansas City, Missouri, Record Group 110; Aaron Lockwood to parents, (no month or day), 1863, Lockwood Family Correspondence, Bentley Historical Library.

9. Mary A. Watters to Iowa Adj. Gen. Nathaniel Baker, Nov. 5, 1862, Mary Ann Watters Correspondence, LOC; Sterling, "Civil War Draft Resistance in the Middle West," 251–52, 257; George H. Keith report, "Historical Reports," 2.

10. Coleman, *The Molly Maguire Riots*, 42–43; Marshall, *American Bastille*, 589.

11. Shannon, *Organization and Administration of the Union Army*, vol. 2, 184–85, 191–92; Fry, "Final Report PMG," 19.

12. Edwin C. Fowler to C. W. West, August 21, 1863, The Civil War in Maryland Collection, Special Collections, University of Maryland Libraries.

13. George Brown to Leander Brown, Sept. 14, 1863, George Brown Family Correspondence, Clarke Historical Library; Josyph, *The Wounded River*, 167, 191; Sterling, "Civil War Draft Resistance in the Middle West," 374; Sarah Keen to Dear Son, July 13 and 18, 1863, Keen Family Letters, William Clements Library.

14. Kirkland, *A Few Words in Behalf of the Loyal Women of the United States by One of Themselves*, 5; Merrill, "Take Your Gun and Go, John."

15. *Lamoille Newsdealer*, Dec. 30, 1863; Seaver, *Historical Sketches of Franklin County*, 279; *Detroit Free Press*, Mar. 5, 1863; Augustus L. Yenner diary, Apr. 9, 1863, Archives and Regional History Collections, Western Michigan University.

16. Waterman Burlingham to "Dear Horace," May 1, 1863, author's collection.

17. Paludan, *A People's Contest*, 168; Hansen and Brebner, *The Mingling of the Canadian and American Peoples*, 148–49; *Weekly Globe* quoted in Landon, *Western Ontario and the American Frontier*, 223.

18. E. A. Parrott to James Fry, June 29, 1863, *O.R.*, ser. 3, vol. 3, 426; E. B. Wolcott and Edward Broadhead to James Lewis, Aug. 26, 1864, *O.R.*, ser. 3, vol. 4, 684; Alfred Sully

to John Pope, Sept. 9. 1864, *O.R.*, ser. 1, vol. 41, pt. 1, 151–52; Fite, *Social and Industrial Conditions in the North during the Civil War*, 35, 39.

19. May, *Three Frontiers*, 74–79.

20. Gates, *Free Homesteads for All Americans*, 7.

21. Marchand, *News from Fort Craig*, 11, 14, 17; Robert Hawxhurst to Bernard Reid, Oct. 11, 1862, Bernard J. Reid Collection, Santa Clara University Library, Archives & Special Collections.

22. James Oakes report, "Historical Reports," 107; Patrick Gallagher to C. H. Hempstead, June 26, 1863, *O.R.*, ser. 1, vol. 50, 495–96.

23. Jewell, *On Duty in the Pacific Northwest*, 77–79; Roberts, *This Infernal War*, 146–47; Rose, *Victorian America and the Civil War*, 90.

24. William Sherman to James Fry, Nov. 8, 1863, *O.R.*, ser. 3, vol. 3, 1006–07; William Sherman to Rear Admiral David Porter, Oct. 25, 1863, US War Department, *Official Records of the Union and Confederate Navies*, ser. 1, vol. 25, 474–75.

25. Taber, *Hard Breathing Days*, 217; Bradley, *Leverett Bradley: A Soldier-Boy's Letters*, 29; Mannis and Wilson, *Bound to Be a Soldier*, 65–66; Feidner, *"Dear Wife": The Civil War Letters of Chester K. Leach*, 159; Soman and Byrne, *A Jewish Colonel in the Civil War*, 150; Charles Tew to Amelia Tew, Sept. 3, 1863, Charles F. Tew Papers, William Clements Library.

26. Linderman, *Embattled Courage*, 66–70; Rankin, *Toward a More Perfect Union*, 281; Gallman, *Defining Duty*, 258.

27. Nash, *Civil War Letters of Jabez L. Huntley to Amy Huntley, 1862–1864*, 32; George Brown to Leander Brown, June 16, 1863, George Brown Family Correspondence, Clarke Historical Library; Henry Truesdell to "Dear Niece Clara," June 20, 1863, Henry J. Truesdell Correspondence, Clarke Historical Library; John Rieley to "Dear Mother and Sister," Apr. 29 [1863], Francis and John Rieley Papers, Western Reserve Historical Society; Phelan, *Tramping Out the Vintage, 1861–1864*, 201–02; Roth, *Well Mary*, 93; Miller, *Collected Writings of Walt Whitman*, vol. 1, 151.

28. Patrick and Willey, *Fighting for Liberty and Right: The Civil War Diary of William Bluffton Miller*, 161–62; Orlando M. Poe to "Dear wife," Oct. 23, 1862, Orlando M. Poe Papers, LOC.

29. Cryder and Miller, *A View from the Ranks*, 155; George Baker to "My Dear Mother," Apr. 17, 1865, George Washington Baker Papers, Southern Historical Collection.

30. Lodge, *Early Memories*, 130–31; Thaddeus Carleton journal, Nov. 21, 1863, William Clements Library; Nevins, *Diary of the Civil War*, 289–90.

31. Styple, *Writing and Fighting the Civil War*, 183; William Sherman to Henry Halleck, Sept. 17, 1863, *O.R.*, ser. 1, vol. 30, pt. 3, 698.

32. Reinhart, *Two Germans in the Civil War*, 40–41; Eben T. Hale to mother, June 9, 1863, Eben Thomas Hale Papers, 1862–1865, Southern Historical Collection.

33. Table No. 6, Recapitulation, Draft of July, 1863, *O.R.*, ser. 3, vol. 5, 730–32; Henry Halleck to William T. Sherman, Oct. 1, 1863, *O.R.*, ser. 1, vol. 52, pt. 1, 717–18.

34. D. Perkins to James Fry, June 24, 1863, *O.R.*, ser. 3, pt. 3, 412–13; Burr and Lincoln, *Town of Hingham in the Late Civil War*, 81–82; *Saginaw Valley Republican* quoted in *East Saginaw Courier*, Dec. 23, 1863.

35. *Bellows Falls Times*, Feb. 20, 1863; Elder, *Love Amid the Turmoil*, 245.

36. *Waynesboro Village Record*, Mar. 6, 1863.

37. Orr, *Last to Leave the Field*, 173.

38. Cook, *A Quiet Corner of the War*, xi–xii, 32, 37, 43.

39. Statement of Osmyn P. Spaulding to Darius Cadwell, [June 1863], Darius Cadwell Papers, Western Reserve Historical Society; *Greencastle Banner*, June 18, 1863, quoted in Canup, "Conscription and Draft in Indiana during the Civil War," 81; Fry, "Final Report PMG," 19; Coakley, *The Role of Federal Military Forces in Domestic Disorders*, 237.

40. Shankman, *Pennsylvania Antiwar Movement*, 143; William B. Lane report, "Historical Reports," 39.

41. Heidelbaugh and Paone, *Between Home and the Front*, 81; J. S. Richards to L. C. Turner, Mar. 17, 1863, *O.R.*, ser. 3, vol. 3, 75; Etcheson, *A Generation at War*, 109; John Newberry to Bennett Hill, July 14, 1863, *O.R.* ser. 3, vol. 3, 488; James M. Allen to James Oakes, July 14, 1863, *O.R.*, ser. 3, vol. 3, 510; Murdock, *One Million Men*, 41; Cook, *A Quiet Corner of the War*, 167; Doc. No. 38, "Casualties among the Employees of the Provost-Marshal-General's Bureau," *O.R.*, ser. 3, vol. 5, 912.

42. Sarah Lundy to unnamed [though John O. Martin], June 8, 1863, Sarah Lundy Correspondence, Ohio History Center Archives & Library. "Butternuts" was the term given to anti-Lincoln, antiwar inhabitants throughout the southern parts of Ohio, Illinois, and Indiana. The term referred to the tannish appearance of their clothing, which was colored from the dye of the butternut tree.

43. Edward Salomon to Edwin Stanton, Nov. 10, 1862, *O.R.*, ser. 3, vol. 2, 761; Coakley, *The Role of Federal Military Forces in Domestic Disorders*, 234–35; Taylor, *Old Slow Town*, 94–101.

44. Dupree and Fishel, "An Eyewitness Account of the New York Draft Riots, July, 1863," 476; Bernstein, *The New York City Draft Riots*, 288–89. For additional modern accounts of the New York City draft riots, see Cook, *The Armies of the Streets* and Schecter, *The Devil's Own Work*.

45. O. A. Mack to Capt. John Godfrey, Aug. 15, 1863, Letters, Logbooks, Registers, and Lists, 1863–1865, RG 110, Records of the Provost Marshal General's Bureau, Chicago, IL; Levine, "Draft Evasion in the North during the Civil War, 1863–1865," 833; Mary Henry diary, Nov. 14, 1863, Smithsonian Institution.

46. Keehn, *Knights of the Golden Circle*, 1–15, 77; also see Weber, *Copperheads*; Towne, *Surveillance and Spies in the Civil War*; and Taylor, "*The Most Complete Political Machine Ever Known*" for modern analyses of these various "secret societies."

47. Quoted in Weber, "Conscription and the Consolidation of Federal Power," 17.

48. *Cincinnati Enquirer*, Aug. 2, 1862; Sarah Keen to Dear Son, July 18, 1863, Keen Family Letters, William Clements Library; Josyph, *The Wounded River*, 224n29.

49. Dayton, "The Raising of Union Forces in Illinois during the Civil War," 434.

50. Sandow, *Deserter Country*, 92.

51. Mannis and Wilson, *Bound to Be a Soldier*, 110–15.

52. Crowell, *The Young Volunteer*, 9–10.

53. McAvoy, "The War Letters of Father Peter Paul Cooney," 220–21.

54. Coddington, "Pennsylvania Prepares for Invasion, 1863," 162–63; Valuska and Keller, *Damn Dutch*, 57, 73; Mattie Conpropst to Hattie Rohrer, June 28, 1863, Zerah Coston Monks Family Papers, Western Reserve Historical Society; Lockwood, *Our Campaign around Gettysburg*, 23; Hoke, *The Great Invasion of 1863*, 211–12.

55. Nevins, *Diary of the Civil War*, 325; "Washington during the Civil War: The Diary of Horatio Nelson Taft," Nov. 18, 1863, https://www.loc.gov/collections/diary-of-horatio -taft/about-this-collection/, accessed Nov. 17, 2021.

56. Craft quoted in Jimerson, *Private Civil War*, 220; George M. Barnard to father, July 4, 1863, George M. Barnard Papers, Massachusetts Historical Society; Taber, *Hard Breathing Days*, 206; Shannon, *Organization and Administration of the Union Army*, vol. 1, 296.

57. Gerrish, *Army Life: A Private's Reminiscences of the Civil War*, 97; George Brown to Leander Brown, Dec. 21, 1863, George Brown Family Correspondence, Clarke Historical Library.

CHAPTER 9

1. Costa and Kahn, *Heroes and Cowards*, 54.

2. Fry, "Final Report PMG," 89–90, 228.

3. Lonn, *Desertion during the Civil War*, 151–52; Gen. Orders No. 31, *O.R.*, ser. 3, vol. 4, 1225.

4. Lonn, *Desertion during the Civil War*, 217; Sandage, *Born Losers*, 206; John Rieley to "Dear Mother and Sister," Feb. 13, 1863, Francis and John Rieley Papers, Western Reserve Historical Society; Ramold, *Baring the Iron Hand*, 254–55; Alotta, *Civil War Justice*, 188.

5. Valentine G. Barney to Maria Barney, Feb. 25, 1863, at "Valentine G. Barney Correspondence—Vermonters in the Civil War," https://cdi.uvm.edu/manuscript/ uvmcdi-90658, accessed Nov. 1, 2021; Hammond to Eliza Quilty, Jan. 20, 1864, Quilty Family Civil War Letters, Special Collections and Archives, Middlebury College Library; Henry W. Halleck to Maj. Gen. Samuel Curtis, July 19, 1862, *O.R.*, ser. 1, vol. 13, 477.

6. Lonn, *Desertion during the Civil War*, 158–60; Meade, *Life and Letters of George Gordon Meade*, vol. 2, 250–51; Miller, *Drum Taps in Dixie*, 144; Billings, *Hardtack & Coffee*, 168.

7. Aldridge, *No Freedom Shrieker*, 45–46, 58–59, 64.

8. Lewis, *My Dear Parents*, 65–67.

9. Abraham Lincoln Gen. Orders No. 252, July 31, 1863, *O.R.*, ser. 2, vol. 6, 163.

10. Samuel J. Gibson diary, June 9 and 28, 1864, Samuel J. Gibson Diary and Correspondence, LOC.

11. *Orleans Independent Standard*, Sept. 2, 1864; Krug, *Mrs. Hill's Journal*, 108.

12. Orlando M. Poe to Eleanor Poe, Nov. 30, 1863, Orlando M. Poe Papers, LOC.

13. *New York Herald*, Nov. 11, 1863; *Star of the North*, Dec. 23, 1863.

14. *Macomb Weekly Journal*, Apr. 3, 1863; Newton Fox to Perrin Fox, Mar. 5, 1863, Fox Family Correspondence, Bentley Historical Library; Ohio soldier quoted in Jordan, *A Thousand May Fall*, 79; Briggs, "Peter Wilson in the Civil War," 353.

15. Basler, *Collected Works of Abraham Lincoln*, vol. 6, 266–67; Klement, *The Limits of Dissent*, 152–58; Hyman, *To Try Men's Souls*, 139. The doctrine of necessity states that normally unconstitutional actions are lawful and proper if by so doing, an even greater danger is thwarted.

16. Phelan, *Who Only Stand and Wait*, 163; *Ohio Repository*, Apr. 29, 1863.

17. Allen, *Forty-six Months with the Fourth R. I. Volunteers*, 188–89; various orders, Feb. 6–13, 1863, *O.R.*, ser. 1, vol. 25, pt. 2, 72–73; Hooker testimony, *Report of the Joint Committee on the Conduct of the War*, vol. 4, 112.

18. *Valley Spirit*, July 16, 1862; Matthews and Wecter, *Our Soldiers Speak*, 144.

19. Lonn, *Desertion during the Civil War*, 134.

20. Ramold, *Baring the Iron Hand*, 244–46; Allen, *Forty-six Months with the Fourth R. I. Volunteers*, 189; Kalmoe, *With Ballots and Bullets*, 86.

21. Carmichael, *War for the Common Soldier*, 52; Mitchell, *The Vacant Chair*, 29–30; Cashin, "Deserters, Civilians, and Draft Resistance in the North," 272; Blight, *When This Cruel War Is Over*, 212; *Counties of Cumberland, Jasper and Richland, Illinois*, 176–77; George H. Keith report, "Historical Reports," 23; Westlake quote in Miller, "To Stop These Wolves' Forays," 215.

22. Jordan, "The Hoskinsville Rebellion," 319–54; Sandow, *Deserter Country*, 145.

23. Lieut. Col. James Oakes to Col. James B. Fry, Apr. 18, 1864, *O.R.*, ser. 1, vol. 32, pt. 1, 630–33; James Oakes telegram to "Gov. Morton or commanding officer," Mar. 30, 1864, Charleston, Illinois, Riot Records, William L. Clements Library.

24. Sauers and Tomasak, *Fishing Creek Confederacy*, 42–45; Shankman, *Pennsylvania Antiwar Movement*, 154–57.

25. Capt. Richard Dodge to Brig. Gen. James B. Fry, Aug, 10, 1864, *O.R.*, ser. 3, vol. 4, 607; Sauers and Tomasak, *Fishing Creek Confederacy*, 42–45, 56, 68–70; Shankman, *Pennsylvania Antiwar Movement*, 154–57.

26. Shankman, *Pennsylvania Antiwar Movement*, 16; Nagler, "Loyalty and Dissent," 351; Schaar, *Loyalty in America*, 60–61.

27. Rhodes, *History of the Civil War, 1861–1865*, 223; Etcheson, *A Generation at War*, 113; Judson W. Bemis to "Dear Steph," Apr. 3, 1864, Bemis Family Papers, Missouri Historical Society Library and Research Center.

28. Samuel Curtis to William Stone, Mar. 1, 1864, *O.R.* ser. 1, vol. 34, pt. 2, 480.

29. Gen. Orders No. 191, June 25, 1863, *O.R.*, ser. 3, vol. 3, 414–16.

30. Reiss, *It Takes a Matriarch*, 335; Charles Tew to Amelia Tew, Nov. 21, 1863, Charles F. Tew Papers, William Clements Library; Palladino, *Diary of a Yankee Engineer*, 75.

31. Thornton and Ekelund, *Tariffs, Blockades, and Inflation*, 66–67; Gallman, *The North Fights the Civil War*, 95–96, 112.

32. Gallman, *The North Fights the Civil War*, 97; Richards, *Village Life in America*, 149; Johann Look to "Dear Children," May 31, 1863, Look Family Papers, Bentley Historical Library; *Detroit Free Press*, Mar. 5, 1864; Frost, "The Home Front in New York during the Civil War," 283; Anderson, *Life and Letters of Judge Thomas J. Anderson and Wife*, 398; Lee, *Discontent in New York City*, 168–69, 171.

33. Almyra C. Barker to "My Dear Charles," Aug. 14, 1864, Lunt Family Correspondence and Photographs, Maine Historical Society.

34. Mitchell, *History of the Greenbacks*, 404; Thornton and Ekelund, *Tariffs, Blockades, and Inflation*, 68–69.

Chapter 10

1. Leeke, *A Hundred Days to Richmond*, xi–xiii.

2. Leeke, *A Hundred Days to Richmond*, xiii; Charles Wilson diary, Apr. 26, 1864, Indiana Historical Society; Johnson, *Warriors into Workers*, 134.

3. Enoch, "One Man's Experience in a One Hundred Day Regiment," 185–201.

4. Sherman, *History of the 133d Regiment, O. V. I.*, 18, 21.

5. Davis, *Affectionately Yours*, 87–88; Aurner, *A Topical History of Cedar County, Iowa, Vol. 1*, 336.

6. Larimer, *Love and Valor*, 271; Massachusetts Historical Society, "Dalton Letters," 485.

7. Larson and Smith, *Dear Delia*, 259–60; Andrew Linscott to "Dear Sir," Sept. 2, 1864, Andrew Linscott Papers, Massachusetts Historical Society; Morse, *Letters Written During the Civil War*, 179–80; Britton and Reed, *To My Beloved Wife and Boy at Home*, 275.

8. Geer quoted in Marvel, *The Monitor Chronicles*, 232; Saltonstall, *Reminiscences of the Civil War*, 69–70; Beale, *Diary of Gideon Welles*, vol. 2, 121.

9. Gen. Orders No. 143, May 22, 1863, *O.R.*, ser. 3, vol. 3, 215–16.

10. Abbott, "Massachusetts and the Recruitment of Southern Negroes," 197–98; *Tribune* quoted in Karamanski and McMahon, *Civil War Chicago*, 228; quoted in Thornbrough, *Indiana in the Civil War Era*, 199; Escott, *"What Shall We Do with the Negro?"* 73.

11. Ulysses S. Grant to William T. Sherman, Apr. 4, 1864, *O.R.*, ser. 1, vol. 32, pt. 3, 245–46.

12. Ulysses S. Grant to George Meade, Apr. 9, 1864, *O.R.*, ser. 1, vol. 33, 827–29; Stoddard, *Inside the White House in War Times*, 178–79.

13. Law, "From the Wilderness to Cold Harbor," 141; Early, *The Campaigns of Gen. Robert E. Lee*, 37; Grant, *Memoirs and Selected Letters*, 588.

14. Gallagher, "The Two Generals Who Resist Each Other," 6, 10; Miller, *Collected Writings of Walt Whitman*, vol. 1, 231.

15. Linderman, *Embattled Courage*, 166–67; Carmichael, *War for the Common Soldier*, 303–04; Horatio Nelson Taft diary, May 12, 1864, https://www.loc.gov/collections/diary-of-horatio-taft/about-this-collection/, accessed Oct. 14, 2021.

16. Rankin, *Toward a More Perfect Union*, 205; Charles Tripp to "Dear Parents," Aug. 14, 1864, Charles A. Tripp Letters, New York Historical Society; Roberts, *This Infernal War*, 223–24; John Sheahan to father, Feb. [no day], 1864, John Parris Sheahan Papers, Maine Historical Society.

17. Murdock, *One Million Men*, 197–98; Fry, "Final Report PMG," 704; George H. Keith report, "Historical Reports," 9; James Fry to Edwin Stanton, June 6, 1864, *O.R.*, ser. 3, vol. 4, 421; Geary, *We Need Men*, 140–41; Public announcement No. 196, July 6, 1864, *O.R.*, ser. 3, vol. 4, 472–74.

18. Orr, "Cities at War," 325; *North Carolina Presbyterian*, Feb. 3, 1864; Phelan, *Who Only Stand and Wait*, 265; James F. Lyman to Benjamin S. Lyman, Aug. 21, 1864, Lyman Family Papers, Special Collections and University Archives, University of Massachusetts

Amherst; Reiss, *It Takes a Matriarch*, 338–40; Dayton, "The Raising of Union Forces in Illinois during the Civil War," 435.

19. Warshauer, *Connecticut in the American Civil War*, 151; Frederick Townsend to James B. Fry, Aug. 5, 1864, *O.R.*, ser. 3, vol. 4, 580; Palladino, *Another Civil War*, 114; Ellen Woodworth to Samuel Woodworth, Aug. 28 and Sept. 26, 1864, Ellen Woodworth Letterbook, Clarke Historical Library; Lyman Blowers to Thaddeus Jackson, Sept. 4, 1864, Lyman Blowers Letter, Indiana Historical Society.

20. McOwen, *Seven Months a Soldier*, 3–4, 70; Geary, *We Need Men*, 140–41.

21. Greene, *Letters from a Sharpshooter*, 258.

22. Quoted in Lee, *Discontent in New York City*, 89–90.

23. Gurowski, *Diary: 1863–'64–'65*, 363; Phelan, *Who Only Stand and Wait*, 260; Reiss, *It Takes a Matriarch*, 415.

24. Denison J. Griffing to Flora A. Weaver, Sept. 24, 1864, Series 26, American Civil War Documents, Manuscripts, Letters and Diaries Collections, Special Collections, Chicago Public Library; Hirshson, *Grenville M. Dodge*, 85; Hancock, "Alexander B. Cooper's Civil War Memories of Camden," 66; Henry Billings Brown diary, Aug. 22–25, 1864, Burton Historical Collection; Nevins, *Diary of the Civil War*, 479–80; M. Ellen Hedrick to Benjamin Hedrick, July 20, 1864, Benjamin Sherwood Hedrick Papers, Rubenstein Library.

25. Anderson, *Life and Letters of Judge Thomas J. Anderson and Wife*, 397–98; William Owner diary, Sept. 7, 1864; H. Alexander Jr. to John Andrew, Aug. 20, 1864, *O.R.*, ser. 3, vol. 4, 631.

26. Murdock, *One Million Men*, 328; Pearson, *The Life of John A. Andrew*, vol. 2, 138–40; Walker, "The Mercenaries," 390.

27. Meade, *Life and Letters of George Gordon Meade*, vol. 2, 211; Athearn, *Soldier in the West*, 205–06; George Anthony to "Dear Brother," Nov. 24, 1864, George T. Anthony Papers, William Clements Library; Grant, *Memoirs & Selected Letters*, 1066.

28. Robertson, *Civil War Letters of General Robert McAllister*, 462–63.

29. Louisa A. Reed to My Dear Husband, Nov. 13, 1864, Louisa A. Reed Papers, William Clements Library; Maria Sargent to Ransom Sargent, July [undated] and Sept. 8, 1864, Sargent, Ransom F., and Emily Maria, Civil War Papers, 1862, Rauner Special Collections Library.

30. Fremantle, *Three Months in the Southern States*, 298–99.

31. Mrs. William Newton Matson to her son, Feb. 20, Mar. 10, Apr. 2, and Aug. 4, 1863, Mrs. William Newton Matson Letters, Connecticut Historical Society Library; Dodge quoted in Burrows and Wallace, *Gotham*, 877; Mcelligott, "'A Monotony Full of Sadness': The Diary of Nadine Turchin," 31; Parker Pillsbury to "My dear friends," July 17, 1864, Parker Pillsbury letter MS Am.1993 (8), Boston Public Library; Taber, *Hard Breathing Days*, 135; Van Tassel, *"Behind Bayonets,"* 65; Phillips and Parsegian, *Richard and Rhoda*, 57.

32. Kamphoefner and Helbich, *Germans in the Civil War*, 68; Bennett and Misselhorn, "Curtis R. Burke's Civil War Journal," 160.

33. Geary, *We Need Men*, 157.

34. Cochran, *The Dream of a Northwestern Confederacy*, 246.

35. *Daily Ohio Statesman*, Mar. 20, 1864; White, *Emancipation, the Union Army, and the Reelection of Abraham Lincoln*, 7; Churchill, "Liberty, Conscription, and a Party Divided," 294–303; "Every Democrat . . ." quoted in Neely, *The Union Divided*, 60.

36. Weber, *Copperheads*, 1; McPherson, *Battle Cry of Freedom*, 766–68.

37. Sarah Lundy to John Martin, June 8, 1864, Sarah Lundy Correspondence, Ohio History Center; Russ Jr., "Franklin Weirick," 251; Throne, "Iowa Doctor in Blue," 109; Henry Miner to "Dear Father," Oct. 11, 1864, Henry Miner Letters, Library of Virginia.

38. Thomas Covert to "My Dear Wife," Oct. 13, 1864, Thomas Covert Papers, Western Reserve Historical Society; Ewing, *From Home to Trench*, 123.

39. Shankman, *Pennsylvania Antiwar Movement*, 190.

40. Weber, "Lincoln's Critics," 40; O. M. Poe to Eleanor Poe, Sept. 7, 1864, Orlando M. Poe Papers, LOC; Dolly A. McDoel to Mrs. Joseph Kidder, Nov. 13, 1864, McDoel-Kidder Letter, Indiana Historical Society; Marie Ester Brandt diary, Oct. 31, 1864, Marie Ester Brandt Collection, Indiana Historical Society.

41. Montgomery, *Beyond Equality*, 107–08; Zornow, *Lincoln and the Party Divided*, 215–16.

42. Waugh, *Reelecting Lincoln*, 354; Zornow, *Lincoln and the Party Divided*, 215–16.

43. McPherson, *Battle Cry of Freedom*, 804–05; White, *Emancipation, the Union Army, and the Reelection of Abraham Lincoln*, 6, 121–28; Tarbell, *A Reporter for Lincoln*, 70.

44. Grimes quoted in Tagg, *The Unpopular Mr. Lincoln*, 462. This book provides a thorough, modern analysis on how and why Lincoln was reviled by many of his contemporaries.

45. "Lili" to Mattie V. Thomas, Dec. 19, 1864, "Prairie Settlement: Nebraska Photographs and Family Letters, 1862–1912," http://memory.loc.gov/cgi-bin/query/r?ammem/ps:@field(DOCID+l011)#N-1, accessed Sept. 14, 2021; Rachel Hunt to Almeda Bennett, Nov. 15, 1864, Bennett-Stites-Fay Families' Papers, Ohio History Center.

CHAPTER 11

1. Flannery and Oomens, *Well Satisfied with My Position*, 86; O'Leary and Jackson, "The Civil War Letters of Captain Daniel O'Leary," 161; Bartholow, *A Manual of Instructions for Enlisting and Discharging Soldiers*, 90.

2. Simeon Freeman to "Dear Emma," Oct. 30, 1864, Simeon Freeman letter, Indiana Historical Society; quoted in McPherson, *For Cause and Comrades*, 81; Jacob Row to Hannah Row, Feb. 28, 1865, Jacob D. Row Letters, Indiana Historical Society.

3. White, *Emancipation, the Union Army, and the Reelection of Abraham Lincoln*, 167–69.

4. William Sherman to Henry Halleck, Jan. 12, 1865, *O.R.*, ser. 1, vol. 47, pt. 2, 36–37; Kamphoefner and Helbich, *Germans in the Civil War*, 246–48; McOwen, *Seven Months a Soldier*, 110; Taber, *Hard Breathing Days*, 437.

5. Albert Harris to "Dear Father" and "Dear Father Mother and All," Jan. 5 and 29, 1865, Albert Harris Papers, Vermont Historical Society; James Bamon to Henry Stroman, Apr. 5, 1865, Henry Stroman Papers, Ohio History Center Archives.

6. Adelbert D. Baughman diary, Jan. 14, 1865, Bentley Historical Library; Catlin, *Civil War Letters of Johannes Van Lente*, 111–13; Charles Cleveland diary, Feb. 7, 11, and 14, 1865, Cleveland Family Papers, Bentley Historical Library.

7. John Giffen to "Dear Father," Feb. 20 and Apr. 18, 1865, Giffen Family Correspondence, Ohio History Center Archives.

8. Marks and Schatz, *Between North and South*, 184.

9. William Doherty to "My Dear Mother Brothers and Sisters," Apr. 10, 1865, Doherty Letter, Clarke Historical Library.

10. McOwen, *Seven Months a Soldier*, 88–89; Carter, *Troubled State*, 181.

11. Edward Warner to "Dear Mother," Mar. 28, 1865, Letter, Library of Virginia, Richmond; McManus, Inglis, and Hicks, *Morning to Midnight in the Saddle*, 234–35; William Barton to Hiram Barton, Feb. 12, 1865, @ "Barton Family Correspondence—Vermonters in the Civil War," https://cdi.uvm.edu/manuscript/uvmcdi-91167, accessed Nov. 2, 2021.

12. Fry, "Final Report PMG," 160.

13. Provost Marshal General's Office Circular No. 9 dated Mar. 27, 1865, *O.R.*, ser. 3, vol. 4, 1253–54; Marks and Schatz, *Between North and South*, 174, 195.

14. Murdock, *Ohio's Bounty System in the Civil War*, 17–18; George Anthony to "Dear Brother," Mar. 3, 1865, George T. Anthony Papers, William Clements Library; Roberts, *This Infernal War*, 239–40; Anderson, *Life and Letters of Judge Thomas J. Anderson and Wife*, 397;

Marshall, *A War of the People: Vermont Civil War Letters*, 254–55.

15. Neely, *Lincoln and the Democrats*, 24–25; Orr, "Cities at War," 18, 265, 282; *Pittsburgh Gazette*, Feb. 17, 1865; Wubben, *Civil War Iowa and the Copperhead Movement*, 129; Murdock, *One Million Men*, 155.

16. Parmenter, *History of Pelham, Mass.*, 209–10.

17. *Detroit Free Press*, Nov. 17, 1864.

18. George A. Douglas to John Robertson, Nov. 26, 1864, and William S. Atwood to John Robertson, Nov. 30, 1864, Thirtieth Michigan Regt. Service Records, Archives of Michigan; Grover S. Wormer to William E. Christian, Dec. 1, 1864, Slafter Family Papers, Michigan State University Archives & Historical Collections.

19. Quoted in Lonn, *Desertion during the Civil War*, 156; Theodore Bronson to Edwin D. Morgan, Apr. 26, 1864, Theodore B. Bronson Letterbook, LOC.

20. Wilkeson, *Recollections of a Private Soldier in the Army of the Potomac*, 1–3.

21. Putnam, *Memories of My Youth*, 286–87; Harriman, *The History of Warner, New Hampshire*, 399; O. Leland Barlow to "Dear Sister," Apr. 11, 1864, O. Leland Barlow Papers, Connecticut State Library; Abbott, "The Civil War and the Crime Wave of 1865–70," 216.

22. Nevins, *Grover Cleveland: A Study in Courage*, 51–52.

23. "The Wrong Way to Get Soldiers," in *The Round Table*, Jan. 16, 1864; Judson, *History of the 83rd Regiment Pennsylvania Volunteers*, 76.

24. John W. Harry to Frank Harry, Sept. 3, 1864, John W. Harry Correspondence, Ohio History Center; Sarah Lundy to John O. Martin, Feb. 28, 1864, Sarah Lundy Correspondence, Ohio History Center; Bender, *Like Grass before the Scythe*, 88, 123; John Voltz to Felix Voltz, Feb. 10, 1865, Felix Voltz Letters, Special Collections, Virginia Tech University; Bensel, *Yankee Leviathan*, 138, n82.

25. Lincoln proclamation, Mar. 11, 1865, *O.R.*, ser. 3, vol. 4, 1229.

26. James Fry to Edwin Stanton, Sept. 11, 1865, *O.R*, ser. 3, vol. 5, 109; Shannon, "State Rights and the Union Army," 63.

27. Murdock, *Patriotism Limited*, 52–53; Shannon, *Organization and Administration of Union Army*, vol. 2, 192.

28. James Fry to Edwin Stanton, Sept. 11, 1865, *O.R.*, ser. 3, vol. 5, 108–09.

29. James Fry to Edwin Stanton, Sept. 11, 1865, *O.R.*, ser. 3, vol. 5, 110–12.

30. Barton and Dorman, *Harrisburg's Old Eighth Ward*, 65.

31. Hyman, *Era of the Oath*, 13; Randall, *Constitutional Problems under Lincoln*, 152 n25; Walker, "Rock Island Prison Barracks," 58.

32. Jordan, *Marching Home*, 43, 54; Montgomery, *Beyond Equality*, 4–5; see Abbott, "The Civil War and the Crime Wave of 1865–70."

33. Jordan, *Marching Home*, 99–100.

34. Rose, *Victorian America and the Civil War*, 245; Cimbala, *Veterans North and South*, xv; Wachtell, *War No More*, 3; Jordan, *Marching Home*, 138–39; Aaron, *The Unwritten War*, xvii.

35. Cook, *Bygone Days in Chicago*, 136; Gallagher, *The Union War*, 120–21; Dubbert, *A Man's Place*, 69–70; Clarke, "'Let All Nations See': Civil War Nationalism and the Memorialization of Wartime Voluntarism," 76–77.

36. "Treasury of Virtue" discussed in Warren, *The Legacy of the Civil War*, 59–64; Sandow, *Deserter Country*, 44–45.

37. Phillips, *Looming Civil War*, 221–22.

38. Nevins, *Diary of the Civil War*, 581; Smith, *Between the Lines*, 33; Cimbala, *Veterans North and South*, 129.

39. Ruehlen, "The Specter of Subversion," 186–87; Beale, *Diary of Gideon Welles*, vol. 2, 590; Josiah Tatman to "Whom it may concern," Aug. 7, 1868, Center for Archival Collections, Bowling Green State University. Tatman's name appears lost to history. His one-sided fragile letter (no location given) looks to have been crumbled and balled up at one time. He concludes by claiming his innocence with the hope that in a later time, his name will be cleared and honored. One cannot help but wonder if this was a suicide note.

40. Blight, *Race and Reunion*, 208; Blakeslee, *History of the Sixteenth Connecticut Volunteers*, 106.

41. Ken Burns (uploaded by Susanna Lee), "Shelby Foote on Union Victory," YouTube video, 0:42, Oct. 25, 2016, https://www.youtube.com/watch?v=H8Iw-j217yk.

CONCLUSION

1. Kalmoe, *With Ballots and Bullets*, 212–13.

2. Weber, "Conscription and the Consolidation of Federal Power," 29.

3. "Waving the bloody shirt" was a popular Republican post–Civil War political strategy that attempted to appeal to voters' emotions by reminding them of the war's horror and suffering, and of the Democratic Party's role in perpetuating that.

4. Carmichael, *War for the Common Soldier*, 305–06; Schaar, *Loyalty in America*, 89; Sandow, *Deserter Country*, 3, 145; Warshauer, "Copperheads in Connecticut," 80.

5. "Most Democrats Say They'd Flee, Not Fight, a Ukraine-Style Invasion," *Wall Street Journal*, Mar. 10, 2022. Also see Polner and Woods, *We Who Dared to Say No to War*.

Bibliography

Manuscript and Archival Sources

Abraham Lincoln Presidential Library and Museum, Springfield, Illinois
Yates, Richard. Family Papers.

Archives and Regional History Collections, Western Michigan University, Kalamazoo
Yenner, Augustus L. Diary.

Archives and Special Collections, University of Pittsburgh, Pennsylvania
McFarland-Hall-Beck Families. Papers.

Archives of Michigan, Lansing.
Regimental Service Records, 1861–65. Michigan Adjutant-General's Department: Thirtieth Michigan Infantry Regimental Service Record.

Author's Collection, Michigan
Burlingham, Waterman. Letters.

Bentley Historical Library, University of Michigan, Ann Arbor
Baughman, Adelbert D. Civil War Diary, 1864–65.
Beers, Isaac. Letter, September 27, 1861.
Cleveland Family. Papers.
Crouse, Robert. Papers, 1846, 1856–1866.
Fox Family. Correspondence, 1863–1866.
Lockwood Family. Correspondence, 1863–1866.
Look Family. Papers, 1851–1903.
McClelland, Robert. Papers.
Potter, Henry Albert. Papers, 1862–1908.

Robinson, George D. Letter, June 12, 1861.
Ryder Family. Papers, 1861–1869.

Boston Public Library, Massachusetts
Anti-Slavery Collection.
Pillsbury, Parker. Letter.

Burton Historical Collection, Detroit Public Library, Michigan
Brown, Henry Billings. Diaries.
Brown, Henry L. Papers.

Center for Archival Collections, Bowling Green State University, Ohio
Carter, Bertha M. Papers—Hood/Pargellis Families.
Conine, Ira B. Correspondence.
Sullivan, William J. Collection/21st Ohio Volunteer Infantry Records.
Tatman, Josiah. Letter.
Weddell Family. Papers.

Clarke Historical Library, Central Michigan University, Mt. Pleasant
Brown, George M. Family Correspondence.
Daley, Thomas. Company book, March–April 1865.
Doherty, William. Letter, April 10, 1865.
Truesdell, Henry J. Correspondence, 1863.
Woodworth, Ellen. Letterbook.

Connecticut Historical Society, Hartford
Matson, Mrs. William Newton. Letters.

Connecticut State Library, Hartford
Barlow, O. Leland. Papers.

Dauphin County Historical Society, Harrisburg, Pennsylvania
Young, Redsecker I. Collection & Diaries, MG 222.

Dayton Metro Library, Ohio
Lowe Family. Papers.

Detre Library & Archives, Senator John Heinz History Center, Pittsburgh, Pennsylvania
Shoemaker Family. Papers.

Ella Strong Denison Library, Scripps College, Claremont, California
Chandler, N. A. Gold Rush Era Letters.

Gilder Lehrman Collection, Gilder Lehrman Institute of American History, New York
Bope, Abraham. Letter.
Churchill, Byron. Letter.
Jackson, Edwin. Letter.
Paull, J. D. Letter.

Indiana Historical Society, Indianapolis
Blowers, Lyman. Letter.
Brandt, Marie Ester. Collection.
Dooley, Rufus. Papers.
Freeman, Simeon. Letter.
McDoel-Kidder. Letter, November 13, 1864.
Row, Jacob D. Letters.
Wilson, Charles. Diaries, 1864–1867.

Kansas Historical Society, Topeka
Reader, Samuel J. Diaries.

Learned T. Bulman '48 Historic Archives and Museum, Washington & Jefferson College, Washington, Pennsylvania
Croft, Samuel W. Letters.

Library of Congress, Manuscripts Division, Washington, DC
Anderson Family. Papers, 1854–1931.
Arnold, John Carvel. Papers.
Badger, Alfred Mason. Papers, 1838–1863.
Bronson, Theodore B. Letterbook, 1863–1865.
Evans, Thomas. Civil War Diary and Memoirs, 1862–1953.
Gibson, Samuel J. Diary and Correspondence.
Owner, William. Diary and Papers.
Patterson, William Franklin. Papers.
Poe, Orlando M. Papers.

Wade, Benjamin F. Papers.
Walker, Henry. Correspondence, 1861–64.
Watters, Mary Ann. Correspondence, 1862.

Library of Virginia, Richmond
Hupman, George S. Letters.
Johnson, Clarence H. Letters, September 21, 1864–1865 May 21, 1865.
Keiholtz, David. Papers.
Miner, Henry. Letters.
Warner, Edward. Letter, March 28, 1865.
Webster, Dow. Papers, 1864–1865, 1891.

Maine Historical Society, Portland
Calderwood, Eben S. Correspondence.
Lunt Family. Correspondence and Photographs.
Sheahan, John Parris. Papers.

Manassas National Battlefield Park Library, Manassas, Virginia
Brown, Charles C. Letters: 1861 and 1862.
Burrill, John H. Letters.
Smart, B. F. Letters.
Thompson, Ai Baker. Letters.

Manuscripts and Archives Division, New York Public Library. Astor, Lenox, and Tilden Foundations
Gross, O. R. Diary, 1861–1862.

Massachusetts Historical Society, Boston
Barnard, George M. Papers.
Linscott, Andrew R. Papers.

Michigan State University Archives & Historical Collections, Lansing
Bamber Family. Letters.
Eaegle Family. Papers.
Farr, George. Autobiography typescript.
Slafter Family. Papers.

Milne Special Collections and Archives, University of New Hampshire Library, Durham
Harris, Leander. Letters.

Missouri Historical Society Library and Research Center, St. Louis
Bemis Family. Papers.

National Archives, Chicago, Illinois
Record Group 110, Records of the Provost Marshal General's Bureau:
  Historical Reports of the State Acting Assistant Provost Marshal General and District Provost Marshals.
  Letters, Logbooks, Registers, and Lists, 1863–1865.

National Archives, Kansas City, Missouri
Record Group 110, Records of the Provost Marshal General's Bureau:
  Letters Received.
  Letters Sent.

National Archives, Washington, DC
Record Group 94, Records of the Adjutant General's Office:
  Case Files of Investigations by Levi C. Turner and Lafayette C. Baker, 1861–1866.

Newberry Library, Chicago, Illinois
Allen Family. Papers.

New-York Historical Society, New York
Bloor, Alfred J. Papers, 1848–1916.
Tripp, Charles A. Letters, 1864.

New York State Library, New York
Morgan, Edwin D. Papers, 1833–1883.

Ohio History Center Archives & Library, Columbus
Bennett-Stites-Fay Families. Papers.
Denig, George W. Memoirs.
Giffen Family. Correspondence.
Harry, John W. Correspondence.
Lundy, Sarah. Correspondence (1862–1865).
Mitchell, William B. Papers.
Smith, William Jay. Papers.
Stroman, Henry. Papers.

Oneida County Historical Society, Oneida, New York
Perry, Daniel. Papers.

Perry, Winfield M. Papers.

Rauner Special Collections Library, Dartmouth College, Hanover, New Hampshire
McCoy, John. Family Papers, 1847–1899.
Sargent, Ransom F., and Emily Maria, Civil War Papers, 1862.

Rubenstein Library, Duke University, Durham, North Carolina
Hedrick, Benjamin Sherwood. Papers.
Pickel, Adam H. Papers, 1859–1866.

Santa Clara University Library, Archives & Special Collections, Santa Clara, California
Reid, Bernard J. Collection 1827–1942.

Schlesinger Library, Harvard University, Cambridge, Massachusetts
Chamberlain-Adams Family. Papers.

Smithsonian Institution, Washington, DC
Mary Henry. Diary, 1858–1863.

Southern Historical Collection, Wilson Library, University of North Carolina, Chapel Hill
Baker, George Washington. Papers, 1856–1888.
Hale, Eben Thomas. Papers.

Special Collections, Chicago Public Library
American Civil War Documents, Manuscripts, Letters and Diaries Collections:
    Series 26: Flora Weaver, 1862–1865.
    Series 29: General Letters, 1847–1924.

Special Collections, University of Maryland Libraries, College Park
The Civil War in Maryland. Collection.

Special Collections, University of Washington Libraries, Seattle
Hoskinson, Riley M. Papers.

Special Collections and Archives, University of California Libraries, Santa Cruz
Fullerton, William B. Civil War Letters.

Special Collections & University Archives, University of Iowa Library, Iowa City
Wise-Clark Family. Papers.

Special Collections and University Archives, University of Massachusetts Amherst Libraries
Lyman Family. Papers.

Special Collections and Archives, Middlebury College Library
Quilty Family. Civil War Letters 1854–1896.

Special Collections and University Archives, Virginia Tech University, Blacksburg
Voltz, Felix. Letters.

Special Collections and University Archives, Wichita State University, Wichita, Kansas
Isely Family. Papers.

State Historical Society of Missouri, Columbia
Scott, Elvira A. W. Diary, 1860–1887.

US Army Heritage and Education Center, Carlisle, Pennsylvania
Ames, John W. Papers.
Fell, Albinus R. Letters. Civil War Document Collection.
Leigh, Lewis. Collection:
Early, Joseph. Letters.
Shorton, L. S. Letter.
Wheeler, A. C. T. Letter.

Vermont Historical Society, Barre
Harris, Albert. Papers, 1862–1869.

Virginia Historical Society, Richmond
Patch, George H. Papers, 1862–1864.

Wellesley College Special Collections, Wellesley, Massachusetts
Mitchill, Catharine. Family Letters.

Western History Collections, University of Oklahoma Libraries, Norman
Kroff, Charles. Diary.

Western Reserve Historical Society, Cleveland, Ohio
Cadwell, Darius. Papers.
Covert, Thomas. Papers.
Cozad, Justus Lafayette. Autobiographical Account.
Leggett, Marilla Wells. Papers.
Monks, Zerah Coston. Family Papers.
Rieley, Francis and John. Papers 1861–1865.

William Clements Library, University of Michigan, Ann Arbor
Anthony, George T. Papers (1858–1890). Schoff Civil War Collection.
Aplin Family. Papers. Schoff Civil War Collection.
Carleton, Thaddeus. Journal (1863). Schoff Civil War Collection.
Charleston (Illinois) Riot records, 1864.
Johnson, Henry J. Papers (1862–1865). Schoff Civil War Collection.
Keen Family. Letters.
Reed, Louisa A. Papers.
Tew, Charles F. Papers.
Wilder, Albert. Papers. Schoff Civil War Collection.

Wisconsin Historical Society, Madison
Bly, Adelbert. Papers.
Quiner, E. B. Scrapbooks.

York County History Center Library & Archives, York, Pennsylvania
Miller, George. Papers.

PUBLISHED STATE AND FEDERAL GOVERNMENT BOOKS AND DOCUMENTS
Baxter, J. H., compiler. *Statistics, Medical and Anthropological, of the Provost Marshal General's Bureau, Derived from Records of the Examination for Military Service in the*

Armies of the United States During the Late War of the Rebellion. 2 vols. Washington, DC: Government Printing Office, 1875.

Boynton, H. V., compiler. *Dedication of the Chickamauga and Chattanooga National Military Park, September 18–20, 1895.* Washington, DC: Government Printing Office, 1896.

Coakley, Robert W. *The Role of Federal Military Forces in Domestic Disorders, 1789–1878.* Washington, DC: US Army Center of Military History, 1988.

Floyd, Dale E., ed. *"Dear Friends at Home . . . ": The Letters and Diary of Thomas James Owen, Fiftieth New York Volunteer Engineer Regiment, During the Civil War.* Washington, DC: US Army Corps of Engineers, 1985.

Fry, James B. "Final Report Made to the Secretary of War by the Provost Marshal General." In *Executive Documents Printed by Order of the House of Representatives, 39th Congress, 1st session, 1865–66.* Washington, DC: Government Printing Office, 1866.

Gates, Paul W. *Free Homesteads for All Americans: The Homestead Act of 1862.* Washington, DC: Civil War Centennial Commission, 1962.

Hamlin, William E. *Report of the United States Provost Marshal of Rhode Island.* Providence, RI: Alfred Anthony Printer, 1863.

O'Brien, Thomas M. and Oliver Diefendorf, eds. *General Orders of the War Department, Embracing the Years 1861, 1862 & 1863.* 2 vols. New York: Derby & Miller, 1864.

State of Michigan. *Annual Report of the Adjutant and Q. M. General of the State of Michigan for the Year 1858.* Lansing, MI: Hosmer & Kerr, 1859.

———. *Annual Report of the Adjutant General of the State of Michigan for the Year 1862.* Lansing, MI: John A. Kerr, 1862.

———. *Annual Report of the Adjutant General of the State of Michigan for the Year 1863.* Lansing, MI: John A. Kerr, 1864.

State of Ohio. *Journal of the House of Representatives of the State of Ohio, for the Second Session of the Fifty-fifth General Assembly.* Vol. 59. Columbus, Ohio: Richard Nevins, 1863.

Terrell, W. H. H. *Indiana in the War of the Rebellion: Report of the Adjutant General.* 1869. Reprint, Indianapolis: Indiana Historical Bureau, 1960.

United States Congress. *Report of the Joint Committee on the Conduct of the War.* 9 vols. 1863–1866. Reprint, Wilmington, NC: Broadfoot Publishing Co., 1998–2002.

———. *Congressional Globe.* 37th Congress.

United States Constitution.

United States War Department. *Field Record of the Officers of the Veteran Reserve Corps, from the Commencement to the Close of the Rebellion.* Washington, DC: Scriver & Swing, 1865.

———. *The War of the Rebellion: A Compilation of the Official Records of the Union and Confederate Armies.* 128 vols. Washington, DC: Government Printing Office, 1881–1902.

———. *Official Records of the Union and Confederate Navies in the War of the Rebellion.* 30 vols. Washington, DC: Government Printing Office, 1894–1922.

NEWSPAPERS

Agitator (Pennsylvania)

American and Commercial Advertiser (Maryland)
American Presbyterian (Pennsylvania)
American Volunteer (Pennsylvania)
Bedford Gazette (Pennsylvania)
Bellows Falls Times (Vermont)
Boston Post (Massachusetts)
Bristol Phenix (Rhode Island)
Burlington Weekly Hawk-Eye (Iowa)
Butler American Citizen (Pennsylvania)
Cambridge Guernsey Jeffersonian (Ohio)
Cass County Republican (Michigan)
Cedar Falls Gazette (Iowa)
Centre Democrat (Pennsylvania)
Chatfield Democrat (Minnesota)
Chicago Daily Tribune (Illinois)
Cincinnati Daily Commercial (Ohio)
Cincinnati Daily Press (Ohio)
Cincinnati Enquirer (Ohio)
Clearfield Republican (Pennsylvania)
Cleveland Plain Dealer (Ohio)
Daily Democrat and News (Iowa)
Daily Gazette (Iowa)
Daily Green Mountain Freeman (Vermont)
Daily Ohio Statesman
Daily Pittsburgh Gazette (Pennsylvania)
Daily State Sentinel (Indiana)
Dayton Daily Empire (Ohio)
Defiance Democrat (Ohio)
Detroit Free Press (Michigan)
Dubuque Herald (Iowa)
East Saginaw Courier (Michigan)
Elkton Cecil Whig (Maryland)
Frank Leslie's Illustrated Newspaper
Franklin Visitor (New York)
Gallipolis Journal (Ohio)
Genesee Valley Free Press (New York)
Grand Haven News (Michigan)
Greencastle Banner (Indiana)
Highland Weekly News (Ohio)
Holmes County Republican (Ohio)
Illustrated London News
Indiana State Sentinel (Indiana)
Indianapolis Daily Journal (Indiana)
Jacksonville Journal (Illinois)

Joliet Signal (Illinois)
Lamoille Newsdealer (Vermont)
Lancaster Daily Intelligencer (Pennsylvania)
Logansport Journal (Indiana)
Macomb Weekly Journal (Illinois)
Miami County Sentinel (Indiana)
Morgan County Gazette (Indiana)
New Albany Daily Ledger (Indiana)
New York Daily Tribune
New York Herald
New York Times
New York World
North Carolina Presbyterian
Ohio Repository
Orleans Independent Standard (Vermont)
Ottawa Free Trader (Illinois)
Pennsylvania Daily Telegraph
Philadelphia Press (Pennsylvania)
Pittsburgh Gazette (Pennsylvania)
Portland Daily Press (Maine)
Putnam Republican Banner (Indiana)
Richmond Palladium (Indiana)
Rockland County Messenger (New York)
Rutland Herald (Vermont)
Saginaw Valley Republican (Michigan)
Saint Johnsbury Caledonian (Vermont)
Star of the North (Pennsylvania)
The Crisis (Ohio)
The Round Table (New York)
Union and Journal (Maine)
Valley Spirit (Pennsylvania)
Vanity Fair (New York)
Wall Street Journal (New York)
Waynesboro Village Record (Pennsylvania)
Western Reserve Chronicle (Ohio)

PUBLISHED PRIMARY SOURCES

Abernathy, Byron R., ed. *Private Elisha Stockwell, Jr. Sees the Civil War.* Norman: University of Oklahoma Press, 1958.

Albert, Allen D., ed. *History of the Forty-fifth Regiment Pennsylvania Veteran Volunteer Infantry 1861–1865.* Williamsport, PA: Grit Publishing Co., 1912.

Alcott, Louisa May. *Hospital Sketches.* Boston: James Redpath Publisher, 1863.

Aldridge, Katherine M., ed. *No Freedom Shrieker: The Civil War Letters of Union Soldier Charles Biddlecom.* Ithaca, NY: Paramount Market Publishing, 2012.

Allen, George H. *Forty-six Months with the Fourth R. I. Volunteers*. Providence, RI: J. A. & R. A. Reid, 1887.

Anderson, James H., ed. *Life and Letters of Judge Thomas J. Anderson and Wife*. Columbus, OH: F. J. Heer, 1904.

Athearn, Robert G., ed. *Soldier in the West: The Civil War Letters of Alfred Lacey Hough*. Philadelphia: University of Pennsylvania Press, 1957.

Baird, Nancy Disher, ed. *Josie Underwood's Civil War Diary*. Lexington: University Press of Kentucky, 2009.

Baker, Cheryl Jackson, ed. *Affectionately Yours: The Civil War Letters of William R. Jackson and His Wife Julia*. Monee, IL: Badgley Publishing, 2014.

Barker, Ernest, ed. *Dear Mother from Your Dutiful Son: Civil War Letters*. Goshen, CT: Purple Door Gallery Press, 2003.

Barnes, Thurlow Weed. *Memoir of Thurlow Weed*. 2 vols. Boston: Houghton, Mifflin and Co., 1884.

Barton, Michael, Carol Brockway-Lieto and Walter Reid Brockway, eds. *Noble Sentiments of the Soul: The Civil War Letters of Joseph Dobbs Bishop, Chief Musician, 23rd Connecticut Volunteer Infantry, 1862–1863*. Bloomington, IN: Xlibris, 2015.

Barton, Michael and Jessica Dorman, eds. *Harrisburg's Old Eighth Ward*. Charleston, SC: Arcadia Publishing, 2002.

Basler, Roy, ed. *The Collected Works of Abraham Lincoln*. 9 vols. New Brunswick, NJ: Rutgers University Press, 1953.

Beale, Howard K., ed. *The Diary of Edward Bates 1859–1866*. Vol. 4, Annual Report of the American Historical Association for the Year 1930. Washington, DC: Government Printing Office, 1933.

———. *Diary of Gideon Welles*. 3 vols. New York: W. W. Norton & Co., 1960.

Beatty, John. *The Citizen-Soldier; or, Memoirs of a Volunteer*. Cincinnati, OH: Wilstach, Baldwin & Co., 1879.

Belmont, August. *A Few Letters and Speeches of the Late Civil War*. New York: Privately printed, 1870.

Bender, Robert P., ed. *Like Grass before the Scythe: The Life and Death of Sgt. William Remmel, 121st New York Infantry*. Tuscaloosa: University of Alabama Press, 2007.

Bennett, Pamela J. and Richard A. Misselhorn, eds. "Curtis R. Burke's Civil War Journal." *Indiana Magazine of History* 66, no. 2 (1970): 110–72.

Billings, John D. *Hardtack & Coffee: Or The Unwritten Story of Army Life*. Boston: George M. Smith & Co., 1887.

Blake, Henry N. *Three Years in the Army of the Potomac*. Boston: Lee and Shepard, 1865.

Blakeslee, B. F. *History of the Sixteenth Connecticut Volunteers*. Hartford, CT: Case, Lockwood, & Brainard Co., 1875.

Blight, David W., ed. *When This Cruel War Is Over: The Civil War Letters of Charles Harvey Brewster*. Amherst: University of Massachusetts Press, 1992.

Bliss, David, ed. *Letters Home to Rehoboth: Bliss Family Writings & Genealogical History*. No place: self-published, 2017.

Blomquist, Ann K. and Robert A. Taylor, eds. *This Cruel War: The Civil War Letters of Grant and Malinda Taylor 1862–1865.* Macon, GA: Mercer University Press, 2000.

Blondheim, Menahem, ed. *Copperhead Gore: Benjamin Wood's Fort Lafayette and Civil War America.* Bloomington: Indiana University Press, 2006.

Bohrnstedt, Jennifer Cain, ed. *Soldiering with Sherman: The Civil War Letters of George F. Cram.* DeKalb: Northern Illinois University Press, 2000.

Bond, Otto F., ed. *Under the Flag of the Nation: Diaries and Letters of a Yankee Volunteer in the Civil War.* Columbus: Ohio State University Press for the Ohio Historical Society, 1961.

Bonner, Robert E. *The Soldier's Pen: Firsthand Impressions of the Civil War.* New York: Hill and Wang, 2006.

Bradley, Susan Hinckley, ed. *Leverett Bradley: A Soldier-Boy's Letters, 1862–1865.* Boston: Privately printed, 1905.

Briggs, John Ely. "Peter Wilson in the Civil War 1863–1865." *The Iowa Journal of History and Politics* 40, no. 4 (October 1942): 339–414.

Britton, Ann Hartwell and Thomas J. Reed. *To My Beloved Wife and Boy at Home: The Letters and Diaries of Orderly Sergeant John F. L. Hartwell.* Madison, NJ: Fairleigh Dickinson University Press, 1997.

Brooks, R. P. "Howell Cobb Papers." *The Georgia Historical Quarterly* 6, no. 4 (1922): 355–94.

Brown, George W. *Baltimore and the Nineteenth of April 1861: A Study of the War.* Baltimore, MD: Johns Hopkins University, 1887.

Bruen, Ella Jane and Brian M. Fitzgibbons, eds. *Through Ordinary Eyes: The Civil War Correspondence of Rufus Robbins, Private, 7th Regiment, Massachusetts Volunteers.* Westport, CT: Praeger Publishers, 2000.

Buckingham, Peter, ed. *All's for the Best: The Civil War Reminiscences and Letters of Daniel W. Sawtelle, Eighth Maine Volunteer Infantry.* Knoxville: University of Tennessee Press, 2001.

Burrows, Sarah Tracy and Ryan W. Keating, eds. *Yours Affectionately, Osgood: Colonel Osgood Vose Tracy's Letters Home from the Civil War, 1862–1865.* Kent, OH: Kent State University Press, 2022.

Burt, Silas W. *My Memoirs of the Military History of the State of New York during the War for the Union, 1861–65.* Albany, NY: J. B. Lyon Co., 1902.

Campbell, Eric, ed. *"A Grand Terrible Dramma": From Gettysburg to Petersburg: The Civil War Letters of Charles Wellington Reed.* New York: Fordham University Press, 2000.

Carter, Gari, ed. *Troubled State: Civil War Journals of Franklin Archibald Dick.* Kirksville, MO: Truman State University Press, 2008.

Castel, Albert. *Tom Taylor's Civil War.* Lawrence: University Press of Kansas, 2000.

Catlin, Janice Van Lente, ed. *Civil War Letters of Johannes Van Lente.* Okemos, MI: Yankee Girl Publications, 1992.

Censer, Jane Turner, ed. *The Papers of Frederick Law Olmsted, Vol. IV, Defending the Union.* Baltimore, MD: Johns Hopkins University Press, 1986.

Chamberlain, Joshua L. "Military Affairs in Maine." In *The Union Army: A History of Military Affairs in the Loyal States 1861–1865,* vol. 1, 20–38. 1908. Reprint, Wilmington, NC: Broadfoot Publishing Co., 1997.

Child, Lydia Marie. *Letters of Lydia Marie Child: With a Biographical Introduction.* Boston: Houghton, Mifflin and Co., 1883.

Church, Charles H. *Civil War Letters.* Rose City, MI: Rose City Area Historical Society, 1987.

Cleveland, Henry. *Alexander H. Stephens in Public and Private: With Letters and Speeches Before, During, and Since the War.* Philadelphia: National Publishing Co., 1866.

Coles, David J. and Stephen A. Engle, eds. *A Yankee Horseman in the Shenandoah Valley: The Civil War Letters of John H. Black, Twelfth Pennsylvania Cavalry.* Knoxville: University of Tennessee Press, 2012.

Collier, Ellen C., ed. *Letters of a Civil War Soldier: Chandler B. Gillam, 28th New York Volunteers.* Bloomington, IN: Xlibris, 2005.

Cook, Frederick F. *Bygone Days in Chicago: Recollections of the "Garden City" of the Sixties.* Chicago: A. C. McClurg & Co., 1910.

Cook, Judy, ed. *A Quiet Corner of the War: The Civil War Letters of Gilbert and Esther Claflin, Oconomowoc, Wisconsin, 1862–1863.* Madison: University of Wisconsin, Press, 2013.

Cox, Jacob D. "War Preparations in the North." In *Battles & Leaders of the Civil War,* vol. 1, edited by Robert Johnson and Clarence Buel, 84–98. New York: The Century Co., 1887.

Cox, Samuel S. *Eight Years in Congress, from 1857–1865: Memoir and Speeches.* New York: D. Appleton and Company, 1865.

Crist, Lynda Lasswell, ed. *The Papers of Jefferson Davis.* 14 vols. Baton Rouge: Louisiana State University Press, 1971–2015.

Croner, Barbara M. *A Sergeant's Story: Civil War Diary of Jacob J. Zorn 1862–1865.* Apollo, PA: Closson Press, 2011.

Crowell, Joseph E. *The Young Volunteer: The Everyday Experiences of a Soldier Boy in the Civil War.* New York: G. W. Dillingham Co., 1906.

Cryder, George R. and Stanley R. Miller, compilers. *A View from the Ranks: The Civil War Diaries of Corporal Charles E. Smith.* Delaware, OH: Delaware County Historical Society, 1999.

Davis, Barbara Butler, ed. *Affectionately Yours: The Civil War Home-Front Letters of the Ovid Butler Family.* Indianapolis: Indiana Historical Society Press, 2004.

Davis, Jack C., ed. *Dear Wife: The Civil War Letters of a Private Soldier.* Louisville, KY: Sulgrave Press, 1992.

DeRosier Jr., Arthur H., ed. *Through the South with a Union Soldier.* Johnson City: East Tennessee State University Research Advisory Council, 1969.

De Tocqueville, Alexis. *Democracy in America.* 2 vols. 1835, 1840. Reprint, Cambridge, MA: Sever and Francis, 1864.

De Trobriand, Regis. *Four Years with the Army of the Potomac.* Boston: Ticknor and Co., 1888.

Donald, David Herbert, ed. *Gone for a Soldier: The Civil War Memoirs of Private Alfred Bellard*. Boston: Little, Brown and Co., 1975.

Donohoe, Patricia A., ed. *The Printer's Kiss: The Life and Letters of a Civil War Newspaperman and his Family*. Kent, OH: Kent State University Press, 2014.

Dupree, A. Hunter and Leslie H. Fishel Jr. "An Eyewitness Account of the New York Draft Riots, July, 1863." *The Mississippi Valley Historical Review* 47, no. 3 (Dec. 1960): 472–79.

Early, Jubal A. *The Campaigns of Gen. Robert E. Lee: An Address by Lieut. General Jubal A. Early before Washington and Lee University, January 19th, 1872*. Baltimore, MD: John Murphy & Co., 1872.

Edmonds, S. Emma. *The Female Spy of the Union Army*. Boston: De Wolfe, Fiske, & Co., 1864.

Elder, Donald C., ed. *Love amid the Turmoil: The Civil War Letters of William and Mary Vermilion*. Iowa City: University of Iowa Press, 2003.

Engs, Robert F. and Corey M. Brooks, eds. *Their Patriotic Duty: The Civil War Letters of the Evans Family of Brown County, Ohio*. New York: Fordham University Press, 2007.

Enoch, Harry G., ed. "One Man's Experience in a One Hundred Day Regiment: Barzilla R. Shaw and the 143d Ohio Volunteer Infantry." *Ohio History Journal* 107 (Summer–Autumn 1998): 185–201.

Escott, Paul D. *"What Shall We Do with the Negro?": Lincoln, White Racism, and Civil War America*. Charlottesville: University of Virginia Press, 2009.

Ewing, Wallace K., ed. *From Home to Trench: The Civil War Letters of Mack and Nan Ewing 1856–1865*. Grand Haven, MI: self-published, 2011.

Farquhar, Arthur B. *The First Million the Hardest: An Autobiography*. Garden City, NY: Doubleday, Page & Co., 1922.

Favill, Josiah M. *The Diary of a Young Officer*. Chicago: R. R. Donnelly & Sons, 1909.

Feidner, Edward, ed. *"Dear Wife": The Civil War Letters of Chester K. Leach*. Burlington: Center for Research on Vermont, 2002.

Fiske, Samuel W. *Mr. Dunn Browne's Experiences in the Army*. Boston: Nichols and Noyes, 1866.

Flannery, Michael A. and Katherine H. Oomens, eds. *Well Satisfied with My Position: The Civil War Journal of Spencer Bonsall*. Carbondale: Southern Illinois University Press, 2007.

Flotow, Mark, ed. *In Their Letters, In Their Words: Illinois Civil War Soldiers Write Home*. Carbondale: Southern Illinois University Press, 2019.

Folmar, John Kent, ed. "Pre–Civil War Sentiment from Belmont County: Correspondence of Hugh Anderson." *Ohio History Journal* 78, no. 3 (1969): 202–10.

Ford, Worthington Chauncey, ed. *A Cycle of Adams Letters, 1861–1865*. 2 vols. Boston: Houghton Mifflin Co., 1920.

Foroughi, Andrea R., ed. *Go If You Think It Your Duty: A Minnesota Couple's Civil War Letters*. St. Paul: Minnesota Historical Society Press, 2008.

Fremantle, Arthur J. *Three Months in the Southern States*. New York: John Bradburn, 1864.

Fry, James B. *New York and the Conscription of 1863*. New York: G. P. Putnam's Sons, 1885.

Gates, Betsey, ed. *The Colton Letters: Civil War Period 1861–1865.* Scottsdale, AZ: McLane Publications, 1993.

Gerrish, Theodore. *Army Life: A Private's Reminiscences of the Civil War.* Portland, ME: Hoyt, Fogg & Donham, 1882.

Gilbert Sr., Daniel R. *Freddy's War: The Civil War Letters of John Frederick Frueauff.* Bethlehem, PA: Moravian College, 2006.

Glaza-Herrington, Linda. *Dear Brother and Sister: Smith-Haviland-Cadwell Fourth Michigan Infantry Civil War Letters.* Grand Rapids, MI: Chapbook Press, 2012.

Goodell, Robert C. and P. A. M. Taylor. "A German Immigrant in the Union Army: Selected Letters of Valentin Bechler." *Journal of American Studies* 4, no. 2 (1971): 145–62.

Goodrich, James W., ed. "Civil War Letters of Bethiah Pyatt McKown, Pts. 1 and 2." *Missouri Historical Review* 67 (January and April 1973): 227–52 and 351–70.

Gordon, Seth C. "The Attitude of the Women of the North and South during and Since the War of the Rebellion" in *War Papers: Read Before the Commandery of the State of Maine, Military Order of the Loyal Legion of the United States, Vol. 4.* Self-published: Lefavor-Tower Company, 1915.

Goss, Warren Lee. "Going to the Front." In *Battles & Leaders of the Civil War*, vol. 1, edited by Robert Johnson and Clarence Buel, 149–59. New York: The Century Co., 1887.

Grant, Ulysses S. *Memoirs and Selected Letters.* New York: Library of America, 1990.

Greene, William B. *Letters from a Sharpshooter: The Civil War Letters of Private William B. Greene.* Belleville, WI: Historic Publications, 1993.

Greenleaf, Margery, ed. *Letters to Eliza from a Union Soldier, 1862–1865.* Chicago: Follett Publishing Co., 1970.

Gregory, John G. "The John Jay Orton Papers." *The Wisconsin Magazine of History* 7, no. 2 (1923): 172–88.

Greiner, James M., Janet L. Coryell and James R. Smither, eds. *A Surgeon's Civil War: The Letters and Diary of Daniel M. Holt, M. D.* Kent, OH: Kent State University Press, 1994.

Gunn, Angus M., ed. *One Man's War: The Civil War Letters of John Large.* West Vancouver, British Columbia: Legacy Press, 1985.

Gurowski, Adam. *Diary, from March 4, 1861 to November 12, 1862.* Boston: Lee and Shepard, 1862.

———. *Diary: 1863–'64–'65.* Washington, DC: W. H. and O. H. Morrison, 1866.

Haas, Ralph. *Dear Esther: The Civil War Letters of Private Aungier Dobbs.* Apollo, PA: Closson Press, 1991.

Hall, Henry. *Cayuga in the Field: A Record of the 19th New York Volunteers, and 3rd New York Artillery.* Auburn, NY: self-published, 1873.

Hamilton, Henry S. *Reminiscences of a Veteran.* Concord, NH: Republican Press Association, 1897.

Hammond, Harold Earl, ed. *Diary of a Union Lady 1861–1865.* New York: Funk & Wagnalls Co., 1962.

Hanchett, William and Joshua Nichols Speed. "An Illinois Physician and the Civil War Draft, 1864–1865 Letters of Dr. Joshua Nichols Speed." *Journal of the Illinois State Historical Society* 59, no. 2 (1966): 143–60.

Hancock, Harold, ed. "Alexander B. Cooper's Civil War Memories of Camden." *Delaware History* 20, no. 1 (Spring–Summer 1982): 50–72.

Hard, Abner. *History of the Eighth Cavalry Regiment, Illinois Volunteers, During the Great Rebellion.* Aurora, IL: none stated, 1868.

Harris, NiNi. *A Most Unsettled State: First-Person Accounts of St. Louis during the Civil War.* St. Louis, MO: Reedy Press, 2013.

Hauranne, Ernest Duvergier. *A Frenchman in Lincoln's America.* 2 vols. Chicago: R. R. Donnelley & Sons Co., 1974.

Haynes, Martin A. *A History of the Second Regiment, New Hampshire Volunteer Infantry, in the War of the Rebellion.* Lakeport, NH: self-published, 1896.

———. *A Minor War History Compiled from a Soldier Boy's Letters to "The Girl I Left Behind Me," 1861–1864.* Lakeport, NH: privately printed, 1916.

Heidelbaugh, Lynn and Thomas J. Paone, eds. *Between Home and the Front: Civil War Letters of the Walters Family.* Bloomington: Indiana University Press, 2022.

Heindel, Ned D., ed. *The 1863 Diary of Beates R. Swift: A Year in the Life of an Easton Youth during the Civil War.* Easton, PA: Northampton County Historical & Genealogical Society, 2004.

Helmreich, Jonathan E., ed. *To Petersburg with the Army of the Potomac: The Civil War Letters of Levi Bird Duff, 105th Pennsylvania Volunteers.* Jefferson, NC: McFarland & Co., 2009.

Hicks, Borden M. "Personal Recollections of the War of the Rebellion." in *Glimpses of the Nation's Struggle: Papers Read before the Minnesota Commandery of the Military Order of the Loyal Legion of the United States*, 6th series. Minneapolis, MN: August Davis, Publisher, 1909.

Hinkley, Julian W. *A Narrative of Service with the Third Wisconsin Infantry.* Madison: Wisconsin Historical Commission, 1912.

Hoffman, Elliott W., ed. *A Vermont Cavalryman in War and Love: The Civil War Letters of Brevet Major General William Wells and Anna Richardson.* Lynchburg, VA: Schroeder Publications, 2007.

Hogan, Sally Coplen, ed. *General Reub Williams's Memories of Civil War Times: Personal Reminiscences of Happenings that Took Place from 1861 to the Grand Review.* Westminster, MD: Heritage Books, 2006.

Hoke, Jacob. *The Great Invasion of 1863; or, General Lee in Pennsylvania.* Dayton, OH: W. J. Shuey, Publisher, 1887.

Holmes, Oliver Wendell. *The Poems of Oliver Wendell Holmes.* Boston: Ticknor and Fields, 1863.

Holmes Jr., Oliver Wendell. *The Common Law.* Boston: Little, Brown and Co., 1881.

Holtmann, Antonius, ed. *A Lost American Dream: Civil War Letters (1862/63) of Immigrant Theodor Heinrich Brandes in Historical Contexts.* Indianapolis: Max Kade German-American Center & Indiana German Heritage Society, 2005.

Houston, Alan Fraser, ed. *Keep Up Good Courage: A Yankee Family and the Civil War.* Portsmouth, NH: Peter E. Randall Publisher, 2006.

Hughes, William E., ed. *The Civil War Papers of Lt. Col. Newton T. Colby, New York Infantry.* Jefferson, NC: McFarland & Co., 2003.

James, James R., ed. *To See the Elephant: The Civil War Letters of John A. McKee (1861–1865).* Leawood, KS: Leathers Pub., 1998.

Jewell, James Robbins, ed. *On Duty in the Pacific Northwest during the Civil War: Correspondence and Reminiscences of the First Oregon Cavalry Regiment.* Knoxville, University of Tennessee Press, 2018.

Johns, Henry T. *Life with the Forty-ninth Massachusetts Volunteers.* Pittsfield, MA: self-published, 1864.

Jones, John B. *A Rebel War Clerk's Diary at the Confederate States Capital.* 2 vols. Philadelphia: J. B. Lippincott, 1866.

Josyph, Peter, ed. *The Wounded River: The Civil War Letters of John Vance Lauderdale, M.D.* East Lansing: Michigan State University Press, 1993.

Judson, Amos M. *History of the 83rd Regiment Pennsylvania Volunteers.* Erie, PA: B. F. H. Lynn, 1865.

Kamphoefner, Walter D. and Wolfgang Helbich, eds. *Germans in the Civil War: The Letters They Wrote Home.* Chapel Hill: University of North Carolina Press, 2006.

Karamanski, Theodore J. and Eileen M. McMahon, eds. *Civil War Chicago: Eyewitness to History.* Athens: Ohio University Press, 2014.

Keating, Ryan W., ed. *The Greatest Trials I Ever Had: The Civil War Letters of Margaret and Thomas Cahill.* Athens: University of Georgia Press, 2017.

Kiefer, W. R. *History of the One Hundred and Fifty-third Regiment Pennsylvania Volunteers Infantry.* Easton, PA: Chemical Publishing, 1909.

Kiper, Richard L., ed. *Dear Catharine, Dear Taylor: The Civil War Letters of a Union Soldier to His Wife.* Lawrence: University Press of Kansas, 2002.

Kirkland, Caroline M. *A Few Words in Behalf of the Loyal Women of the United States by One of Themselves.* New York: Loyal Publication Society, 1863.

Kohl, Lawrence F., ed. *Irish Green and Union Blue: The Civil War Letters of Peter Welsh.* New York: Fordham University Press, 1986.

———. *The Politics of Individualism: Parties and the American Character in the Jacksonian Era.* 1989. Reprint, New York: Oxford University Press, 1991.

Krug, Mark M., ed. *Mrs. Hill's Journal—Civil War Reminiscences.* Chicago: The Lakeside Press, 1980.

Laas, Virginia Jeans, ed. *Wartime Washington: The Civil War Letters of Elizabeth Blair Lee.* Urbana: University of Illinois Press, 1991.

Lapham, William B. *My Recollections of the War of the Rebellion.* Augusta, ME: Burleigh & Flynt, 1892.

Larimer, Charles F., ed. *Love and Valor: The Intimate Civil War Letters between Captain Jacob and Emeline Ritner.* Western Springs, IL: Sigourney Press, 2000.

Larson, Michael J. and John David Smith, eds. *Dear Delia: The Civil War Letters of Captain Henry F. Young, Seventh Wisconsin Infantry.* Madison: University of Wisconsin Press, 2019.

Law, Evander M. "From the Wilderness to Cold Harbor." In *Battles & Leaders of the Civil War*, vol. 4. New York: The Century Co., 1888.

Lensink, Judy N., ed. *"A Secret to Be Burried": The Diary and Life of Emily Hawley Gillespie, 1858–1888*. Iowa City: University of Iowa Press, 1989.

Lewis, A. S., ed. *My Dear Parents: The Civil War Seen By an English Union Soldier*. New York: Harcourt Brace Jovanovich, Publishers, 1982.

Livingstone, Charles B., ed. *Charlie's Civil War: A Private's Trial by Fire in the 5th New York Volunteers and 146th New York Volunteer Infantry*. Gettysburg, PA: Thomas Pub., 1997.

Lockwood, John. *Our Campaign around Gettysburg: Being a Memorial of What Was Endured, Suffered, and Accomplished by the Twenty-third Regiment (N.Y.S.N.G.) and Other Regiments Associated with Them*. Brooklyn, NY: A. H. Rome & Brothers, 1864.

Lodge, Henry Cabot. *Early Memories*. New York: Charles Scribner's Sons, 1913.

Logan, Mrs. John A. *Reminiscences of a Soldier's Wife: An Autobiography*. New York: Charles Scribner's Sons, 1913.

Longacre, Edward G., ed. "'Come Home Soon and Don't Delay': Letters from the Home Front, July, 1861." *Pennsylvania Magazine of History and Biography* 100, no. 3 (July 1976): 395–406.

———. *From Antietam to Fort Fisher: The Civil War Letters of Edward King Wightman, 1862–1865*. Rutherford, NJ: Fairleigh Dickinson University Press, 1985.

Lowenfels, Walter, ed. *Walt Whitman's Civil War*. New York: Alfred Knopf, 1961.

Macsherry, Helen Drury, ed. *Pastime: Life & Love on the Homefront during the Civil War, 1861–1865*. Union Mills, MD: Union Mills Homestead Foundation, 2013.

Mannis, Jedediah and Galen R. Wilson, eds. *Bound to Be a Soldier: The Letters of Private James T. Miller, 111th Pennsylvania Infantry, 1861–1864*. Knoxville: University of Tennessee Press, 2001.

Marchand, Ernest. *News from Fort Craig, New Mexico, 1863: Civil War Letters of Andrew Ryan*. Santa Fe, NM: Stagecoach Press, 1966.

Marks, Bayly Ellen and Mark Norton Schatz, eds. *Between North and South: A Maryland Journalist Views the Civil War: The Narrative of William Wilkins Glenn, 1861–1869. Rutherford, NJ: Fairleigh Dickinson University Press, 1976*.

Marlatt, Helen S. M., ed. *Stuart Letters of Robert and Elizabeth Sullivan Stuart and Their Children, 1819–1864*. 2 vols. N.p.: privately printed, 1961.

Marshall, Jeffrey D., ed. *A War of the People: Vermont Civil War Letters*. Hanover, NH: University Press of New England, 1999.

Martin, Edward Sandford. *The Life of Joseph Hodges Choate, as Gathered Chiefly from His Letters*. 2 vols. London: Constable and Co., 1920.

Massachusetts Historical Society. "Dalton Letters." In *Proceedings of the Massachusetts Historical Society*, vol. 56. Boston: self-published, 1923.

Matthews, William and Dixon Wecter. *Our Soldiers Speak 1775–1918*. Boston: Little, Brown and Co., 1943.

Mayberry, Virginia and Dawn E. Bakken, eds. "The Civil War Home Front: Diary of a Young Girl, 1862–1863." *Indiana Magazine of History* 87 (March 1991): 24–78.

Mayhue, Justin T. *A Civil War Journey: The Letters of John W. Brendel.* Hagerstown, MD: self-published, 2006.

McAvoy, Thomas. "The War Letters of Father Peter Paul Cooney of the Congregation of Holy Cross (Continued)." *Records of the American Catholic Historical Society of Philadelphia* 44, no. 3 (1933): 220–37.

McCabe Jr., Selden P., ed. *The Civil War: A Soldier's Letters Home 1861–1863.* Bloomington, IN: Xlibris, 2009.

McCune, Julia, ed., *Mary Austin Wallace: Her Diary, 1862.* Lansing: Michigan Civil War Centennial Observance Commission, 1963.

Mcelligott, Mary Ellen, ed. "'A Monotony Full of Sadness': The Diary of Nadine Turchin, May, 1863–April, 1864." *Journal of the Illinois State Historical Society* 70, no. 1 (1977): 27–89.

McManus, Christopher D., Thomas H. Inglis and Otho J. Hicks, eds. *Morning to Midnight in the Saddle: Civil War Letters of a Soldier in Wilder's Lightning Brigade.* Bloomington, IN: Xlibris, 2012.

McMurtry, Gerald, ed. "Everybody is afraid of being drafted . . ." *Lincoln Lore* no. 1564 (June 1968).

McOwen, Mary Ellen, ed. Seven Months a Soldier: A Civil War Story Told by the Letters of Pvt. Arnold Southwick and Mariah Harper Southwick. Bloomington, IN: AuthorHouse, 2014.

Meade, George. *The Life and Letters of George Gordon Meade.* 2 vols. New York: Charles Scribner's Sons, 1913.

Melville, Herman. *Battle-Pieces and Aspects of the War.* New York: Harper & Brothers, 1866.

Merrill, H. T., composer. "Take Your Gun and Go, John." Chicago: Root & Cady, 1863.

Michie, Peter. "Reminiscences of Cadet and Army Service." In *Personal Recollections of the War of the Rebellion: Addresses Delivered Before the New York Commandery of the Loyal Legion of the United States*, vol. 2. New York: G. P. Putnam's Sons, 1897.

Miller, Delavan S. *Drum Taps in Dixie: Memories of a Drummer Boy 1861–1865.* Waterford, NY: Hungerford-Holbrook Co., 1905.

Miller, Edwin Haviland, ed. *The Collected Writings of Walt Whitman: The Correspondence. Vol. 1.* New York: New York University Press, 1961.

Mohr, James C., ed. *The Cormany Diaries: A Northern Family in the Civil War.* Pittsburgh, PA: University of Pittsburgh Press, 1982.

Morse, Charles F. *Letters Written During the Civil War, 1861–1865.* No place: Privately printed, 1898.

Murphy, Kevin C., ed. *The Civil War Letters of Joseph K. Taylor of the Thirty-Seventh Massachusetts Volunteer Infantry.* Lewiston, NY: Edwin Mellen Press, 1998.

Mushkat, Jerome, ed. *A Citizen Soldier's Civil War: The Letters of Brevet Major General Alvin C. Voris.* DeKalb: Northern Illinois University Press, 2002.

Nash, Linnabell H. *Civil War Letters of Jabez L. Huntley to Amy Huntley, 1862–1864.* Whiting, KS: Privately printed, 1962.

Nevins, Allen, ed. *A Diary of Battle: The Personal Journals of Colonel Charles S. Wainwright, 1861–1865.* New York: Harcourt, Brace, & World, 1962.

———. *Diary of the Civil War 1860–1865: George Templeton Strong*. New York: Macmillan Co., 1962.

Newman, Simon P. "A Democrat in Lincoln's Army: The Civil War Letters of Henry P. Hubbell." *The Princeton University Library Chronicle* 50, no. 2 (1989): 155–68.

Nicolay, John G. and John Hay. *Abraham Lincoln: A History*. 10 vols. New York: The Century Co., 1890.

Olcott, Henry S. "The War's Carnival of Fraud." In *The Annals of the War Written by Leading Participants North and South*, 705–23. Philadelphia, PA: Times Publishing, 1878.

O'Leary, Jenny and Harvey H. Jackson. "The Civil War Letters of Captain Daniel O'Leary, U.S.A." *The Register of the Kentucky Historical Society* 77, no. 3 (1979): 157–85.

Orr, Timothy J., ed. *Last to Leave the Field: The Life and Letters of First Sergeant Ambrose Henry Hayward, 28th Pennsylvania Volunteers*. Knoxville: University of Tennessee Press, 2011.

O'Shaughnessy, Mary Searing, ed. *Alonzo's War: Letters from a Young Civil War Soldier*. Lanham, MD: Fairleigh Dickinson University Press, 2012.

Palladino, Anita, ed. *Diary of a Yankee Engineer: The Civil War Story of John H. Westervelt, Engineer, 1st New York Volunteer Engineer Corps*. New York: Fordham University Press, 1997.

Patrick, Jeffrey L. and Robert J. Willey, eds. *Fighting for Liberty and Right: The Civil War Diary of William Bluffton Miller, First Sergeant, Company K, Seventy-Fifth Indiana Volunteer Infantry*. Knoxville: University of Tennessee Press, 2005.

Pease, Theodore C. and James G. Randall, eds. *The Diary of Orville Hickman Browning, Volume I, 1850–1864*. Springfield: Illinois State Historical Library, 1927.

Peck, George W. *How Private George W. Peck Put Down the Rebellion*. Chicago: Belford, Clarke & Co., 1887.

Pelka, Fred, ed. *The Civil War Letters of Colonel Charles F. Johnson, Invalid Corps*. Amherst: University of Massachusetts Press, 2004.

Phelan, Helene C., ed. *Tramping Out the Vintage, 1861–1864: The Civil War Diaries and Letters of Eugene Kingman*. Interlaken, NY: Heart of the Lakes Publishing, 1983.

———. *Who Only Stand and Wait: Civil War Letters of David and Ann Smith 1863–1865*. Interlaken, NY: Heart of the Lakes Publishing, 1990.

Phillips, Marion G. and Valerie Phillips Parsegian, eds. *Richard and Rhoda: Letters from the Civil War*. Washington, DC: Legation Press, 1981.

Polner, Murray and Thomas E. Woods Jr. *We Who Dared to Say No to War*. New York: Basic Books, 2008.

Priest, John M., ed. *Turn Them Out to Die Like a Mule: The Civil War Letters of John N. Henry, 49th New York, 1861–1865*. Leesburg, VA: Gauley Mount Press, 1995.

Putnam, George Haven. *Memories of My Youth, 1844–1865*. New York: G. P. Putnam's Sons, 1914.

Rankin, Charles E., ed. *Toward a More Perfect Union: The Civil War Letters of Frederic and Elizabeth Lockley*. Lincoln: University of Nebraska Press, 2023.

Reinhart, Joseph R., ed. *Two Germans in the Civil War: The Diary of John Daeuble and the Letters of Gottfried Rentschler, 6th Kentucky Volunteer Infantry.* Knoxville: University of Tennessee Press, 2004.

Reiss, Stephen W., ed. *It Takes a Matriarch: 780 Family Letters from 1852 to 1888 Including Civil War, Farming in Illinois, Life in St. Louis, Life in Sacramento, Life in the Theater, Wagon Making in Davenport, and the Lost Family Fortune.* Bloomington, IN: AuthorHouse, 2009.

Rhoades, Nancy L. and Lucy E. Bailey, eds. *Wanted—Correspondence: Women's Letters to a Union Soldier.* Athens: Ohio University Press, 2009.

Richards, Caroline Cowles. *Village Life in America 1852–1872.* New York: Henry Holt and Co., 1913.

Roberts, Timothy Mason, ed. *"This Infernal War": The Civil War Letters of William and Jane Standard.* Kent, OH: Kent State University Press, 2018.

Robertson Jr., James I. *The Civil War Letters of General Robert McAllister.* New Brunswick, NJ: Rutgers University Press, 1965.

Rood, Hosea W. *Story of the Service of Company E and the Twelfth Wisconsin Regiment.* Milwaukee, WI: Swain & Tate, 1893.

Roth, Margaret Brobst, ed. *Well Mary: Civil War Letters of a Wisconsin Volunteer.* Madison: University of Wisconsin Press, 1960.

Rundell Jr., Walter, ed. "'Despotism of Traitors': The Rebellious South Through New York Eyes." *New York History* 45, no. 4 (1964): 331–67.

Sala, George A. *My Diary in America in the Midst of War.* 2 vols. London: Tinsley Bros., 1865.

Saltonstall, William Gurdon. *Reminiscences of the Civil War and Autobiography.* No place: privately printed, 1913.

Sanborn, Alvan F., ed. *Reminiscences of Richard Lathers: Sixty Years of a Busy Life in South Carolina, Massachusetts and New York.* New York: Grafton Press, 1907.

Sauers, Richard A., ed. *The Civil War Journal of Colonel William J. Bolton 51st Pennsylvania.* Conshohocken, PA: Combined Publishing, 2000.

Sears, Stephen, ed. *For Country, Cause & Leader: The Civil War Journal of Charles B. Haydon.* New York: Ticknor & Fields, 1993.

Seward, Frederick W. *Seward at Washington as Senator and Secretary of State: A Memoir of His Life, with Selections from His Letters, 1861–1872.* New York: Derby and Miller, 1891.

Sheldon, Mrs. Georgie. *Sibyl's Influence; Or, the Missing Link.* New York: Street & Smith Publishers, 1888.

Sherman, Caroline B., ed. "A New England Boy in the Civil War." *The New England Quarterly* 5, no. 2 (1932): 310–44.

Sherman, S. M. *History of the 133d Regiment, O. V. I. and Incidents Connected with its Service during the "War of the Rebellion."* Columbus, OH: Champlin Printing Co., 1896.

Silber, Nina and Mary Beth Sievens. *Yankee Correspondence: Civil War Letters between New England Soldiers and the Home Front.* Charlottesville: University Press of Virginia, 1996.

Silliker, Ruth, ed. *The Rebel Yell & the Yankee Hurrah: The Civil War Journal of a Maine Volunteer.* Camden, ME: Down East Books, 2014.

Simpson, Brooks D. and Jean V. Berlin, eds. *Sherman's Civil War: Selected Correspondence of William T. Sherman, 1860–1865.* Chapel Hill: University of North Carolina Press, 1999.

Simpson, Brooks D., Stephen W. Sears and Aaron Sheehan-Dean, eds. *The Civil War: The First Year Told by Those Who Lived It.* New York: Literary Classics of the United States, 2011.

Skinner, J. F. *Little Incidents of the Battle of Lexington, Mo. by the Old Fife Major.* Wichita, KS: Eagle Press, 1890.

Skipper, Marti and Jane Taylor, eds. *A Handful of Providence: The Civil War Letters of Lt. Richard Goldwaite, New York Volunteers, and Ellen Goldwaite.* Jefferson, NC: McFarland & Co., 2004.

Smith, Hampton, ed. *Brother of Mine: The Civil War Letters of Thomas and William Christie.* St. Paul: Minnesota Historical Society Press, 2011.

Smith, Henry B. *Between the Lines: Secret Service Stories Told Fifty Years After.* New York: Booz Brothers, 1911.

Soman, Jean P. and Frank L. Byrne, eds. *A Jewish Colonel in the Civil War: Marcus M. Spiegel of the Ohio Volunteers.* 1985. Reprint, Lincoln, NE: Bison Books, 1995.

Stanley, Carry. "The Volunteer's Wife." *Peterson's Magazine* 40, no. 4 (1861): 256–59.

Stillwell, Leander. *The Story of a Common Soldier of Army Life in the Civil War, 1861–1865.* N.p.: Franklin Hudson Publishing, 1920.

Stoddard, William O. *Inside the White House in War Times.* New York: Charles L. Webster & Co., 1890.

Stone, Charles P. "Washington on the Eve of War." In *Battles & Leaders of the Civil War*, vol. 1, edited by Robert Johnson and Clarence Buel, 7–25. New York: The Century Co., 1887.

Styple, William B., ed. *Writing and Fighting the Civil War: Soldier Letters from the Battlefront.* Kearny, NJ: Belle Grove Publishing Co., 2004.

Sutherland, Kate. "The Laggard Recruit." *Arthur's Home Magazine* 19 (January–June 1862): 9–12.

Taber, Thomas R., ed. *Hard Breathing Days: The Civil War Letters of Cora Beach Benton.* Albion, NY: Almeron Press, 2003.

Tatum, Margaret Black. "'Please Send Stamps': The Civil War Letters of William Allen Clark Part III." *Indiana Magazine of History* 91, no. 3 (1995): 288–320.

Throne, Mildred, ed. *The Civil War Diary of Cyrus F. Boyd, Fifteenth Iowa Infantry, 1861–1863.* 1953. Reprint, Baton Rouge: Louisiana State University Press, 1998.

———. "Iowa Doctor in Blue: The Letters of Seneca B. Thrall, 1862–1864." *Iowa Journal of History* 58, no. 2 (1960): 97–188.

Tyler, Mason Whiting. *Recollections of the Civil War.* New York: G. P. Putnam's Sons, 1912.

Union League Club. *In Memoriam, Henry Whitney Bellows D.D.: New York, April 13, 1882.* New York: Union League Club, 1882.

Vallandigham, Clement L. *The Record of Hon. C. L. Vallandigham on Abolition, the Union, and the Civil War.* Columbus, OH: J. Walter & Co., 1863.

Van Alstyne, Lawrence. *Diary of an Enlisted Man*. New Haven, CT: Tuttle, Morehouse & Taylor, 1910.

Verter, Bradford. "Disconsolations of a Jersey Muskrat: The Civil War Letters of Symmes H. Stillwell." *The Princeton University Library Chronicle* 58, no. 2 (1997): 231–72.

Volwiler, A. T., ed. "Letters from a Civil War Officer." *The Mississippi Valley Historical Review* 14, no. 4 (1928): 508–29.

Wallace, Isabel. *Life & Letters of General W. H. L. Wallace*. Chicago: R. A. Donnelley & Sons Co., 1909.

Walton, William. *A Civil War Courtship: The Letters of Edwin Weller from Antietam to Atlanta*. Garden City, NY: Doubleday & Co., 1980.

Ward, Artemus. *Letters of Artemus Ward to Charles E. Wilson 1858–1861*. Cleveland, OH: The Rowfant Club, 1900.

Ward, Eric. *Army Life in Virginia: The Civil War Letters of George G. Benedict*. Mechanicsburg, PA: Stackpole Books, 2002.

White, Jonathan, ed. *A Philadelphia Perspective: The Civil War Diary of Sidney George Fisher*. New York: Fordham University Press, 2007.

White, Jonathan W. and Daniel Glenn, eds. *Untouched by the Conflict: The Civil War Letters of Singleton Ashenfelter, Dickinson College*. Kent, OH: Kent State University Press, 2019.

Whiteaker, Larry H. and W. Calvin Dickinson, eds. *Civil War Letters of the Tenure Family, Rockland County, New York 1862–1865*. New City, NY: Historical Society of Rockland County, 1990.

Whitman, Walt. *Specimen Days & Collect*. Philadelphia: David McKay, 1882.

Wickman, Donald H., ed. *Letters to Vermont from Her Civil War Soldier Correspondents to the Home Press, Vol. 1*. Bennington, VT: Images from the Past, 1998.

Wilder, Frank, composer. "The Invalid Corps." Boston: Henry S. Tolman & Co., 1863.

Wilkeson, Frank. *Recollections of a Private Soldier in the Army of the Potomac*. New York: G. P. Putnam's Sons, 1886.

Wilkie, Franc B. *The Iowa First: Letters from the War*. Dubuque, IA: Herald Book & Job, 1861.

———. *Pen and Powder*. Boston: Ticknor and Co., 1888.

Wills, Charles W. *Army Life of an Illinois Soldier*. Washington, DC: Globe Printing, 1906.

Winther, Oscar O., ed. *With Sherman to the Sea: The Journal of Theodore F. Upson*. Baton Rouge: Louisiana State University Press, 1943.

Wistar, Isaac J. *Autobiography of Isaac Jones Wistar 1827–1905*. 2 vols. Philadelphia: Wistar Institute, 1914.

Wister, Fanny Kemble and Sarah Butler Wister. "Sarah Butler Wister's Civil War Diary." *Pennsylvania Magazine of History and Biography* 102, no. 3 (1978): 271–327.

PUBLISHED SECONDARY SOURCES

Aaron, Daniel. *The Unwritten War: American Writers and the Civil War*. New York: Alfred A. Knopf, 1973.

Abbott, Edith. "The Civil War and the Crime Wave of 1865–70." *Social Service Review* 1, no. 2 (1927): 212–34.

Abbott, Richard H. "Massachusetts and the Recruitment of Southern Negroes, 1863–1865." *Civil War History* 14, no. 3 (1968): 197–210.

Alotta, Robert I. *Civil War Justice: Union Army Executions under Lincoln.* Shippensburg, PA: White Mane Publishing, 1989.

Anbinder, Tyler. "Which Poor Man's Fight? Immigrants and the Federal Conscription of 1863." *Civil War History* 52 (December 2006): 344–72.

Andrews, William G. *Civil War Brockport: A Canal Town and the Union Army.* Charleston, SC: The History Press, 2013.

Arieli, Yehoshua. *Individualism and Nationalism in American Ideology.* 1964. Reprint. Baltimore, MD: Penguin Books, 1966.

Aurner, C. Ray, ed. *A Topical History of Cedar County, Iowa, Vol. 1.* Chicago: S. J. Clarke Publishing, 1910.

Ayers, Edward L. *In the Presence of Mine Enemies: War in the Heart of America, 1859–1863.* New York: W. W. Norton & Co., 2003.

Bahde, Thomas. "'Our Cause Is a Common One': Home Guards, Union Leagues, and Republican Citizenship in Illinois, 1861–1873." *Civil War History* 56 (March 2010): 66–98.

Baker, Jean. *Affairs of Party: The Political Culture of Northern Democrats in the Mid-Nineteenth Century.* Ithaca, NY: Cornell University Press, 1983.

Barrett, James R. *The Irish Way: Becoming American in the Multiethnic City.* New York: Penguin Press, 2012.

Bartholow, Roberts. *A Manual of Instructions for Enlisting and Discharging Soldiers.* Philadelphia, PA: J. B. Lippincott & Co., 1863.

Baynes, John. *Morale: A Study of Men and Courage.* New York: Frederick A. Praeger, Publishers, 1967.

Benedict, George G. *Vermont in the Civil War: A History.* 2 vols. Burlington, VT: The Free Press Assoc., 1886–1888.

Bensel, Richard Franklin. *Yankee Leviathan: The Origins of Central State Authority in America, 1859–1877.* New York: Cambridge University Press, 1990.

Benton, Elbert J. *The Movement for Peace without a Victory during the Civil War.* 1918. Reprint, New York: Da Capo Press, 1972.

Bernard, Kenneth H. "Lincoln and the Civil War as Viewed by a Dissenting Yankee of Connecticut." *Lincoln Herald* 76, no. 4 (1974): 208–15.

Bernstein, Iver. *The New York City Draft Riots: Their Significance for American Society and Politics in the Age of the Civil War.* 1990. Reprint, Lincoln: University of Nebraska Press, 2010.

Bingham, Harold J. *History of Connecticut.* 4 vols. New York: Lewis Historical Publishing Co., 1962.

Blair, William. "We Are Coming, Father Abraham—Eventually: The Problem of Northern Nationalism in the Pennsylvania Recruiting Drives of 1862." In *The War Was You and Me: Civilians in the American Civil War*, edited by Joan E. Cashin, 183–208. Princeton, NJ: Princeton University Press, 2002.

———. *With Malice toward Some: Treason and Loyalty in the Civil War Era.* Chapel Hill: University of North Carolina Press, 2014.

Blanchard, Charles, ed. *Counties of Morgan, Monroe, and Brown, Indiana: Historical and Biographical.* Chicago: F. A. Battey & Co., 1894.

Bledsoe, Andrew S. *Citizen-Officers: The Union and Confederate Volunteer Junior Officer Corps in the American Civil War.* Baton Rouge: Louisiana State University Press, 2015.

Blied, Rev. Benjamin J. *Catholics and the Civil War.* Milwaukee, WI: self-published, 1945.

Blight, David W. *Race and Reunion: The Civil War in American Memory.* Cambridge, MA: Harvard University Press, 2001.

Boatner III, Mark Mayo. *The Civil War Dictionary.* 1958. Reprint, New York: Vintage Books, 1991.

Boggs, Colleen Glenney. *Patriotism by Proxy: The Civil War Draft and the Cultural Formation of Citizen-Soldiers.* New York: Oxford University Press, 2020.

Brandt, Dennis W. *From Home Guards to Heroes: The 87th Pennsylvania and Its Civil War Community.* Columbia: University of Missouri Press, 2006.

Bratt, Peter. "A Great Revolution in Feeling: The American Civil War in Niles and Grand Rapids, Michigan." *Michigan Historical Review* 31, no. 2 (2005): 43–66.

Briggs, "The Enlistment of Iowa Troops during the Civil War." *The Iowa Journal of History and Politics* 15, no. 3 (1917): 323–92.

Brock, Peter. "When Seventh-day Adventists First Faced the Draft: Civil War America" In *Against the Draft: Essays on Conscientious Objection from the Radical Reformation to the Second World War*, by Peter Brock, 109–18. Toronto, Canada: University of Toronto Press, 2006.

Buck, Stephen J. "'A Contest in Which Blood Must Flow like Water': Du Page County and the Civil War." *Illinois Historical Journal* 87, no. 1 (1994): 2–20.

Bulla, David W. *Lincoln's Censor: Milo Hascall and Freedom of the Press in Civil War Indiana.* West Lafayette, IN: Purdue University Press, 2008.

Burr, Fearing and George Lincoln. *The Town of Hingham in the Late Civil War.* Boston: Town of Hingham, 1876.

Burrows, Edwin G. and Mike Wallace. *Gotham: A History of New York City to 1898.* New York: Oxford University Press, 1999.

Butterfield, C. W. *The History of Waukesha County, Wisconsin.* Chicago: Western Historical Co., 1880.

Canup, Charles E. "Conscription and Draft in Indiana during the Civil War." *Indiana Magazine of History* 10, no. 2 (1914): 70–83.

Carmichael, Peter S. *The War for the Common Soldier: How Men Thought, Fought, and Survived in Civil War Armies.* Chapel Hill: University of North Carolina Press, 2018.

Carnahan, Burrus M. *Act of Justice: Lincoln's Emancipation Proclamation and the Law of War.* Lexington: University Press of Kentucky, 2007.

Cashin, Joan E. "Deserters, Civilians, and Draft Resistance in the North" In *The War Was You and Me: Civilians in the American Civil War*, edited by Joan E. Cashin, 262–85. Princeton, NJ: Princeton University Press, 2002.

Churchill, Robert. "Liberty, Conscription, and a Party Divided: The Sons of Liberty Conspiracy 1863–1864." *Prologue: The Journal of the National Archives* 30, no. 4 (Winter 1998): 294–303.

Cimbala, Paul A. "Soldiering on the Home Front: The Veteran Reserve Corps and the Northern People." In *Union Soldiers and the Northern Home Front*, edited by Paul A. Cimbala and Randall M. Miller, 182–218. New York: Fordham University Press, 2002.

———. "Federal Manpower Needs and the U.S. Army's Veteran Reserve Corps." In *Scraping the Barrel: The Military Use of Sub-Standard Manpower, 1860–1960*, edited by Sanders Marble, 5–27. New York: Fordham University Press, 2012.

———. *Veterans North and South: The Transition from Soldier to Civilian after the American Civil War*. Santa Barbara, CA: Praeger, 2015.

Cimbala, Paul A. and Randall M. Miller. *The Northern Home Front during the Civil War*. Santa Barbara, CA: Praeger, 2017.

Cirillo, Frank. "Waiting for the Perfect Moment: Abby Kelley Foster and Stephen Foster's Union War." In *New Perspectives on the Union War*, edited by Gary W. Gallagher and Elizabeth R. Varon, 9–38. New York: Fordham University Press, 2019.

Clark, Dan E. *Border Defense in Iowa during the Civil War*. Iowa City, IA: State Historical Society of Iowa, 1918.

Clarke, Frances M. and Rebecca Jo Plant. "No Minor Matter: Underage Soldiers, Parents, and the Nationalization of Habeas Corpus in Civil War America." *Law and History Review* 35, no. 4 (November 2017): 881–927.

Cochran, William C. *The Dream of a Northwestern Confederacy*. Madison: State Historical Society of Wisconsin, 1916.

Coddington, Edwin B. "Pennsylvania Prepares for Invasion, 1863." *Pennsylvania History: A Journal of Mid-Atlantic Studies* 31, no. 2 (1964): 157–75.

Cohen, Joanna. "'You Have No Flag Out Yet?': Commercial Connections and Patriotic Emotion in the Civil War North." *The Journal of the Civil War Era* 9, no. 3 (2019): 378–409.

Cohen, Michael D. *Reconstructing the Campus: Higher Education and the American Civil War*. Charlottesville: University of Virginia Press, 2012.

Coleman, J. Walter. *The Molly Maguire Riots: Industrial Conflict in the Pennsylvania Coal Region*. 1936. Reprint, New York: Arno & the *New York Times*, 1969.

Cook, Adrian. *The Armies of the Streets: The New York City Draft Riots of 1863*. Lexington: University Press of Kentucky, 1974.

Costa, Dora L. and Matthew E. Kahn. *Heroes and Cowards: The Social Face of War*. Princeton, NJ: Princeton University Press, 2008.

Counties of Cumberland, Jasper and Richland, Illinois: Historical and Biographical. Chicago: F. A. Battey & Co., 1884.

Cranmer, Gibson Lamb. *History of the Upper Ohio Valley, Vol. 1*. Madison, WI: Brant & Fuller, 1891.

Cunliffe, Marcus. *Soldiers and Civilians: The Martial Spirit in America 1775–1865*. Boston: Little, Brown and Co., 1968.

Current, Richard N. *The Civil War Era, 1848–1873: History of Wisconsin, vol. II*. Madison: State Historical Society of Wisconsin, 1976.

Curti, Merle. *The Roots of American Loyalty*. 1946. Reprint, New York: Russell & Russell, 1967.

Daly, John Patrick. *When Slavery Was Called Freedom: Evangelicalism, Proslavery, and the Causes of the Civil War*. Lexington: University Press of Kentucky, 2002.

Davenport, David and Gordon Lloyd. *Rugged Individualism: Dead or Alive?* Stanford, CA: Hoover Institution Press, 2017.

Goodman, Carl and Susan Dawson. *William Dean Howells: A Writer's Life*. Berkeley: University of California Press, 2005.

Dayton, Aretas A. "The Raising of Union Forces in Illinois during the Civil War." *Journal of the Illinois State Historical Society* 34, no. 4 (1941): 401–38.

Du Bois, W. E. Burghardt. *Black Reconstruction: An Essay toward a History of the Part Which Black Folk Played in the Attempt to Reconstruct Democracy in America, 1860–1880*. New York: Russell & Russell, 1935.

Dubbert, Joe L. *A Man's Place: Masculinity in Transition*. Englewood Cliffs, NJ: Prentice-Hall, 1979.

Duggan, Joseph C. *The Legislative and Statutory Development of the Federal Concept for Military Service*. Washington, DC: Catholic University of America Press, 1946.

Dunning, William A. "Disloyalty in Two Wars." *The American Historical Review* 24, no. 4 (1919): 625–30.

Eddy, T. M. *The Patriotism of Illinois: A Record of the Civil and Military History of the State in the War for the Union*. Chicago: Clarke & Co., 1865.

Edel, Leon. *Henry James: The Untried Years*. Philadelphia: J. P. Lippincott Co., 1953.

Ekirch Jr., Arthur A. *The Civilian and the Military: A History of the American Antimilitarist Tradition*. 1956. Reprint, Oakland, CA: Independent Institute, 2010.

Ernst, Kathleen A. *Too Afraid to Cry: Maryland Civilians in the Antietam Campaign*. Mechanicsburg, PA: Stackpole Books, 1999.

Etcheson, Nicole. *A Generation at War: The Civil War Era in a Northern Community*. Lawrence: University Press of Kansas, 2011.

Fahs, Alice. *The Imagined Civil War: Popular Literature of the North and South, 1861–1865*. Chapel Hill: University of North Carolina Press, 2001.

Fish, C. R. "Social Relief in the Northwest during the Civil War." *The American Historical Review* 22, no. 2 (1917): 309–24.

Fite, Emerson D. *Social and Industrial Conditions in the North during the Civil War*. New York: Macmillan Co., 1910.

Foner, Eric. *Free Soil, Free Labor, Free Men: The Ideology of the Republican Party before the Civil War*. New York: Oxford University Press, 1995.

Foote, Lorien. *The Gentlemen and the Roughs: Violence, Honor, and Manhood in the Union Army*. New York: New York University Press, 2010.

Ford, S. R. "Letter to the Little Folks." *Ford's Christian Repository* 38, no. 5 (1884): 389–91.

Frank, Joseph Allan. *With Ballot and Bayonet: The Political Socialization of American Civil War Soldiers*. Athens: University of Georgia Press, 1998.

———. *Martial Metaphors: Soldiers' Perspectives on the Civil War*. Lanham, MD: University Press of America, 2016.

Frassanito, William A. *Grant and Lee: The Virginia Campaigns 1864–1865*. New York: Charles Scribner's Sons, 1983.

Fredrickson, George M. *The Inner Civil War: Northern Intellectuals and the Crisis of the Union*. New York: Harper & Row, 1965.

———. *Racism: A Short History*. Princeton, NJ: Princeton University Press, 2015.

Fritsch, James T. *The Untried Life: The Twenty-Ninth Ohio Volunteer Infantry in the Civil War*. Athens: Ohio University Press, 2012.

Frost, James A. "The Home Front in New York during the Civil War." *New York History* 42, no. 3 (1961): 273–97.

Fry, Zachery A. *A Republic in the Ranks: Loyalty and Dissent in the Army of the Potomac*. Chapel Hill: University of North Carolina Press, 2020.

Furniss, Jack. "To Save the Union 'in Behalf of Conservative Men': Horatio Seymour and the Democratic Vision for War." In *New Perspectives on the Union War*, edited by Gary W. Gallagher and Elizabeth R. Varon, 63–90. New York: Fordham University Press, 2019.

Gallagher, Gary W. *The Union War*. Cambridge, MA: Harvard University Press, 2011.

———. "The Two Generals Who Resist Each Other: Perceptions of Grant and Lee in the Summer of 1864." In *Cold Harbor to the Crater: The End of the Overland Campaign*, edited by Gary W. Gallagher and Caroline E. Janney, 1–32. Chapel Hill: University of North Carolina Press, 2015.

Gallagher, Gary W., ed. *The Richmond Campaign of 1862: The Peninsula & the Seven Days*. Chapel Hill: University of North Carolina Press, 2000.

Gallman, J. Matthew. *The North Fights the Civil War: The Home Front*. Chicago: Ivan R. Dee, 1994.

———. *Defining Duty in the Civil War: Personal Choice, Popular Culture, and the Union Home Front*. Chapel Hill: University of North Carolina Press, 2015.

Garrity, Timothy F. "'We Respect the Flag but . . .': Opposition to the Civil War in Down East Maine." *Maine History* 48, no. 1 (2014): 23–55.

Gates, Paul W. *Agriculture and the Civil War*. New York: Alfred A. Knopf, 1965.

Geary, James W. *We Need Men: The Union Draft in the Civil War*. DeKalb: Northern Illinois University Press, 1991.

Giesberg, Judith. *Army at Home: Women and the Civil War on the Northern Home Front*. Chapel Hill: University of North Carolina Press, 2009.

———. *Civil War Sisterhood: The U.S. Sanitary Commission and Women's Politics in Transition*. Boston: Northeastern University Press, 2000.

Girardi, Robert I. "'I Am for the President's Proclamation Teeth and Toe Nails': Illinois Soldiers Respond to the Emancipation Proclamation." *Journal of the Illinois State Historical Society* 106, no. 3–4 (2013): 395–421.

Goodheart, Adam. *1861: The Civil War Awakening*. New York: Alfred A. Knopf, 2011.

Goodspeed, Weston A. "History of Warren County." In *Counties of Warren, Benton, Jasper and Newton, Indiana: Historical and Biographical*, 31–156. Chicago: F. A. Battey & Co., 1883.

Gordon, Lesley J. *"I Never Was a Coward": Questions of Bravery in a Civil War Regiment*. Milwaukee, WI: Marquette University Press, 2005.

Gray, Wood. *The Hidden Civil War: The Story of the Copperheads*. New York: Viking Press, 1942.

Greenberg, Amy S. *Manifest Manhood and the Antebellum American Empire*. New York: Cambridge University Press, 2005.

Greenberg, Irwin F. "Charles Ingersoll: The Aristocrat as Copperhead." *Pennsylvania Magazine of History and Biography* 93, no. 2 (1969): 190–217.

Greenslet, Ferris. *The Lowells and Their Seven Worlds*. Boston: Houghton Mifflin Co., 1946.

Guelzo, Allen C. *Fateful Lightning: A New History of the Civil War & Reconstruction*. New York: Oxford University Press, 2012.

Haidt, Jonathan. *The Righteous Mind: Why Good People Are Divided by Politics and Religion*. 2012. Reprint, New York: Vintage Books, 2013.

Hallock, Judith Lee. "The Role of the Community in Civil War Desertion." *Civil War History* 29, no. 2 (1983): 123–34.

Hamand, Lavern M. *Coles County in the Civil War*. Charleston: Eastern Illinois University, 1961.

Handley-Cousins, Sarah. *Bodies in Blue: Disability in the Civil War North*. Athens: University of Georgia Press, 2019.

Hansen, Marcus Lee and John B. Brebner. *The Mingling of the Canadian and American Peoples, Volume 1*. New Haven, CT: Yale University Press, 1940.

Harper, Judith E. *Women during the Civil War: An Encyclopedia*. New York: Routledge Press, 2004.

Harriman, Walter. *The History of Warner, New Hampshire*. Concord, NH: Republican Press Assoc., 1879.

Hess, Earl. J. *Liberty, Virtue, and Progress: Northerners and Their War for the Union*. New York: New York University Press, 1988.

Hirshson, Stanley P. *Grenville M. Dodge: Soldier, Politician, Railroad Pioneer*. Bloomington: Indiana University Press, 1967.

Holzer, Harold. *Lincoln President-Elect: Abraham Lincoln and the Great Secession Winter 1860–1861*. New York: Simon and Schuster, 2008.

Hsieh, Wayne Wei-siang. *West Pointers and the Civil War: The Old Army in War and Peace*. Chapel Hill: University of North Carolina Press, 2009.

Hubbart, Henry Clyde. "'Pro-Southern' Influences in the Free West 1840–1865." *The Mississippi Valley Historical Review* 20, no. 1 (June 1933): 45–62.

Huston, James L. *The Panic of 1857 and the Coming of the Civil War*. Baton Rouge: Louisiana State University Press, 1987.

Hyman, Harold M. *Era of the Oath: Northern Loyalty Tests during the Civil War and Reconstruction*. Philadelphia: University of Pennsylvania Press, 1954.

———. *To Try Men's Souls: Loyalty Tests in American History*. Berkeley: University of California Press, 1960.

Ignatiev, Noel. *How the Irish Became White*. New York: Routledge Classics, 2009.

Janney, Caroline E. *Remembering the Civil War: Reunion and the Limits of Reconciliation*. Chapel Hill: University of North Carolina Press, 2013.

Jimerson, Randall C. *The Private Civil War: Popular Thought During the Sectional Conflict*. Baton Rouge: Louisiana State University Press, 1988.

Johnson, Russell L. "'A Debt Justly Due': The Relief of Civil War Soldiers and Their Families in Dubuque." *The Annals of Iowa* 55 (1996): 207–38.

———. *Warriors Into Workers: The Civil War and the Formation of Urban-industrial Society in a Northern City*. New York: Fordham University Press, 2003.

Jones, Gregory. "Violence on the Home Front: Democracy and Disunity in Southeastern Ohio during the American Civil War." In *Lesser Civil Wars: Civilians Defining War and the Memory of War*, edited by Marsha R. Robinson, 59–78. Newcastle Upon Tyne, UK: Cambridge Scholars Pub., 2012.

Jordan, Brian Matthew. *Marching Home: Union Veterans and Their Unending Civil War*. New York: Liveright Publishing, 2014.

———. *A Thousand May Fall: An Immigrant Regiment's Civil War*. New York: Liveright Publishing, 2021.

Jordan, Wayne. "The Hoskinsville Rebellion." *Ohio History Journal* 47 (Oct. 1938): 319–54.

Kahan, Paul. *Amiable Scoundrel: Simon Cameron, Lincoln's Scandalous Secretary of War*. Sterling, VA: Potomac Books, 2016.

Kalmoe, Nathan P. *With Ballots and Bullets: Partisanship and Violence in the American Civil War*. New York: Cambridge University Press, 2020.

Kashatus, William C. *Abraham Lincoln, the Quakers, and the Civil War: "A Trial of Principle & Faith."* Santa Barbara, CA: Praeger, 2014.

Keating, Ryan W. *Shades of Green: Irish Regiments, American Soldiers, and Local Communities in the Civil War Era*. New York: Fordham University Press, 2017.

Keehn, David C. *Knights of the Golden Circle: Secret Empire, Southern Secession, Civil War*. Baton Rouge: Louisiana State University Press, 2013.

Kelley, Brooks M. "Fossildom, Old Fogeyism, and Red Tape." *Pennsylvania Magazine of History and Biography* 90, no. 1 (1966): 93–114.

Kent, Arthur A., ed. *Three Years with Company K: Sergt. Austin C. Stearns Company K*. Rutherford, NJ: Fairleigh Dickinson University Press, 1976.

Kettleborough, Charles. "Moratory and Stay Laws." *American Political Science Review* 12, no. 3 (1918): 458–61.

Kettner, James H. *The Development of American Citizenship, 1608–1870*. Chapel Hill: University of North Carolina Press, 1978.

Kimmel, Stanley. *Mr. Lincoln's Washington*. New York: Coward-McCann, Inc., 1957.

Klement, Frank L. *The Limits of Dissent: Clement L. Vallandigham & the Civil War*. Lexington: University Press of Kentucky, 1970.

———. *Wisconsin in the Civil War*. Madison: State Historical Society of Wisconsin, 1997.

Kreiser Jr., Lawrence A. *Marketing the Blue and Gray: Newspaper Advertising and the American Civil War*. Baton Rouge: Louisiana State University Press, 2019.

Kurtz, William B. *Excommunicated from the Union: How the Civil War Created a Separate Catholic America*. New York: Fordham University Press, 2016.

———. "The Union as It Was: Northern Catholics' Conservative Unionism." In *New Perspectives on the Union War*, edited by Gary Gallagher and Elizabeth Varon, 91–113. New York: Fordham University Press, 2019.

Lande, R. Gregory. *Psychological Consequences of the American Civil War*. Jefferson, NC: McFarland & Co., 2017.

Landon, Fred. *Western Ontario and the American Frontier*. 1941. Reprint, Russell & Russell, 1970.

Lare, W. A. and W. M. Hartzell. *The Rebellion Record of Allegheny County from April, 1861, to October, 1862.* Pittsburgh, PA: A. A. Anderson, 1862.

Lawson, Melinda. *Patriot Fires: Forging a New American Nationalism in the Civil War North.* Lawrence: University Press of Kansas, 2002.

Leach, Jack F. *Conscription in the United States: Historical Background.* Rutland, VT: Charles E. Tuttle, 1952.

Lee, Brother Basil Leo. *Discontent in New York City 1861–1865.* Washington, DC: Catholic University of America Press, 1943.

Leeke, Jim, ed. *A Hundred Days to Richmond: Ohio's "Hundred Days" Men in the Civil War.* Bloomington: Indiana University Press, 1999.

Lehman, James O. and Steven M. Nolt. *Mennonites, Amish, and the American Civil War.* Baltimore, MD: Johns Hopkins University Press, 2007.

Levine, Peter. "Draft Evasion in the North during the Civil War, 1863–1865." *The Journal of American History* 67, no. 4 (1981): 816–34.

Linderman, Gerald F. *Embattled Courage: The Experience of Combat in the American Civil War.* New York: The Free Press, 1987.

Longacre, Edward G. *Joshua Chamberlain: The Soldier and the Man.* 1999. Reprint, Cambridge, MA: Da Capo Press, 2003.

Lonn, Ella. *Desertion during the Civil War.* 1928. Reprint, Gloucester, MA: Peter Smith, 1966.

Love, William DeLoss. *Wisconsin in the War of the Rebellion; A History of All Regiments and Batteries.* Chicago: Church and Goodman, 1866.

Luebke, Peter C. "'To Transmit and Perpetuate the Fruits of This Victory': Union Regimental Histories and the Great Rebellion in Immediate Retrospect." In *New Perspectives on the Union War,* edited by Gary Gallagher and Elizabeth Varon, 186–99. New York: Fordham University Press, 2019.

Maas, David. *Marching to the Drumbeat of Abolitionism: Wheaton College in the Civil War.* Wheaton, IL: Wheaton College, 2010.

Mahoney, Timothy R. *From Hometown to Battlefield in the Civil War Era: Middle Class Life in Midwest America.* New York: Cambridge University Press, 2016.

Manning, Chandra. *What This Cruel War Was Over: Soldiers, Slavery, and the Civil War.* New York: Alfred A. Knopf, 2007.

Marrin, Albert. *Unconditional Surrender: U. S. Grant and the Civil War.* New York: Atheneum, 1994.

Marshall, John A. *American Bastille: A History of the Illegal Arrests and Imprisonment of American Citizens during the Late Civil War.* 1869. Reprint, Philadelphia: Thomas W. Hartley, 1876.

Marten, James. *Sing Not War: The Lives of Union and Confederate Veterans in Gilded Age America.* Chapel Hill: University of North Carolina Press, 2011.

Marvel, William, ed. *The Monitor Chronicles: One Sailor's Account: Today's Campaign to Recover the Civil War Wreck.* New York: Simon & Schuster, 2000.

Marvel, William. *Mr. Lincoln Goes to War.* Boston: Houghton Mifflin, 2006.

———. *Lincoln's Darkest Year: The War in 1862.* Boston: Houghton Mifflin, 2008.

———. *Lincoln's Autocrat: The Life of Edwin Stanton*. Chapel Hill: University of North Carolina Press, 2015.

———. *Lincoln's Mercenaries: Economic Motivation among Union Soldiers during the Civil War*. Baton Rouge: Louisiana State University Press, 2018.

Massey, Mary E. *Bonnet Brigades: American Women and the Civil War*. New York: Alfred A. Knopf, 1966.

Masur, Louis P. *Lincoln's Hundred Days: The Emancipation Proclamation and the War for the Union*. Cambridge, MA: Belknap Press, 2012.

Matteson, John. *A Worse Place Than Hell: How the Civil War Battle of Fredericksburg Changed a Nation*. New York: W. W. Norton & Co., 2021.

May, Dean L. *Three Frontiers: Family, Land, and Society in the American West, 1850–1900*. New York: Cambridge University Press, 1994.

McCaffrey, James M. *Army of Manifest Destiny: The American Soldier in the Mexican War, 1846–1848*. New York: New York University Press, 1992.

McClintock, Russell. *Lincoln and the Decision for War: The Northern Response to Secession*. Chapel Hill: University of North Carolina Press, 2008.

McElroy, John. *Andersonville: A Story of Rebel Military Prisons*. Toledo, OH: D. R. Locke, 1878.

McKay, Ernest A. *The Civil War and New York City*. Syracuse, NY: Syracuse University Press, 1990.

McPherson, James M. *Ordeal by Fire: The Civil War and Reconstruction*. New York: Alfred K. Knopf, 1982.

———. *Battle Cry of Freedom: The Civil War Era*. New York: Oxford University Press, 1988.

———. *For Cause & Comrades: Why Men Fought in the Civil War*. New York: Oxford University Press, 1997.

Meier, Kathryn S. *Nature's Civil War: Common Soldiers and the Environment in 1862 Virginia*. Chapel Hill: University of North Carolina Press, 2013.

Menand, Louis. *The Metaphysical Club: A Story of Ideas in America*. New York: Farrar, Straus and Giroux, 2001.

Miller, Jason. "To Stop These Wolves' Forays: Provost Marshals, Desertion, the Draft, and Political Violence on the Central Illinois Home Front." *Journal of the Illinois State Historical Society* 105, no. 2–3 (2012): 202–24.

Miller, Kerby A. *Emigrants and Exiles: Ireland and the Irish Exodus to North America*. New York: Oxford University Press, 1988.

Miller, Randall M. "Catholic Religion, Irish Ethnicity, and the Civil War." In *Religion and the American Civil War*, edited by Randall M. Miller, Harry S. Stout, and Charles R. Wilson, 261–96. New York: Oxford University Press, 1998.

Miller, Richard F. *Harvard's Civil War: A History of the Twentieth Massachusetts Volunteer Infantry*. Lebanon, NH: University Press of New England, 2005.

Mitchell, Wesley Clair. *A History of the Greenbacks: With Special Reference to the Economic Consequence of Their Issue: 1862–65*. Chicago: University of Chicago Press, 1903.

Mitchell, Reid. *Civil War Soldiers*. New York: Viking Penguin, 1988.

———. *The Vacant Chair: The Northern Soldier Leaves Home*. New York: Oxford University Press, 1995.

———. "From Volunteer to Soldier: The Psychology of Service." In *The Civil War Soldier: A Historical Reader*, edited by Michael Barton and Larry M. Logue, 354–85. New York: New York University Press, 2002.

Moers, Ellen. *The Dandy: Brummell to Beerbohm*. New York: Viking Press, 1960.

Montgomery, David. *Beyond Equality: Labor and the Radical Republicans 1862–1872*. New York: Alfred A. Knopf, 1967.

Moody, W. R. *The Life of D. L. Moody by His Son*. New York: Fleming Revell Pub., 1900.

Mujic, Julie A. "'Ours Is the Harder Lot': Student Patriotism at the University of Michigan during the Civil War." In *Union Heartland: The Midwestern Home Front during the Civil War*, edited by Ginette Aley and J. L. Anderson, 33–67. Carbondale: Southern Illinois University Press, 2013.

———. "'We Are Setting the Terms Now': Loyalty Rhetoric in Courtship." In *Contested Loyalties: Debates Over Patriotism in the Civil War North*, edited by Robert M. Sandow, 107–36. New York: Fordham University Press, 2018.

Murdock, Eugene C. *Ohio's Bounty System in the Civil War*. Columbus: Ohio State University Press, 1963.

———. "New York's Civil War Bounty Brokers." *The Journal of American History* 53, no. 2 (1966): 259–78.

———. *Patriotism Limited 1862–1865: The Civil War Draft and the Bounty System*. Kent, OH: Kent State University Press, 1967.

———. *One Million Men: The Civil War Draft in the North*. Madison: State Historical Society of Wisconsin, 1971.

Murphy, Michael B. *The Kimberlins Go to War: A Union Family in Copperhead Country*. Indianapolis: Indiana Historical Society Press, 2016.

Nagler, Jörg. "Loyalty and Dissent: The Home Front in the American Civil War." In *On the Road to Total War: The American Civil War and the German Wars of Unification, edited by* Stig Förster and Jörg Nagler, 329–56. Cambridge, NY: Cambridge University Press, 1997.

Nash, Eugene A. *A History of the Forty-fourth Regiment, New York Volunteer Infantry, in the Civil War, 1861–1865*. Chicago: R. R. Donnelly & Sons, 1911.

Neely Jr., Mark E. *The Fate of Liberty: Abraham Lincoln and Civil Liberties*. New York: Oxford University Press, 1991.

———. *The Union Divided: Party Conflict in the Civil War North*. Cambridge, MA: Harvard University Press, 2002.

———. *Lincoln and the Democrats: The Politics of Opposition in the Civil War*. New York: Cambridge University Press, 2017.

Neff, Stephen C. *Justice in Blue and Gray: A Legal History of the Civil War*. Cambridge, MA: Harvard University Press, 2010.

Nevins, Allan. *Grover Cleveland: A Study in Courage*. New York: Dodd, Mead & Co., 1933.

Newell, Clayton R. and Charles R. Shrader. *Of Duty Well and Faithfully Done: The Regular Army on the Eve of the Civil War*. Lincoln: University of Nebraska Press, 2011.

Noe, Kenneth W. *The Howling Storm: Weather, Climate, and the American Civil War.* Baton Rouge: Louisiana State University Press, 2020.

Noll, Mark A. *The Civil War as a Theological Crisis.* Chapel Hill: University of North Carolina Press, 2006.

O'Connor, Harvey. *Mellon's Millions, the Biography of a Fortune: The Life and Times of Andrew W. Mellon.* New York: The John Day Co., 1933.

O'Connor, Thomas H. *Civil War Boston: Home Front and Battlefield.* Boston: Northeastern University Press, 1997.

Palladino, Grace. *Another Civil War: Labor, Capital, and the State in the Anthracite Regions of Pennsylvania 1840–68.* Urbana: University of Illinois Press, 1990.

Paludan, Phillip Shaw. *"A People's Contest": The Union and Civil War 1861–1865.* New York: Harper & Row, 1988.

Parmenter, C. O. *History of Pelham, Mass. From 1738 to 1898, Including the Early History of Prescott.* Amherst, MA: Press of Carpenter & Morehouse, 1898.

Parish, Peter J. *The North and the Nation in the Era of the Civil War.* New York: Fordham University Press, 2003.

Pearson, Henry Greenleaf. *The Life of John A. Andrew.* 2 vols. Boston: Houghton, Mifflin and Co., 1904.

Perri, Timothy J. "The Evolution of Military Conscription in the United States." *The Independent Review* 17, no. 3 (2013): 429–39.

Philadelphia Club. *The Philadelphia Club, 1834–1934.* Philadelphia: Privately printed, 1934.

Phillips, Christopher. *The Rivers Ran Backward: The Civil War and the Remaking of the American Middle Border.* New York: Oxford University Press, 2016.

Phillips, Jason. *Looming Civil War: How Nineteenth-Century Americans Imagined the Future.* New York: Oxford University Press, 2018.

Phillips, Christopher and Jason L. Pendleton. *The Union on Trial: The Political Journals of Judge William Barclay Napton, 1829–1883.* Columbia: University of Missouri Press, 2005.

Prokopowicz, Gerald J. *All for the Regiment: The Army of the Ohio, 1861–1862.* Chapel Hill: University of North Carolina Press, 2001.

Quigley, Paul. "Civil War Conscription and the International Boundaries of Citizenship." *Journal of the Civil War Era* 4, no. 3 (2014): 373–97.

Rable, George C. *Fredericksburg! Fredericksburg!* Chapel Hill: University of North Carolina Press, 2002.

———. *God's Almost Chosen Peoples: A Religious History of the American Civil War.* Chapel Hill: University of North Carolina Press, 2010.

Rael, Patrick. *Eighty-Eight Years: The Long Death of Slavery in the United States, 1777–1865.* Athens: University of Georgia Press, 2015.

Ramold, Steven J. *Baring the Iron Hand: Discipline in the Union Army.* DeKalb: Northern Illinois University Press, 2010.

Randall, James G. *Constitutional Problems under Lincoln.* New York: D. Appleton and Co., 1926.

Randall, J. G. and David Donald. *The Civil War and Reconstruction,* second edition. Lexington, MA: D. C. Heath and Co., 1969.

Raus Jr., Edmund J. *Banners South: A Northern Community at War.* Kent, OH: Kent State University Press, 2005.

Rawley, James A. *The Politics of Union: Northern Politics during the Civil War.* Hinsdale, IL: Dryden Press, 1974.

Raymond, Henry J. *History of the Administration of President Lincoln.* New York: Derby & Miller, 1864.

Reardon, Carol. "'We Are All in This War': The 148th Pennsylvania and Home Front Dissension in Centre County during the Civil War." In *Union Soldiers and the Northern Home Front*, edited by Paul A. Cimbala and Randall M. Miller. New York: Fordham University Press, 2002.

Reed, Thomas J. *America's Two Constitutions: A Study of the Treatment of Dissenters in Time of War.* Madison, NJ: Fairleigh Dickinson University Press, 2017.

Reid, Brian H. and John White. "'A Mob of Stragglers and Cowards': Desertion from the Union and Confederate Armies, 1861–65." *Journal of Strategic Studies* 8, no. 1 (1985): 64–77.

Rhodes, James Ford. *History of the Civil War, 1861–1865.* New York: Macmillan Co., 1917.

Richard, Patricia L. *Busy Hands: Images of the Family in the Northern Civil War Effort.* New York: Fordham University Press, 2003.

Risse, Guenter B. *Mending Bodies, Saving Souls: A History of Hospitals.* New York: Oxford University Press, 1999.

Robertson, John, comp. *Michigan in the War.* Lansing, MI: W. S. Clarke & Co., 1882.

Robertson Jr., James I. *Soldiers Blue and Gray.* Columbia: University of South Carolina Press, 1988.

Robinson, Corrine Roosevelt. *My Brother Theodore Roosevelt.* New York: Charles Scribner's Sons, 1921.

Rodgers, Thomas E. "Hoosier Women and the Civil War Home Front." *Indiana Magazine of History* 97, no. 2 (2001): 105–28.

Rose, Anne C. *Victorian America and the Civil War.* New York: Cambridge University Press, 1992.

Rugoff, Milton. *The Beechers: An American Family in the Nineteenth Century.* New York: Harper & Row, 1981.

Russ Jr., William A. "Franklin Weirick: 'Copperhead' of Central Pennsylvania." *Pennsylvania History: A Journal of Mid-Atlantic Studies* 5, no. 4 (1938): 245–56.

Sandage, Scott A. *Born Losers: A History of Failure in America.* Cambridge, MA: Harvard University Press, 2005.

Sandow, Robert M. "The Limits of Northern Patriotism: Early Civil War Mobilization in Pennsylvania." *Pennsylvania History: A Journal of Mid-Atlantic Studies* 70, no. 2 (2003): 175–203.

———. *Deserter Country: Civil War Opposition in the Pennsylvania Appalachians.* New York: Fordham University Press, 2009.

Sauers, Richard A. and Peter Tomasak. *The Fishing Creek Confederacy: A Story of Civil War Draft Resistance.* Columbia: University of Missouri Press, 2012.

Saxton, Alexander. *The Rise and Fall of the White Republic: Class Politics and Mass Culture in Nineteenth-Century America.* 1990. Reprint, New York: Verso, 2003.

Schaar, John H. *Loyalty in America*. Berkeley: University of California Press, 1957.

Schecter, Barnet. *The Devil's Own Work: The Civil War Draft Riots and the Fight to Reconstruct America*. New York: Walker & Co., 2005.

Schlosser, Mickey and John Robortella, eds. *Writing Home: Civil War Letters from the Hinchey Family Archive*. Gates, NY: Gates Historical Society, 2013.

Schneider, Paul. *Old Man River: The Mississippi River in North American History*. New York: Henry Holt and Co., 2013.

Schulman, Vanessa Meikle. "The Pleasure of the Parlor: Mocking the 'Home Guard' in Civil War Visual Culture." *Studies in American Humor* 7, no. 1 (2021): 105–27.

Schultz, Jane E. *Women at the Front: Hospital Workers in Civil War America*. Chapel Hill: University of North Carolina Press, 2004.

Scott, Sean A. *A Visitation of God: Northern Civilians Interpret the Civil War*. New York: Oxford University Press, 2011.

Sears, Stephen W. *To the Gates of Richmond: The Peninsula Campaign*. New York: Ticknor & Fields, 1992.

Seaver, Frederick J. *Historical Sketches of Franklin County and Its Several Towns*. Albany, NY: J. B. Lyon Co., 1918.

Shankman, Arnold M. *The Pennsylvania Antiwar Movement, 1861–1865*. Rutherford, NJ: Fairleigh Dickinson University Press, 1980.

Shannon, Brent. "Refashioning Men: Fashion, Masculinity, and the Cultivation of the Male Consumer in Britain, 1860–1914." *Victorian Studies* 46, no. 4 (2004): 597–630.

Shannon, Fred A. "State Rights and the Union Army." *The Mississippi Valley Historical Review* 12, no. 1 (1925): 51–71.

———. *The Organization and Administration of the Union Army 1861–1865*. 2 vols. Cleveland, OH: Arthur H. Clark Co., 1928.

Silber, Nina. *Daughters of the Union: Northern Women Fight the Civil War*. Cambridge, MA: Harvard University Press, 2005.

Silkenat, David. *Raising the White Flag: How Surrender Defined the American Civil War*. Chapel Hill: University of North Carolina Press, 2019.

Skidmore, Joe. "The Copperhead Press and the Civil War." *Journalism Quarterly* 16, no. 4 (1939): 345–55.

Smith, Adam I. P. *No Party Now: Politics in the Civil War North*. New York: Oxford University Press, 2006.

Smith, Diane M. *Fanny & Joshua: The Enigmatic Lives of Frances Caroline Adams & Joshua Lawrence Chamberlain*. 1999. Reprint, Hanover, NH: University Press of New England, 2013.

Smith, John David and William Cooper Jr., eds. *A Union Woman in Civil War Kentucky: The Diary of Frances Peter*. Lexington: University Press of Kentucky, 2000.

Smith, Michael Thomas. *The Enemy Within: Fears of Corruption in the Civil War North*. Charlottesville: University of Virginia Press, 2011.

———. "Abraham Lincoln, Manhood, and Nineteenth-Century American Political Culture." In *This Distracted and Anarchical People: New Answers for Old Questions about the Civil War–Era North*, edited by Andrew L. Slap and Michael T. Smith, 29–41. New York: Fordham University Press, 2013.

Snell, Mark A. "If They Would Know What I Know It Would Be Pretty Hard to Raise One Company in York." In *Union Soldiers and the Northern Home Front*, edited by Paul A. Cimbala and Randall M. Miller, 69–118. New York: Fordham University Press, 2002.

Snow, Donald M. and Dennis M. Drew. *From Lexington to Baghdad and Beyond: War and Politics in the American Experience*. Armonk, NY: M. E. Sharpe, 2010.

Spann, Edward K. *Gotham at War: New York City, 1860–1865*. Wilmington, DE: Scholarly Resources, 2002.

Spar, Ira. *Civil War Hospital Newspapers: Histories and Excerpts of Nine Union Publications*. Jefferson, NC: McFarland & Co., 2017.

Stanley, R. H. and George O. Hall. *Eastern Maine and the Rebellion*. Bangor, ME: R. H. Stanley & Co., 1887.

Sterling, Robert E. "Civil War Draft Resistance in Illinois." *Journal of the Illinois State Historical Society* 64, no. 3 (1971): 244–66.

Stevenson, Louise L. *The Victorian Homefront: American Thought and Culture, 1860–1880*. 1991. Reprint, Ithaca, NY: Cornell University Press, 2001.

Stinson, Byron. "The Invalid Corps." *Civil War Times Illustrated* 10, no. 2 (1971): 20–27.

Stout, Harry S. *Upon the Altar of the Nation: A Moral History of the Civil War*. New York: Viking Books, 2006.

Tagg, Larry. *The Unpopular Mr. Lincoln: The Story of America's Most Reviled President*. New York: Savas Beatie LLC, 2009.

Tarbell, Ida M. *A Reporter for Lincoln: Story of Henry E. Wing, Soldier and Newspaperman*. 1926. Reprint, New York: Book League of America, 1929.

Taylor, Amy Murrell. *The Divided Family in Civil War America*. Chapel Hill: University of North Carolina Press, 2005.

Taylor, Paul. *"Old Slow Town": Detroit during the Civil War*. Detroit, MI: Wayne State University Press, 2013.

———. *"The Most Complete Political Machine Ever Known": The North's Union Leagues in the American Civil War*. Kent, OH: Kent State University Press, 2018.

Thompson, Francis M. *History of Greenfield, Shire Town of Franklin County, Massachusetts. Vol. 1*. Greenfield, MA: New England Historic Genealogical Soc., 1904.

Thornbrough, Emma Lou. *Indiana in the Civil War Era, 1850–1880*. Indianapolis: Indiana Historical Bureau & Indiana Historical Society, 1965.

Thornton, Mark and Robert B. Ekelund Jr. *Tariffs, Blockades, and Inflation: The Economics of the Civil War*. Wilmington, DE: Scholarly Resources, Inc., 2004.

Towne, Stephen. *Surveillance and Spies in the Civil War: Exposing Confederate Conspiracies in America's Heartland*. Athens: Ohio University Press, 2015.

Tynan, Jane and Lisa Godson, eds. *Uniform: Clothing and Discipline in the Modern World*. London: Bloomsbury Visual Arts, 2019.

Valuska, David L. and Christian B. Keller. *Damn Dutch: Pennsylvania Germans at Gettysburg*. Mechanicsburg, PA: Stackpole Books, 2004.

Van Tassel, David with John Vacha. *"Behind Bayonets": The Civil War in Northern Ohio*. Kent, OH: Kent State University Press, 2006.

Wachtell, Cynthia. *War No More: The Antiwar Impulse in American Literature, 1861–1914*. Baton Rouge: Louisiana State University Press, 2010.

Walker, Mack. "The Mercenaries." *The New England Quarterly* 39, no. 3 (1966): 390–98.

Walker, T. R. "Rock Island Prison Barracks." In *Civil War Prisons*, edited by William B. Hesseltine. Kent, OH: Kent State University Press, 1962.

Walls, Stephanie M. *Individualism in the United States: A Transformation in American Political Thought*. New York: Bloomsbury, 2015.

Walsh, Chris. *Cowardice: A Brief History*. Princeton, NJ: Princeton University Press, 2014.

Warren, Robert Penn. *The Legacy of the Civil War: Meditations on the Centennial*. New York: Random House, 1961.

Warshauer, Matthew. *Connecticut in the American Civil War*. Middletown, CT: Wesleyan University Press, 2011.

———. "Copperheads in Connecticut: A Peace Movement that Imperiled the Union." In *This Distracted and Anarchical People: New Answers for Old Questions about the Civil War–Era North*, edited by Andrew L. Slap and Michael T. Smith, 60–80. New York: Fordham University Press, 2013.

Waugh, John C. *Reelecting Lincoln: The Battle for the 1864 Presidency*. New York: Crown Publishers, 1997.

Weber, Jennifer L. *Copperheads: The Rise and Fall of Lincoln's Opponents in the North*. New York: Oxford University Press, 2006.

———. "Lincoln's Critics: The Copperheads." *Journal of the Abraham Lincoln Association* 32, no. 1 (2011): 33–47.

———. "Conscription and the Consolidation of Federal Power." In *Civil War Congress and the Creation of Modern America: A Revolution on the Home Front*, edited by Paul Finkelman and Donald R. Kennon. Athens: Ohio University Press, 2018.

Whisker, James B. *The Rise and Decline of the American Militia System*. Selinsgrove, PA: Susquehanna University Press, 1999.

White, Jonathan W. *Emancipation, the Union Army, and the Reelection of Abraham Lincoln*. Baton Rouge: Louisiana State University Press, 2014.

Wiley, Bell Irvin. *The Life of Billy Yank: The Common Soldier of the Union*. 1952. Reprint, Baton Rouge: Louisiana State University Press, 1971.

Williams, Kipling D. *Ostracism: The Power of Silence*. New York: The Guilford Press, 2001.

Williams, Kipling D. and Steve A. Nida, eds. *Ostracism, Exclusion, and Rejection*. New York: Routledge Press, 2017.

Wilson, Mark R. *The Business of Civil War: Military Mobilization and the State, 1861–1865*. Baltimore: Johns Hopkins University Press, 2006.

"Wisconsin Home Guards during the Civil War." *The Wisconsin Magazine of History* 2, no. 2 (1918): 212–14.

Wood, Forrest G. *Black Scare: The Racist Response to Emancipation and Reconstruction*. Berkeley: University of California Press, 1968.

Wright, Edward. *Conscientious Objectors in the Civil War*. Philadelphia: University of Pennsylvania Press, 1931.

Wubben, Hubert H. *Civil War Iowa and the Copperhead Movement*. Ames: Iowa State University Press, 1980.

Zornow, William F. *Lincoln and the Party Divided*. Norman: University of Oklahoma Press, 1954.

DISSERTATIONS AND THESES

Feeney, William R. "Manifestations of the Maimed: The Perception of Wounded Soldiers in the Civil War North." Ph.D. diss., West Virginia University, 2015.

Foster, John Michael. "Defenders of the Home Front: State Militias, Home Guards, Emergency Troops, and Home Protection in the Civil War North." Ph.D. diss., Purdue University, 2014.

Kautz, Craig L. "Fodder for Cannon: Immigrant Perceptions of the Civil War—The Old Northwest." Ph.D. diss., University of Nebraska, 1976.

Logothetis, Kathleen Anneliese. "A Question of Life or Death: Suicide and Survival in the Union Army." M.A. thesis, West Virginia University, 2012.

Meneely, A. Howard. "The War Department, 1861: A Study in Mobilization and Administration." Ph.D. diss., Columbia University, 1928.

Olsen, Jonathan Andrew. "'We Come Not to War On Opinions, But to Suppress Treason': Ypsilanti, Michigan during the Civil War." M.A. thesis, Eastern Michigan University, 2002.

Orr, Timothy Justin. "Cities at War: Union Army Mobilization in the Urban Northeast, 1861–1865." Ph.D. diss., Pennsylvania State University, 2010.

Ruehlen, Christopher R. "The Specter of Subversion: Fears, Perceptions, and Reactions to Civil War Dissent in the Civil War North, 1861–1865." Ph.D. diss., University of Florida, 2015.

Schindler, Mauren. "Dismantling the Dichotomy of Cowardice and Courage during the American Civil War." M.A. thesis, Kent State University Press, 2018.

Sterling, Robert E. "Civil War Draft Resistance in the Middle West." Ph.D. diss., Northern Illinois University, 1974.

Welsko, Chuck. "Copperheads and Blacksnakes: Divided Loyalty in Eastern Pennsylvania." M.A. thesis, West Virginia University, 2014.

White, Jonathan. "'To Aid Their Rebel Friends': Politics and Treason in the Civil War North." Ph.D. diss., University of Maryland, 2008.

DIGITAL AND VIDEO SOURCES

"1860 Census: Population of the United States." US Census Bureau. https://www.census.gov/library/publications/1864/dec/1860a.html.

"A. H. Marsh Civil War Letters." Fenton Historical Society, Fenton, MI. http://fentonhistsoc.tripod.com/index.html.

Burns, Ken. "Shelby Foote on Union Victory," YouTube video, 0:42, Oct. 25, 2016, https://www.youtube.com/watch?v=H8Iw-j217yk.

"Civil War Casualties." American Battlefield Trust. https://www.battlefields.org.

"Civil War Letters." Delaware County NY Genealogy and History Site. https://www.dcnyhistory.org/milcwlettersbloomvillemirror.html#taylornote.

"Civil War Letters of Aaron Jones Fletcher." https://www.actonmemoriallibrary.org/civilwar/fletcher/fletcher-intro.html.

"Civil War Letters of Henry Clay Long, 11th Maine Infantry." https://henrylong687641266.wordpress.com.

"Civil War Letters of Hubert Dwight Smith of Litchfield." https://www.hillsdalehistoricalsociety.org/smith-civil-war-letters.

"Civil War Letters and Journal of Charles F. Weller." New York Heritage Digital Collections. https://nyheritage.org/collections/civil-war-letters-and-journal-charles-f-weller.

"Civil War Voices: Soldier Studies." http://www.soldierstudies.org.

"Eugene F. Hawley Civil War Letters." Connecticut Digital Archive. https://collections.ctdigitalarchive.org/islandora/object/150002%3A9268.

"George C. Burmeister Diary, 1861." Iowa Digital Library. https://diyhistory.lib.uiowa.edu.

Hart, Peter J. "The White Feather Campaign: A Struggle with Masculinity during World War I." http://www.inquiriesjournal.com/a?id=151.

"Irish in the American Civil War." https://irishamericancivilwar.com.

"Letters of Bernt Olmanson: A Union Soldier in the Civil War 1861–1865." http://www.olmanson.org/BerntO/index.html.

Martinovich, Milenko. "Americans' Partisan Identities Are Stronger than Race and Ethnicity." Stanford News, Aug. 31, 2017. https://news.stanford.edu/2017/08/31/political-party-identities-stronger-race-religion.

"Massachusetts in the Civil War." Massachusetts Historical Society. https://www.masshist.org/.

Plante, Trevor K. "The Shady Side of the Family Tree." National Archives. https://www.archives.gov/publications/prologue/1998/winter/union-court-martials.

"Prairie Settlement: Nebraska Photographs and Family Letters, 1862–1912." Library of Congress American Memory. http://memory.loc.gov/ammem/award98/nbhihtml/pshome.html.

"Private Voices: Corpus of American Civil War Letters." https://altchive.org/private-voices. https://www.archives.gov/publications/prologue/1998/winter/union-court-martials.

"Sarah Waldsmith Bovard Diary." http://freepages.rootsweb.com/~haefner/genealogy/Bovard.

Tappin, Ben M. and Ryan T. McKay. "The Illusion of Moral Superiority." Social Psychology and Personality Science. https://journals.sagepub.com/home/spp.

"U.S. Business Cycle Expansions and Contractions." National Bureau of Economic Research. https://www.nber.org/cycles.

"The Valley of the Shadow: Two Communities in the American Civil War." https://valley.lib.virginia.edu.

VandeCreek, Drew E. "Economic Development and Labor in Civil War Illinois." Northern Illinois University Digital Library. https://digital.lib.niu.edu/illinois/civilwar/economic#footnote1_pynkcws.

"Vermonters in the Civil War." University of Vermont Libraries' Center for Digital Initiatives. https://cdi.uvm.edu/collection/uvmcdi-uvmcdicivilwar.

Wade, Lisa. "Irish Apes: Tactics of De-Humanization." https://thesocietypages.org/socimages/2011/01/28/irish-apes-tactics-of-de-humanization.

"Washington during the Civil War: The Diary of Horatio Nelson Taft, 1861 to 1865." Library of Congress. https://www.loc.gov/collections/diary-of-horatio-taft/about-this-collection.

INDEX

Note: Page numbers for figures are in italics.

AAPMG. *See* Acting Assistant Provost Marshal General
abolitionism: anti-abolitionism, 163–67; Black people and, 174–75; propaganda against, 201; radical, 187; slavery and, 38–42; war and, 92–93
"Abundant Disqualification" (cartoon), *78*
Acting Assistant Provost Marshal General (AAPMG): in Connecticut, 206, 236; in Illinois, 206, 214, 228–29, 265–66; in Maryland, 199; in Michigan, 240; in Pennsylvania, 239; for Union, 192, *193*, 194
Adams, Charles, Jr., 54
Adams, Charles Francis, Sr., 54
Adams, Henry, 54
Alexander, H., Jr., 290
Allen, Gideon, 79
Alvord, Henry, 33
Ames, John, 133
Anderson, James, 126
Anderson, Robert, 1

Anderson, Thomas, 271, 288, 290–91
Andersonville prison, 257–58
Anthony, George, 291, 312
anti-abolitionism, 163–67
anti-Black immigrants, 242
anti-draft movement: history of, 197–98; in Northern society, 230–35, *234*, 309–10; politics of, 294–96; in social culture, 238–41; to Southern society, 233–35, *234*
Antietam (battle), 159–61, *161*, 169–70
apathy, of soldiers, 273–76, *277*, 278–79
Armprister, Henry, 37
assassination, of Lincoln, A., 300, 307, 325–26
Atwood, William, 314

bachelors, 190–91
Badger, Frank, 83
Baker, George W., 233
Baker, Henry, 94–95

Mellon, Thomas, 54

Melville, Herman, 105

memory, social culture and, xiv

men: business and, 18; in
community, 28–33, *32*;
masculinity, 24, *25*, 26–28;
religion and, 155–56; voting
by, 34

Merrill, Samuel, 30

Mexican War: to Connecticut, 19;
to US, 2, 17; veterans of, 22–23,
64, 263; War of 1812 and, 31

Mexico, 242

Michie, Peter, xvii–xviii

Michigan: AAPMG, 240; Civil
War and, 6; Ohio and, 314–15;
riots in, 241; social culture of,
91; University of Michigan, 80;
Volunteer Infantry, 314

militarism, 196

military service: draft for, xiv–xvi,
xv; hierarchies in, 23–24; in
Northern society, xiii–xviii, *xv*;
planning for, 3–4

Militia Act (1795), 5–6

Militia Act (1862), 112–18, *114,
117*, 156–57, 191–92, 330. *See
also* draft

militiamen, 4–6, 9, 21, 45

Miller, James, 82, 230, 246

Miller, John, 102

Miller, William, 232

Milroy, Robert H., 172

Miner, Henry, 297

Minnesota, 83

Mississippi, 26

Missouri, 168

Mitchell, Silas, 326

Mitchell, William, 75

Moler, Nelia, 3

Molter, John, 226

Moody, Dwight L., 90

Moody, Emma, 27

moral nationalism, 92

Morford, Henry, 61

Morgan, Benjamin, 217–18

Morgan, Edwin, 58, 86, 88,
133, 315

Morgan, John Hunt, 11, 181

Morris, Alvin, 28

Morse, Charles, 276

Morton, Oliver, 116, 179

Naill, Henry C., 199

Napton, William, 178

nationalism: militarism and, 196;
moral, 92; in Union, 34

Native Americans, 11, 40

"The Naughty Boy Gotham"
(cartoon), *243*

Navy, US, 252, 276, *277*, 278

Newberry, John, 240

New Hampshire, 195–96, 208–9

New York: advertising in, *183*;
draft in, xviii–xix; farming in,
81; Infantry, 26, 30; militiamen
in, 6; New York City, 34, 37–38,
151; press in, 286–87

Noe, Kenneth, 46–47

Sutherland, Kate, 60–61
Sutton, Mary, 184
"The Sweet Little Man" (poem), 13–14
"Sweet Little Men of '61" (cartoon), *14*
Swift, Beates, 174–75

"Take Your Gun & Go, John" (song), 224–25
Tatman, Josiah, 326, 367n39
taxation, 270, 308, 312–13
Taylor, Joseph K., 105
Taylor, Netta, 75
Taylor, Tom, 105
Tebbetts, William, 32
teenagers, 29, 33, 132–33
Tennyson, Lord, 34
Tew, Charles, 230–31, 269
Thomas, Clarence, 49
Thompson, Ai Baker, 28, 82–83
Thrall, Seneca, 175–76
Tocqueville, Alexis de, 53, 185
Tod, David, 147, 222–23
Tomlinson, Eliza, 27
Trachpy, Godfrey, 95
Tracy, Osgood, 16
treason, 152–53, 179–80, 187, 194
Tripler, Charles S., 110–11
Tripp, Charles, 283
Trobriand, Regis de, 134
Trotsky, Leon, 332
Truesdell, Henry, 231
Tunnicliff, Joseph, 213–14
Turchin, John, 293

Turner, John W., 142

Ukraine, 332
Underwood, Josie, 181
Union: AAPMG for, 192, *193*, 194; at Bull Run creek, 47; Confederacy and, 2, 8, 36, 43–44, 98–99, 172–73, 213, 273–74, 313–18, 320–22; conscription in, xii; culture of, 249; desertion to, 188, 318–19; disloyalty to, xvii; draft and, 112–18, *114*, *117*; economics of, 19–20; Emancipation Proclamation to, 167–70, 353n11; enlistment to, 283–85, 304–5; farming to, 10; ideology of, 40–41, 49–50; immigrants to, 37; Lincoln, A., and, 273–74; loyalists, 49–50; morale in, 111–12; nationalism in, 34; Northern society and, 195–96; optimism in, 101; Overland campaign by, 279–83; patriotism in, 230–31; planning by, 5–6; politics in, 267–72; press and, 56, 61–62; propaganda for, 2–3, 17; psychology of, 156–57; recruitment for, 26, 46–47, 320–21; Rock Island Prison for, 322; slavery to, 159–67, *161*, 168; soldiers to, xviii–xix, 3–4, 245–46; succession from, 346n57; uniforms in, 10;

About the Author

Paul Taylor is a retired insurance professional and an author/editor of eight previous books on the American Civil War era. His biography of O. M. Poe, titled *Orlando M. Poe: Civil War General and Great Lakes Engineer*, was a recipient of the Library of Michigan's 2010 Notable Books Award, the 2010 State History Award from the Historical Society of Michigan, and the Society of Midland Authors 2010 Honorable Mention Award for Biography. His Civil War–era history of Detroit, titled *"Old Slow Town": Detroit during the Civil War*, was a recipient of the 2013 ForeWord Reviews Book of the Year Award in the War and Military category and the 2014 State History Award from the Historical Society of Michigan.